Publicity photograph, 1969.

Famous Enough: A Hollywood Memoir
© 2014 Diane McBain and Michael Gregg Michaud. All Rights Reserved.

No part of this book may be reproduced in any form or by any means, electronic, mechanical, digital, photocopying or recording, except for the inclusion in a review, without permission in writing from the publisher.

Unless otherwise noted, all photographs are from the personal collection of Diane McBain.

Published in the USA by:
BearManor Media
PO Box 1129
Duncan, Oklahoma 73534-1129
www.bearmanormedia.com

ISBN 978-1-59393-576-4

Printed in the United States of America.
Back cover photographs from the collection of Michael Gregg Michaud.
Book design by Brian Pearce | Red Jacket Press.

Famous Enough
A Hollywood Memoir

Diane McBain
and Michael Gregg Michaud

"Then God explodes from his hiding place."
MARIA-RAINER RILKE

Publicity photograph, 1962. COLLECTION OF MICHAUD

Table of Contents

Epiphany | 9

Part I: Starlight | 19

Part II: Stardom | 77

Part III: Starburst | 263

Part IV: Star Shine | 339

Fade To: Light | 419

Film and Television Credits | 423

Acknowledgments | 439

Authors' Profiles | 443

Epiphany

In 1982, I attended a Christmas Eve party at a friend's house in the San Fernando Valley. My young son Andrew was staying with his father for the holiday. The company was charming, and the house festively decorated. We enjoyed a potluck dinner and exchanged gifts. After a career lull, I was enjoying a recurring role as a madam named Foxy Humdinger on the long-running soap opera, *Days of Our Lives*. After the party, I drove home alone, appreciative of the nearly deserted freeways after midnight.

I had to get out of the car to open the garage door before heading into the darkened space. Watching from a fast-food stand on the boulevard corner opposite my apartment building, two Latin men with sober features tracked my progress. I was completely unaware of them, except that in the corner of my mind I was cognizant of some people at the stand. The men must have followed my actions from the time I pulled up to the garage and opened the door. The food stand was a nuisance and somewhat of a local landmark. Open twenty-four hours a day, Oki Dog was a popular spot for young, aimless people to hang out. The building was painted bright orange and was bathed in orange neon light. The glow could be seen from miles around.

Once I pulled into the garage, I suddenly realized I was not alone. A male voice called out, "We're the police!" I knew they were not police officers, but I couldn't lock my car door because the handle had been broken by a car wash attendant earlier that day. The two men grabbed me and yanked me from the driver's seat. As they clutched my hair, I could hear the roots being ripped from my skull.

My first reaction was to fight back, which proved to be a mistake. They attacked me with a viciousness I had never imagined. A week earlier, I had read an article in *Cosmopolitan* magazine about what a woman should do in the event of an assault. The writer suggested digging her fingers into the aggressor's eyes and pulling downward. Instead, they dug *their* fingers into *my* eyes. Astonished, I tried to scream, but they slapped me and punched me in the face to quiet me. My lip was busted open in the fracas and bled heavily. Out of the corner of my eye, I could see a few people sitting in orange light at a picnic table by the food stand. They could not hear my cries for help over the Christmas music blasting on the establishment's radio. As one of the men held me, the other closed the garage door and I knew in the blackness of anonymity there was nothing I could do to stop them. Illuminated by the headlights' glare from my car, I saw intense hatred in their faces and for an instant I wondered where it came from. They didn't know me, nor I them. They called each other Luis and Ricardo.

They pushed and pulled me around, slamming me against the side of the car. They called me vulgar names as I struggled until I finally relented when they had entangled my flailing arms with their own. I pleaded with them, "You don't want to do this," but they tore my clothes away and both held me upright as one of the men forced himself into me. After a while, they turned me around, jammed me against the car, and forced me to bend over. "Get down, get down," they yelled at me. Between my knees, I could see the bowed legs of one of my assailants. Suddenly, one of them brutally sodomized me until I nearly lost consciousness.

I became numb to what was going on. The garage had become very quiet, though I could hear my heart pounding in my chest. I could smell mildew and motor oil, and taste my own blood. I could feel the force and pain of their kicks and punches, but my body finally went into shock. My lack of resistance didn't seem to affect their criminal resolve. Still, I wanted to be a good witness. I tried to pay close attention and look each man in the face. They were young — in their twenties. They were about my height, and dressed like gauchos. They spoke English and Spanish, and they were sober.

The horrific attack lasted about forty-five minutes. My attackers did everything they could to hurt and humiliate me. I remained temporarily unmoved and steely. I wanted to burn their images into my brain so that I could later identify them. Before they fled, they beat me to the ground. They dragged me by my hair and by one of my arms, scratching my knees and buttocks on the rough concrete floor. Then, they tied me to the bumper of my car using one leg of my panty hose. The other leg was used to wrap around my neck and mouth so I couldn't scream. Until then, I hadn't feared for my life. One of them said, "You're lucky we're not going to kill you," before they left in the darkness.

It wasn't easy to free myself from the maze of nylon without choking. When I finally emerged from the garage, they had disappeared. I staggered up the stairs to my apartment and called the sheriff's station. It was nearly two o'clock on Christmas morning.

The operator connected me to a rape trauma counselor from Cedars-Sinai Victim Response Center. While I waited for authorities to arrive, she gave me invaluable information about what and what not to do. I followed her instructions. I later realized that she was working from her home. She was counseling me from the edge of her bed.

When the sheriff officers stormed in, their huge frames seemed to fill my small living room. Law enforcement, strongly influenced by women's rights advocates, had come to a better understanding of rape victims and their special needs. The officers were kind, comforting, and helpful as I slowly began emotionally to disassemble. My earlier steely resolve melted away as their strength gave me the chance I needed to fall apart.

The rapists had stolen a photograph album from my car, which somehow became the greatest loss of the night. It contained pictures (and the negatives) of dear, lifelong friends I had recently visited in Berkshire, England. The album became the focus of all my feelings of desolation. There was no way to retrieve the precious photos. They were lost forever, just as the innocence that allows hope to survive was seemingly gone forever. I felt inconsolable by the loss, which seemed so wanton. What use did they have for those photographs? What use did they have with my body, my mind, and my soul? What did they get out of this horrible experience? Was it domination and humiliation of a woman?

Despite the horror and pain of the attack, there was reason to feel that all was not lost. I called upon two dear friends, an actor named Ty Henderson and an artist named Vera Desmond, and they came running to my aid. The representative from the trauma center came to the hospital on that early Christmas morning to help me through the difficult evidence-gathering examination. Following my sexual assault, a rape kit was used by medical personnel to collect and preserve any physical evidence. This "kit" consisted of small boxes, microscope slides, and plastic bags for storing evidence — such as clothing fibers, hairs, and any bodily fluids, including blood and semen. These samples could be used to later identify my attacker. In 1982, DNA testing (commonly used today) was several years away from being utilized. I laid under glaring lights for a process that took hours. Both of my eyes were swollen shut. They took X-rays because I'd been battered. The medical examination was tedious, meticulous, clinical, and mechanical, and could easily be perceived as an extension of the physical violation already suffered by the victim. The woman from the trauma center held my hand while doctors sewed up my torn lip. Hours after the attack, I was still trembling. The warmth and reassurances from this wonderful person, who was an unpaid volunteer at the Rape Trauma Center, were comforting beyond anything I could remember since my mother had held me as a child. The support I received from everyone, as each learned what had happened to me, was tremendous and invaluable to my slow recovery.

The physical damage was shocking. I was unrecognizable at first, and thought I would never look the same. As my friend, Vera, drove me to her house to convalesce, I was both embarrassed and devastated to see a man's shocked reaction to seeing my face as we drove past him. In a few weeks, the ugly facial cuts and bruises began to heal, the swelling abated, and I was able to return to work.

Years later, I was certain I recognized one of my assailants working at an auto shop just doors away from my apartment. I found out his name was Luis. When I called the police to report my suspicions, I was shocked to learn that all the evidence collected in relation to my case had either been lost or discarded. I was overcome when I learned that this mishandling of evidence in rape cases was not uncommon because of the volume of cases that overwhelm law enforcement agencies.

I had been "date-raped" many years before. A naïve nineteen in 1960, I was enjoying a surge in popularity as my fledgling career was just about to take off. I had been assigned to play the title character in a film at Warner Bros. called *Claudelle Inglish*. It was a tremendous opportunity for me.

Amidst the excitement, I was feeling a little too big for my britches. I placed myself in an untenable position, and when the assault was over, erroneously felt that my poor judgment had earned me what I deserved. Most rape victims feel this way, a fact that I would not understand until much later. In the ensuing years, I blamed myself and excused my rapist, who became a famous and powerful man, until that Christmas morning.

The two rapists had been strangers, which made the attack easier to deal with. I didn't feel the shame that many women associate with assault, especially "stranger rape." I didn't believe the rape was my fault at all. What was there to be ashamed of when the men were clearly committing the crime? Wearing a modest pantsuit, I couldn't be accused of tempting my assailants by my sexy clothing, which is often the excuse rapists and their lawyers use to rationalize the abhorrent behavior. Shame was incomprehensible to me in this case, but there was something deeper going on that I didn't recognize at the time.

Since I had not called the earlier instance a rape when I was forced by my date to have sexual intercourse, I had never associated the symptoms of irrational anxiety and deep depression I experienced from that encounter to be the result of sexual assault. I had suffered from Rape Trauma Syndrome then, and was swept away by the same feelings again.

After some therapy, I realized how victimized I had been by the first rape, and I decided to write about both attacks for *Cosmopolitan* magazine. I also decided to reveal the name of the now famous man who had forced himself upon me so many years before. Unabashedly, I told my friends his name, which was very unlike me. But I began to hate myself for my accusatory stand. The assault had happened so long before. Perhaps he was repentant and I didn't know it.

My contrite heart reached out in remorse to God for airing my anger in the media. I had rationalized the revelation by telling myself that I was doing a service to the female public. I wanted to assure them that their feelings of shame following such an attack are not unusual. The feelings result from a mishandling of our femininity — rape — whether by a trusted confidant, a relative, or a stranger. Shame and self-loathing are frequent psychological side effects. There are negative spiritual elements, as well. Abject fear overcomes the positive spiritual energy that we cultivate in our soul. As part of the healing process, I recommended that women be open about what had happened to them and not feel any guilt. Fear doesn't live in the light of knowledge. In 1982, rape was still considered shameful in many corners of America. Women needed to be freed from the fear that *they* are essentially evil and cause men to rape them. Such fears are often based on social or religious presumptions.

Ironically, I felt guilty for doing the very thing I was recommending — going public. This feeling made my resolution more difficult. I'd heard rumblings that industry people perceived my public stance as some sort of ploy for publicity by a pathetic has-been. I felt just guilty enough to wonder if they were right. Confused, I sought forgiveness and understanding from my God.

My West Hollywood apartment was quiet. My son was still at school and I had a few minutes to unwind before he came home. I had struggled all day with the article I was writing for *Cosmopolitan*, my feelings constantly vacillating. I felt retribution was appropriate, and at the same time, I was unable to bring myself to believe that I was not somehow responsible, too.

It was far more than heavenly understanding I received in return. I fell into a meditative state as I stared out the window. I was vaguely aware of the television playing in the background. Quite by surprise, an unusually bright beam from the setting sun flashed in through my bedroom window and exploded into an astonishing clash of light that seemed to come from the middle of my forehead. An eruption of incandescence suddenly surrounded me and, all at once, emanated from me. At first, it was very bright, like a burst of blinding white sunlight. I heard a crackling sound inside my head, and when I closed my eyes, there was a fire that didn't burn yet seemed to consume. Two green, doe-eyed-shaped orbs glowed in the midst of the flame. When I opened my eyes again, light beams emanated from all around me.

My reaction was astonishment. At first, I thought I was having a stroke, but I had no physical pain and I hadn't become disabled in any way. The sound from the television provided a distraction as I witnessed the glowing emanations begin to dissipate. The early evening news provided a timetable. The entire broadcast transpired as I sat there radiating light. This was certainly unlike anything I had experienced or heard before.

My son returned from school. He opened my bedroom door and said, "Hi, Mom."

Andrew was a scrawny twelve-year-old with a freckled face, blue eyes, sandy hair, and a winning smile. Even though he was essentially handsome, he was going through one of those awkward stages.

"Hi, honey," I answered. "I was just watching a little television." I hesitated to say what was really on my mind, but I wondered if the radiating light I felt was apparent to him. "Do you notice anything different?" I asked.

"No. Why? Anything wrong?"

"Uh-uh. I was just — uh, oh — feeling odd and wondered if it was noticeable."

He said he was going out to skateboard as he closed the door behind him. He had entered as he always had, checked in with me as usual, and left without a thing seeming different. The contrast between the ordinariness of the day's usual progression and what I had just experienced was stunning. This was truly extraordinary, and I wasn't sure what to think.

The event did change my life, but not all at once. At first, I no longer felt guilty about the rapes and my angry response, and over time, my most self-destructive attitudes changed. I felt at peace with how I should proceed with the article. Mentioning the name of the perpetrator in that particular venue now seemed superfluous to my intention, so I decided it was not the time or place to do so. More importantly, I came to the conclusion that I had met the Holy Spirit "face to face". Still, I was clueless to what my "other-worldly" encounter meant.

As is usual with spiritual events, defining exactly what had happened — except in reference to what my religious traditions dictated — was impossible. For the first time, I came to a conscious awareness and understanding of the concept of the Holy Spirit. The subject had, of course, come up in my Episcopalian training thousands of times before — in the readings of the liturgy, in hymns and sermons — but I'd never recognized the Holy Spirit as something so real. As an adult, I'd perceived Bible scriptures as being indicative of a subjective reality, an inner enlightenment. I thought the halos in religious art drawn around the heads of Jesus and the saints were poetic expressions of inner knowledge and nothing more.

Since I'd never considered the Holy Spirit as something objectively real, I had never been consciously aware of the scriptures that described it. Or I had dismissed them as primitive descriptions of something so unusual to the people of that time that they were described in mythical terms. I had vague memories of "tongues of fire," faces that glowed with light, and "baptism by fire," but not enough to connect the dots until I went to church one Pentecost Sunday soon after my encounter with the glowing green orbs.

Suddenly, like a bolt out of the blue, I heard in the reading of the scriptures how the apostles were blessed with an infusion of the Holy Spirit as they awaited the risen Christ in the upper room. In the New Revised Standard Version of the Bible, Acts 2:2-4, I read in part, "And suddenly from heaven there came a sound like the rush of a violent wind, and it filled the entire house where they were sitting. Divided tongues, as of fire, appeared among them, and a tongue rested on each of them. All of them were filled with the Holy Spirit…"

Once they were doused by the fire that consumes but does not burn, the apostles were able to speak in tongues. I didn't speak in tongues, but after my unusual experience, I felt I could better understand the human heart. I was able to communicate back my interpretation of those feelings, which was often helpful to others. I grew more discerning, too. I was able to see things I hadn't noticed before. I had an uncanny capacity to see through lies, distractions, and artifice. Often, I didn't believe myself, but as time wore on, I was more and more able to discern the truth in any situation without questioning my probity.

People's auras or halos became visible under certain circumstances. I was surprised to find auras around the heads of all sorts of people, even self-proclaimed atheists. At church, in classrooms, at the theater, people would suddenly glow as their lives lit up with the Creative Spirit. All at once, as if someone had turned on a heavenly light, I could see the Holy Spirit everywhere.

Artistry became easier for me. Whatever artful endeavor I attempted, the results were quite good. My acting became deeper, also. It seemed that the Holy Spirit was working with me because creativity was so effortless.

Over time, I came to believe that the "fire" of the Holy Spirit had burned away my sins, my bad karma, everything negative from my past. I no longer felt guilty because I realized that everything that had happened in my past led me to that incredible moment when I was open and humbled enough to receive God. How could I feel guilty? For what? All that was left to do was grapple with forgiveness — to forgive everyone I thought had harmed or hindered me in any way. How could I not when I felt so forgiven?

I know I am not alone. There are other people who can relate to what I experienced. And there are others who have come to know the Holy Spirit in a similar manner. Nevertheless, I was initially hesitant to speak about this phenomenon. I worried that my imagination might have taken over. Maybe I was making it all up. But each time I considered the incident I came to the same conclusion. What happened to me was real. Part of my reluctance to talk about my perception was the fear that I might diminish its importance through needless chatter. Rather, I chose initially to share my realization only with close friends. (I think they thought I was a little crazy.)

Why was I reluctant to spread the news? Was I, like Peter in the Bible, denying my Lord by not acknowledging Him? In the final analysis, I was a "doubting Thomas." I also had serious issues with the "Jesus Movement" as it was then expressing itself. The beliefs of many of those followers were too Bible-literal and incomprehensible to me — a self-professed twentieth-century woman. I envied "born-again" people whose simple belief systems didn't demand logic. They could swallow the Bible hook, line, and sinker. I could not. I questioned everything.

Later, I realized the Holy Spirit is implied in the *entire* Bible. In fact, the point of the two books — the Old and New Testaments — is the story of The Light and how it works to infuse all of creation with the light of His spirit. I believe we are an arrogant and stiff-necked people. When we let go of our self-righteous judgments and humble ourselves before God, His light can enter. The liturgies are replete with this message.

For me, complete clarity did not come at once. It took me a long time to recognize what was in front of my nose all along. The Holy Spirit is a Presence that I can feel moving within me from the base of my spine upward and outward to my extremities. Still, I didn't identify the feeling then in quite the same way I do now. It took a long time to process the experience, and I endeavored to trust and believe my own senses.

After my journey with the light, there were many changes I would have to undergo. I've been way up and I've been way down. Through it all, I found it was the Light I was seeking. That realization is the story of my life, in and out of Hollywood.

Practicing my "cheesecake pose" at the age of seven in Glendale, California.

Starlight

Chapter 1

A teenager during the Depression, my mother, Cleo Ferguson, had two dresses, one to wear and another to wear while laundering the first. Her parents were divorced when she was very young, and her life had been tough. Suffering from a broken heart when the love of her life broke off their engagement, she married the man who would be my father, Walter McBain, on the rebound. She made a commitment to him, though her heart really wasn't convinced. Born on May 18, 1941 in Cleveland, Ohio, I came into the world feet first. Mine was a breech birth. My mother always said I was born "bass-ackwards." I was an only child.

My mother made her own clothes and mine. From an early age, I determined that I didn't want to make the kind of sacrifices my mother had made. I didn't want to let the love of my life get away, and settle for a man, though handsome and strong, who would never be able to satisfy my deepest longings. My mother tried to put her life in perspective, but I could tell her choices ate at her.

Unlike many other girls I knew, I had a great relationship with my mother. She was essentially a homemaker who had to work when she could to help with family finances. My father loved to play the horses, and often lost at the track what little money they managed to save.

In 1944, shortly after my third birthday, my father was called to serve in the Navy during the final days of World War II. I was bereft to see him leave, and that feeling of abandonment never really left me. I can't remember a time when I wasn't fearful that men would abandon me. My mother, Grandma Ray, Aunt Dorothy (my father's sister), and my paternal grandmother, who I called Nonny, decided they'd had enough of the dreadful winters in Cleveland, and chose to move to California.

We traveled to the West Coast by train. My only memory of the trip is seeing Santa Claus, a white-whiskered old man with long ivory-colored hair and red trousers with suspenders, standing near the side of the tracks and waving at all the children as the train came into the station. I believed there was, in fact, a Santa Claus, and he was living in California.

At the foot of the Verdugo Mountains, the Los Angeles suburb of Glendale was a lovely, middle-class, all-white community in 1944. It was always sunny, and the air was sweet with the perfume of nearby, blossoming orange trees. The city was family-friendly, and the home of Bob's Big Boy Restaurant and Baskin-Robbins ice cream parlors.

Women were empowered by the war. "Rosie the Riveter" became an icon for American women working in factories to support the war effort. Women missed their men, but they learned to become more self-reliant as they had to fend for themselves and their children. My mother was no exception.

Aunt Dorothy bought a small, two-bedroom house on Harvard Street in Glendale. There was a tiny, one-bedroom bungalow in the back where my mother, Grandma Ray and I would live. I soon realized that the women in my family took matters into their own hands. Aunt Dorothy was divorced, and was a single parent to her two teenage sons. She worked as a bookkeeper. Grandma Ray got a job at the nearby Gladding, McBean & Co. factory making ceramic dinnerware.

My mother sent my father a letter explaining we had moved to California. She told him where to find us when he returned after the war. Years later, my mother told me his stint in the Navy had provided them with a trial separation.

The women in my family were as devoted to going to church as they were to surviving on their own. They attended the Episcopal Mass regularly. I spent a lot of time in Sunday school. I remember moving a Popsicle stick across a piece of a paper as the black and white image of Jesus and his followers sitting on a hillside magically appeared on the page. The scene was of the Sermon on the Mount, which became apparent as my Popsicle stick urged the dark images out of the white paper. My world was equally black and white. There were no shades of gray, then. It was either black or white, right or wrong, or good or evil. Christianity, as it was taught to me then, was at the core of such simplistic thought. I was a curious child, but the adults in my world taught me more about right and wrong than they did about the wonderful possibilities of life. They were more worried about the size of my ego than whether I developed the healthy self-confidence needed to succeed.

My father's return from the war in 1946 presented an awkward problem at home. I had missed him, but he seemed like a stranger to me, and I to him. He didn't know how to handle a child, especially a girl. I didn't see him as a very sentimental man and I found it difficult to trust him, fearing he might abruptly leave again.

Our little bungalow suddenly seemed even smaller. My father displaced me from the bedroom I had shared with Mom. My grandmother and I slept in the dining area off the kitchen. I hit my head on the corner of the table whenever I got up in the middle of the night.

Once my mother had discovered she could take care of herself, her newfound independence determined her marriage from then on. I

Left: *Mom, Dad and me in Cleveland in 1944 on the day Dad left to serve in the Navy.* Right: *Nonny, Grandma Ray, Mom and me. Easter Sunday in Glendale.*

remember watching my father sit in an armchair with a radio to each ear. One broadcast a golf tournament and the other a ball game. While he listened, he buried his face in the sports pages of the newspaper. After we bought our first television set, he watched wrestling matches. I'd watch him from the kitchen as I helped my mother and grandmother prepare meals. It seemed like two different worlds under one roof, and nothing I did appeared to interest my father as much as his beloved sports programs.

Even the safest communities, can harbor dangers for a child. There was a factory at the end of the street we lived on in Glendale. On the weekends, when the business was closed, a security guard was stationed at a small gatehouse at the entrance. I played with my friends, or often alone, on the street. The guard invited me into his little kiosk. Sometimes he had candy, but usually just seemed a jovial sort. I'd sit on his lap and before long he began to fiddle with my genitals. He never tried to kiss me or penetrate me, just wanted to play "touch." This went on for a short time. I came to learn that many of the children in the neighborhood were victimized by this man. He was an equal opportunity molester, luring both little girls and little boys into his kiosk. He was well-practiced, and like most molesters, he knew the type of child he could assault. I suppose I liked the attention in some way. Being a child, I had no idea of the seriousness of his offence or what may have been behind his impropriety.

When I was a little girl, child abuse was secretive and rarely spoken of. Oftentimes the child victim was not believed. When I told my parents what had happened, their reaction surprised me. They didn't seem to believe me or think that it was important. Perhaps their natural shock prevented them from outwardly reacting. Child sexual abuse finally became a public issue in the 1970s and 1980s with the enactment of mandatory laws that required physicians to report their suspicions of child abuse to authorities. Not surprisingly, it's difficult to talk about, and the victim often feels shamed. I'm not an expert on this subject, and I've never fully understood the extent of any issues I may have had in dealing with the molestation. I never even considered the ramifications until I spent time with a therapist later in my life, but arguably, the childhood encounters subconsciously informed my choices.

Since I spent so much of my time alone, I felt unprotected. Although my mother, father, and loving extended family were nothing for me to be afraid of, another unsettling thing happened to me in my neighborhood. In addition to the incidences with the security guard, a few local teenage boys took me behind a shed one afternoon. They pinned me on the ground and sat on me. I didn't know what their intentions were, but before the assault could become sexual, they had a change of heart and let me go. The experience frightened me. They had overpowered me, and I had felt trapped and completely vulnerable. Once they released me, I ran home. I told my parents. Again, they seemed to shrug it off.

Though I never thought what to make of the assaults I endured at the time, I nevertheless felt the need to protect myself. Instinctively, my mind set to work on some kind of defense. The name "Diane" seemed like such a grownup name when I was born that my family nicknamed me "Danny." The name stuck. Danny, who is essentially my true self, is a mischievous child. She's a tomboy. She loves to ride bikes and play sports with the boys. She prefers to wear comfortable cotton in simple gingham and plaid patterns. She has a wicked sense of humor and loves to shock people with the things she says.

On the other hand, Diane, self-created, is righteous and controlling. A bit uptight and icy, she loves to dress like a princess. Diane dislikes getting dirty, and cannot tolerate the feel of wool against her skin. She is not happy unless she is getting her way, and she's not very fond of anyone. In my innocent subconscious, I depended upon Diane to protect Danny.

Oddly, my mother preferred Diane, who was more reserved and dutifully studied ballet, a pursuit my mother abandoned many years before. Danny, who was Daddy's little girl, was quite the opposite. She was much less disciplined, and could hardly be controlled.

One Sunday, when I was about six years old, my father decided to take us for an outing to Indian Springs. With a swimming hole, picnic tables and concession stands, the tiny oasis in the Angeles National Forest was a fun place to go on a hot summer day. I was so excited. I wanted to take my Cocker Spaniel, Corey, with us. She was my pal even though she really belonged to my grandmother, who was going with us that day. I loved the way Corey's shaggy bottom wagged when she got excited. My father insisted we leave the dog behind. I was disappointed, but the decision was made.

As we pulled away from our house, I peered out the back window and saw Corey running after us. She looked as if she had a smile on her face when she saw me watching her. Suddenly, I realized we were approaching an intersection. I screamed, "Daddy, Daddy! Stop! It's Corey!" My father wouldn't stop. He ignored me and continued to talk with my mother.

"Daddy, Daddy," I screeched, "Please stop!"

But it was too late. Corey was struck in the intersection. She looked like a little golden ball tossed into the air. She disappeared under the wheels of a car and from my life. I was devastated. Nonny clutched me as I cried uncontrollably. My father moved Corey's lifeless body to the side of the road. Undeterred, he drove on to Indian Springs.

When I was in the third grade, I got a terrible case of poison oak. My cat brought it in on her fur, into which I had buried my face. By the time I was aware of the itching, it was too late. I was one big itch from head to toe. My mother lathered me with calamine lotion. She was working, so my father had to take me to my elementary school to pick up my homework assignments.

It was impossible to attend school in my condition, but for some reason he insisted that I accompany him into the classroom. I was certain everyone would stare at the white, glistening lotion covering my face, arms and legs. I was terribly self-conscious and knew everyone would laugh at me while I stood in the doorway next to my father. I wanted to run back to the car, but he kept me there while the teacher gave him my homework. Perhaps sensing my discomfort, he treated me to a movie matinee before we went home. He wanted to see *Bwana Devil*, a 3-D film starring Robert Stack about lions in the wild. The lions were jumping off the screen at me as my skin crawled with fear, and ached with the painful itch of poison oak.

When I was ten, I became a Brownie, the female equivalent of a Cub Scout. We earned merit badges, like the older Girl Scouts. In order for me to earn a badge for "Industry," I had to tour a local factory. Again, my father took charge. He took me to a brassiere factory. I was mortified as we toured the facility and watched seamstresses carefully stitching away. Lacy cups and elastic straps with tiny hooks and eyes were assembled to look like a woman's breast. My father was much more interested in what was going on there than I was. When we got home, I blanked out our tour and couldn't remember a single thing. Consequently, my father wrote the report I was to present at the troop meeting the following day. I was too embarrassed to even review what he had written. When the time came for me to read the assignment aloud, I couldn't decipher his handwriting. I was embarrassed and humiliated when the other girls realized I hadn't done the assignment. I know he was only trying to help me, but I felt betrayed.

Mom often encouraged me and Dad to try to get along. Once, my father decided to give me golf lessons. I wasn't the least bit interested and failed miserably.

I think my father was frustrated by his life choices. He drove a bus for the City of Glendale because he had to earn a living, but would have preferred something else like a job related to his interest in sports. Insolent bus passengers, low pay, and less than comfortable working conditions angered him. He often took his frustration out on us at home. Although he never laid a hand on any of us, once he put his fist through the wall in a rage. I felt as though I was walking on eggshells around him as his temper could flare at any moment.

I know my father meant well, but we struggled to establish a father-daughter relationship. I had created a world without him when he was away, which seemed adequate to my needs. I had lots of girl friends, but I preferred the company of the neighborhood boys. Electric train sets were more interesting to me than dolls. I preferred to run with the boys, climb trees, play softball, tackle, and hide and seek, and Danny loved playing "doctor" with the boys.

"Do as I say, not as I do" was a lesson mightily challenged when I was young. I discovered our pastor had feet of clay. Some kids in the neighborhood discovered the pastor of our church swam naked in his backyard pool. Located directly off the street and barely obscured by a fence and bushes, they watched him skinny-dipping in the glorious sunshine. Word spread fast, and he became quite a topic of conversation.

I had a rich imagination. I never really applied myself in school. My head was in the clouds. Teachers told my parents that I was a daydreamer, more interested in gazing out the window than reading a book. I was bored beyond measure. My lack of focus would much later be diagnosed as Attention Deficit Disorder. To keep myself entertained, I conjured up all sorts of scenarios for myself. I wanted to be a reporter like Brenda Starr in the comic strips. I wanted to be a nurse in the midst of war who cared for the dying men who lay in her arms. I wanted to be heroic like Joan of Arc, and I wanted to be a businesswoman like those played by Joan Crawford in the movies. I pictured myself walking into an office suite filled with staff who would greet me, "Good morning, Miss McBain. And how are you today, Miss McBain?" I would graciously smile as I swept into my office that had a sweeping view of Manhattan, and took my seat at a well-appointed desk. Of course, I had no idea then what a businesswoman did, other than light a cigarette and bark orders into the telephone.

My mother had numerous jobs, including working as a clerk for the Southern California Gas Company. Since Grandma Ray worked as well, I was often left to my own devices after school. I never minded playing in the deserted schoolyard. I climbed on the jungle gym and swung on the monkey bars. I loved riding my bicycle down the beautiful, tree-lined streets, and feeling the wind blow through my hair.

Because my father was a bus driver, all his fellow drivers looked out for me and made sure I got home safely after school. "Okay, Danny," the driver would say as I stepped off the bus, "now go right home." I let myself into the house, fixed a snack, and practiced the piano, which I hated. Even though I was unsupervised, I felt obligated to practice. My mother frequently reminded me how expensive the lessons were. There were days when the blisters on my fingers from my tomboy after-school play made piano playing nearly impossible.

My father's reckless gambling created a lot of friction between my parents. His debts caused us to move several times. Eventually, my mother pulled enough of her savings together to purchase a small house in the Glendale hills. I shared a bedroom with Grandma Ray, but I had my own bed. There were two massive oak trees in the front yard and some colorful maple trees in the back. It was a picturesque yet simple life. Rarely was there dinner-table talk about the economy or politics. We talked about school, work, and church.

I continued to spend a lot of time at church, perhaps more out of obligation and habit than interest. Still, there was something comforting and reassuring about our faith. My first encounter with the Holy Spirit happened on a camp out with my fellow Girl Scouts. We sat around the campfire, sang songs, and listened to stories about the loving nature of Jesus. Though I had been attending Episcopal Church in Glendale for years, I had never heard Jesus described in this way. I knew scripture, but the idea of accepting Him into my life as my personal Savior was new to me.

At that time, the Girl Scouts taught Christian-based lessons. When I was young, I thought there were only Catholics and Protestants. There was one Jewish boy in my school who made me realize there was something other than Christianity to believe in, but in my neighborhood, Judaism was considered very weird and foreign. Since the little boy actually looked different to me, I assumed such a silly belief was true.

Sitting around the campfire that night was the first time I became aware that Protestants had different views and interpretations of scripture than other Christians. Sitting next to my schoolmate, Phyllis, I was overcome by the loving message. When we were asked to accept Jesus into our hearts and make Him our Savior, we agreed and hugged one another to seal the promise. There was much camaraderie around the camp that evening. The feelings of love and belonging were palpable and comforting. The stories of Jesus' life demonstrated the healing power of unconditional love, and I vowed I would follow His selfless example.

Later that evening, jealous Diane reared her mischievous head. Inexplicably, I stole another girl's wallet and hid it deep inside my sleeping bag. I was perplexed by the desire to have what the other girl had. I was overtaken by the sin of envy, and I couldn't control my terrible impulse. I was dismayed and ashamed of my behavior, but still I could not control my powerful desire.

I had stolen money before from the moneychanger on my father's bus. I was also caught stealing from the corner drug store a short time earlier and the merchant reported the crime to my parents. We didn't have a lot of money then, and the Diane in me had felt deprived.

I wanted to buy my own clothes, rather than wear those my mother made. Danny didn't care about clothing, but the simple homemade dresses embarrassed Diane. My mother sternly lectured me about stealing, but I was more concerned with what other children had, than weighing the morals of theft.

My spiritual and material desires were obviously at odds, but once I decided to follow the example of Jesus, I experienced an awakening of sorts. I recognized that theft hurt someone else. The stolen wallet was returned when I got home. My mother grounded me for a couple of weeks. My days as a young thief were over. Jesus had made an impression.

My reputation as a homerun-hitting softball player was solidified by the time I entered the Sixth Grade. Such sports were not considered "lady-like." Not only did I like playing, I excelled as a player and was the envy of my male classmates. At the same time, I earned my first "A" in school for a research paper I wrote about Nova Scotia. The terrific grade affected me profoundly. Though bright, I did not do especially well in school. I was beginning to think I had no brains. My hair was so lightly colored that it was almost white, and my eyebrows were so pale they could barely be seen. Having heard about "dumb blondes" all my life, I was beginning to think I was one.

Having a good swing on the field was handy, though. My skill earned me a lot of attention from the boys in school. I was eventually invited to play on the, up until then, all-boy team. At last, my father took an interest in what I was doing. He attended my games and cheered me proudly from the bleachers. I hadn't realized how much I craved his attention.

It didn't take long before my ball-playing days came to an end. I had my first period. "Young ladies," my mother informed me, "don't play ball." Danny was crushed. Diane was relieved.

My athletic skills didn't seem to frighten the boys away. I had fallen in love for the first time when I was thirteen. My boyfriend, Joe, was a schoolmate who belonged to the ROTC. After months of dating, he decided to enroll in a military school in New Mexico. My parents allowed me to ride to Albuquerque with his family to see him off. I cried on his father's shoulder while we watched him walk away onto the campus. It was the second time the military had taken away the man I loved. First, it was my father in WWII, and then my boyfriend.

When I was a teenager, I was confirmed in the church my mother and grandmother attended. I enjoyed services, and sang in the choir. My voice matured then, actually cracking like a boy's voice does when he hits puberty. I quickly developed a very low, sultry adult voice.

At this time, I became more curious about God and all things spiritual. There were things in life that confounded me. Making sense of them became a goal. Coming from a Christian background, I assumed many things about the outside world that I would later learn were simply not true. A small voice from a deep spiritual reservoir inside me spoke. I was not sure whether to believe my inner voice because it often contradicted what I had been taught to believe, but it always proved to be profoundly loving, piercingly honest, entirely forgiving, and sometimes difficult to listen to. Later, I consoled myself that the voice, although inside me, was not of me. The voice didn't *think* my thoughts, it *guided* my thoughts. I was in the flow of life, or in a kind of rhythm, and I felt that ideas came out of the sky. The experience had a meditative quality.

Though schooled in certain religious dogma, I soon realized that I was developing my own sense of spirituality. Being open to this experience was what made my life worth living.

Chapter 2

My father's gambling debts caused us to lose our lovely home in the hills. We moved back to the flats of Glendale. My parents rented an apartment near Bob's Big Boy drive-in restaurant on Colorado Boulevard. Living so close to "double-deck" hamburgers, fries, and milk shakes did not make me unhappy. My friends and I loved to hang out at Bob's.

There were few career choices available to women in 1956, and none of them really interested me. As a teenager, I had a few odd jobs. I worked as Santa's assistant in an outdoor holiday tree lot during one Christmas season. My mother was determined that I pursue a higher education. She wanted me to be independent and self-reliant. When I was fifteen years old, I was still a tomboy at heart. To "feminize" me, my mother and grandmother pooled their resources and enrolled me in the John Robert Powers Modeling School (soon to be called the Loretta Young Charm School) in Pasadena. Until I decided upon a proper career, they thought I could earn money modeling and pay for my eventual college tuition. I really wasn't interested in modeling. Actually, it was something I had never considered.

Nevertheless, I dutifully attended the modeling classes and quickly got my first job. Actress Jayne Mansfield was to be photographed with her infamous pink Cadillac at the docks in Long Beach, a port city south of Los Angeles. I was hired to be one of a bevy of bathing beauties who were instructed to stand in a line around Jayne and her glistening convertible. The night before, I decided that my legs were too white and in need of a tan. On the drive to Long Beach, I slathered some makeup on my legs, hoping to disguise the white skin. I hadn't noticed that the makeup was actually *pink* colored. Once at the location, there was nothing I could do but pose coyly next to the car. In the color photographs, my legs are as pink as Jayne's Caddie!

The modeling school began to send me out for auditions. I soon found a commercial agent interested in representing me. I was always self-conscious and hyper-critical of my looks. The beauty others saw in me was a complete mystery to me. I knew I was attractive, but people told me I was truly beautiful. I couldn't see it, and since I had nothing to do with my looks — God and my parents' good genes were the cause — I never felt it was something I could claim or for which I could take credit.

On a dare, I entered a beauty contest and, to my astonishment, I won. Oddly enough, being crowned "Miss Realty of Glendale" presented a new conundrum. At that time, the Glendale real estate industry was dominated by white, middle-class people. No one outwardly said that people of color were discriminated against. However, I learned city fathers actively sought to keep anyone who wasn't Caucasian out of town. Many legal screening methods were used to discourage people of color and even people with accents from owning or just renting property in Glendale. The blatant discrimination offended me, and I was unused to feeling embarrassed by something so out of my control. I was also disappointed to realize that I had been reared in this milieu of prejudice all my young life. In 1956, assuming the mantel of "Miss Realty of Glendale" was the beginning of my consciousness about racism, which came to play a big role in my adult life.

During the next year, I entered several local beauty contests and was crowned "Miss Beautiful," "Miss Catalina Grand Prix," and "Miss Glendale." My picture first appeared in the *Los Angeles Times* on April 1, 1957, when I was photographed presenting a trophy to the owner of a Cocker Spaniel that won "Best in Show" at the "Spring All-Breed Dog Show and Obedience Trial" staged by the Glendale Kennel Club.

Shortly after my sixteenth birthday, I was named "Miss Days of Verdugos" at a coronation ball attended by more than five hundred people. I received my first telegram on May 29 from the celebrity dance instructor Arthur Murray. My new "title" had earned me a $200 mambo course at his Glendale dance studio.

On June 4, I sat atop the royal float in the tenth annual Days of Verdugos Parade. A record 65,000 people lined Brand Boulevard. Smiling and waving in a beautiful gown and glittering crown, I again appeared in a photograph in the *Los Angeles Times*. I had become a bit of a celebrity to my classmates at Glendale High School, which was frivolous but fun. Danny was mortified, and Diane was in her element.

That fall, a family friend suggested I audition for the role of the ingénue lead at the Glendale Centre Theatre. The theater accepted me. Months later in March 1958, I was cast in *Love Comes in Many Colors* at the tiny theater on Colorado Boulevard. I received my first review as an actress in the *Glendale News Press* on March 27, when reporter Wanda Owen wrote, "Lovely blonde Miss McBain makes a perfect defiant teenager." The play ran for several weeks, and I was then cast in another production titled, *Return to Autumn*.

That spring, I began to work frequently as a "Sweet Sixteen" model, eventually appearing on the covers of dozens of national magazines, including *True Love, True Confessions, True Experience, True Story,* and

Riding atop the royal float as "Miss Days of Verdugos" on June 4, 1957.

Modern Romance. No more baseball bats or band-aid covered fingers for me. I also appeared in a number of national television commercials for Colgate Toothpaste ("Luscious lye toothpaste makes your teeth glisten, knocks those nasty germs out of bounds, and tastes good too!"), Max Factor, the National Dairy Association, and Bobbie Home Permanent. One of the less glamorous assignments was posing with the thirty-five

On stage at the Glendale Centre Theatre in Return to Autumn.

millionth tire made by the B. F. Goodrich Tire Co. to commemorate thirty years of tire-making on the West Coast.

My mother was conflicted by my sudden success. She wasn't sure how this would affect the pursuit of a college education, but she never discouraged me. In fact, she was my chaperone whenever needed. My father, on the other hand, loved it all. He was very proud of me, which pleased me, too.

A couple of magazine covers typical of my "Sweet Sixteen" modeling days.

Shortly before my seventeenth birthday, I signed an exclusive contract with Revlon. The opportunity came so fast. This was a profession that never interested me before and one I didn't pine for. Maybe because I didn't take it very seriously, I quickly became comfortable in front of a camera. I seemed to land most of the auditions I went out for. Still, I was just a teenager and my real interests were centered on school, teenage fun, and boys. The prospects of this burgeoning career were heady, but I was often separated from my peers, which tended to make me feel vulnerable and alone.

I embraced any chance I had to socialize with my high school friends. On Easter vacation, my friends and I rented a boat to spend the week at Catalina Island. It was a big tub of a vessel and bounced like a beach ball in the notoriously choppy waters between the California coast and the tiny island. I was plagued by seasickness and could do nothing more than lay about the boat and eat saltine crackers. I got terribly sunburned, suffered a heatstroke, retained water, and blew up like a balloon.

When I waddled onto the set the following Monday morning for my first shoot for Revlon, I was fired on the spot. Easy come and easy go. Diane was mortified. Danny was relieved.

I husbanded my modeling income, which my parents considered my own, and at last was able to shop in proper stores for fashionable clothing, shoes, and costume jewelry. After living with so little resources, my earnings seemed like a small fortune to me. Once I started shopping, it was very hard to stop. I wasn't very good at putting money aside for college. I did like the attention, but I found modeling to be a mindless activity. The few television commercials I landed and my work at the Glendale Centre Theatre proved to be much more interesting.

In the fall of 1958, a theatrical agent named Bill Barnes expressed an interest in representing me as an actress. He assured my mother and me that television acting was easy. He priggishly said, "Anyone can do it!" I read for and won a small role on Robert Young's hit TV program, *Father Knows Best*. Playing his daughter's high school friend, I had only a few lines, but I loved the newness of the experience, and the activity on the sound stages at Columbia Studios in Hollywood piqued my interest. So did the $200 paycheck.

Father Knows Best profiled the classic wholesome American family. The CBS-TV situation comedy was a fan favorite. I don't think such a perfect family ever really existed; it certainly didn't exist in my home. Robert Young and Jane Wyatt, the stars of the show, were very nice and easy to work with. Most of my scenes were with Elinor Donahue, who played their eldest daughter, Betty, and she was a joy, too.

I was invited to take acting, diction and poise classes at Universal-International Studios. These were professional classes and not conventional academic lessons. "It is not *snot*, dear. It is *it's not*. Did you say, *chew*, dear? Surely you meant to say, *it's you*, dear. No, it is not, *lemme*, dear. It is *let me*. You must pronounce your 'ts,' dear. If you think it is correct to say *awright*, then surely you will not be *all right* in this business, dear. And be sure to end your sentences with *lift*. You don't want to depress us by ending *down*, dear."

When I was seventeen, before I graduated from high school, I met a man. Richard Monte was ten years my senior and had just graduated from medical school. He was a doctor, and his plan was to complete his residency at the Presidio in San Francisco while taking care of his military obligation. He had been drafted, and he could kill two birds with one stone, as he liked to say. He was tall, good-looking, intelligent, romantic, and everything any young woman would dream about — and he was in love with me.

Danny liked Dr. Monte but, never thoroughly convinced of her own intelligence, was afraid she might not be bright enough to be the wife of a physician. Diane thought he was handsome and had possibilities, but she wasn't the least bit ready to settle down and give up the new, exciting opportunities that were coming her way.

I was smitten, but my mother fell in love with him. She thought he was the "one" and pushed me, *shoved* me really, to go out with him. Soon after he left the Los Angeles area for San Francisco, he talked my mother into allowing me to visit him there, alone. He assured her I would have my own quarters. He promised to take good care of me, and arranged for my overnight passage on the train.

I was quite surprised my mother would allow me to go away with any man. He charmed her, and she believed his intentions were honorable. More importantly, she was taken with the idea that her daughter might marry a doctor. Although she was an independent-minded woman, she had misgivings about my ability to properly support myself in show business. I think she didn't want me to struggle as she had. I also thought that Dr. Richard Monte was the type of man she would have chosen for herself if given such a chance.

I excitedly packed my bags. I was very young and had yet to do much traveling without an adult escort. I was just too excited to sleep that night on the train.

The moon was full over the Pacific as the train wended its way north from Union Station in Los Angeles to San Francisco. I remember gazing out the window watching the moonlight dance on the ocean water, when I noticed a massive black curtain of fog ahead. It was a wall that slowly swallowed the white glow of the moon, turning it yellow at first, then orange before it disappeared completely in the consuming darkness. The train ahead actually disappeared, too, slowly car by car. Soon, the fog swallowed up the car I was in, and I could see myself getting swallowed up by a marriage I didn't really want.

Suddenly, the acting business was loudly calling, and Danny's wishes for marriage were forgotten. Besides, San Francisco was too far away from my family. I did care for Richard very much, though, and I tried to remain open. I spent the time there trying to fit in.

One evening, we visited another couple who were his friends. They, too, were about ten years older than I. Though I considered myself quite sophisticated for my age, I was a country bumpkin compared to these very intelligent people. The man was also a doctor, and his girlfriend was a nurse. After a while, I got the strange feeling that Richard had brought me there to show me how happy a doctor and his nurse-wife could be. Richard was campaigning hard. However, the evening had the opposite effect. The prospect of marriage made me feel diminished as a person, rather than lifted up into some sort of equally loving partnership.

His friends had recently been in Alaska, still just an American territory. He obviously admired their military service and the adventure it offered.

"What was the biggest problem you ran into while you were up there?" Richard asked.

"Cabin fever."

"What's cabin fever?" I piped, thinking it was some sort of strange illness native to Alaska.

The brief, but painfully embarrassing silence was enough to convince me that I was out of my league. The blank look on their faces made me feel like a stereotypical "dumb blonde." I could have disappeared into the couch. I knew I didn't stand a chance with people like that, and I was a long way from being a nurse. I was simply not the caregiver type.

Later that night, we made our way back to the room where I was staying. Feeling quite vulnerable by that time, and unsure of myself, I craved the cuddling my family gave me when I felt distressed. I was also consumed with a fear that marriage to Richard would be a terrible mistake. The mixed message must have been very confusing for him. He must have thought that I wanted to be intimate, and though I wanted to be comforted, I wasn't ready for sex. His advances frightened me because I was unused to such an experienced man. The most physical contact I had at the time was kissing, hugging, and simple petting at the drive-in with boys my own age. When Richard revealed his erect penis, I pulled away and cried for him to leave. He gathered his clothes and left immediately, probably feeling mislead and embarrassed.

I was extremely glad to be returning to Glendale the next day, to the protective arms of my mother and father.

Solly Biano, a talent scout for Warner Bros., had seen me in a play in Glendale. Biano attended every public event, beauty contest, and local theater production searching for kids with looks and talent. Some people said he actually visited local soda fountains. He had discovered many stars, including Lana Turner, Burt Lancaster, Debbie Reynolds, Tab Hunter, and a dear friend to-be, Sharon Hugueny. Biano invited me to Warner Bros. to read for the casting department.

After a few auditions, I was cast as Charlotte in "Passage to Fort Doom," an episode of the hit Western television series *Maverick*. Paul Henreid, the actor who starred in *Casablanca*, was the director. Though I was vaguely familiar with the name, not being a movie fan by nature, I didn't really know anything about him, though he was a very skillful and patient director. *Maverick*, a big hit for ABC, was filmed at Warner Bros.

With a playful James Garner in Maverick. PHOTO COLLECTION OF MICHAUD.

in Burbank. The hour-long show was smart, often funny, and a star-maker for the very charming James Garner, who played the role of Bret Maverick.

Warner's backlot was sprawling. It was fun to be driven past the various permanent sets built to look like big city blocks, small town streets, exotic ports, lagoons, and lush jungles. The Western-style sets of *Maverick*, located on fictional "Laramie Street," were surprisingly realistic, until the first time I opened a set door to see absolute nothingness behind the facade. Handsome horses were tethered to wooden hand railings along boardwalks that fronted the sheriff's office, a general mercantile, the hotel, and a rollicking saloon. The sets were fake, but the dusty dirt on the road was real, and so was the stinky horse manure. We filmed some scenes on the backlot, and to control the light and sound, on massive soundstages where the elaborate interior sets were constructed, including a full size riverboat. There were so many sets that Stages 22, 25, and 28 were all used for *Maverick*. The experience was truly magical to this teenage girl.

"Passage to Fort Doom" was set in 1878 and told the story of a group of hapless travelers who survived a dangerous wagon-train ride through the Badlands to a remote Army outpost. I had a great time in my period costume as a proper young lady on her adventurous way to marry her man. My diction and poise classes helped me create the prim character of Charlotte. The set was a bit of a boy's club, but I had a ball. The episode aired on March 8, 1959.

Playing the part of Maverick's brother, Bart, actor Jack Kelly gave me my first screen kiss. My parents were in awe. Their daughter had kissed Jack Kelly! I was the talk of the neighborhood and the envy of my senior girlfriends at Glendale High School. Daddy loved *Maverick* and was terribly proud about my appearance on the show. He bragged about me to all the passengers on his bus. Mother was a little embarrassed by his antics, but she, too, was proud. When she told me her friends assured her that I was destined to make it big in Hollywood, she couldn't help but beam.

I continued with my final year of high school classes in Glendale, lessons at Universal-International, more and more frequent modeling assignments, and television auditions during the next few months. My schedule was hectic, but I liked the frenetic pace.

I was next cast in an episode of *77 Sunset Strip*, a hugely successful one-hour detective series. This show was the prototype for glamorous private-detective series that would dominate television in the late 1950s and early 1960s. The stories revolved around two Los Angeles private dicks who were both former government secret agents. Their office was located at 77 Sunset Strip, next door to Dean Martin's real life hangout,

Dino's Lodge. Rather than a hard-edged drama, *77 Sunset Strip* was laced with self-deprecating humor. The show was shot primarily on Stage 14. We also worked on Stages 17 and 21, which contained "generic sets" that were used for many of the television series shot at the studio. If our TV audiences were astute enough, they could easily recognize the same sets that appeared on different shows.

With Efrem Zimbalist Jr. in "Six Superior Skirts." This was my first appearance on 77 Sunset Strip. PHOTO COLLECTION OF MICHAUD.

My episode, "Six Superior Skirts," concerned a jewel theft at a charity bazaar. I played the role of a debutante. The imperious, eye-patch-wearing Andre De Toth directed the episode. The series starred Efrem Zimbalist Jr., Roger Smith, and Edd Byrnes, who was insufferably egotistical. I loved Efrem, though. He was mannered, stylish, and sophisticated. I had never met a man like him before. I had just graduated from high school when I first worked on this show, and Efrem was very considerate and sweet to me. I enjoyed working with him, and we playfully flirted on the set. "Six Superior Skirts" aired months later on October 16.

My mother had to accompany me on set as I was still a minor. Any fears or misgivings she had were quickly allayed by the professional atmosphere at the studio. In her way, I know she enjoyed herself. To find ourselves in such a situation was surreal. This was a profession so many people dream about and tirelessly seek. In a peculiar way, it almost hurled itself at me. I felt more like a witness than a participant.

My mother visits me on the set of Maverick *in November, 1959.*

Chapter 3

Shortly after my eighteenth birthday I signed a seven-year contract with Warner Bros. Studios. I had talked it over with my parents, who were enthusiastic, and we decided to accept the generous offer that provided me with a beginning salary of $250 a week. Most young contract players were paid a similar amount at signing, with escalating salary clauses kicking in each successive year. The business was a male-dominated; the men's beginning salary was $25 more per week. The contract provided for forty weeks of work with a twelve-week paid hiatus. There were no bonuses promised, and no bonuses were paid to me during my time at the studio. Every contract actor's status was reviewed each six months. If the actor wasn't producing, or had become a troublemaker, the studio could terminate his contract at the end of each six-month period.

Louella Parsons reported in her entertainment column, "Cinderella stories are still happening in Hollywood and the latest beauty to find the glass slipper fits is 18-year-old Diane McBain. Jack Warner, sitting in a Warner projection room looking at one of the *77 Sunset Strip* chapters, spotted Diane in a brief role, and signed her to a screen contract."

I have no idea how it came to be that I was offered a long-term contract, and I never met Jack Warner to ask him. Like Cinderella in the fairy-tale, it was by the grace of something that seemed entirely outside of me that I was catapulted from a life of sweeping up the ashes to the center of attention. Like all magic, it was not by my own wits or being, and it was illusory.

When I was much younger, as we sat on the porch after dinner, Nonny pointed out the Hollywood searchlights that crisscrossed the night sky. Glamorous movie premieres were frequent in those days. Hollywood was just over the hill, but it seemed a million miles away!

"Look there," Nonny said. "They are looking for you." She smiled at the fantastic idea. "Those lights swirling around up there are looking for you, Diane." Those were the only times she called me Diane. Unlike my mother who preferred Diane, Nonny was enamored with Danny.

In my heart, I am Danny. In the beginning, before the glittering world of Hollywood beckoned, I wanted to marry and have a family. Though Danny has a wild side, there are conventional ends to her means. Diane is too independent to ever settle down with a mate. She is not a caregiver.

Life didn't really begin for Diane until I took that first step onto a sound stage. The mesmerizing power of mystery encased within its soundproof walls, the secrets it contained, the untold history it preserved, captivated me beyond measure. I imagined all the actors and actresses who had graced the sets and stages and made them come alive with their craft. Diane wanted to be one of them, and she made that her goal.

The times were fast-changing. By the time I signed my contract the studio contract system that defined the Golden Age of Motion Pictures was huffing and puffing to its painful death. The advent of television and the government-enforced antitrust action (that resulted in the loss of studio-owned movie theater chains) had completely changed the business of making movies from that time forward. In 1956, Albert and Harry Warner, two of the four founding brothers, sold most of their shares in the company. The venerable Jack L. Warner, the youngest of twelve children of Jewish immigrants and one of the "Founding Four," remained the studio boss and its largest single stockholder. He ruled with an iron fist.

Founded in 1923, Warner Bros. had actually started twenty years earlier in 1903 as a nickelodeon in a small town in Pennsylvania. Gradually, the studio expanded into distribution, as well as production, and in 1925, it gobbled up Vitagraph and First National Pictures. Vitaphone, a subsidiary, was formed in 1926. In association with Western Electric, Vitaphone developed a "sound-on-disk" system, and the talking picture was born. *The Jazz Singer*, the first film with synchronized songs and dialogue, was released in 1927, and overnight Warner Bros. became a leading player in movie production.

Films about the common man were the mainstays at Warner during the 1930s. The expensive and extravagant musicals and comedies were left to MGM. Along with studio head Jack Warner, Darryl Zanuck and Hal Wallis became top producers. Gangster pictures, social dramas, and prominent film biographies were their forte. Their list of contract players was most impressive: James Cagney, Edward G. Robinson, Humphrey Bogart, Paul Muni, Errol Flynn, Bette Davis, Joan Crawford and Olivia de Havilland led the pack. Even so, Mr. Warner was interested in economy. Consequently, films were produced at a frantic pace, lower salaries defined the day, and production values were tight and unadorned.

The 1940s were particularly successful years, highlighted by the swashbuckling adventure films of Errol Flynn, Joan Crawford's overblown melodramas, and many classic mystery-dramas. Bogie became a movie icon. The marvelous Chuck Jones helped create some of the biggest animated stars for the studio cartoon department, and managed to win three Academy Awards for Bugs Bunny, Porky Pig, Daffy Duck, Tweetie Pie, Speedy Gonzalez, Road Runner and Wile E. Coyote! Apparently anyone, or any "thing," could become a star in Hollywood.

Enter Diane.

By the late 1950s, the glamorous days of promise were no more. Warner Bros. was struggling, like most other studios, to keep its proverbial head above shark-infested waters. Instead of capitulating to the enemy (the new medium of television) the studio created a television department that would rival all other contenders for several years to come. Studio executive William T. Orr was the head of television production on the lot. He was very powerful, and it didn't hurt that he was married to Jack Warner's stepdaughter. In spite of

This is one of my first publicity photos taken at Warner. Me with the biggest bunny star in history. PHOTO COLLECTION OF MICHAUD

inside charges of nepotism, Bill Orr was a very astute businessman. Up until that time, most television production had been based in New York City. Orr moved Warner's nascent New York based television division to their Los Angeles studios, thereby creating more revenue for the company as well as more jobs. He negotiated an exclusive deal with the ABC television network to broadcast new series produced at Warner. And introducing television production on the lot was a good way to keep busy the studio's new crop of young contract players, and ostensibly nurture them for movie stardom. Bill Orr supervised the ten leading series then produced by the studio for broadcast on ABC.

Following a remarkable roster of stars, I, and a few actors and actresses who would become friends and co-workers, were the last of the Hollywood contract players comprising a long list of copycat, episodic television serials. We didn't realize it at the time, but we would later fight a battle of enormous proportions to save our careers. Most of us would lose.

In July 1959, I was assigned a role in my first feature film. Edna Ferber wrote a bestselling, epic novel about the dramatic debate over Alaska Statehood. Alaska had become the forty-ninth state several months earlier on January 3. *Ice Palace* was a complicated, three-generation story about gender and race, which chronicled the loves and losses of two brave families in the frozen Northwest. The core conflict of the story concerned two men; one who loved Alaska and one who loved money. The money-lover used mechanized fishing boats to catch salmon thereby endangering the delicate environmental balance. The title of the book came from a twelve-story, aluminum and glass building called the Ice Palace in Baranof, the author's fictional Alaskan city. The Northward Building in Fairbanks would double for it in the film.

The studio already had a success in 1956 with their adaptation of Edna Ferber's *Giant*, starring James Dean in what was to be his final role. The studio was equally excited about *Ice Palace*, and before even reading the book, Jack Warner paid the author $350,000 to secure the rights to the film. In her review of the novel, Dorothy Parker said the two male leads were "crashing bores." So is the novel, which proved very difficult to adapt to film. Several writers and producers had tried unsuccessfully to write a screenplay.

The day I walked onto the soundstage to test for the part of Christine Storm, I felt anticipation on the part of the film's director, Vincent Sherman. I sensed he was looking for something in particular. No one had given me a script, and I hadn't read the novel at the time. I only knew the character was the granddaughter of the two male leads played by Richard Burton and Robert Ryan. In fact, the script was still being written by Sherman and the film's producer, Harry Kleiner, as the actors were being cast.

I was carefully coiffed and dressed in a beautiful costume, then shoved in front of the camera. I'd spent enough time in front of cameras to feel comfortable, but I had never screen-tested before. I thought the purpose of a screen test was to determine acting ability. I was wrong.

As it turned out, Mr. Sherman wasn't as worried about my acting skills as he was my looks. The character of Christine Storm was the daughter of a blonde, blue-eyed girl played by Shirley Knight, and a dark-skinned Eskimo played by George Takei. My own mixed-up heritage of Scot, German, and Native American served me well. I looked the part.

Sherman, Jack Warner, and the film's producer, Henry Blanke, reviewed my test in a studio screening room. "The projection room was dark," reported *Screen Stars* magazine. "The film had not yet begun to roll. Studio officials sat tensely waiting to see whether a new star was about to be born.

"The anxiety was high at this first viewing of Diane McBain's screen test. Star quality was rare and the lack of it could make or break a studio production. Perhaps here, at last, was a girl with an 'aura.' The film began to roll... [and] soon the screen test was over. The lights came on in the projection room and there was silence among the producers and directors who made up the audience. Slowly, quietly, they began to talk.

'It's unbelievable...' 'She's right out of the thirties — when a woman was *all* woman.' 'She has sex appeal oozing out of every pore...I haven't seen anything like it since Jean Harlow...' 'More subtle than Harlow. There's a touch of Grace Kelly and the look that makes every man feel she's looking right at *him*, that he's the only man who can have her...'"

Oh, brother. All very nice, but Vincent Sherman should have been more concerned with my acting skills. My first day on the set, I found myself in heady company. Sherman was an accomplished director responsible for such films as *The Young Philadelphians*, *Mr. Skeffington*, and *Affair in Trinidad*. He had been blacklisted by the House Un-American Activities Committee for his supposed political affiliations for several years in the early 1950s. Sherman was short, compact, handsome, and bossy. The cast included Martha Hyer, Jim Backus, Carolyn Jones, and Ray Danton.

I was eighteen years old and a little overwhelmed. My mother helped me decorate my little dressing room on the lot. I had no idea what I was supposed to do or what was expected of me.

Filming began on August 3. The director and most of my fellow actors were very cordial and helpful. I tried to make friends with the other actors on the set. Speaking in his Mr. Magoo voice, Jim Backus kept us laughing, Robert Ryan, a consummate professional, kept us on our toes, and Martha Hyer with her picture-perfect posture set the standard for ladylike behavior. Carolyn Jones tried to teach me to cry on cue. Her huge, bug-like eyes made her look stern and imposing, but she was nice to me.

This was a time for learning, and the lessons came fast and hard. The studio medic, Dr. Hank, took a liking to me. He was also a chiropractor, and I loved the way he rubbed my feet, which responded poorly to movie footwear. I became addicted and craved his foot massages all the time.

He was so eager to please me, and I easily took advantage of him. One day I was on call on the set and could not leave, so I called Dr. Hank for a massage. When he arrived, he was visibly upset. He was frightened that something serious had happened to me, which required his emergency services. He had actually abandoned a patient in his studio office to accommodate me. "There isn't anything I wouldn't do for you, Diane," he sighed. I felt awful. I felt spoiled. Chagrined, I sent him back to his patient and promised never to make such a selfish request again.

Snowy sets were created in two huge soundstages on the studio lot. In mid-August, we flew to Alaska for location shooting in Juneau and Fairbanks, and Petersburg, a salmon fishing center on Mitkof Island. Petersburg was located on the Wrangell Narrows, a watery channel that opened up into Frederick Sound. Quaint, wood-framed cottages were built in the wooded hillside. Norwegians had immigrated there years earlier, and the language was spoken by many of the residents. The little town had a hotel (where we all stayed), a general store, a café, a barbershop and a few saloons. Though real, it all looked remarkably like a movie set. A giant cannery stood on stilts in the water, and a long pier jutted out into the fast flowing current. The air was pungent with the smell of fish. I am not a fish eater, and the odor put me off.

Warner's makeup supervisor, a lovely man named George Bau, who was a little bald and a lot rotund, took over the town barbershop and made it our makeup facility. George was a terrific and talented guy. He loved his work and followed us all around the set carrying his little makeup box for on-the-spot touch-ups.

Alaska was starkly and ruggedly beautiful. In the summer, the sun barely set during the two weeks I was there. Fairbanks and Juneau were as different as night and day. Fairbanks was a moderately sized city. Juneau, the capital, was more of a fishing village and mining outpost.

Ray Danton played my love interest in the film. He was very handsome, but very stiff. I remember staring into his eyes as we played star-crossed lovers. We sat on the rocky beach of a lake at Mendenhall Glacier. This incredible scene, with the vast ice flows in the background, was breathtaking. The nearby lake, fed by melting snow, appeared lifeless to me. Ray stared back at me with the same lifelessness. He didn't project any emotion at all. He tried to smile, but his face nearly cracked with effort. Such an amazingly romantic setting, and I felt like I was courting a frozen fish stick.

Richard Burton played the role of my grandfather, though he was only thirty-two years old. Married with one daughter, Burton excelled in British theater and was an acclaimed classical actor. He had starred in many notable films, including *The Robe* and *Look Back in Anger*. I didn't know who he was, though I could tell by his skill and bearing that he was a very experienced movie star.

With Ray Danton looking frozen on location in Alaska for the film Ice Palace.

The day I met Richard, we filmed a scene where our characters were at loggerheads. The orphaned Christine begs her paternal grandfather to reconcile with her maternal grandfather. She wants them to settle a long-running feud so she can stop being shuffled from one to the other.

Perhaps Richard was a little enchanted by my obvious naïveté and lack of experience. Or, maybe he couldn't resist a pretty, young face. Perhaps it was part of his seduction process, but he was kind and very patient. I had a terrible time learning my lines. Poise and diction may have been taught at the studio, but oddly, the fundamentals of acting were not part of the studio's curriculum. I was simply in over my head. Unbeknownst to me at the time, Richard saved my job on the film. The director wanted to fire me because I had such a hard time memorizing the dialogue. Several times, Richard sensed I was struggling and purposefully muffed his own lines so I wouldn't be blamed for holding up the take.

In all of this turmoil, I was served a sizeable portion of the Richard Burton charm. He had the uncanny ability to make a girl feel like she was the only woman on earth. When he gazed into my eyes, he made me feel like I was the only woman in his *life*. It was impossible to resist his

Jim Backus, Richard Burton and me on the studio set of Ice Palace. *Richard has his nose in a book. Reading was one of his favorite pastimes.*

attention. Both Diane and Danny loved it.

I fell in love with him. The sandy, tasseled hair teasing the brow just above his clear, green "I've Got a Secret" eyes, was more than I could resist. I was dreadfully young, and didn't dream such a man would have any interest in me. He followed me around like a lost puppy, and in a sense, was present from that moment on. He wanted to have dinner with me that first evening. I took the bait.

When Richard picked me up at home, my mother followed me to his car, which was idling at the curb. He jumped out of the driver's seat to greet her. Within minutes, she was utterly charmed by him. They laughed together, he complimented her good looks, and he congratulated her for raising such a lovely and talented daughter.

We went to dinner at the Sportsman's Lodge in the San Fernando Valley, a rambling, rustic restaurant with a pond where you could actually catch your own fish, and we talked for hours. He was a raconteur and an amazing story-teller. He talked about having lunch with Picasso and quarreling with Hemingway. I was swept away.

I soon discovered Richard had quite a reputation with the ladies. Being a husband and father didn't seem to slow him one bit. He flirted with other women on the set, but he seemed a bit more entranced with me. I was just out of high school, and I was a virgin. Diane was terrified of sex. Danny was enthusiastic, but unsure. My mother's advice about men and my religious principles were blatantly ignored.

Richard and I had dinner many times, and one day he invited me to his agent's house on the beach in Malibu. Hugh French and his girlfriend, Marta, were charming hosts and we met there quite often thereafter. We had a wonderful time. We ate delicious food and drank Scotch. The two men talked about philosophy and politics while Marta and I listened intently from the sidelines.

Richard encouraged me to read, and gave me a list of books to consider. He advised me to find novels and stories that could be suitable for future roles and present them to my agent. He wanted me to find a better agent, too. He felt I shouldn't have signed a studio contract, and he tried to think of ways to break it.

I listened to him because he was a reasonable and brilliant man. He read a book every day, he told me. A chronic insomniac, he often read through the night.

Often, when we were alone, he pulled me onto his lap and held me. I felt happy and contented like never before. I was so safe in his arms, cradled against him. I knew I was in love. Sometimes he spoke to me in Welsh. It was the most beautiful, lyrical language I had ever heard. The sound of his voice was transcendent.

One night after dinner at Romanoff's in Beverly Hills, Richard took me back to his house for the first time. The English Tudor style residence was situated in a cove off Sunset Boulevard in Pacific Palisades. His wife, Sybil, and his daughter, Kate, had recently relocated to their home in Switzerland. I didn't know very much about his married life except he had confessed to me that he no longer had sex with his wife and he wasn't sure his marriage would survive. Richard was my first "adult" love and my first adventure in adultery. I believed him because I *wanted* to believe him. The fact that his wife was pregnant with his second child was something I chose to ignore.

The large house was dark and cold when we first entered. The den was comfortably furnished with overstuffed leather chairs, a couch, and a baby grand piano. He started a fire in the fireplace and lit a few candles around the room. He poured me a drink, then took my hands and led me to a lush green-leather couch. He sat next to me and brushed his lips against mine. "Give us a kiss," he whispered… and I did.

Soon I was nestled into the couch, smothered in his kisses. He then went to the piano and played Beethoven's "Moonlight Sonata." The night was so romantic, and the piano playing so seductive, I found myself completely open to his persistent sexual advances. I was ripe for the picking.

I needed help. "Marta!" I cried into the phone in the bathroom. "I tried a tampon and it hurt like hell. If I can't get one of those inside me, how on earth am I going to manage…well, you know?"

She laughed and calmly explained that Richard would make me ready to receive him no matter how large his penis appeared. I didn't believe her, of course. I ached to talk with my mother, but how could I? To admit contemplating sexual activity at my age and before marriage was unacceptable. Richard, fourteen years my senior, was married. I was sure she would try to talk me out of it, and out of his house. My mother tried to allow me to make my own mistakes, but this was more than she could have handled. Marta tried to reassure me, but I was inconsolable. Finally, I was able to get off the telephone.

Richard was very gentle and I was beginning to believe what Marta had said. Perhaps he could make me more receptive to him than I had been to that dry tampon. His mouth traveled up and down my naked body with wet lush kisses and when his tongue found my vagina… I was horrified!

"You can't do that!" I screamed as I pushed him away. I couldn't imagine why anyone would want to do that. "I mean," I stammered, "I go to the bathroom from there!" How could I let him put his mouth where I wouldn't even put my hands?

He was insistent. "I want to do that to you," he said. "I want to make you feel things you've never felt before." I relented, and he did. His mouth was amazing, but I found the size of his penis to be too overwhelming. He was unable to move past my resistance enough to have intercourse.

I saw Richard regularly, and we were intimate to a point. Soon, I became aware of his many sexual escapades. He told me he was unable to look upon love in any kind of exclusive way. He told me he was "amoral," something I'd never heard of before. In his view, there was no right or wrong when it came to sex. It was just good.

The more I heard about his wicked ways, the more I became numb to any feelings of jealousy. Such a feeling wouldn't change him; in fact, it may even jeopardize whatever true feelings he had for me. I denied my feelings, and refused to express my rage.

I was juggling a budding career and my first love affair. My studio contract called for me to work steadily on whatever film or Warner Bros.-

The "Deb Stars" of 1959, posing with Bob Hope for his television special. I'm seated next to Bob, to his left. PHOTO COURTESY OF MICHAUD

produced ABC television series was available. I had no choice. In the fall, I happily returned to work on *Maverick* in an episode about a murder frame-up gone awry. "The Fellow's Brother" aired on November 22.

"Deb Stars" were chosen annually by journalists as up and coming stars of the future. They were formally introduced at the annual Deb Stars Ball in Hollywood, a benefit that funded the Make-up and Hairstylists Guild's chosen charity. The ball was little more than a publicity event, but always attracted a great deal of press coverage. On November 9, I was one of ten "Deb Stars" introduced by Bob Hope on his one-hour NBC-TV special. Sheilah Graham wrote in her "Hollywood Gadabout" column, "Diane McBain, doing nicely in television. Here is a very pretty blond who hails from Cleveland, Ohio. Diane was one of the 10 Hollywood debs on Bob

Hope's last special. She walked down the stairs with more poise and charm than any of the others on the show."

I was then assigned the role of Paula Harding in "The Starlet." This episode of *77 Sunset Strip* called for the detectives to prove that the apparent suicide of a despondent actress was actually murder. "The Starlet" was broadcast a couple of months later in February.

With Kay Elhardt in "The Starlet." PHOTO COURTESY OF MICHAUD

As the *Ice Palace* production came to a close in December, Richard informed me he would return to his home and wife in Switzerland. We had exchanged gifts earlier. Mine was a beautiful white sweater with a white fox collar. I gave him a white sweater with a red and blue strip around the neck. We laughed at the unlikelihood of giving each other virtually the same gift.

The night before he was scheduled to depart, his manager, Valerie, threw a party for him at her home. In a curious move, she invited each of the women he had bedded during his stay. An older woman, Valerie seemed to be envious of his lovers. Perhaps she felt if she couldn't have him herself, she would provide all the beautiful women he wanted, thereby maintaining some sense of control.

Perhaps each of the women expected to spend the night, as we all arrived in taxis. At the gathering, Richard paid no attention to the others. When the party drew to a close, he asked me to spend the night with him. I felt smug when the other women (Carolyn Jones, Martha Hyer, and Shirley Knight) marched out grumbling.

There was no sleep that night. Richard and I were both consumed with passion. We attempted intercourse, yet again. At last, he was able to break through my hymen, passionately and painfully. My body could not accommodate his penis, though, so he was not able to fully penetrate me and complete the sex act. We talked through the night, cradled in each others' arms. The next morning, I went with him to the airport. He promised his undying love, and I cried until he had to board the jet that would take him home to Switzerland and out of my life.

Soon after he arrived home, his wife gave birth to a girl who was severely brain damaged. I wondered if some kind of divine retribution influenced his life. The countless women, the debauchery, and the alcoholism were all distinct indications that something was amiss. Richard later said, "The minute you start fiddling around outside the idea of monogamy, nothing satisfies anymore." Perhaps he came to a deeper understanding about the need for monogamy as time wore on.

My inner voice assured me that God's forgiveness is complete. Richard was more innocent that I realized. He behaved defensively, like a wounded animal.

Now, I had to face my own indiscretions. I had lost my virginity, had an affair with a married man, and deceived my parents. I fell in love with Richard, but I had to come to terms with my behavior.

Several months later in the summer of 1960, *Ice Palace* opened with a thud. In a *New York Times* review dated June 30, Bosley Crowther called it "as false and synthetic a screen saga as has rolled out of a color camera" and "no more authentic than cornstarch snow on a studio set." On July 28, Philip K. Scheuer wrote in the *Los Angeles Times*, "*Ice Palace* leaves viewers cold. Despite its two hours and twenty-three minutes, it never seems much more than a synopsis for a picture the studio may really get around to making someday."

Trying to look cool in a studio "fur coat" promoting Ice Palace. *It was about 110 degrees under the lights!*

The trade papers were a bit kinder to me. On June 15, the *Hollywood Reporter* wrote that I was one among other "standouts as the younger generation…" *Variety* added, "…Diane McBain particularly decorative in support."

Ice Palace was a commercial and critical failure. The studio lost millions of dollars, and I lost my heart.

Chapter 4

In early 1960, I moved from my parent's home on Verdugo Road in Glendale into a spacious two-bedroom apartment with Sherry Jackson. We met on the set of *77 Sunset Strip*, were the same age, and struck up an instant friendship. Sherry had made a few films and starred in the popular television series, *Make Room for Daddy*. Montgomery Pittman, her stepfather, was a terrific writer/director on *77 Sunset Strip*. After all that had happened in the previous six months, I was feeling grown-up and independent. I wanted to explore what it was like to live on my own as an adult woman. I also felt guilty for being less than honest with my mother and wanted to get away from her watchful eyes. The apartment on Scenic Drive in Hollywood was in an old building that looked like a French chateau with turrets and towers.

My lifestyle began to reflect my increasing profile as an actress. Even though my weekly payroll of $250 was a good chunk of money at the time, I was unable to pay for the many extravagances I craved. Credit was easy to obtain, and, sadly, I used it indiscriminately.

I was also assigned a studio publicist. We were told never to engage in a dialogue with a critic or a gossip columnist. That's what the studio publicists were supposed to handle. Sometimes they did. The lesser stars were often sacrificed, though, for the studio's icons. The bigger the star, the more they were likely to get away with bad behavior. I didn't think my behavior was any better or worse than anyone else's. I never thought it was anyone's business what I did in my private life. There were times when I thought the studio threw me under the bus when the gossip got hot and heavy.

Don Ryber was the studio publicist who handled me. He was good at spinning stories and well-practiced at keeping a secret. Don was gay and lived with his boyfriend, Ray. I liked Don very much, and I spent Christmas at his house assembling a miniature train-village beneath the holiday tree. The time spent reminded me of childhood days playing with neighborhood train sets. Don had collected wintry props, including houses, storefronts, fir trees, streetlights, and other miniatures reminiscent of Christmas villages with tiny trains moving through snowy vistas. Danny loved it.

Don was a great friend and a clever publicist. Through the years, I gave him plenty of gossip to handle. He eventually moved on to work with singer Johnny Mathis, whose determination to remain in the closet made Don's job especially tricky.

My family was conservative, and even though one of my best high school friends was gay, I was surprised to meet and work with so many homosexual men at the studio. They were involved in every creative aspect of movie making, including hair, make up, costuming, music, art and set design, lighting, and writing. Of course, many actors were gay, but they lived in the closet for fear of sabotaging their career goals. Making movies was profoundly infused with homosexual aestheticism. I think their cultural influence was so powerful, it's mystifying to me that so many people — people who loved the movies — harbored homophobic prejudices. I never understood it.

The studio publicity department fawned over me, delightedly making up stories about the young actress fresh out of high school, while I blithely put to rest such absurdities.

On December 13, 1959, Louella Parsons wrote for the *Los Angeles Examiner*, "'How did you get into motion pictures?' I expected her to say, 'All my life I wanted to be an actress.' But instead, Diane, who hasn't yet learned to embroider the facts and make them into a beautiful make-believe story, said she never particularly wanted to be an actress. In fact, she told me she had never written fan letters nor been excited over the stars."

I don't even remember talking with her, but what she said was true, though it made me sound haughty and cold. That was Diane.

I became a parade float decoration once again on January 1, 1960, when I was chosen "Queen of the Range" by the United States Navy and rode on the Pacific Missile Range float in the Rose Parade in Pasadena. I thought I would freeze to death. I manically waved at the thousands of spectators in an attempt to keep warm. The spectacular float was comprised of a massive twisting dragon made of fragrant yellow roses and a thirty-foot-tall mock missile decorated in red, white, and blue flower blossoms! A few days later, James Johnson, Commander of the US Navy, wrote a letter of thanks to William Hendricks, Director of Publicity at Warner Bros. Johnson wrote in part, "I'm taking this opportunity to write you on behalf of the entire staff of the Pacific Missile Range and in particular Admiral Monroe and myself. We all feel that our chosen Queen of the Range, Diane McBain, proved herself worthy of the title beyond any shadow of a doubt by 'sticking to her guns' despite the extreme climatic conditions and discomfort of not being able to sit down throughout the parade route. It is the unanimous feeling of all that not only was Diane the most beautiful young lady in the area, but the most gracious as well." Commander Johnson concluded his letter with an appealing offer to me, "Please feel free to call on the Navy here at Point Magu in the event we can be of any assistance to you in the future." That was one of the best offers I had ever received — what eighteen-year-old young woman wouldn't want the US Navy at her beck and call!

Newly crowned "Queen of the Range," I have my first dance with Admiral Monroe on January 1, 1960.

My career seemed on the fast track, famous Hollywood columnists like Hedda Hopper, Louella Parsons, and Sheilah Graham wrote about me, I had completed my first feature film, I experienced my first love affair, and I moved into an apartment building that looked like a castle. I felt like Cinderella.

It wasn't Prince Charming who swept me off my feet, though. It was television. The casting department handed me one television role after another for the next few months. I quickly became accustomed to the low-budget, tight-scheduled conveyor belt production system. This was a particularly touchy time for television production. A strike was called on January 16, 1960 by the Writers Guild of America. The conflict concerned the writer's share of revenue paid to them by the studios from the lease or sale of movies to television. The devastating strike was not settled until June 10, making it the longest writers' strike in history up to that time.

During the strike, the studio used previously produced television scripts and simply adapted them to suit another of their series. In the credits, the writer of those particular recycled scripts was listed as "W. Hermanos." The "W" stood for Warner, and "hermanos" is the Spanish word for "brothers." For us actors, after a while, all the shows seemed to run into one another. We just changed costumes.

The first show I was shoveled into was *The Alaskans*, which starred Roger Moore as a fortune hunter in Skagway, Alaska during the 1890s Gold Rush. It also starred as a saloon singer Dorothy Provine, and my fellow contract player, Ray Danton. From *Ice Palace* to *The Alaskans*, poor Ray couldn't seem to extricate himself from the snow.

In Warner's terms, the show was a "big production." Massive Stage 12 was completely transformed into a snow-covered Yukon setting. There were fake mountains, and fake evergreen trees nailed to the floor. White sheets covered the floor, and then those sheets were covered in fake snow. "Movie snow" was made of gypsum and cornflakes. Tons of fake snow would cascade down from the ceiling at the appropriate cue. The crew was actually equipped with masks and goggles. The rest of us had to have our eyes flushed with saline after each snow-burdened scene. The supposed frozen town of Skagway was created on the backlot with drifts of fake snow sweeping up against the buildings. We were all dressed in fur boots, heavy parkas, gloves, hats, and woolen scarves. Outside, it was eighty degrees.

Roger Moore was thirty-two years old. I didn't pay attention to him, and he didn't pay attention to me. He was too busy having an affair with his leading lady, Dorothy Provine. Dot was a brassy blonde and a good-time girl with legs to spare. She loved to laugh, and I liked her, though I felt a little competitive with her professionally. Roger was born in England. His handsome looks made it easier to accept the idea that the Alaskan adventurer he portrayed had a pronounced English accent.

In *The Alaskans*, I played Harriet Pemberton in an episode called "Behind the Moon," which had something to do with gold prospectors and Indians. The one-hour episode was broadcast on March 6, 1960.

I then filmed three episodes of *Bourbon Street Beat*. This was another detective series using Warner's formula of a requisite team of detectives, an aspiring third detective, and an attractive female character. Contract players Andrew Duggan, Richard Long, and Van Williams starred in this program set in colorful New Orleans. Their fictional detective agency was located in the French Quarter above a real restaurant called Absinthe House. Thinking that this series would be a winner (which it wasn't), the studio actually bought an interest in the historic Bourbon Street restaurant. The show was shot on Stages 17 and 18, and utilized the dusty, dark Vieux Carre sets originally created for *A Streetcar Named Desire*.

In the first episode, I played the role of a missing beauty contestant who was victimized by a blackmailer. "The Missing Queen" aired on

March 14. I was again directed by the suave Paul Henreid. This episode was written by two women, Doris Gilbert and a mystery novelist named Dorothy B. Hughes. At that time, there were very few women working as television writers.

In the second episode, about a man's suicide that led the detectives to a strange island controlled by an even stranger blackmailer, I played

With my dear friend Robbie at the Coconut Grove in Los Angeles. He was my "date" on Valentine's Day in 1960.

Lorraine Elliot. "Wall of Silence" was broadcast two weeks later.

"Ferry to Algiers" concerned the investigation of an elderly shopkeeper blackmailed by hoodlums who wanted to buy his property. Obviously, blackmail was a recurring theme on this show. I played Christina in the episode that aired on June 6. The best thing to come out of my three appearances on *Bourbon Street Beat* was the beginning of my longtime professional association and lifetime friendship with Van Williams.

When *Bourbon Street Beat* was cancelled a few months later, two of the leading characters moved directly into other Warner Bros. /ABC series, playing the same roles. Richard Long's character moved from New Orleans to Los Angeles to join the detectives on *77 Sunset Strip*. Van Williams' character, Ken Madison, moved to Miami Beach and formed his own agency in a new series to be called *Surfside Six*.

In the midst of my many television assignments, I was invited to model Oscar-nominated costumes on the 32nd Annual Academy Awards telecast on April 4. The location of the spectacle was the Pantages Theatre in Hollywood, which had never looked more sparkling and illuminated before. My friend Robbie, who was actually more excited to be there than I, was my date. Although all the actresses looked beautiful in their gowns and diamonds, couture designers were not yet scrambling to "loan" their latest and most glamorous creations to be worn by celebrities on the red carpet for publicity purposes. I wore a beautiful pink satin gown that my mother actually made for the occasion. Her skills as a dress-designer and seamstress had improved remarkably over the years.

Sugarfoot called for my services next. Shot on Stage 22, this one-hour Western starred Will Hutchins as the title character named Tom "Sugarfoot" Brewster. Will was tall, lanky, cute, and funny, and he played the role of a bumbling, "shit-kicking" boob so well. It was a pleasure to work with him and the show was terribly popular. I played Joan in a twice-told tale about a crooked mayor and a young man charged with murder. "Return to Boot Hill" aired on March 15.

On May 6, I appeared in another episode of *77 Sunset Strip* called "Fraternity of Fear." I guest-starred with Shirley Knight and Gary Vinson. The studio publicity department linked me romantically with Gary, which was a complete fabrication. I didn't find him attractive or even interesting. The gossip was good for promoting the episode, though.

With barely a moment to breathe, I appeared on an installment of *The Lawman* called "The Judge." I played Lilac, a woman on the plains, who helped the title character when he's shot while searching for a criminal humorously called The Actor. The clever teleplay was written by Montgomery Pittman. A granite-jawed John Russell starred as the lawman. He was seemingly made of stone. During production, he went on a carrot juice diet for some reason and literally turned orange before our eyes. The makeup department was seeing red. Peter Brown played Russell's young deputy. Peter was an incredibly handsome man, and no one appreciated his good looks more than he.

In the midst of working twelve-hour days in sound stages and on the studio backlot, I was expected to be available for interviews, photo shoots, and personal appearances. I still craved substantive acting lessons, but oddly nothing of the sort was available on the studio lot. I had little time to pursue anything on my own when I was working.

The studios employed still photographers, who were invited on movie and television sets to take staged photos of the goings-on. There were also some talented portrait photographers, who took head and glamour shots of the studios' stars. All these photos were then sent to various photo agencies, where the images were sold to movie magazines and periodicals. The purposes were to promote the film or television show in production or to promote the contracted stars.

One of the first things a person notices when they become a celebrity is that the people around them suddenly treat them differently. I enjoyed the special treatment. Diane loved being driven around in limousines and was naturally delighted to be adorned in fabulous clothing. The studio's chief costume designer, Howard Shoup, created spectacular outfits for me. His unfailing sense of color, pattern, and flattering lines was reflected in his own impeccable personal style. Howard was a delightful gay man, who was beloved by everyone at the studio. He would create costumes for most of my Warner films. Howard was one of the dearest men I ever met in Hollywood, which says a lot. He was always respectful of me, and treated me with deference.

Another very talented gay man named John Brandt became my personal clothing designer. He created everything from cocktail casual to formal wear.

I loved being dressed to the nines and walking into the studio commissary, where all eyes watched me while I ate. The dining room was a great place to make a grand entrance. Danny was particularly delighted by that kind of attention. I often ordered an ice cream cone for dessert and licked it in such a way that forks dropped and napkins suddenly tumbled onto men's laps. It was fun to tease and get such a reaction.

Chapter 5

Mildred Savage published her first novel, *Parrish*, in 1958. The steamy story about rival tobacco farmers in Connecticut was a bestseller. Jack Warner purchased the rights to adapt the novel to the screen. Originally, Joshua Logan was attached to the project. He wanted Clark Gable and Vivien Leigh to play the parents, and he tested many young actors, including Warren Beatty and Jane Fonda. Logan's plans fell through when he rejected the first draft screenplay, and the project languished for a short time.

The film was green-lighted at the end of 1959 and set to star several screen veterans, including Oscar winners Dean Jagger and Karl Malden, and film legend Claudette Colbert. Troy Donohue was cast as Parrish, a rebellious young man at odds with his ruthless stepfather. Connie Stevens and Sharon Hugueny were cast as two young women chasing after Parrish's affections. The studio was looking for Troy's third leading lady. I tested and easily landed the role of Allison Post, Dean Jagger's manipulative and truculent daughter. It was a choice role, and I was thrilled to be a part of the film.

Delmer Daves was set to write and direct *Parrish*. Though Westerns were his forte, he had written and directed several hit films, including *Dark Passage*, *A Summer Place*, and *An Affair to Remember*. He was a towering man, at well over six feet tall, and he had a reputation as a director who brandished a velvet whip.

Claudette Colbert was a total mystery to me. Though diminutive in stature, the Oscar winner was the biggest movie star with whom I had worked. I didn't know what to expect when I came face to face with her on the first day on the set. The star of film classics, such as *It Happened One Night*, *The Palm Beach Story*, and *Since You Went Away*, she was treated like royalty at the studio. *Parrish* would provide her with her final performance in a feature film. She was a fit fifty-seven years old, tidy, and solid. There was a sturdiness to her that seemed unbending. Sometimes she spoke in a stentorian tone that caused everyone to drop what they were doing and run to accommodate her. She was outwardly nice to me, at times friendly, but not very warm. She certainly had the aura of a movie star. I think she had formed something of an opinion of me before we met. She didn't have to wait long for me to confirm her worst fears.

After some work at the studio in late April, the production moved to Windsor, Connecticut for location work in fields of Connecticut shade tobacco. We arrived in May. Though the countryside was beautiful, it was

With Troy Donahue in Parrish.

hot and muggy. I experienced the same difficulty learning my lines as I had on *Ice Palace*. I had yet to figure out a method of memorization, which was plaguing my ability to act. In television production, it didn't seem to matter as much, but on the big screen it mattered a lot — especially working with such respected and award-winning actors. When I got nervous, I lost my concentration. Lacking proper training, I didn't know how to control my nerves.

Each night before I was due on the set I read and re-read my scenes, covering the lines with my hand and trying desperately to remember. All night, I struggled with the lines. I barely got any sleep, and when I finally dozed off, I was overcome with terrifying nightmares.

Of course, acting isn't just about remembering lines. Since I had no formal training, my acting lessons consisted of listening to the director.

I watched my fellow actors and gleaned what I could by example. Daves was an "old school" director. "Method-style" acting was more and more popular in film work, but Daves said that there was no such thing as a system suitable for all actors. In my case, his direction took the tone of mental conditioning. He told me to "think hard" about Troy (my leading man) during the day and "even dream about him at night." He said he

With the venerable Claudette Colbert in Parrish.

wanted me to "know" Troy "like you would know a man who has changed your whole life." He continued, "then when you look at Troy in a scene, your face will show an understanding of him, and reflect past your feelings discovered in the rehearsal immediately before." His direction of me was simple — dream and daydream about Troy Donahue. "Keep notes on Troy," he said, "and on your own experiences in life paralleling those in the script. The results will surprise you." He was right in that regard. I think Miss Colbert was surprised, as well.

One day, a scene required me to smoothly descend a sweeping circular staircase — no "bouncing" — while letting Miss Colbert's character know in no uncertain terms how I felt about spending the evening with her and my hapless father. The spoiled Allison wanted instead to spend time with the handsome son of her father's business rival.

I was required to deliver a monologue while walking. I couldn't remember the damned lines standing still and looking at the script, much less while gracefully descending a long, curving stairway. In addition, I had to time it so that my last line of dialogue was delivered when I took my last step to the floor. All the while, Miss Colbert stood stoically at the foot of the stairs, staring at me.

With Troy Donahue in Parrish.

I tried and tried, but I was never able to conquer the complicated task of delivering the words and moving in precision. Take after tedious take, Miss Colbert stiffened before my eyes. I could feel the chill off her as if she was an iceberg. Daves became more and more velvety with his emotional whip. Finally, they decided to scrap the entire scene. I was embarrassed beyond words, I realized I had a lot of work to do, and I could see the job wasn't going to be easy. Throughout this painful ordeal, Miss Colbert didn't say a word, but if looks could kill, I would have been buried in a tobacco field outside Hartford, Connecticut.

Still I managed to have fun with Troy, Connie, and especially Sharon. I celebrated my nineteenth birthday on location with the director, the cast, and crew. I remember eating my first "Steak Diane" — a delicious flambé affair — then drinking succulent Cabernet Sauvignon and finally being the toast of the entire room atop the Huntington Hartford Hotel. My new young actor friends and the crewmembers, who had now become colleagues, surrounded me. I always loved the guys on the crew. It's because of their hard labor that movies get made at all. Though the public never seems to care about them, they are the "real" people in the film industry.

Me as Allison Post in Parrish.

My special birthday dinner was memorable, and I often wish I could go back to that night. Alas, the sword at the entrance to the Garden is flaming and impassable. One can never go back.

During the making of the film, gossip columnists began to take swipes at me in the press. Hedda Hopper, often supportive in the past, reported in the *Los Angeles Times* months later on August 19, 1960, that her associate in Connecticut reported, "Picture industry should be proud of Delmer Daves and *Parrish* company. They filmed many days in our community and were friendly and warm and won our hearts. Sharon Hugueny, Connie Stevens and Troy Donohue delightful, but Diane McBain could learn from them: she was the only one who was distant."

My looks put me on magazine covers and, eventually, into the movies. From an early age, people stared at me. Being uncomfortable with that attention and superficial interest, I ignored their stares and was usually oblivious to them. I never meant to be rude; I just didn't know how to handle ogling eyes.

The film was beautifully photographed in color, and Max Steiner created a captivating musical score, but at 138 minutes, the movie was overlong. In spite of my struggles with lines, I garnered a few decent reviews when the film was released in 1961. On March 21, *Variety* wrote, "…the strikingly beautiful and glamorous Miss McBain is effective as Jagger's spoiled daughter." The *Hollywood Reporter* added, "Diane McBain was vivid." On June 29, the *Los Angeles Examiner* wrote, "…Diane McBain, a real beauty, becomes a genuine actress as Jagger's dissolute daughter." The following day, the *Los Angeles Times* added, "Miss McBain, an unusually good looking girl, might, if she can handle light comedy, be the next Carol Lombard." Oh, my God!

Warner Bros. Publicity Photo. COURTESY OF MICHAUD

Stardom

A typical studio publicity photograph from 1960.

Chapter 6

In 1960, I was on my contractual hiatus for most of the summer. Though I wasn't required to act in front of a camera, I was still expected to magnanimously grant interviews and pose for movie magazine pictorials. My dating habits were very casual, and I still thought of Richard Burton now and then. I especially reconsidered his advice in terms of my studio contract. In August, the casting department at Warner Bros. informed me I would be starring as a regular in a new, one-hour detective series set in Miami Beach called *Surfside Six*. Under the contract system, an actor had little to say about his or her roles. I could have objected, but legally I was required to comply with the studio's demands or face suspension. Richard had warned me that if the studio over-exposed me by too many television appearances, it would destroy my chances for a real career as a motion picture star. In a way, I felt as though I was being put out to pasture.

Surfside Six was created by studio chief William T. Orr and writer Hugh Benson. The storylines centered around a Miami Beach detective agency that used a sixty-foot, two-story houseboat as a home and office. "Surfside 6" was the telephone exchange that also included the marina slip number where the boat was docked. The detective team featured Troy Donahue as Sandy Winfield II, Van Williams as Ken Madison, and Lee Patterson as Dave Thorne. I was cast as Daphne "Daffy" Dutton, a "kooky socialite," whose yacht was parked next to the boys' houseboat. Margarita Sierra played Cha Cha O'Brien, a singer, who worked the Boom Boom Room at the majestic Fontainebleau Hotel across the street. The series also gave the studio another opportunity to use their contract players on a weekly basis. Perhaps the most memorable thing about the show was the popular theme song written by Jerry Livingston and David Mack.

Though I was billed as a regular, I didn't appear in all seventy-four episodes broadcast over the next two years, but I did appear in most. The show gave the three handsome leading men plenty of opportunity to take their shirts off, Margarita to shimmy and shake, and me to prance around like a zany debutante in outlandishly stylish clothing.

The show was filmed on Stages 20 and 24 at Warner, as well as on the backlot. There were only two permanent sets specific to *Surfside Six* — the boys' houseboat and the hotel lobby and adjoining nightclub. In the summer, we traveled to Miami Beach and filmed "B-roll" for a couple of weeks. "B-roll" was additional footage that could easily be cut into the primary film. In our case, it was little more than "stock footage" for the

Troy Donahue, Margarita Sierra, Lee Patterson, me, and Van Williams. The cast of Surfside Six. PHOTO COLLECTION OF MICHAUD

producers and directors to use and re-use. For the most part, our Miami location scenes consisted of the boys and me driving up to or away from the houseboat, or dashing back and forth across the busy boulevard that separated the boat from the hotel. Costuming had to be simplified since those shots were later edited into whatever was filmed at the studio to give the viewers the mistaken idea that the entire program was filmed on location in Florida. I usually wore a tennis outfit, and the boys wore shorts or simple t-shirts and jerseys to make it easier for the sake of continuity to match the costumes in the edited shots. This is why the boys were bare-chested in so many scenes. No costumes were required to match one bare-chested shot to another.

The work environment on set was jovial; we all got along very well. There was a lot of teasing and laughter. Our natural chemistry and playfulness made the show easy to watch. The boys had a great time together, and their camaraderie was apparent on the screen. I loved them all for different reasons. Troy was billed as the star of the show. He was a good-natured, gentle soul. He didn't take himself or his blonde, Ivy-League good looks seriously. Van was a gentleman and a cool cat. He was happily married with kids, and always in a good mood. Lee was very independent. He was from Canada, and possessed no "movie-star" attitude at all. He

On the set of Surfside Six *with Troy, Lee, and Van.* PHOTO COLLECTION OF MICHAUD

was a different kind of actor for me. Margarita Sierra was adorable. She was sweet and very funny, and we all loved her. I never experienced or witnessed any ego issues with the cast members.

The order in which our scenes were filmed usually caused us to be on the set at different times. I might have had only a few scenes in an entire episode, so they tried to film all of them on the same day. Sometimes it took a couple of days. Of course, with me being a contract actor, they could have called me at midnight to come in and work, and they sometimes did.

Since there were four of us credited as "stars" of the show, each one of us was featured in individual episodes on a rotating basis. Each of those storylines was centered on a particular lead character. These shows were often filmed simultaneously at the studio. The producers realized that by doing so they could crank out more episodes without incurring a marked increase in production costs. Sometimes, we actually shot two or three shows at the same time. There were days when I had no idea what the story concerned that I was working on. I still don't know, because I rarely watched the finished product.

I actually saw more of my co-stars at lunchtime in the studio commissary. Besides providing us all with a break from work, it was a great time to socialize and catch up with our co-workers and friends. It was also important to be "seen" in the commissary to remind the powers-that-be that you were still there and anxious to work. The commissary provided us the rare opportunity to sit and chat with the casting personnel about any upcoming feature films on the lot.

The storylines on *Surfside Six* were less than lightweight. Some of the highlights of the first season included stories about a hated dictator living in exile in Miami Beach who was murdered at a birthday party by a performing clown named Pepe; a mind-reader in a trance, who was instructed to commit a heinous murder; a diver who turned up dead after he claimed a portion of the gold coins he discovered in a shipwreck; a voodoo-practicing poison snake importer, who killed someone at a carnival in Jamaica; a performer in a water-ski show, who blackmailed her ex-boyfriend into forfeiting his multi-million dollar inheritance; a Treasury Department money engraver, who was kidnapped on his honeymoon and forced to work for a counterfeiter. Very heady stuff. You get the picture.

Ray Danton, playing an ex-con, guest-starred in our premiere episode titled, "Country Gentleman," which aired on October 3, 1960. My friend, Sherry Jackson, appeared in our second episode titled "High Tide," which was written and directed by her stepfather, Montgomery Pittman. Sherry played a "bored stenographer on vacation," who enlisted the boys' help after she discovered she was being followed by a couple of thugs played by Max Baer Jr. and Chad Everett.

Monty Pittman was not just a talented writer with infallible directing instincts. He looked like a character out of central casting. He was frumpy, and he could easily have played the role of a vagabond. What he lacked in formal education he made up for with his wit, his gregarious nature, and down-to-earth sensibility. The stinky odor of his cigar always heralded his entrance. He adored Sherry and doted on her. Historically, the importance of writers in Hollywood has been all but entirely dismissed. Writers are at the bottom of the Hollywood food chain, yet Monty was an exception. He was a wonderful and reliable writer, and the studio treated him with a bit of reverence.

We had been on the air for just a few months, when the *Pittsburgh Press* put our show into perspective on January 1, 1961. They wrote, "One of the few bright spots of *Surfside Six* is the good looks of Diane McBain. *Surfside Six* is a detective series with a Miami Beach locale. It has the quality of a game being played by a group of attractive youngsters, with luxurious cars, boats, and clothes as toys. As with many games of childhood, the players' reasons for doing whatever they do are vague, sort of made up as they go along, to create action and excitement. Diane appears every week, and approximately each fifth week has a major part. The rest of the time she is largely decorative." I couldn't have said it better myself. We didn't showcase serious material like that featured on *Studio One* or *Omnibus*. *Surfside Six* was created for the youth market. We presented good old "T&A," and for a time, the audience hungrily tuned in.

Surfside Six was successful, and like the stars of most successful television shows, we all quickly became household names. In a short time, I was deluged with fan mail, and movie magazine polls named me a fan favorite. The studio was thrilled with the advertising dollars and the marketing revenue from books, posters, photographs, and other merchandise tie-ins. A firm in Miami built and sold replicas of the "Surfside Six" houseboat. The actors, though, were paid no more as a result of this windfall. We had no share of advertising or merchandizing revenue. For the first time, I realized the downside of fame. I couldn't walk down the street without someone calling out to me, "Hey, Daffy!" Suddenly, my opinion of men was questioned in the press, and my dating advice was sought after by columnists. I began to think Richard was right about me becoming a television actress. My fear was, "familiarity breeds contempt."

I sensed a change in the way the studio intended to market me before we shot our first episode. Studio photographers were summoned, and the boys and I were readied for a new round of glamour shots. My poses and wardrobe changed when I began work on *Surfside Six*. Warner decided to promote me as a sex symbol. Suddenly, my couture, picture-perfect wardrobe was cast aside in exchange for revealing one-piece bathing suits. This became another part of my life I had to surrender for the sake of my contract. I had to go where they told me to go, and I had to pose for the pictures they wanted me to pose for. So, for the next two years, I submitted myself to do cheesecake photos for the sake of my craft. Cheesecake (and beefcake in the case of the boys on the show, who were also required to strip down) was studio slang for something erroneously characterized as bathing suit art. I stood in a six foot square "sand box" (filled with questionably clean sand) and flirtatiously sipped ice-tea through a straw, played with an oversized beach ball, struck a coquettish pose beneath an umbrella, or straightened my sunglasses for countless, and at times leering, photographers.

It was impossible to express my concerns in the press without looking like an ungrateful bitch. A profile of me in *TV Guide* was titled "Exiled to 'Siberia' — Diane McBain feels that way about her role in *Surfside*

Looking cheesy for the Studio's Publicity Department.

Six." I indelicately expressed my dissatisfaction with the series and how it would interfere with a film career. Actors, such as Jane Fonda, smartly refused to do television because they feared the medium would chew them up and spit them out. It was a legitimate fear at the time, but I sounded a bit disingenuous and ungrateful to say so in the magazine that celebrated television.

With Lee (left), *and with Margarita* (right) *on the road to publicize* Surfside Six. PHOTO COLLECTION OF MICHAUD

As the show took off, so did I. Fan letters poured in by the thousands. Color postcards of me in a bathing suit, pre-printed with my autograph, were sent to clamoring fans across the country. Periodically, the studio delivered boxes of fan letters to my home. Sometimes I perused the mail, but usually I didn't have the time for such an indulgence.

The studio sent me on press junkets around the country to visit radio and television stations and submit to interviews for the local press. For the purpose of publicizing the show, I attended movie openings, county fairs, sporting events, golf and tennis tournaments, and other innocuous happenings, such as ribbon cuttings for store openings. I never got paid for these countless appearances. Warner Bros. charged from $5,000 to $10,000 for my personal appearance at an event, but I never got a dime of those fees. I met countless people, all of whom began to look alike. I attended countless honorary banquets and ate the blandest meals of my life — breast of white chicken, white mashed potatoes, white bread and butter, white succotash and cauliflower, iceberg lettuce with creamy white dressing, vanilla ice cream and a glass of milk.

I was on countless television and movie magazine covers. My name began to appear regularly in gossip columns. Articles (most of which were doctored by the studio press department) appeared about me and my dating habits. Most celebrity dates that I had were arranged by the studio for publicity purposes. One studio press release read, "Now that Diane has gotten 'that man' out of her system, she is once again footloose and fancy free. She did have a serious romance but it had complications. She prefers to date with no strings attached. When the time comes she will gladly settle for wifehood." All the things fans apparently wanted to read about me, and all the things I never said!

When we weren't working at the studio, we were often dispensed to the most popular restaurants and nightclubs in Hollywood, where more photographers captured us glamorously enjoying a night on the town. Actresses and actors were often "set-up" on dates with other up-and-comers in the business. I went on so many of these arranged dates that I lost count early in the game. Some of the men were pleasant, but some were unbearably self-centered with an eye cocked for the ever-present cameras. They were all handsome, but good-looks in Hollywood is not a gift; it's a given. I don't know who actually paid for the date. Some of the establishments were terribly expensive. Perhaps the ambitious young man submitted an expense report to his management team for reimbursement. I've seen so many photographs of me in night spots with other actors I met only once — oddly recorded by photographers, who just happened to be there during the ten seconds it took for us to exchange "How do you dos?" Thousands of photographs were taken of us throughout the course of each year. We did not have "photo approval" on images that were published. We relied on the supposed good judgment of the studio's publicity department.

News of my "dating" was relentless. I was linked with Richard Beymer, Tab Hunter, Bobby Darin, Tod Windsor, Peter Brown, Skip Ward, Vince Edwards, Jerry Orbach, Jack Haley, Jr., and Rod Taylor. With a few exceptions, I never even met most of those men. I did have a crush on Richard Beymer, but anyone who knew Tab Hunter (who was a nice man) knew he didn't date women. Jack wasn't interested in the opposite sex, either. Rather than making me sound interesting, I thought it all made me sound like a slut.

I had become friendly with Troy Donohue during the making of *Parrish*. He was a few years older than me, and charmingly naïve. We dated a few times, and one evening, after laughing a lot and having a few drinks, we tumbled into bed. It just didn't seem right. We were working together on *Surfside Six*, and we both decided to stay friends and forget about romance. I enjoyed Troy's companionship, and we formed a very good and lasting friendship.

A bigger mistake than fooling around with dear Troy was my ill-thought-out fling with my other co-star, Lee Patterson. I dated Lee a very short time during the first season of *Surfside Six*, but as soon as he got what he wanted, which was getting laid, the thrill was gone for both of us.

A publicity shot with Bobby Darin in the studio parking lot.

In 1958, Erskine Caldwell published his novel, *Claudelle Inglish*. Caldwell had written many books, including the modern classics *Tobacco Road* and *God's Little Acre*. He wrote about poverty and racism in his native South. The critics loved him, but many Southerners resented the way he depicted the people of the region. *Claudelle Inglish* was a provocative, big-selling book, which did not disappoint Caldwell's fans. Jack Warner quickly optioned the novel for his studio.

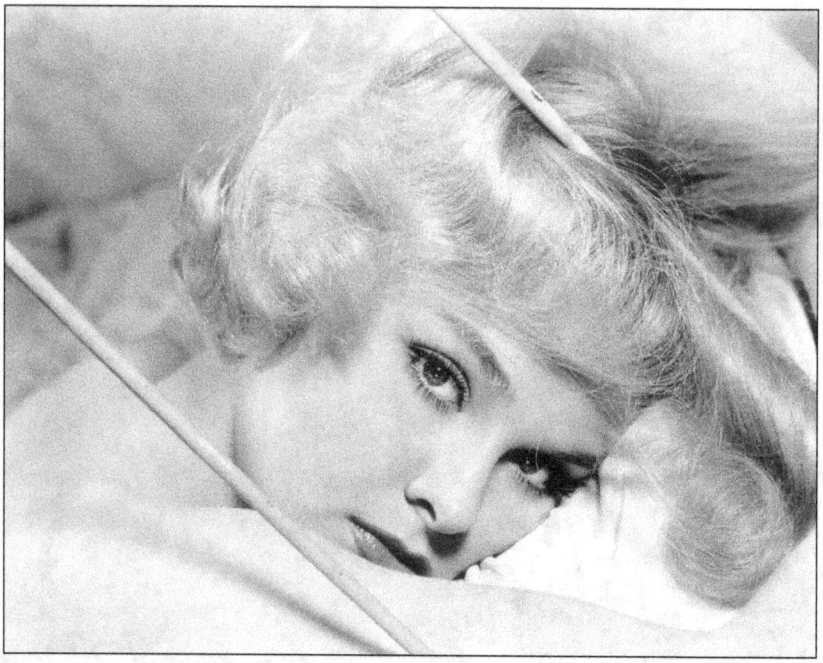

My first starring role in Claudelle Inglish.

Claudelle Inglish was the sordid tale of the teenage daughter of Georgia sharecroppers who became the town tramp after she received a "Dear Jane" letter from her true love, a common farmhand who had been inducted into the service. She then took every man she met to the cleaners, destroying several families (including her own), and herself in the process.

The promotional tagline couldn't have explained the plot any more succinctly. "When she was seventeen there wasn't a man she'd let near her. When she was eighteen there wasn't one she'd keep away. She liked boys looking at…and thinking…and then she'd take her delicious kind of revenge on them all! This is Erskine Caldwell's most misbehavin' female… the child-woman who took revenge the only way she knew how."

A potboiler, for sure. Danny was thrilled.

Veteran director Gordon Douglas was tapped to direct the film. Douglas had directed dozens of films, including many *Our Gang* short comedies in the 1930s and the classic science fiction film, *Them!* The turgid film adaptation would be written by prolific television writer Leonard Freeman.

Casting began in November. Constance Ford and five-time Oscar nominee Arthur Kennedy were cast as Claudelle's parents. Claude Akins,

Gordon Douglas rehearses a scene with Arthur Kennedy, dialogue director Ken Rose, me, and Constance Ford. The man fiddling with Arthur's hair is makeup man Lou Phillippe.

Frank Overton, my friend Will Hutchins, and an uncommonly handsome and sweet Chad Everett completed the cast.

Several actresses at the studio tested for the plum role of Claudelle. Shirley Knight, with whom I had previously worked, tested the same day as I did. She was a fine actress, originally from New York, which then seemed to hold sway with casting agents in Hollywood, and she had a bit of a reputation as a nymphomaniac. I don't know how much of that was fabricated gossip, but she did have a fling with Richard Burton while we were all making *Ice Palace*. If gossips were saying things like that about her, I could only imagine what they were saying about me. Whatever her personal reputation may have been, she was definitely a very talented actress, and I was worried that I would come in second.

The studio press release boldly stated, "The very pretty blonde Diane McBain had an early Christmas present when Jack L. Warner told her that she is to play the title role in *Claudelle Inglish*, from Erskine Caldwell's novel. Many girls were tested but Warner was impressed with Diane's beauty and acting ability in *Parrish*…"

Filming began in mid-December 1960 at Warner Bros., and after the holiday, moved to a few locations in Stockton, California. While I was making the film, *Surfside Six* went on without me for several weeks.

Unexpectedly, I felt anxiety and a huge responsibility in assuming the title role in a film for the first time. The role couldn't have come at a more inopportune moment. I still felt the sting of my ill-fated romance with Richard Burton. I was anxiously scouting for someone to love, and in spite of the gossip-column chatter to the contrary, my dating was sporadic at best. I felt tainted by my physical inability to accommodate Richard's lovemaking advances, and I began to wonder if I'd ever be able to completely love a man. I knew so little about sex, I wasn't really sure women were actually supposed to enjoy it. Up until then, sex had not been pleasurable or satisfying. The more I worried, the more uncomfortable sexual intercourse became. I actually feared that my failure to have complete intercourse indicated that something physical may be wrong. It never occurred to me to consult a gynecologist. Finally, a girl friend told me if I just relaxed, sexual intimacy might be more enjoyable.

When Mark Nathanson, the handsome son of a wealthy Palm Springs real estate tycoon, insinuated himself into my life, I suspected I had met up with the devil's agent. It wasn't the profession that he shared with his father that vexed me, but his "used car salesman" slippery demeanor. When he wasn't pressing me for sex, he was trying to sell me off to someone or something else! Celebrity fascinated him and he wanted to be a movie mogul. He knew a lot of people, some who actually were in a position to help him.

We dated a few times, but soon, and inexplicably, he wanted to introduce me to a man I will call William Shitsky. His friends called him Bill. I'll call him "B.S." for short. B.S. was a struggling actor and had minor roles in a few films. He never caught on as a thespian. He had higher aspirations in the film business, but had temporarily stepped away from moviemaking to work with a friend, who was trying to establish a fashion company. I'd seen him in a film and thought that, though he was no actor, he was handsome. So, I agreed to go out with him.

B.S. first took me out for dinner, and I wasn't very impressed. For a thirty-year-old man with few personal accomplishments, he seemed a little too full of himself. He spoke with a phony New York Upper East Side accent, and I was soon bored with his egocentric conversation. There was no one else knocking on my door at the time, however, so I agreed to see him again and again. I was not responsible with the money I earned, and I had been living beyond my means for some time. I liked the things money could buy, such as steak dinners in fancy Beverly Hills restaurants, something I could ill afford. I needed someone to buy me things. My attitude was selfish and self-absorbed, and it was time for nineteen-year-old Diane to receive a "come-uppance."

In the midst of filming *Claudelle Inglish*, B.S. asked me to take a weekend off and accompany him to Las Vegas. "We'll just gamble, see a couple of shows and come home," he said.

"Will we stay over? Will I have my own room?" I asked warily. "I don't know you well enough to share a room."

He laughed as if my request was silly and childish, but promised I would have my own room.

His invitation was tempting. I'd never been to Las Vegas without my parents, and I was fascinated by all the lights, glitter, and entertainment. When I was a child, we drove through the city, but my mother wouldn't allow us to stop and get caught up in the gambling. She was right, of course, because my father had a weakness for betting. Since then, Las Vegas had become a much more glamorous place, and besides, I felt like I needed a diversion. The hot desert sun sounded appealing after I spent so many days on dark movie studio stages. I agreed to go and we planned to leave early on a Friday when my work schedule allowed.

We boarded a plane, and sipped champagne during the short flight. It felt like stepping into a steaming oven when we disembarked. I instantly hated the arid wasteland. The heat made me feel woozy. Thankfully, everywhere we went was air-conditioned, and the excitement was undeniably heady. B.S. traveled in style.

After a sumptuous dinner at the hotel, a glamorous show with bare-breasted women (totally unexpected and a bit shocking to me), and too much alcohol, we headed for the tables.

I loved the look of the rich green velvet that covered the black jack table. In contrast, my fingernails were painted a gorgeous blood red, and the Cubic Zirconia ring I wore glittered in the intense spotlights that flooded the table. It felt good to handle the cards as they were dealt, and I liked the sense of power that came with going out on a limb, and of course — winning. I could feel the lure my father must have experienced. B.S. left me with a hundred dollar bill. "Have fun," he said. "If you need anything, you'll find me over there at the craps table."

He faded away into the crowd, and I cashed in the money for a stack of chips. I was happy to be left alone. Since I was gambling his money, having the courage to risk losing my own was not an issue. Playing black jack was seductive, stimulating, and magical. By the time I was finished, I had won $2,000! I gave him the hundred dollars he had fronted me, and we headed for our rooms and some much needed sleep.

On the way to our rooms, I felt saucily proud that I had done so well. $2,000 was a lot of money at that time, and it seemed to happen so easily. I felt buoyant because I could pay off some onerous, long-standing debts. Chatting happily with him about my plans, I felt lucky as we made our way through the seemingly endless hotel corridors.

When we arrived at our "rooms," I realized I had been naïve. The accommodation was actually a single suite with two separate bedrooms. Still a little drunk, I decided to ignore the warning signs and headed for the first bedroom, giving him a light kiss on the cheek. "Goodnight," I said as cheerily as possible. "See you in the morning."

I went into the bathroom to change into my nightgown, and when I emerged, B.S. was laying naked on my bed.

Stunned, and wishing I had been smarter about the accommodation issue, I said, "Oh, gosh, I thought this was supposed to be my bed."

"It is," he laughed. "You don't expect me to bring you all the way to Vegas, give you all that money, and get nothing in return for my trouble, do you?"

"Well, yes. Actually, I did," I said. "I gave you back your hundred, so what's up?"

"The plane trip, the room, the dinner and show came to hundreds of dollars. Will you pay me that, too?"

"I don't know why you would assume that I could pay for it, but I don't sleep with a man just because of money. I'd have to have feelings for you."

That, apparently, was the wrong thing to say. The comment made him very angry. He persisted, ignored my protestations, grabbed my wrists, and pulled me to the bed. I struggled, but felt strangely obligated to him, and somehow guilty for taking something that didn't belong to me. For a brief moment, I felt as if I owed him what he demanded. Soon, he was holding my legs apart and painfully thrusting himself into me. I was completely unprepared for the physical assault. I froze. My nightgown was pushed up around my neck, and his spittle and perspiration slathered all over my body. I wanted to throw up as I stared at the ceiling. As soon as he was done, which was thankfully soon, he rolled off me without saying a word, and disappeared into the other bedroom.

In shock, I stumbled into the bathroom. The alcohol had worn off, but I still felt dizzy and a little disoriented. I was covered in his sticky phlegm and semen. Curling up on the tile floor of the shower, I dowsed myself in the steaming hot water.

I tried to rationalize what had happened. *Maybe this was divine punishment*, I thought, as I slowly returned to the bed and tried to sleep. I had put myself in a compromising position and had taken things that didn't belong to me. This was the result.

We returned to Los Angeles the next day. I was in a daze, and we hardly spoke a word to one another. He called a few days later, and I begged off his dinner invitation. "I don't think we will be seeing each other again very soon," I said.

"I'm getting the brush off, aren't I?" he asked coldly.

"Look, don't take it personally. I'm working. I don't have time right now." I was thoroughly in denial, and decided what happened that horrible night in Las Vegas was my fault. I didn't want to think about it, and I had no tears to spare on myself. Still, I felt utter anxiety about the weekend, and about B.S.

He suddenly became indifferent and hung up.

I hoped that would be the end of him, but by the tone of his voice, I feared it would not. Soon, he called again. "Please," he said, "I need to see you. There is something I need to tell you."

"Will it take much time?" I asked, frustrated.

"Not really. Maybe half an hour." He was using his charming voice. "Come on over for a drink this afternoon."

I acquiesced just to get him off my back. *One visit*, I reasoned. We would talk things over, clear the air, and then I could really move on. I wanted to get this off my mind as soon as possible so it wouldn't interfere with my work. My role in *Claudelle Inglish* was too important to mess up. I still had difficulty memorizing my lines, and now, on top of that, I had to deal with this lecher.

His apartment, sparsely furnished with brown and beige colored furniture, carpeting, and drapes, was located on Sunset Plaza Drive above the Sunset Strip. The room was incongruously dark on an otherwise bright, sunny day. He was talking on the telephone and motioned for me to sit in a chair facing him. He rudely continued to talk on the phone, eventually whispering to me that he was speaking with Mark, the man who had originally introduced us.

B.S. was slumped in the sofa, legs crossed with the phone receiver casually cradled against his shoulder. His eyes were Cimmerian and sooty, and his black, pomade-thick hair was combed straight back from his darkly tanned face. He looked greasy. He exuded an air both uncaring and indifferent. If someone was casting the devil, he would have been a good choice. I looked at him and wondered what I had ever seen in him and what had I gotten myself into.

When he finally hung up the phone, he said, "I asked you to come here to let you know how disappointed I am that you blew me off so coldly the other day. Breaking up on the phone just isn't nice. I didn't like it and I want my clothes back."

"What?" I was incredulous. He had given me some things from his friend's fledgling clothing company. "Used clothes are worthless. Why on earth would you want them back?" I didn't know quite how to react. Though his request was almost humorous, I felt an inkling of fear. I had worn the clothing in public and had been photographed in them. This was good advertising for his friend's company, which is why I thought he gave the items to me in the first place. I didn't feel I owed him anything.

"I also want my money back," he said flatly.

"What money?" My immediate feeling of astonishment quickly turned to discomfort. He didn't have to answer my question. I knew what money he referred to.

"The $2,000 you won for me off my investment."

"Excuse me, but you won nothing. I won that money because you gave me something to gamble with so you could get rid of me while you played craps. I gave you back your hundred."

The truth was (as I had explained my intentions to him in Las Vegas) I spent the $2,000 when I got home. I used every cent to pay off bills. I wanted to forget the awful weekend and decided to use the winnings to get out of debt. I didn't have any money to give back to him even if I had wanted to.

"If I don't see the clothes and the money by the end of the week, I am going to call the press and let them know what a whore you are. I took care of my tracks, so don't think you can get me on statutory rape charges," he said calmly. "I made sure there was no evidence that I took you to Vegas, and I took care of the concierge so he and his porters will not identify you and me together."

My head was spinning. The threat of blackmail had never occurred to me. I was barely out of high school, and I had naively allowed myself to get caught up in a compromising situation. The thought of my mother's fears filled me with remorse. I wished I had heeded her sound advice.

"So," I countered, "how are you going to tell the press we were in Vegas together if you don't admit you took me there?"

"Who said I would tell them that? I'll tell them you were there on your own looking for a hit with some bucks."

"What's that?" I asked, angling for time to think of something clever to say that would stop him.

With a satanic grin on his face, he said condescendingly, "You were looking to roll a big spender."

My mind flashed back to a strange man who approached me on the *Claudelle Inglish* set several days earlier and asked if I had called him the night before, around one or two in the morning. I hadn't called him, and I didn't know him, but he insisted that a woman calling herself Diane McBain with a deep voice like mine had called and propositioned him in the middle of the night. I swore it wasn't me, but he seemed unconvinced. A couple of days later, another stranger stopped me at the studio and asked the same question. He laughed when I said, "No. I wouldn't do that." He walked away before I could explain that I wasn't that kind of person. Evidently, there was someone making provocative phone calls in my name.

It worried me that his threats and the odd confrontations at the studio could blow up into some kind of weird Hollywood story with me at the center of some awful, career-smashing scandal. I, like all contract players, had a morals clause in my contract that the studio could exercise at will. The clause was a means of holding the actor or actress to a certain behavioral standard that would not create a scandal or reflect poorly on the studio. Forbidden activity included the abuse of alcohol and prescription drugs, the use of illegal drugs, and any illegal or illicit sexual activity. I don't know how often any such violation was actually used to fire an actor. The clause was probably more effectively used as a threat. Of course, who at the studio was the arbiter of "illicit sexual activity" was never clear to any of us. I knew I was not an important enough star to withstand an ugly scandal or even unfounded accusations. B.S. wasn't just threatening me to get money and his clothes back. In my young mind, it sounded like blackmail. If so provoked, the studio could simply fire me and I would have little recourse.

I felt his threats carried real weight. After all, he had premeditated the trip so that he would not have to own up to anything untoward. He was aware of the Mann Act and the seriousness of taking an underage girl (twenty-one was the age of majority then) across state lines for the purpose of sex. He had purchased the plane tickets in the names of a married couple. The hotel suite had been reserved in those names as well. He was far cleverer than I. I took him very seriously.

I went home completely confounded. His intimidation was yet another assault after what he had done to me in Las Vegas. I was terrified. My stomach was in knots. All I could think about was gathering up the clothes he gave me and throwing them outside. I would never be able to wear them again, anyway.

"Your stupid clothes are on the front lawn," I told him over the phone, "but I don't have the money, so you'll have to wait."

"I said by the end of the week and I meant it," he growled. "I'll have my man come and pick up the clothes."

The clothing was gone by the next morning.

I didn't have a clue what to do. I tried the banks, but I didn't qualify for an unsecured loan. The only collateral I had was the few months left on my optioned contract at the studio. I was paid too little money. By then, I was in the second year of my contract and was only making $350 a week. Studio contracts were reviewed every six months. I had been busy at the studio, and *Surfside Six* was popular, so I had a certain level of comfort that my option would be picked up. Still, contract players were often told how expendable we were. Bigger stars than I had previously been dumped by the studio. If the morals clause was compromised, I felt certain I would be shown the door. Reluctantly, and without explaining my situation, I asked the studio for a loan or advance, but was turned down.

I believed I deserved to be in the situation I found myself. I had been stupid, and spent every dime I'd ever earned and more. I felt compelled to look and live like a star. I wanted to live in the right neighborhood, wear the right clothes and jewelry, and drive the right car. In those days, a celebrity never left the house without wearing makeup, perfectly coiffed hair, and fashionable clothing. It was an expensive undertaking that the studio did not underwrite. On the little money I made, it was impossible to keep up the appearance of a star.

I panicked as this bastard's deadline approached. If my trip to Las Vegas became public knowledge, I would take the fall.

Nevertheless, I had no money. My family didn't have it, either, even if I had the nerve to ask them, but I didn't want my parents to know about my foolish, reckless behavior. As I waited, I actually became physically ill.

Soon, I received another call from B.S. while I was on set at the studio. "Where is my money?" he snapped.

"I don't have any money."

"You'd better get a hold of my $2,000, or the next thing you know I will be having a conversation with your mother. She will find the information I have about you to be... well, it would be unfortunate news."

My mother, I thought. *My God! He was threatening to drag my mother into this mess. How would this affect her?* She would hate me for being so impulsive, and she would be hurt that I would do something so foolish after all her warnings. As understanding as my mother was, this would not sit well with her. I was certain she would be devastated. I could hardly think. *What could I do to stop him?* I was compelled to act in desperation because I loved my mother too much to hurt and disappoint her. Still I couldn't seem to recognize the fact that this slimy man had raped me!

I borrowed the money from my dear friend Robbie Utzinger's father. Robbie was my friend from high school and the best gay male friend a girl could ever have. B.S. sent an assistant to pick up the blood money. I met that man again many years later. He approached me at a restaurant and told me that being the courier had made him sick. He'd known B.S. was blackmailing me and he didn't like the idea. With sincere regret in his eyes, he apologized for his part in the shakedown. When he told me that, I experienced an enormous relief. For years and years, I had never talked about the incident. Breaking the silence with someone else who knew what had transpired was like being released from a solitary prison.

My way of dealing with the rape and subsequent blackmail was to deny the horrors ever happened. I thought the repulsive episode was completely my fault, and that I deserved what I had coming. There were no tears. I ignored the shame and pain. I thought I was a tainted woman, a tart who had pursued a married man. My affair with Richard Burton had made me an adulterer, plain and simple. I was guilty. Justice had been meted out, but to me, not to the man who was really responsible.

It wasn't the loss of money, though, that bothered me. The real loss was much deeper. I questioned my self-confidence and my decision-making. I was incapable of choosing the right sort of man. I was stupid and put myself in terrible situations. As I looked around and considered my new friends, I began to question their feelings and concerns about my welfare. I wondered if they were just hangers-on, looking to hang around a movie star. Diane and Danny were torn and seemed to be at odds in my head and heart. I stuffed the hurt inside. There was nothing left to feel, and a black emptiness consumed me.

The studio publicity department worked tirelessly to keep my name in the news. I wanted to crawl in a hole and hide, but every time I looked at a newsstand, numerous movie magazines carried purported interviews with me about life and love. I was surely the last person on earth to give anyone advice about love!

I did date a few men. Though the press had a heyday, in reality, my love life was a disaster. In the midst of the storm, I got a call from Richard Burton. His voice was heaven sent.

He had begun what would become a hugely successful and legendary engagement on Broadway in *Camelot*. He was alone and he said he missed me. He wanted me to come to New York to see the play. He wanted to show me the town. I needed no urging. I marched into the front office and asked for time off.

Unbeknownst to me, studio executives called my mother and asked if she knew I wanted to go to New York and asked if we had any relatives or friends there I might visit. My mother said "no." They presumed I wanted to see Richard, and my mother concurred. The studio was displeased with my interest in a married man and ultimately refused to let me travel to New York. I was distraught.

As if things weren't absurd enough, Harrison Carroll wrote in the *Los Angeles Herald Express* on February 10, 1961, "Diane McBain's poodle is, of all things, a hepatitis victim." Two weeks later, he reported "Diane McBain is heartbroken. Her poodle died of hepatitis." The press was as accurate in reporting my dating habits as the terrible fate of my beloved black poodle. In truth, Cherie, the toy poodle Sherry Jackson had given me for Christmas, had disappeared from our front yard. The publicity department at Warner, never to be accused of missing a story they could run with, reported my lost dog to the trade papers and provided a studio phone number for callers to report any news of sightings.

On February 5, the *Los Angeles Times* printed a long interview I gave Hedda Hopper. The gossip queen titled her piece, "Too Pretty to Act?" It was fluff of the first order, arranged by the studio, but heady nonetheless for a nineteen-year-old girl. Hopper wrote, "Diane McBain is one of Warner's rocketing stars. She's 19, has already played in two major films: *Ice Palace* and *Parrish* and has had a running part in the *Surfside Six* television series. Now she has the title role in *Claudelle Inglish*. This is something of a record even today where the speed-up to fame and fortune makes movie methods of a decade ago seem like snail's pace." That much was true enough.

She added, "When Diane starts work on a picture she tells all her boyfriends that she's out of circulation until it's finished and not to expect any of her time." I had no boyfriends at all. I had few friends, as well. There was so little time to collect my thoughts, and less time to create a stable home life.

In March, the press reported that I was about to star in a new film about the fabled stripper Gypsy Rose Lee called *Gypsy*. On March 7, Sidney Skolsky wrote in the *Citizen News*, "Diane McBain and Angie Dickinson are battling it out for the [stripper] role in the movie version of *Gypsy*." Mike Connolly wrote for the *Hollywood Reporter*, "Darlin' Diane McBain is whipping up a hurricane at Warners with her bumps & grinds; a mighty pitch for the top stripper spot in *Gypsy*." Months later, John L. Scott again reported the story for the *Los Angeles Times*. Ridiculous. I didn't know Angie Dickinson. I didn't "bump & grind" for anyone. I didn't sing. Moreover, I wasn't suited for the part. I can't believe the studio ever really considered me, either.

The Eighteenth Annual Golden Globe Awards presentation was produced on March 16, 1961, in the Grand Ballroom of the Beverly Hilton Hotel in Beverly Hills. I appeared as "Miss Golden Globe," an honor bestowed upon a young, promising actress each year. My responsibilities included looking glamorous and poised, and carrying each award trophy to the celebrity presenters on stage. On March 30, Hedda Hopper wrote about the award show in her column in the *Los Angeles Times*, "Diane McBain as hostess was a dream walking."

Sleep walking was more like it. I was numb with depression.

Chapter 7

My self-confidence and self-worth seemed to vanish before my eyes. I was completely lost. Without thinking, I dated an actor named Ralph Taeger a few times. Ralph was very tall, dark, and ruggedly handsome. He starred on a television series called *Klondike*. I wasn't that interested in him. He was just a diversion at a terrible time, but again, my poor judgment took its toll. My roommate Sherry had dated Ralph previously. They had broken up, but it was poor form for me to date my girlfriend's ex. The situation at our apartment became awkward and uncomfortable. Emotionally spent, I moved out and into a little one-bedroom, where I buried my head under the pillow. Literally.

It was hard for me to care about anything. With little effort, I had fallen into a profession that countless people dream about. *My* dream, though, was to find the love of my life. This pursuit had only led me down a dead end road. The one thing I truly cared about was not simply allusive — it broke my heart. Of course, I couldn't then see the folly of my choices. I was chasing dead ends; that was the problem. I thought love could cure any problem and make the world perfect. All I had to do was love my world and the people in it, but another ending seemed to be true.

I also began to worry about my career. I was working steadily, but none of my few feature films were impressive box office hits. My overexposure on television had turned me into a common household name, with "common" being the operative word. Many people warned me this would have a negative impact on a career in films. It seemed to be true. No man was asking me to marry him, either. Danny felt alone and confused. Diane was icily silent and in complete denial.

With limited coping mechanisms, trying to deal with these issues and the emotional baggage of the unacknowledged rape made me exhausted and somnolent. Lightheadedness and heavy eyelids drew me into a nocturnal web. Sleeping became my escape. I could avoid dealing with my feelings if I was asleep. Soon, I was sleeping almost all of the time. I barely got out of bed, and when I did, I longed to be asleep again so I didn't need to focus on anything. I existed in a dark, oppressive fog.

I had met an agent named Fred Amsel, and we casually dated a few times. He was a lovely fellow and a fine gentleman. He was the sort of man I should have been seriously interested in, but wasn't. Seeing that I was in such a funk, he invited me to see a production of the musical *Carousel* in San Diego. I wanted to see the show and we both thought the trip would be a welcome diversion. I slept in the car all the way to San Diego… and through the performance. I slept all the way back to Los Angeles. Poor Fred didn't know what to make of me.

It was nearly impossible for me to focus on reality, much less deal with it. Immersed in the past and crippled by depression, my situation dragged me down and whirled me around so I could never get my footing. Rather than deal with the real issues, I thought I could just ride it out. Little by little, I began to function again, although never at full capacity. The joy of life had been sucked out of me, and I didn't know how to retrieve it.

I had all but ignored God for some time, as well. I had forgotten to pray. I no longer considered what God might have wanted from me. Actually, had I thought about it, I would have realized that was the problem. As anyone who has experienced a "living hell" knows, it is difficult to see the problem when you are living so far away from the Light. I was so caught up in my pain and self-loathing that I couldn't have seen God if He was standing right in front of me. Without my acknowledgement and consent, God couldn't do anything for me either. Acceptance of God's love and care is a prerequisite to healing, much like allowing the doctor through your door.

I did see a doctor of sorts, however. This sad cliché of a "Hollywood" doctor supplied me with an endless supply of diet pills. Plagued with weight problems, since studio bosses had earlier insisted I drop my "baby fat," dieting had become a regular part of my life. The pills would help "pick up my spirits," the good doctor explained. He failed to tell me that diet pills were essentially legal amphetamines, and very addictive.

It might have been wise for me to advise him that I had become somewhat of a drinker. Alcoholism wasn't considered the illness that it is today. My aunt had a problem with alcohol, though, and I prided myself in being able to drink any man under the table. So I did. Mixing diet pills and booze was a very good recipe for disaster, and the problem was yet another one that I was ill-equipped to deal with.

Then, I went shopping. There was something about a spree at Saks, perhaps the self-indulgence that was soothing. I loved combing through stores and finding great-looking clothing. Having outfits designed for me at the studio didn't give me the same feeling of satisfaction. Shoes, jewelry, lingerie, and perfumes, anything luxurious and beautiful that could be purchased in an elegant setting, took my mind off the pain. These distractions hid the pain for a time. However, they depleted my bank account and kept me from addressing my emotional dilemma.

The 50th Annual Indianapolis 500 Race was held on Memorial Day Weekend in 1961 in Speedway, Indiana. To commemorate the event, many Hollywood stars were flown in to attend the race and lend some glamour to an already exciting occasion. I sat beside actor George Montgomery on the flight from California to Indiana. Alcohol was freely flowing on the plane, and by the time we got to the hotel in Indianapolis, George was all over me like a wet rag. I liked him, and he was smitten enough to control himself when I chastised him, so I was open to meeting him again the following day.

We rode in the pacing car for one of the preliminary qualifying races, and Danny was in her element. Sitting on the back of the convertible, with my hair blowing in the wind, was like being back in my old Glendale neighborhood flying down the street on my bicycle. What a thrill it was to watch the racing cars behind us, revved up and ready to take off. Then, off they roared, as we pulled to the side of the track. The rush was incredible, and I wanted to drive one of those cars!

During the next few days, as I became inundated with interviews, photo shoots, and luncheons with strangers, George became the one recognizable and friendly face in the crowd. We ended up spending the week together.

George was a massive, handsome, forty-five-year-old man, and a cowboy at heart. Since I didn't keep up with the private lives of movie stars, I was only vaguely aware that George was married to someone important. "Oh, that's right, Dinah Shore, the Chevrolet lady," I chortled when someone mentioned this small but salient fact. "Someone's in the kitchen with Dinah, right?" That was pretty much my feeling for Dinah Shore. I never thought she could sing, and I marveled that she had been popular for so long. She didn't appeal to me, so the fact that her husband was having trouble keeping his hands off me wasn't exactly startling. I had the sense that he'd married her for some reason other than love. I'd heard just about every speech a man used by then, and George never told me just exactly what his relationship with Dinah was. Of course, I never posed the question.

It was much more fun to be in denial. I was enjoying his company, and the rollicking sex was good. With no strings attached, the recreational thrill of sex was addictive. I rationalized that if he was hanging around with me, then what he had with his wife couldn't possibly be enough. His commitment to his marriage would not be honored whether I was involved or not. I might have been right about that, but it didn't make my actions right. I turned a blind eye to my complicity. George was living quite separately from Dinah by the time I met him, but he was nonetheless still married, and I was injudicious to see him in the middle of what he told me was their separation.

My friend Robbie was a big fan and wanted more than anything to meet George and see where Dinah Shore lived. One day, George asked me up to the house he shared with Dinah on Drury Lane in Trousdale to go for a swim. He told me he needed to pick up the last of his things. Dinah was away. George invited Robbie to join us. While we romped in the Olympic-size pool of the sprawling, stone and glass mansion that George actually built with his own hands, Robbie kept a lookout for any unexpected visitors or prying cameras.

George's marriage was on the rocks before I hit the scene, but the rumor mongers decided I was the cause. Once Hedda Hopper got wind of the story, she was like a dog with a bone. *Screen Stories* reported, "Diane McBain's green-blue eyes looked clouded, her face troubled, as she hung up the receiver. She was in the smart apartment in Hollywood where she lives alone, and had just heard a shocking rumor about herself. A newspaperman had called to ask if it was true — as the town was buzzing — that she was responsible for the breakup of the Dinah Shore/George Montgomery marriage. Gossip had it that she had dated George and was 'the other woman'... but no matter how fiercely she denied it, she couldn't stop loose talk."

No one knew, least of all me, that I was a wounded human being writhing in unacknowledged emotional pain. The denial I was living with was taking a toll. I quickly became inured to the kind of careless, even reckless life I was living. Dates and intimate relations with men I didn't care about were becoming the rule rather than the exception. So, too, were the lies to the press. I wouldn't admit it, but I was becoming jaded and my self-loathing was deepening.

In August, production resumed on the second — and thankfully last — season of *Surfside Six*. We again filmed a couple of weeks on location in Miami, and then we were sentenced to the cavernous Warner Bros. sound stages. Our second season provided more ridiculous storylines concerning marital triangles, mobsters, mistaken identities, and murderous high school reunions. Some of the more absurd plots included a ventriloquist whose dummy was kidnapped for a ransom, the mentally unstable head of a flourishing swim suit company who vanished when her husband turned up dead (this episode's real claim to fame was that Margarita, Troy, and I introduced a new dance called the "Cha Cha Twist" in the Boom Boom Room), and the director of a lingerie show who became the main suspect in the murder of one of his models. Some of our many interesting guest

Back to Surfside Six. *Van, Lee and me.*

stars included Dennis Hopper, Lon Chaney, Jr., Bruce Dern, Mary Tyler Moore, Sally Kellerman, Ellen Burstyn, Jack Cassidy, Harvey Korman, George Kennedy, John Marley, and Chad Everett.

About midway through our second season, we filmed a "crossover" episode that featured two main characters (played by Roger Smith and Edd Byrnes) from the hit series, *77 Sunset Strip*. This was a common tactic used

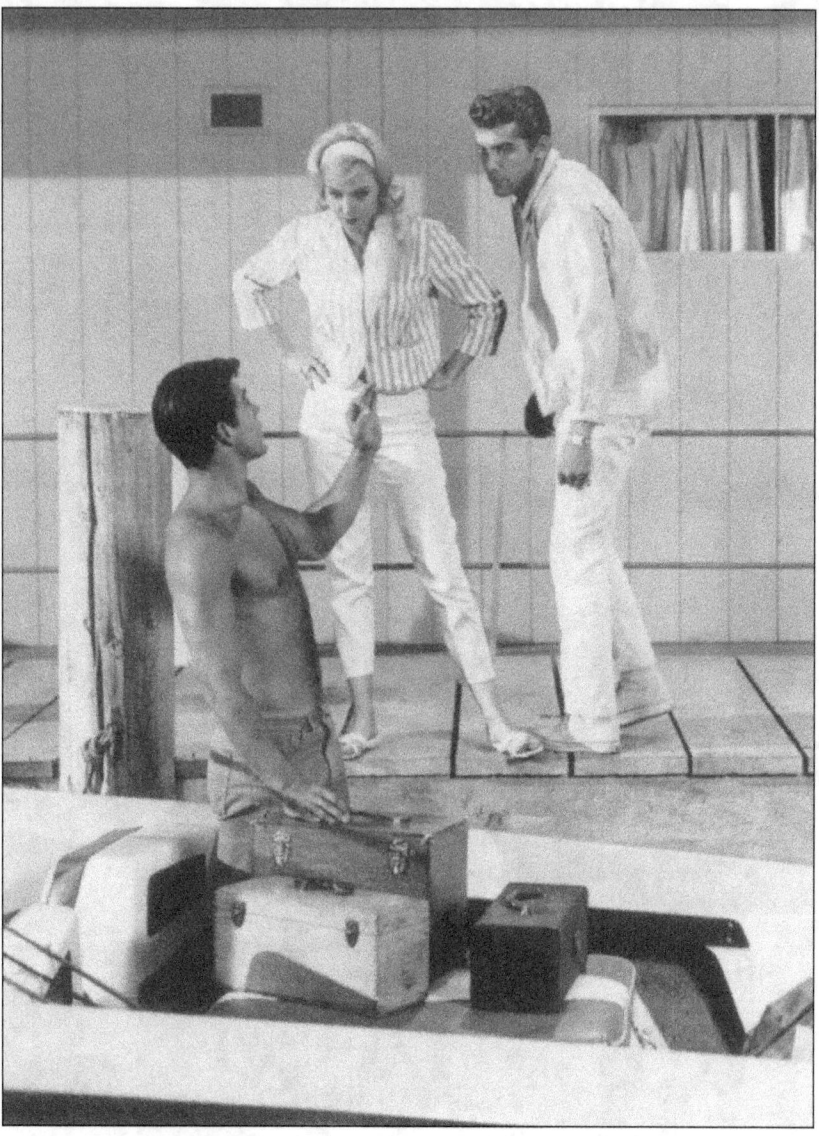

On the sound stage at Warner with Van and Lee in Surfside Six.

by the television production department at the studio to bolster interest in a show that was failing in the ratings. Our ratings had begun to sag after riding a wave of popularity that had lasted for a little more than a year. The idea was that viewers would tune in to see their favorite characters from *77 Sunset Strip* appear in an episode of *Surfside Six*. Dean Riesner wrote the clever episode titled, "Love Song for a Deadly Redhead." The producers thought the show would be the ratings boon that we needed. They were wrong.

As our ratings declined, so did our production budget. The editors began to use "stock-footage" of our reaction shots from previous episodes. Several times, Margarita's musical production numbers were reused in the second season. If viewers were paying attention, they would have seen the same singing interludes previously broadcast. Continuity was nonexistent. Production values were abandoned. The sets were so poorly constructed that the walls wobbled.

My character, Daffy, was featured in several episodes during our second season; Daffy befriended five retired, elderly crooks who shared a house and were victimized by a young hoodlum they had taken in, Daffy was kidnapped on the way to attend her friend's wedding in Nassau, Daffy fell in love with a mysterious young nomad, and Daffy took detective measures into her own hands when one of her party guests was murdered.

One of my favorite lines is said when Troy's character roles an "acey-deucy" three times in a row at the Fontainebleau Hotel. Daffy says, "Those dice aren't trained, they're educated."

With a role, dialogue, and storylines like those, did I have anything to worry about with my career? You bet I did.

Claudelle Inglish was released in October, 1961. I began to see the light at the end of the tunnel. It was such a thrill seeing my name on the marquee. My hometown theater had put my name on their marquee when *Parrish* was released, but in this new film, I played the title character and felt the honor was more deserved. I tried to be off-hand about all the attention, but in truth, I loved it.

Claudelle Inglish produced some good press. On October 12, the *Hollywood Citizen News* reported, "Diane McBain as Claudelle has distinguished herself in her demanding role, her best dramatic vehicle to date." *Films in Review* noted, "Diane McBain has a future in films. She photographs as well in black and white as she did in color, and she seems to be learning about acting." John P. Scott wrote in the *Los Angeles Times* on

October 13, "Diane McBain, a pretty blonde, plays the ill-starred heroine and, with more experience, should go places." On September 6, *Motion Picture Herald* wrote, "Miss McBain, a newcomer seen previously as the rich girl in *Parrish* makes an attractive Claudelle, if an overly sophisticated one." Danny laughed, but Diane was rather flattered to be called "overly sophisticated."

Cozying up to Will Hutchins in Claudelle Inglish.

The newspaper from my hometown, the *Glendale News Press*, was naturally the kindest of all. George Raborn wrote, "Gorgeous Diane McBain, who two years ago was a student at Glendale High School, now seems destined to become one of Hollywood's biggest movie stars. She proves that she has learned to act in *Claudelle Inglish*."

The film eventually raked in several million dollars and managed to

With Chad Everett in Claudelle Inglish.

turn a profit for the studio. Dear Howard Shoup was nominated for an Academy Award for his "black and white" costume design, and my performance as a down-home bad girl earned me a Golden Laurel Award nomination for "Top Female New Personality." Howard and I both lost.

Little Danny from Glendale took a back seat to Diane McBain the movie star as my fame grew. Diane became enamored with Hollywood life on the wild side. I was lavished with gifts, flowers, candy, and adoration, yet I was still wet behind the ears. My name and likeness popped up in the tabloids alongside Elizabeth Taylor, Grace Kelly, Tony Curtis, Natalie Wood, Debbie Reynolds, and Warren Beatty. There was hardly a hint of "normal" life left for Danny.

An article about me in the November 1961 issue of *TV's Top Ten* magazine took a rather reverent tone. "'Lead us not into temptation,' these powerful, prayerful words are words Diane McBain must live by. For she's a beautiful girl, a serious actress, the stakes are high, and the temptations almost overwhelming. Diane shares her greatest struggle with millions of girls whose reason, which tells them what is right and good in the long run, is constantly at war with their feelings, which ache hungrily for what seems so very, very right at the moment." It sounded more like a sermon than a celebrity profile!

The article continued, "Give in to that moonlight and roses feeling and you must risk possible heartache and embarrassment the next day. Place your future in the hands of a man instead of counting on your own talents, ambitions and ideas, and you may end up far from your goal. It takes courage and strength and a solid, long-range view to balance heart and head. So far, Di's stayed on the right road."

Well, just barely. I had taken a sharp turn off that "right road." In the 1950s, teenagers became both empowered and emboldened. Girls began to exert their own independence. When I began my young adult life, I wanted to free myself from the bonds of society's repressively religious sexual attitudes. I grew away from the God of my fathers, the patriarchal God that sought punishment of the so-called wicked, wanton women. My contemporaries began to question the old values because the Christian version of sin always seemed to have sex at its core. I questioned this, too. I thought, as the lessons were taught me, that Jesus was more concerned with our *judgments* of other people's sexual practices and not so much the deeds themselves. I felt there was an insidious double standard afoot. Men could be in the priesthood, but women could not. Men could steadily climb the corporate ladder, but women invariably ran into a "glass ceiling" along their way. Single men could have sex whenever and with whomever they wanted, and women were expected to remain virgins until marriage.

I had no intention of living under those rules. Marriage didn't really appeal to me at that moment, especially since Diane seemed to be in control of things. I felt I was too young for such a big commitment, anyway. However, becoming sexually active occupied my thinking. It seemed only fair that I should be able to pursue the same physical ambitions and joys that men pursued.

Television production dominated the studio, and feature film work became more difficult to secure. Earlier, I had been mentioned in the press to star in *The Chapman Report* for Warner. The film, based on the popular book by Irving Wallace, was directed by George Cukor, and starred Jane

Fonda and Shelly Winters. The studio also considered lending me out for *Term of Trial*, a movie filmed in England. The dramatic story about a schoolteacher who fell in love with a young student would star Laurence Olivier and Simone Signoret. I was considered for the role of the student, which was eventually played by Sarah Miles. I would love to have been in either film.

With Philip Carey in Black Gold.

Instead, I was cast in a programmer about oil drilling in Oklahoma in the 1920s. I'd heard that the studio often purposefully invested in possible failures to get some sort of tax break. Written by husband and wife team, Bob and Wanda Duncan, this cinematic yawn was called *Black Gold*. I co-starred with Philip Carey, a wonderful person with countless film credits. The film did have a great cast of supporting players including Claude Akins, James Best, Fay Spain, and Iron Eyes Cody. The entire film was shot on the backlot at the studio. This movie was a sure-fire flop from the beginning. Even I, a supposed newcomer to show business, could see it.

Black Gold was directed by Leslie Martinson, arguably the most neurotically dramatic director I ever worked with. The drama was confined to behind the cameras, though, and rarely made it to the screen! Like a raving lunatic, Leslie would fly off the handle over the silliest things. Diane didn't like him at all, but Danny loved the eccentric director and watched him in bemused amazement. I'd worked with him in television before and knew what to expect. While others were ranting and raving about Leslie's lack of control and screaming histrionics, I just sat back and watched the foolishness play out.

My Dad visits me on the dusty backlot set of Black Gold.

There was little to come away with in this movie. The only experience I remember while filming was learning to drive a Model T Ford. The automobile was a fascinating contraption with peddles, gears, and pulleys. It was truly a challenge to make the thing work without appearing to be a novice, but I mastered the old Ford rather well. My father loved watching us shoot those scenes when I roared down the dusty road in that old tin bucket. He found any excuse to come to the set as often as he could.

1961 came to a close with me in a celluloid wasteland.

Chapter 8

No matter how busy, tired, or uninterested I may have been, I was expected to cooperate with the publicity department and accommodate interview requests. There were always more interviews scheduled during the production of a film, since there was a real reason to talk with reporters — i.e., advance publicity.

Movie magazines served a purpose for the studios and the fans. The monthly publications provided a perfect place for publicity departments to plant stories about up-and-coming films and stars. They were arbiters of taste, and a source of celebrity gossip. Their popularity can be attributed to the fact that they provided the average reader a way into the glamorous world of Hollywood and its stars. The magazines were used by the studios to *start* rumors, and then to try and squelch them!

In December 1961, during the filming of *Black Gold*, the studio arranged an extensive interview with Rose Perlberg from *Modern Screen* magazine. Perlberg's mission was to ferret out the "real" Diane McBain, whoever she was. Of course, such publicity was supposed to boost a career. In my case, such stories often had the opposite effect. In the press, I was usually depicted as a whore who stole women's husbands, or as an enigmatic iceberg. My take on myself was of little help. If my assailant, B.S., hadn't wrecked my career, then on some subconscious level, I would.

Perlberg wrote, "During a break from shooting *Black Gold*, Diane McBain lunched with a reporter in the Warner's commissary. She wore a low-back, chartreuse gown of the Twenties — her costume for the movie. It was one of those filmy, flimsy things and, as she gestured in conversation, it kept sliding off one shoulder. Three TV actors, sitting two tables away, apparently found it, and what it conferred, much more interesting than what was on their plates. Since Diane's arrival, their attention had definitely not been on the Green Room's specialty of the day."

Perlberg did seem to have a handle on the genesis of gossip. She certainly contributed to it by throwing logs on the flames, but still the studio publicity department was more interested in just keeping their contract players' names in the papers.

"It was a sure bet that within forty-eight hours the anecdote would be incorporated into the mushrooming 'McBain Legend'," she astutely wrote. "First, of course, it would be wickedly whispered through the ranks of lesser stars, gathering the usual *artistic* embellishments along the way. By the time it was laid to rest as 'history,' any resemblance to the original would be quite coincidental. That would hardly bother the chroniclers." Of course, Miss Perlberg was one of those chroniclers!

Though publicity is important, there is indeed such a thing as bad publicity. It is doubtful that anyone in movie production, or in the movie business for that matter, had the time or interest to read movie magazines but fans seemed to gobble up the stories –and the more fanciful the details, the better. "Diane McBain has a reputation," Perlberg declared. "Not only around her own studio, but in the big (area-wise), little (gossip-wise) town known as Hollywood. The statuesque blonde with the penetrating blue eyes and the low, husky voice, is probably the first new personality to be strapped on the lead horse on the gossip-go-round since tempestuous Tuesday Weld proclaimed her Declaration of Nonconformity several years ago.

"She is depicted as flighty, fickle, and flippantly flirtatious. She is said to dangle men of all ages like a professional puppeteeress, love 'em and leave a trail of broken hearts in her wake. She is most of all condemned as an aloof, cold snob. 'Look at those eyes,' her critics say smugly, 'That girl is made of ice.' 'She thinks she's some kind of goddess; she rarely deigns to come down to your level,' others snort."

"It is rather unfortunate, but not unusual, that the people who talk most about Diane know the least about her." Perlberg seemingly leapt to my defense. "The image they paint may delight the gossip-hungry, but it is not very accurate. It is based mainly on hearsay or a fleeting first impression, and it has about as much depth as a reflection on a pool of water."

Then Perlberg interviewed my friends. "'I had *heard* that she was a cold and very distant person,' said Louise Myers, Diane's stand-in on *Surfside Six* and her closest girl friend. 'People who had worked with her said she was very strange and you couldn't quite get to her; she was kind of above it all. Diane did give that *impression*, but not because she was stuck up; she was just plain scared. At that time, she was barely nineteen. She hadn't been in the business long and she wasn't at all sure of herself. She was desperately afraid of doing the wrong thing in her work, and in her relationships with people. That was a year and a half ago. She's still scared, but she's come a long way.'"

My friend Robbie Utzinger had changed his last name to Singer and got a job as a publicist at ABC. He actually worked on publicizing *Surfside Six*. Robbie told Perlberg, "If Diane seems cold and aloof, it's just a cover-up for her basic shyness. When she was younger, she trusted the wrong people. She was hurt too many times. Now she's afraid to let people get close to her." Robbie was right.

I had learned early on to be cautious with my words in interviews. Nevertheless, if fans read between the lines, they'd discover more about me than I intended.

"She seemed remarkably poised for a twenty-year-old who'd been acting professionally for barely two years. You listened to her and you began to wonder if anything ever ruffled her consistent composure. 'I guess,' she confessed, 'I leave myself wide open for gossip. I date older men. It's not for publicity, but simply because I feel more at ease with them. I've always felt more comfortable with older people. Also, I need security. I'm not in a very secure profession. To balance this, in my private life I need a man who can give me something solid and substantial. And despite what you may have heard, I don't deliberately lead *any* man on…'"

The Perlberg interview continued in the little trailer I was assigned as a dressing room during the filming of *Black Gold*. The trailer was easily moved from one backlot location to another. "She flopped down on the couch and kicked off her shoes," Perlberg wrote. "She ran her hand through her shoulder-length wavy blonde hair and she began to talk. This time the words weren't filtered through the fine mesh of her defense mechanisms.

"She started reflectively, 'The last few years have been kind of confusing. Everything has been happening so fast. So much success in two years. There have been a lot of surprises, too.'"

In reference to the roles I'd played, I explained, "Maybe they're all me. I'm a sort of chameleon. If the situation in *real life* calls for the aloof sophisticate, I find myself automatically being that. If it calls for a more down-to-earth girl, I can be that, too. When I try to analyze myself, I get scared and I start to worry if what I was, at a given time, was the *real* me, or something phony. I've finally convinced myself that there can't be *one* image — I'm a combination of things. I hope I'm not kidding myself."

Modern Screen magazine may have thought it had uncovered the "real" me and any secrets I may have harbored. They were wrong, of course.

Perlberg continued. "Diane's voice trailed off. The distant look glazed her eyes. She drifted into her own private world. You sat in the smoky, cluttered little trailer and you studied her. Her hair was mussed, her make-up smudged, her dress wrinkled. There was a mountain of cigarette butts in the one, chipped ashtray. She had been talking for almost two hours, and her defenses were still at low tide." Of all the journalists who interviewed me, Rose Perlberg was the most creative. What she crafted sounded like an opening scene written by Raymond Chandler for a pulp novel.

"You watched her in this off-guarded moment," Perlberg concluded. "In a few minutes, she'd get up and straighten her hair and her make-up and her dress, because she was due back on the *Black Gold* set. You knew that when she set foot outside the trailer, her head would be high, her back would be straight, and her step would be steady. She'd *appear* cool, confident, completely composed. But you knew that *inside* she'd be a little shaky; that when she came to a corner, she'd hesitate for a fraction of a second and brace herself, just in case a stranger was waiting around the bend to engage her in conversation.

"You thought about everything she'd told you and what you'd observed in the last couple of hours. And you began to wonder how you could most accurately describe her. Then you remembered a statement made by the man who's known her for a long time. At first, it had merely aroused your curiosity. But now, you realized it was probably the best thumbnail summation ever made of Diane McBain.

"'She has the cool, classic beauty of a Lana Turner or a Jean Harlow', he had said. 'She comes across as a sophisticated woman of the world. But I always think of her as a frightened little girl, who is trying terribly hard to live up to the impression she creates when she walks into a room.'"

Those were Robbie's words. He was speaking as my dear friend. And publicist.

"The new and lighter ash tint in Diane McBain's blonde hair makes her even prettier," Louella O. Parsons wrote in the *Los Angeles Herald Examiner* on January 25, 1962. "She said she had a very exciting weekend in Washington where she was Pat Di Cicco's date at the Democratic Ball."

I had met Di Cicco at a party and we dated casually a few times. He told me he was an agent. He was in his early fifties, and he certainly "knew" lots of people. At the time I met him, I had no idea who he really was. Pasquale "Pat" Di Cicco was born in Queens, and was a bootlegger and pimp when he was a young man. His first cousin was Albert "Cubby" Broccoli, who later became a successful movie producer responsible for most of the "James Bond" movies. Di Cicco moved to Los Angeles in the early 1930s. He was married to actress Thelma Todd and to heiress Gloria Vanderbilt. Both women divorced him, charging him with physical and mental abuse. Legend had it that he was associated with Hollywood mobsters "Lucky" Luciano and "Bugsy" Siegel. At one time, Di Cicco was employed by Howard Hughes. He propositioned beautiful young women on the millionaire's behalf and arranged their clandestine meetings. Later, he earned the reputation of procuring beautiful women for President John F. Kennedy. He was responsible for introducing Marilyn Monroe to the President.

Di Cicco claimed to have ubiquitous ties to "big business," though his talk about his various enterprises was always quite vague. Since his history was unknown to me at the time, I accepted his invitations. He was charming and generous, and I liked him to a point. He invited me to accompany him to the party for Kennedy in Washington, D.C., and he seemed very enthusiastic about the trip. He insisted I find an eye-catching ball gown for our evening with the politicos. When we got to Washington, I spent the day shopping and finally found a fabulously rich gown in stunning magenta. It was bare-shouldered, and the slim bodice billowed out into a profusion of satin over stiffening crinoline.

I was so excited to go to the White House, but alas, the ball was held in a building that looked more like an empty warehouse than a glamorous banquet hall. The tables were made of rough, splintery wood and covered with over-sized, round white cotton clothes that dragged on the floor. People were running about in daytime attire, some hurriedly setting the tables and arranging flowers. I felt horribly out of place. An aide escorted us to our table and we were seated in the front row. We both sat stiffly in our formal clothes and anxiously waited for more people to arrive.

Soon, "Hail to the Chief" loudly played and the now full room stood as the President and his wife made their entrance. Kennedy was handsomely dressed in a tuxedo, and Jackie looked statuesque and ethereal in a flowing, white Grecian-style gown. The bright spotlights caused her diamond earrings to sparkle like the setting sun on the ocean. They were seated on the dais directly in front of our table. We were separated from the First Couple by less than ten feet. I felt very privileged to be seated so close. Before long, the President was audaciously flirting with me right under his wife's nose. I couldn't believe he could be so reckless. His attention to me didn't seem to bother De Cicco at all, and I wondered who else noticed the Commander-In-Chief's blatant flirtatiousness.

At that time, most television news programs were broadcast in black and white. I had never seen Kennedy in "living color" before. He was stunningly handsome. His skin was tanned, his pale brown eyes sparkled with mischief, and his tasseled, sandy-colored hair made him look even younger than his forty-five years. I melted into the *foie gras*.

As he casually chatted with his wife, he pointed out people in the audience that I imagined they both knew. His teasing eyes intermittently darted in my direction. His gleaming white teeth flashed through his warm smile. It was exciting to have this flirtation with the most powerful man in the world.

I never met him. He was whisked away before we had the opportunity to be introduced. After the party, Di Cicco and I returned to our rooms at the nearby Mayflower Hotel. He had designs on me that evening, but I had no intention of repeating the terrible experience I had with B.S. in Las Vegas. Di Cicco went to bed with only his bruised ego that night.

The gossip columns continued to link me with many, many men. "Diane McBain keeps her name in print shedding beaus weekly," Walter Winchell reported in his "Man About Town" column in the *Los Angeles Herald Examiner* on February 21. The columnists kept my name in print, I didn't.

I did date singer Jimmy Boyd a couple of times. When Jimmy was thirteen years old, he had recorded a #1 hit song, "I Saw Mommy Kissing Santa Claus." He was a couple of years older than I was, but he looked much younger. He was cute, but some of my friends thought that his red hair, freckles, and protruding ears made him look a little like Howdy Doody. Jimmy had a great sense of humor and loved to laugh. He tickled my funny bone, but that's as intimate as we ever got.

I dated Charlie Feldman, a producer, a few times, too. Charlie was charming, and I loved playing gin rummy with him. Glenn Ford invited me to his house for dinner one night and I was bored out of my mind. Dinner with Vince Edwards was as exciting as watching paint dry.

I met actor Laurence Harvey, newly divorced from his actress wife Margaret Leighton, and ended up in his hotel room in Beverly Hills one evening. He was droll, fey, and affected. I did my best to seduce him, but discovered he was interested in the same thing as Tab Hunter — men. I should have known something was up when he introduced to me James Woolf, his manager (and rumored long-term lover), with whom he shared his suite.

In the March, 1962 issue of *Movieland and TV Times*, Will McCamy wrote, "Like a diamond, Diane McBain has many facets. She'll change from one personality to another whenever she thinks it's necessary. 'With every man I meet, I change,' she told me. 'If I go out with a country boy, I'll act like the girl next door. The next night I might go out with a tall, suave sophisticate. Then I'll become sophisticated myself. And if I date someone with a terrific sense of humor, I'm a million and one laughs.'"

I cringe when I'm reminded of the stupid things I said to the press. Of course, Danny thought it was deliciously funny to have reporters look back at me in shock.

One of the most spectacularly ridiculous stories about my love life concerned the Prince Ali Salman Aga Khan. It seemed the Aga was gaga over me. Gossip columnists also reported I was actually feuding with actress Dolores Hart over the leader's affections. I never met the Prince and I didn't know Dolores Hart. Later, Dolores left Hollywood and became a nun. Smart move.

Still, the silly story persisted, and months later *Hollywood Star's Yearbook* updated the fans in an article about me entitled, "She Turned Down the Aga Khan!" The article read, "Hollywood was stunned when Diane McBain refused to date young and handsome Aga Khan who is not only a billionaire but one of the most hunted and desirable bachelors in the world. 'I'll admit I was tempted,' smiled the beauteous Diane, 'but, I also knew he was wife-shopping and I refused to stand in line.' The gossips insist that the young Muslim ruler was so smitten with the blonde actress that he had her watched by detectives. When questioned about it, Diane flipped: 'Ridiculous, but exciting.' When asked what type of man she does prefer, the publicity-wise doll informed: 'I like millionaires, pirates with their own boats, empire builders with their own building blocks — rich, reckless and romantic men. Money isn't everything,' she insisted, 'but poverty is death to romance.'"

I never said one word that had been attributed to me in this laughable tabloid.

As if those stories weren't silly enough, on February 23, Bill Kennedy had written in his "Mr. L.A." column for the *Los Angeles Herald Examiner*, "It's a dog's life. Diane McBain of the *Surfside Six* series plunked down $100 for a wardrobe for her pet pooch, Coquette, a tiny French poodle. It includes a hooded reversible raincoat, a pink angora turtle neck sweater, a mink-lined car coat, and for evening, a jeweled velvet job with a matching jeweled hat." This wasn't reported in a nonsensical gossip magazine. It was reported in a *newspaper!*

April 1, 1962 the *Los Angeles Times* named me one of "3 New Faces Goin' Places." "Pretty Diane McBain improves the scenery Mondays on Warner Bros.' *Surfside Six*, which, at times, can stand a face-lifting." I'm glad they felt I was going places. Mired in the television series, I thought I was going nowhere fast, professionally.

Nevertheless, *Surfside Six* made me a recognizable star. The studio was swamped with adoring fan mail, so the publicity department decided to use me as a "professional celebrity." The United Jewish Welfare Fund sponsored a fund-raiser on April 5, hosted by Steve Allen. I joined many stars in making radio and TV spots on behalf of their $8 million campaign. On April 12, I appeared with more than 100 stars in something called the "Super Circus Spectacle" produced by the Thalians to benefit emotionally disturbed children. Steve Allen acted

With my beloved little scene-stealer, Coquette, on the set of Surfside Six.

as the celebrity ringmaster. The International Super Circus, a genuine three-ring affair, played at the Los Angeles Sports Arena and starred performing chimps, dancing bears, lions and tigers, elephants, and the famous clown, Emmett Kelly.

The studio may not have considered me a top-earning *movie* star, but I was *cast* as one in "Leap, My Lovely," an episode of *77 Sunset Strip*. I played Nina Maran, a star who was blackmailed by a hypnotist named Ferini, and who implored her movie producer (played by silent film veteran actor Neil Hamilton) to pay off her extortionist and save her career. The storyline was a little too close for comfort. The show was filmed in April at Warner, and aired many months later on October 19.

After a couple of years of negotiations, Hall Bartlett secured the rights to make a film based on the 1959 novel, *The Caretakers*, written by Dariel Telfer. Hall and Jerry Paris wrote a story based upon the book, and Henry F. Greenberg adapted the story for the screen. The legendary Joan Crawford was interested in the film. She secured an important role and signed on to executive produce the motion picture.

Hall Bartlett was a very talented director with a social conscience. It was not surprising that the subject matter of *The Caretakers* — the problems of caring for mentally ill patients — would attract his interest. His previous films included *Navajo*, which focused attention on the plight of American Indians; *Unchained*, a film about the terrible living conditions in a men's prison; and *All The Young Men*, starring Sidney Poitier, which concerned an African-American man's struggle to achieve first class citizenship.

On May 28, Philip K. Scheuer reported in the *Los Angeles Times*, "... beauteous Diane McBain is being borrowed from Warner Bros. by Hall Bartlett to supply Robert Stack's romantic interest in *The Caretakers*. She is a nurse's aide to his psychiatrist."

I was not "borrowed" from the studio. I was "rented out." An actor's contract allowed him to be "lent-out" to another studio or producer for an approved project. The actor was paid his contracted salary without interruption, but his studio lent him out at an inflated rate, thereby making money on the deal.

I began work on *The Caretakers* in mid-May at Paramount Studios in Hollywood. As originally written, my role as Alison was a good part, and I was excited to work in a film that seemed important.

The story of *The Caretakers* was set in a mental hospital. A young, progressive-minded psychiatrist, played by Robert Stack, believed his mentally ill patients could benefit from group therapy. I played the role of his supportive nurse, and romantic interest. Joan Crawford played the unyielding head nurse of the facility, who preferred the more inhuman traditional treatment — straight jackets and padded cells (the only person in need of a straight jacket and padded cell was Miss Crawford). The determined psychiatrist eventually prevailed. Polly Bergen, Janis Paige, Barbara Barrie, and Ellen Corby played the mental patients. Herbert Marshall,

With Roger Smith in "Leap My Lovely." PHOTO COLLECTION OF MICHAUD

Constance Ford, Sharon Hugueny, Susan Oliver, Robert Vaughn, and Van Williams completed the cast.

We had an interesting mix of actors. Marshall was seventy-two years old and fragile, and he filmed his few scenes early in the day with the help of his old friend, Joan Crawford. I was happy to work again with Constance, Sharon, and my good friend, Van.

With Robert Stack in The Caretakers.

Sharon was an emotional wreck. She was trying to recover after what she described as a miserable five-month marriage to a minor actor named Robert Evans. She was seventeen years old when she married thirty-one-year-old Evans in May 1961. Sharon and I had become good friends when we made *Parrish* together a year earlier. She commiserated with me on the set of *The Caretakers* about what she called her "torturous" marriage. He took her to live in New York, and the studio suspended her without pay. She told me that Evans had forced her to have daily waxing treatments to rid her entire body of hair. He couldn't stand any hint of hair on her flesh, and she couldn't bear the painful treatments. Without her friends and family, and without her career, she had been miserable. She said Evans arranged for a quickie divorce in Mexico and left her high and dry without alimony. She had been forced to walk away from a career on the rise, and she was never able to reestablish her place in the business. I felt so sorry for what she said she had suffered.

Joan Crawford played the evil counterpart to the kindly, progressive psychiatrist played by Stack. She played the part well. The wardrobe department dressed her in a drab, white nurse's uniform. It accentuated her harsh, unforgiving stiffness. Her long, middle-aged face was awash in wrinkles and she looked a little like a horse. Moreover, her outfit only worsened her appearance. Crawford, herself, was a miserable woman, filled with jealousy and bitterness.

I hadn't been on set very long before Robbie asked me to have lunch with him and afterward introduce him to, as he worshipfully called her, "The Great Joan Crawford." He was madly in love with celebrity. For reasons I suspected could be problematic, he asked me to wear a beautiful new picture hat and a pretty beige sheath that I had recently purchased.

When the day arrived, we had a sumptuous Mexican feast at Lucy's El Adobe Restaurant on Melrose Avenue across the street from Paramount Studios. After our lunch, we wandered over to the set. The actors and crew were just returning from their lunch, too, and the giant doors to the movie stage were wide open. As we entered, I was backlit with the blinding sunlight, and framed perfectly in my sexy hat and sleek sleeveless dress. At that very moment, Joan emerged from her dressing room on the set, dressed severely in her nurse's costume.

Later, Robbie gleefully described the moment. "Her eyes turned red with hatred, becoming slits like a snake's, and a gooey, green jealousy oozed from her pores."

She looked like she had been slapped in the face with a dead fish. Clearly, she was enraged to be confronted by her young, out-of-the-cradle competition. Of course, Robbie didn't care what she thought of me. He pushed forward with his hand outstretched, certain he would ingratiate her. She politely, but coolly shook his hand, ignored me, and quickly brushed past us on her way to rehearsal. She reminded me of what I call "L.A. road hogs." They are motorists who are usually past their prime. They drive with their minds on the car behind them and do their best to block its way. They will break any laws and drive slower and slower to prevent the person behind them from going by. They will even go so far as to run a person off the road rather than let them proceed. As I tried to pass, Joan Crawford was trying to run me off the road.

As a producer, she succeeded. She managed to have most of my scenes edited or even cut out of the final film. The shoot was a struggle. I'd never found myself in the middle of such jealousy and dissension on a set before.

One of the things I had loved about the job of acting was the camaraderie performers seemed to have when they worked together. On this film, it was every woman for her self.

Never before had I run into so many women in a single film, either. With few exceptions, they all behaved as if they had something to protect. At times, the nonsense degenerated into ugly bitch fights. I half expected to find clumps of hair on the floor of the set. It really surprised me because, coming from my background, I always had such a high regard for women. The women in my family were heroines. They were kind and courageous. I found it very disconcerting and discouraging to realize that such vicious cattiness between women could be so real. Perhaps I should have taken a hint from the girls and been more protective of myself.

Joan Crawford turned me into her personal vendetta. Since she was the producer, and the completion bond (the money held in trust to guarantee the film's completion) was her personal money, my role in the movie was in grave jeopardy. She was on the Board of Directors of Pepsi Co., and when she wasn't trying to place bottles of Pepsi on every flat surface she could find (she even had bottles delivered to everyone's dressing room daily), she manipulated the director in a plan of sabotage. She orchestrated all of our scenes together so that I could easily be excised from the film. By the time she was finished, my part in the movie was nearly non-existent. My love scenes with Robert Stack were also cut out, so that the real purpose of my character in the film faded away! I was eventually reduced to a nurse in the background with a line here or there.

In the days leading up to the "wrap" party to celebrate the conclusion of principal photography, the planned soiree had become something of an event. Many Hollywood personalities ended up on the RSVP list. Everyone in town wanted to go. Except me. After the unnecessary backroom drama on the movie set, I didn't want to spend an evening socializing with the cast. A gentleman named Richard Gully coaxed me to attend the party. Gully was a rather dapper Englishman who had worked as Jack Warner's "aide-de-camp" during the 1950s. He was a "professional social director" in the movie colony, and knew every rumor, innuendo and incriminating story in town. Gully said I could mingle with the producers and directors who were also on the guest list. He promised to place me at a "wonderful table." I sat with Bob Stack and his lovely wife, and estimable directors Vincente Minnelli and Otto Preminger, and their wives. My tablemate was director Jean Negulesco who had apparently left his wife at home.

At some point during the evening, Hall Bartlett asked me to dance. Going to the party was my first mistake. My second was dancing with Hall. Within minutes, his jealous wife accosted us on the crowded dance floor. She grabbed her husband's arm and yelled, "You're coming home with me and you're going to stay away from that prostitute!" Activity on the dance floor abruptly halted and a hush fell over the room. I was mortified. Another man graciously took my arm and danced me away from the embarrassing scene.

Once I returned to my table, I quickly excused myself and left. I could feel the faces and eyes follow me on the way out the door. I couldn't even drive home. I stopped at my friend and *Surfside Six* stand-in Louise Myer's apartment to cry on her shoulder.

In spite of trying to put the galling episode behind me, the foolish fray made the newspapers. On June 29, Hedda Hopper wrote in the *Los Angeles Times*, "Producer Hall Bartlett and his Latin wife Anna Maria had a misunderstanding when he spent too much time at a party, dancing with Diane McBain." The rumors spread throughout the community, especially after my fling with George Montgomery before he divorced Dinah Shore.

The studio publicity department was forced to deal with the Montgomery story in the June issue of *Screen Stories*. The publicist wrote that I denied my involvement with George. In fact, they reported I barely admitted to knowing him. "I realize that this is one of the hazards of being an unmarried young actress in Hollywood," they imaginatively wrote. "Every kind of date with a man gets blown up, distorted, talked about and gossiped about." Still, these stories dogged me.

Nelson Hughes wrote in the *Independent Journal* on July 12, "Hall Bartlett gave a party at Lucy's in honor of Joan Crawford. Diane McBain, also in the picture, danced with Hall and here in Hollywood there's a rumor going around that there's more to it than those four silly little ole' Twists…"

The public must have thought that I was on the prowl for married men. Every time I turned around, my choices led me into another fiasco. Unconsciously, I was sabotaging my best efforts. I was reaching out for something I could never quite claim as my own. I was pursuing men I knew were unavailable. Perhaps some deeply held fear of being disappointed determined my choice in men. It was such a conundrum to have everything so many young women dreamed of, but I was unable to get what I really needed.

The gossip magazines were relentless and sometimes frightfully astute. A profile of me in the July 1962 issue of *Screen Album* began, "In the past, one friend said sadly, all Diane's troubles have been the kind that would make most girls delirious with joy. She was so pretty in high school that she wasn't popular; she's so popular with Hollywood men that the women don't like her. The only serious problem she's ever had is that some columnists in town like to make up stories about her. Now it looks as if she's trying to prove they were right after all."

No one, friend or foe, knew how distressed I really was. Even I didn't know at the time. Wanting to be an ordinary person, while hoping to be sought after, was, to say the least, confusing. Actually, I was quite mixed-up about a lot of things. I acted like the ice queen with most people, but I was just trying to hide how terrified and uncertain I really was.

"She's beautiful," the articled continued, "like a rare piece of Dresden china, but the consensus around Hollywood has been that she's as cold as a handsome piece of Dresden left in the deep freeze too long. Disturbed by this kind of talk, Diane denies it, 'I'm not cold, I'm cautious,' she protests."

While Diane desired to possess beautiful things and enjoy the advantages of celebrity, Danny was worried that money would be a stumbling block to heaven. Though my spiritual beliefs took a back seat in those tumultuous times, I still considered my religious upbringing now and then. I often thought about the young rich man in the Bible, who goes to Jesus asking if he can become his disciple. Jesus asks him if he diligently follows the laws of Moses, and the young man answers yes. "Then give away all that you have to the poor and come follow me," Jesus instructs. The man departs dejected because he cannot give up all his worldly possessions. There is only one God and, like the young man in the story, I feared I was in danger of worshipping money instead.

Money, too, had become a sore point between me and some of my less fortunate friends. Diane was happy to be the one who picked up the check when we were out. Being generous served my ego well. However, Danny felt it made my friends feel uncomfortable. She would never be happy until all the people in the world had plenty of money, too.

The two sides of my personality were in endless conflict over more than just money. They wouldn't agree on men. A part of me felt the time had come to find a nice man, get married, and start a family. However, I never met a man I liked who wasn't involved with someone else. Either he was married, or gay, or some other particular reason kept him out of my reach. Diane sabotaged Danny's desires because they were at cross-purposes to her own, and Danny skillfully played her part in messing up Diane's best-laid plans!

I did attract some men, of course. Usually, though, they were "hangers-on" — men who needed my *influence* more than they needed me. They were takers, not givers. I wouldn't have minded if they had come to the table with some good ideas or a strong sense of self and independence, but they mostly came empty-handed. A truly nice man who was single, funny, responsible, and smart didn't seem to be the sort of man I attracted.

On July 14, I was the guest of honor at the Coronado Film Festival near San Diego. I was glad to be finished with *The Caretakers*, Joan Crawford, and jealous, bitchy women on the set. Moreover, I was happy for any excuse to get out of town, and away from wagging tongues.

"Midnight for Prince Charming," the last episode of *Surfside Six*, aired with little fanfare on June 25, 1962. I hoped the studio would think I had paid my dues and would concentrate on feature film assignments for me. I had gained some excellent experience in the pressure-cooker atmosphere of episodic television production. We had worked with some wonderful directors, including Monty Pittman, Irving Moore, Charles Rondeau, Sidney Salkow, Richard Benedict, Jeffrey Hayden, and Robert Altman. Dean Riesner, a terrific writer, who went on to write several hit feature films for Clint Eastwood, had given us several funny scripts. Still, I was happy and relieved to move on to more satisfying projects — hopefully.

Left to right: *Grandma Ray, Mom, me, Daddy, Robbie, and Aunt Dorothy. My 21st birthday at Edna Earle's Fog Cutter Restaurant in Hollywood.*

Chapter 9

One of the embarrassing residual effects of being a familiar television star was displayed on the evening of August 7. Troy Donahue and I attended the gala premiere of *The Wonderful World of the Brothers Grimm* at the Warner Theater in Hollywood. Throngs of fans crowded the sidewalk and spilled into the street. When Troy and I arrived, a boisterous group of teenage fans went berserk. Their screams were deafening. We got a bigger reception than the film's stars, Barbara Eden and Laurence Harvey, who preceded us on the red carpet.

Since I fulfilled my professional obligations, I decided to take advantage of my hiatus. I went to Hawaii. I arranged a five-day cruise to the islands, hoping the dramatic change of scenery and people would do me good. I traveled first-class with my business manager and his family on the luxurious Matson Line *S.S. Lurline*. My dress designer, John Brandt, whipped together a wardrobe any young woman would envy. There were delicate, floating chiffons, shimmering taffetas, lush brocades, and daywear in linen and cotton, all of which made me look like a princess. The trip was a nearly perfect, except for my lack of a "prince charming." There was a young man onboard with whom I partied and danced, but we parted company as soon as the ship arrived in Honolulu Harbor.

Awaiting us was a genuine character who called herself Carla Dupree Beach. She was the Elsa Maxwell of the Hawaiian Islands and loved to greet celebrities when they arrived by plane or ship. She adorned us with fragrant leis and took us on a charming tour of Oahu. She knew the loveliest shops, the most delectable restaurants, and the most inviting bars and nightclubs. She was originally from Spain, and moved to Hawaii, where she became involved with the famed restaurateur, Don the Beachcomber. Perhaps sensing my vulnerable condition, Carla took me under her wing and ferried me around town. She showed me the time of my life. With macadamia nuts, Mai Tais, and the aquamarine sea, it was easy to succumb to the blandishments of the island, and hard to be depressed in such an exotic paradise.

Carla introduced me to a particularly intriguing man, who was "flying solo" in Oahu. Alan Shepard, a handsome, thirty-eight-year-old, was one of the original seven Mercury astronauts. He piloted Freedom 7 and became the first American to travel into space on May 5, 1961. After his successful return, he was celebrated as a national hero. He had an adorable, full-faced grin, and a mouthful of teeth. He joined us at the Outrigger

With astronaut Alan Shepard on the beach in Oahu.

Beach Club. He laughed a lot, but seemed lonely and in search of company. I was very happy to oblige him. We had lunch, drank island martinis, and played in the surf. He was cool and a little cocky, but a genuine sort of fellow. We talked a little about his career, and about his wife and kids. I knew he was attracted to me, but he was loyal to his wife. Still, he asked for my phone number. He was enigmatic. I caught him during a rare time when his feet were literally on terra firma. He was an astronaut between missions. In 1971, he would command Apollo 14 and become the fifth person to walk on the moon. Not long after I returned to the mainland, Alan called me and dropped by my apartment. We chatted for a long time and had another interesting evening together. He still seemed a little lonely. He was very self-confident, which I found incredibly attractive, but he never made a move on me. I wish he had. Perhaps he was waiting for *me* to make the first move. I wish *I* had.

My dear buddy, Robbie, flew to Hawaii and joined me. We met some fascinating people, who became life-long friends, especially a wonderful woman named Mary Muirhead and her young daughter, Leslie. Ralph Riskin, a theatrical agent and son of the famous film producer, Everett Riskin, was on the island at the time. He was cute, with freckles and a prominent nose that saved his baby-face from looking silly. Ralph was cool. He knew how to behave in public and wasn't swayed by my celebrity or the attention I attracted. His charm seduced me. We had a carefree island romance.

Warner Bros. took advantage of my trip to Hawaii by casting me in an episode of their successful show, *Hawaiian Eye*. The program starred Robert Conrad, Connie Stevens, and my pal, Troy Donohue, in a recurring role. "Hawaiian Eye" was the name of a combination private security firm and detective agency located in the Hawaiian Village Hotel. Though the storylines were routine, the exotic locations and pretty people made the show a hit for ABC. I extended my stay in Hawaii to work a few days on the "Pursuit of a Lady" episode.

Connie Stevens and I had worked together a few times and we had sort of a professional rivalry at the studio. We were both under contract. Some gossip columnists tried to create contention between us, but she was easy to work with, and she was always cordial to me. We had actually met when I was appearing in a play at the Glendale Centre Theatre. She was dating a young man who was also in the play, and frequently hung around the theater to be near him.

Feeling better about life and reinvigorated after the wonderful stay in Hawaii, upon my return, I rented a spacious two-bedroom apartment in a French Gothic style building in West Hollywood. Mary and her daughter Leslie, my new friends from Hawaii, soon moved in with me. Actually, Mary sent her young daughter ahead while she straightened her affairs. I was ill-equipped to care for a small child, but I did my best for the few weeks Leslie was in my care.

Mary taught me how to paint with oil and watercolors and helped me overcome my fear of failure. She was a very good influence in my life. She was boldly honest and one of the few friends I could count on to tell me the truth.

A young actress named Sharon Tate moved into the apartment next to mine. She was so wide-eyed and beautiful. We chatted once in awhile in the yard and shared our adventures in Hollywood. Sharon was very naïve, and I thought she had jumped into the shark tank with no defenses, but her smile and endless optimism were contagious.

Ralph Riskin broke up with me soon after we returned to California, but I hadn't invested any real emotion into the relationship. Apparently, he hadn't either. He said he had been put off by my stoicism on our dates. He didn't seem impressed with my intellect, either. He was being honest, but I didn't appreciate his criticism.

There wasn't much work for me, so I threw myself into painting my new apartment. John Brandt volunteered to help me decorate. He went a little overboard, and his tastes were a bit garish for me, but we had a great time working on the place.

Providence sent me back to Honolulu in late September to film another episode of *Hawaiian Eye* called "Pretty Pigeon." In this one, I played a mystery writer who set herself up to be a ruse in a Hawaiian Eye investigation.

I loved working again with Troy, but the show's star, Robert Conrad, was another matter. He was so stuck on himself, I just couldn't abide him. He was very short, which presented a problem for any men or women who appeared in the same scene with him. His ego would not allow him to stand on an apple crate to appear taller than the others in a scene. Instead, the crew had to dig holes in the sand for us to stand in so it appeared as though Conrad towered over us! I didn't like standing in a hole for anyone.

I had an instinctual feeling about certain actors. I could sense an arrogance in some of them that turned me cold. Conrad was one, and so was Edd Byrnes. I was contractually bound to work with both of them several times. Another smug actor who turned me off completely was a man some nutty manager renamed Ty Hardin. Actually, his birth name was Orison Whipple Hungerford Jr., so perhaps his manager wasn't so nutty. We called him "Ty Hard-On" because he walked around the Warner lot carrying a Bible, which he actually used to seduce women. He approached young women on the lot and told them that God wanted him to lay them, and his ploy worked! I was very resentful of him and his blasphemous exploitation of a holy book.

I had a glorious (though illogical) wardrobe for "Pretty Pigeon." While others were running around in bikinis and muumuus, I breezed through my scenes in picture hats, taffeta, and chiffon.

The studio didn't know what to do with me, it seemed. So, the publicity department tossed a bone to the columnists. "Diane McBain flew back from Hawaii without island industrialist Woody Woods," Harrison

Carroll wrote in the *Los Angeles Herald Examiner* on October 1, "but she'll meet Woods in San Francisco in three weeks. Meanwhile, she'll be dating famed golfer, Arnold Palmer."

I did spend some time with Woods in Honolulu, but I had no plans to see him again. Although my father would have loved his daughter dating Arnold Palmer, it never happened. I don't believe I ever met the man!

Back to the beach for me in Hawaiian Eye.

In the fall of 1962, Richard Gully called me. He wanted to set me up on a date with an acquaintance of his named Ralph Stolkin. Gully was an interesting Hollywood type. He was not a celebrity, but he fit in with Hollywood royalty, and bore a certain underworld chic. Since he had worked for Jack Warner, I was a little less suspicious of his motives. I was mistaken. We all met at a Beverly Hills restaurant. Ralph was twenty-three years older and married. He was a millionaire entrepreneur, and reminded me of the fact many times. He was ostentatious, and he seemed to know most people in Hollywood.

Ralph had a curious past. When he was a young man in Chicago, he had borrowed $15,000 to begin a mail-order business. He peddled fake coonskin caps, cheap transistor radios, and ballpoint pens. He had parlayed his small investment into a multi-million dollar business called Empire Industries. Along with his father-in-law, Chicago-based businessman, Abe Koolish, Ralph owned the National Video Corporation, which manufactured television tubes. When Ralph sold his mail-order business for a staggering profit, he traveled to Texas, hooked up with some wildcatters, and struck oil.

He had bigger things in mind, though. Hollywood beckoned, as it does to so many people. Howard Hughes had decided to sell his failing movie studio, RKO Pictures. Enter Ralph. In September of 1952, Ralph formed a business partnership with his father-in-law, and two other investors, Edward Burke and Ray Ryan, both of San Antonio, Texas. The Stolkin investment team purchased RKO Studios from Howard Hughes for about $7 million. The deal was not an outright sale, though. It was an option contract that called for Ralph and his friends to pay Hughes $1.25 million up front. The balance was to be paid in increments during the next two years. If Ralph's group defaulted, Hughes would get his faltering movie studio back and keep the down payment.

Within weeks, the Hollywood press revealed Ralph's rather checkered past. His shady business practices had gotten him into trouble with numerous Better Business Bureaus across the country. The Federal Trade Commission (FTC) accused him of fraudulent sales practices, and the United States Post Office charged him with illegal use of the mails and selling mail-order punchboards, a bogus cardboard lottery game used by conmen. Furthermore, the *Wall Street Journal* reported that he and his business partners were tied to racketeering charges and organized crime in Chicago. Ryan was connected to mobster Frank Costello's bookie operations in Florida. Koolish had been indicted in 1949 by the FTC for mail fraud.

Hollywood insiders were shocked. The stockholders at RKO balked and production was suspended at the studio. Ralph resigned from the RKO board in October because he had no desire to have his past business dealings investigated by the Securities and Exchange Commission. Within a month, the rest of his investment team resigned. Ralph and his partners could not make the second payment due Howard Hughes, so in February, 1953, the illusive Hughes took back control of the studio. Ralph and his partners lost their $1.25 million investment.

Like a cat, Ralph landed on his feet. He became involved in real estate development and other businesses, though he could never shake his reputation as an underworld figure.

Ralph was rich, powerful, and married. I couldn't resist.

One night, he took me home to his sprawling modernist Bel Air mansion. The spectacular house was filled with designer furniture and priceless fine art. There were bodyguards and security cameras on the property. When we went to his bedroom, he took out a handgun and casually tossed it on an upholstered chair near me. "I just want you to know," he said, "I have guards here." I was taken aback, and wondered why he'd done that. At the time, I didn't know anything about his past, other than what little he had shared with me. He was not much of a lover. Perhaps the accoutrements made him feel more like a man.

He had a home in Palm Springs, too. His wife traveled frequently. She based her life in Chicago. It was obvious to me that they lived separate lives. There was never a hint of her presence at the Bel Air mansion or the house in the desert.

I began to date Ralph steadily. He had many provocative and interesting friends, and people deferred to him wherever we went. Laurence Harvey, the man who had graciously spurned my advances, was one of Ralph's drinking buddies. He may not have been interested in me, but he was a charming man nonetheless, and we socialized with him on occasion. Edd Byrnes was another of Ralph's friends, and I did my best to avoid him.

Though we openly socialized in public, we managed to avoid the press. We ate wonderful dinners at Chasen's and Perrino's, and watched from the front table at Ciro's some of the greatest nightclub performers. He gave me an enormous diamond and pearl ring and glittering diamond bracelets. I got caught up in his wealth. Of course, Ralph had the ability to pay off the nosey reporters, which probably was the case. Occasionally, a movie magazine tiptoed around our affair. Late in 1962, *Movietown* magazine reported, "'Do you think I'm completely crazy?!' laughed the lovely Diane McBain, as she teasingly flashed her much discussed pearl and diamond ring. 'Wild horses couldn't drag out of me the name of the gentleman who placed it there,' she continued.

"There is a ring on Diane's finger — a ring that has adorned her hand for several months — yet no one, we repeat, **no one** has been able to tie the correct name of the giver to the sparkling collection of gems, **or** what its full meaning on her hand conveys — romance, engagement, or marriage?

Left to right: *Unknown gentleman, actress Myrna Fahey, Don the Beachcomber, Carla Beach, me, Robbie, and Myrna's mother enjoying the exotic beauty of Hawaii.*

"*Movietown* has always considered the private life of the fabulous Greta Garbo as the most intriguing and mysterious of all stars. But young Diane is rapidly cloaking her own personal affairs in much the same manner."

I certainly was. I was ashamed of myself in fact. Diane was in the driver's seat and Danny was lucky to hang off the rear bumper.

Chapter 10

On January 15, 1963, Jack Warner announced the motion pictures planned for the upcoming year at his studio. The *Los Angeles Times* reported, "The President of Warner Bros. Studios predicted Tuesday that 'exceptional production and release plans' in the next year will make the studio Hollywood's center of activity."

Warner proclaimed his optimism. "These are motion pictures, which we believe will spark the whole industry. We offer them as conclusive evidence that Warner Bros. intends to lead the way to the best and most exciting entertainment goals."

Several promising movies were about to be released by the studio, including *Gypsy*, *Critic's Choice*, and *Spencer's Mountain*. *My Fair Lady* was scheduled to begin filming on the lot later in the summer. Other films planned were *Youngblood Hawke*, *Camelot*, and *Sex and the Single Girl*.

The first film scheduled to begin principal photography, though, was a Broadway hit play written by Jean Kerr called *Mary, Mary*. The comedy had opened on Broadway in 1961 and played more than 1,500 performances. Veteran producer/director Mervyn LeRoy was set to direct the adaptation written by Richard L. Breen. LeRoy was responsible for some of the greatest films in Hollywood history, including *Little Women*, *The Bad Seed*, *No Time for Sergeants*, and the perennial classic, *The Wizard of Oz*. Debbie Reynolds, America's movie sweetheart, Barry Nelson, and the sophisticated British actor Michael Rennie were signed to star in the film. Both gentlemen had starred in the Broadway production. I was cast in the pivotal role of Tiffany. This project sounded wonderful on paper, and I was very excited to work in what I thought could be a very good motion picture.

A few months earlier, entertainment trade papers had reported that I would appear in a Warner film titled *Palm Springs Weekend*. The cast included my fellow contract actors, Robert Conrad, Troy Donahue, Ty Hardin, and Connie Stevens. Written by Earl Hamner Jr., (who later wrote the acclaimed television series *The Waltons*), *Palm Springs Weekend* was about a bunch of unruly college kids on spring break in Palm Springs. I thought we were all too old to be playing college kids. So did Troy. He refused the assignment, and he was promptly suspended by the studio. Fortunately for me, I had previously been cast in *Mary, Mary*, which filmed at the same time, so my schedule saved me from being stuck in the desert with Conrad and Hardin. We were all shocked that the studio was so intractable, and dismissive of Troy's reasonable concerns. It was disconcerting to think that the studio would so quickly dump a popular actor who had proven to be a box office asset. His suspension was a portent of things to come.

In a short time, Troy found it impossible to live the life of a movie star with no income. He relented and accepted the role of a college basketball player in *Palm Springs Weekend*. To drown his frustration, he drank very heavily during the making of the film. Later, he admitted that he had been drunk in every scene.

Principal photography for *Mary, Mary* began on the lot in February 1963. The work experience was pleasant with no in-fighting. Barry was fun, Michael was charming, and Debbie was "movie star" personable, completely prepared and professional. I brought my little dog to the set often, and when the film wrapped in March, Debbie gave me a super-duper pooper-scooper as a gift.

The humorous plot of *Mary, Mary* focused on a divorced couple who met in the ex-husband's apartment with an attorney to discuss financial matters. Inconveniently, they were snowed in with a handsome movie star who lived next door and the newly divorced husband's much younger fiancé.

Mervyn LeRoy had an overpowering personality. I liked him, but he was a little rough around the edges. He was a man of few words, and the few words he spoke were delivered with a slight stutter. Mervyn was at the end of his impressive directing career, and spent most of his time on the telephone or in the toilet because he couldn't hold his water. It was tough to get him on the set to do a take. He made the creative decision to film the movie using essentially one set on a stage on the lot, which felt confined and claustrophobic. There was one brief exterior scene shot in the snow, but all the rest of the action took place in the living room of Barry's character. It seemed lazy and lacking in any real thought or planning. The studio had a full plate of productions scheduled for the upcoming year, and money was an issue. I was stunned when I learned that for this film I was paid less than one percent of Debbie's $350,000 salary. The producer felt the funny story and impressive star appeal of Debbie Reynolds were enough to interest an audience. The producer was wrong.

I was awkwardly miscast as little more than a live mannequin for Oscar-winning costume designer, Bill Travilla, who had famously designed costumes for Marilyn Monroe. With such an ambitious production schedule at the studio, I couldn't understand why I was cast in such consistently poor films. Surely studio big-wigs knew stage adaptations rarely worked. New film and sound technology made it possible for

Me as Tiffany in Mary, Mary.

filmmakers to be more creative than ever. Location shooting was more and more common, and the visual possibilities of photographing the movie in New York City would only have improved the finished product. Producers didn't need to rely upon painted back drops and unconvincing sets any longer. As a consequence of those short-cut measures, the movie ultimately didn't compete well in the marketplace.

I thought the studio had lost touch with their audience. The world was changing rapidly, and movie-goers' tastes changed, as well. People were more politically aware, more hip to what was happening in the world, and they were more involved. This new awareness manifested itself in the music, books, and movies people wanted to experience. The youthful culture had an entirely different take on the world. I was born on the cusp of this great "cultural revolution," and though it took me a while, I eventually joined the revolt.

The Sherman anti-trust suits filed against studio conglomerates beginning in the 1950s eventually broke movie studio monopolies, which had produced a condition of creative ennui. Earlier, the studios had also owned the means of film distribution and the theaters in which their movies were shown. As a result, independent film makers were virtually shut out when it came to booking their films in theaters. Studio-owned theaters only showed their own product. Government regulators stepped in ostensibly to make the market more competitive. It didn't accomplish that for a number of years, and in the meantime, the movie business completely changed to suit the new regulations. One of those changes was the end of the contract system that had given me the opportunity to forge a career in acting. None of us understood the ramifications. It didn't occur to me then that this would adversely affect my work. I never thought that celebrity life could ever come to an end. I may not have starred in "top-ten" movies, but I thought I was an asset at the studio.

On March 5, I was a presenter at the 20th Annual Golden Globe Awards in Hollywood. I was in good company; my fellow presenters included Joan Blondell, Bette Davis, Irene Dunne, Charlton Heston, Maureen O'Hara, Eleanor Powell, Ronald Reagan, Barbara Stanwyck, and Jane Wyman, among other top stars. Fueled by free-flowing champagne, the celebration was a raucous and glamorous event that was telecast live in Los Angeles.

A few days later, I guest-starred with Richard Long on another episode of *77 Sunset Strip* titled, "Nine to Five." Richard played the role of a New York City engineer, who enlisted the help of his friend Stu (Efrem Zimbalist Jr.) in dealing with his "pretty but unruly" wife. I liked playing "unruly."

On April 10, I attended at the Chinese Theater the star-studded benefit premiere of Judy Garland's return to the screen in *I Could Go on Singing*. There was pandemonium on the streets, but the frenzy wasn't for the dozens of stars in attendance. A few weeks earlier, Garland overdosed on sleeping pills in her Manhattan hotel suite. I don't know where she was the night of the Hollywood premiere, but her rabid fans went berserk shoving and clawing each other trying to see if she was in attendance. The police struggled to maintain order, while we all tried to push our way into the theater. People were knocked to the pavement and trampled. It was an unnerving experience reminiscent of such a scene in Nathanael West's wonderfully dark novel about Hollywood, *Day of the Locust*.

I was actually quite moved when I was invited back to where I had started to be the Grand Marshal of the 16th Annual Days of the Verdugos Fiesta Parade. The mile-long, two-hour parade consisted of thirty floats, marching bands, as well as several other Hollywood celebrities. I had a great time and was thrilled to see more than 125,000 people line Brand Boulevard to see the spectacle.

Philip K. Scheuer let the news slip in the *Los Angeles Times* on July 1 that I would soon *star* in Warner's *Sex and the Single Girl*. The film was based on the #1 best-selling book of the same title by Helen Gurley Brown. I should have been excited, but when I read the first draft of the script, I was disconcerted. His announcement was a bit premature, but there was little time to worry about that. At the end of June, I had been shipped off to New Mexico to begin work on *A Distant Trumpet*.

Work began in Gallup, and several weeks later, the company moved to Arizona. We made our home base in Flagstaff, but shot nearby in the spectacular Painted Desert and at Grand Falls on the Little Colorado River. My co-stars included Suzanne Pleshette, and my old friends Troy Donahue and Claude Akins. Completing the cast were James Gregory, Kent Smith, and William Reynolds. Many Navajo Indians were used as extras. In August, we moved back to the studio, where the film was eventually completed in September.

John Twist wrote the screenplay based on the novel by Paul Horgan about the American Southwest after the Civil War. Troy played a West Point graduate with a conscience, who tried to whip a cavalry troop into shape before they relocated a band of Apache Indians. The story was trite as Westerns go, just a tale of Indian vs. white man in the Wild West, but there was a love triangle to spice up the dusty desert. I played the role of Troy's fiancé, and Suzanne played the role of the "other woman." Love bloomed on the set, but not for me. Troy and Suzanne fell in love and quickly married. They divorced several months later. I thought it was an odd affair from the start. Suzanne was too much woman for Troy. He was such a soft spoken, pliable man, and she was a "ball buster." I couldn't imagine the dynamic in that union, but they were smitten with each other on the set.

Back in Troy Donahue's arms in A Distant Trumpet.

Suzanne Pleshette was a different kind of woman to me. She had the foulest mouth I'd ever heard on anyone in my life — man or woman. "Truck-driver-mouth" was an apt and deserved description. The word "fuck" was new to me at the time. I was sensitive to its usage, especially by a woman. In fact, I was shocked. But I was very fond of Suzanne, her uninhibited self-expression, and her deep, throaty laugh. The women's movement then was responsible for some very odd behavior. Suzanne and I, along with many other young actresses, felt a need to break through all the male-designed social barriers of the day. We engaged in behaviors that purposely flew in the face of convention. Suzanne turned defiance into an art.

This cinematic "horse opera" we found ourselves in was horseshit. The studio seemed to be depending on old, worn-out ideas, and it looked to me like they had an old contractual obligation with Raoul Walsh that they wanted to dispense with in any way they could. Walsh was certainly a respected director with many great films under his belt, but by 1963, he was an eye-patch-wearing old man literally on his last leg. A tax loss must have been their goal. At least this one was in Technicolor.

As I finished work on *A Distant Trumpet* on the backlot, I began work on the five-part, final-season opener of *77 Sunset Strip*, called "Five." Written by Harry Essex, a veteran science fiction writer, the intriguing story chronicled Stuart Bailey's globe-trotting journey that began when his friend called him to New York following the death of the friend's younger brother. In an effort to buy his late brother's way to heaven, the friend asked Bailey to make amends to those his departed brother had wronged during his squandered life. Bailey's search, which took him around the world, involved a missing treasure. Eventually he ended up back in New York for a shocking conclusion.

While we worked at the studio, second units filmed in Paris and Rome. The impressive international guest-cast of twenty-four actors included Luther Adler, Tony Bennett, Jacques Bergerac, Victor Buono, Leonid Kinskey, Peter Lorre, Burgess Meredith, Marisa Pavan, Cesar Romero, Joseph Schildkraut, Walter Slezak, and Ed Wynn! It was a great working experience, and Bill Conrad was a terrific director.

During the summer months, Jack Warner decided to shake up the television department. What had saved the studio in the late 1950s nearly destroyed it in the early 1960s. The studio had spent too much time and money producing average television series, while the other big Hollywood studios invested in motion pictures geared to a new and younger audience.

Jack Webb replaced Bill Orr as executive producer of *77 Sunset Strip*, the one remaining Warner/ABC-TV series. The long-running hit would air its final episode in six months. In addition, most of the studio contract players' options were being dropped systematically. I could recognize the warning signs, especially when I was told earlier that I would next appear in little more than a cameo role as a secretary in *Sex and the Single Girl*.

The Caretakers was finally released in August 1963 to mediocre reviews. My notices were less than stellar. On August 15, 1963, *Variety* wrote, "Diane McBain and Susan Oliver as nurses, and Sharon Hugueny, as a young patient, do nicely." James Powers wrote in the *Hollywood Reporter*, "Diane McBain and Susan Oliver are good as young nurses." Margaret

Harford reviewed the film for the *Los Angeles Times* on August 23. "Susan Oliver and Diane McBain," she wrote, "are just plain frazzled as bewildered, overworked younger nurses." Miss Harford really got it; I *was* frazzled and bewildered.

The film was a disappointment at the box office. However, President Kennedy requested the movie be shown on the floor of the Senate. I believe this was the first time a film had been screened for Senators in the Capitol Building. Soon after the screening, the President's mental health bill passed without a dissenting vote!

I took comfort in knowing that our painstaking film had done some good. However, my option at the studio was in jeopardy, and I knew the lousy reviews would not help my cause.

Chapter 11

I was heartbroken when I heard the terrible news that my dear friend and *Surfside Six* co-star, Margarita Sierra, died on September 6, 1963. She was twenty-seven-years-old. She had experienced heart problems and did not survive the corrective heart surgery performed on her at St. Vincent's Hospital in Los Angeles. I was truly shocked. She was so lively, such a delightful ball of fire. I couldn't believe the news. A few days later, I attended her funeral at a Catholic church in Encino. Troy Donohue, Van Williams, Chad Everett, and Margarita's studio publicist, Mort Lichter, were pallbearers. It was a very sad day for all of us.

Though there was no work for me at the studio, the public didn't have time to miss me. On September 20, the first of the five-consecutive-episode premiere of *77 Sunset Strip* was broadcast to a very receptive television audience. The final episode, shown on October 18, included ghostly hauntings and an elaborate costume party. Little did I know that this would be my swansong at the studio.

Throughout the summer, work had continued on the script of *Sex and the Single Girl*. David R. Schwartz and Joseph Heller completed their adaptation of the best-selling book in the fall. Heller was the author of the successful novel, *Catch-22*.

On October 21, Philip K. Scheuer wrote in the *Los Angeles Times*, "Beauteous Diane McBain will have a starring role, along with Natalie Wood and Tony Curtis, in Warner's *Sex and the Single Girl* already rolling under the direction of Richard Quine. The character is that of a brash, young magazine editor."

The impressive cast included Henry Fonda, Lauren Bacall, and Mel Ferrer, but Mr. Scheuer's report was inaccurate. I did not have a *starring* role in the film. To make matters worse, *Mary, Mary* opened to lousy reviews. To add insult to injury, the movie opened at Radio City Music Hall in Manhattan while the blockbuster play was still showing at the nearby Helen Hayes Theatre.

Bosley Crowther wrote in the *New York Times* on October 25, 1963, "Obviously Mervyn LeRoy did a little bit more than merely place his camera in the Helen Hayes Theatre and shoot a straight running photograph of a performance of *Mary, Mary* to get a film of the Jean Kerr comedy. But you would hardly be able to tell it from the rigidly set-bound quality of his film version of the long-run stage play, which came to Radio City Music Hall yesterday."

Mr. Crowther didn't care for the film. About me, he wrote, "A sleek and conventional female rival is poured into slacks by Diane McBain." That was it. On September 4, the *Hollywood Reporter* had written, "Diane McBain is glacially attractive as Nelson's interim romance." *Product Digest* wrote on September 18, "Diane McBain most attractive as the health-conscious other woman." On October 31, John G. Houser wrote in the *Los Angeles Herald Examiner*, "Diane McBain, a blonde beauty hasn't a lot to do, but her lines are important and she handles the role like it was written expressly for her." The *Los Angeles Times* was clearly unimpressed, and wrote on November 1, "More serious miscasting is that of Diane McBain as Tiffany Richards, the chatterbox socialite with a passion for money and dried apricots. Miss McBain is a beauty but no kook in Tiffany fashion. It's doubtful if Mrs. Kerr would even recognize her as the exasperating, over-solicitous girl in the play… *Mary, Mary* loses all her bloom in transit to the screen."

The sting of the negative reviews was compounded by indolence on the part of Warner Bros. To capitalize on the free publicity (such as it was) generated by the opening of *Mary, Mary*, Warner jumped the gun and touted my upcoming role in *Sex and the Single Girl*. A photograph of me was released by the Publicity Department to all the news wire services, and appeared in most American newspapers. The tiny caption below the photo read, "Diane McBain [will be] playing the provocative part of Tony Curtis' sensuous, dumb-like-a-fox secretary in Warner's film version of Helen Gurley Brown's bestseller." What was especially galling to me was the bold-print headline above my photo, which read, "DUMB-LIKE-FOX"! I'd heard of "crazy like a fox" and "sly as a fox", but what did "dumb like fox" mean? In my mind, this was more like a disparaging editorial comment than a movie teaser.

The *Chicago Sun-Times* newspaper printed an interview with me on December 1. "There was a time when the average schoolgirl in this country dreamed of becoming a screen star. She pictured herself in a world of gold, glitter and glamour, besieged by handsome leading men, adoring movie fans, and charming, ardent lovers.

"To judge by the decreasing number of screen-struck girls who come to Hollywood nowadays, that dream has gone out of fashion. All these yesteryear stars have money, memories, but no husbands — none at least with whom they are currently living in a happy marriage. If this is what film fame does to the private lives of stars, who wants stardom?

"That's today's thinking, and no one expresses it better than Diane McBain, a tall (5 feet 7) blue-eyed blonde, currently starring in *Sex and the Single Girl*, a film with nothing to do with the book of the same name.

"Warner Brothers has told Diane that she has 'everything to become another Marilyn Monroe.' But, aware of Marilyn's demise, all Diane wants 'is some nice, pleasant, sincere, honest young man who would like to marry and take care of me. You see,' she explains, 'what happens to a girl is this: she gets caught up in the film business, and she becomes an actress, and automatically this makes her appealing to a lot of men. They want to take her out, not because she's a good girl or a smart girl or a witty girl. They take her out because they want to be seen with a pretty face. It does something for their ego.

"'For a while it's fun. But then it dawns on you that these men are dating you as a showpiece and not because they're genuinely interested in you as a person.

"'Last year,' Diane says, 'I realized a very shocking truth — men of character, men of achievement shy away from actresses, especially motion picture actresses. I'm talking now about doctors, lawyers, corporation executives, men of substance. They don't want to marry actresses — especially actresses who'd like to continue their acting careers.'"

I was having second thoughts about marriage being my primary goal. Though I came into show business with little planning, I had developed a sense of self during the process of becoming a credible actress. I had slowly come to the realization that my career was important to me. Acting was, after all, the best way for me to earn a living.

There was something to be learned from Helen Gurley Brown's book, *Sex and the Single Girl*. The outspoken author had always been a proponent of women's liberation. Unfortunately, the wisdom of her book didn't make it into the screenplay. Aside from Natalie Wood's starring role in the film, there was only one other part for a young woman. For the past several years, the studio pushed me so hard. The system had created and nurtured a star, and now, I was expected to play the bit part of a secretary. In the screenplay I was given to read, the character didn't even have a name!

The casting department never thought I would be foolish enough to turn down the only role offered to me at the studio. With my exercise in free will came the studio's option to put me on suspension, and ultimately to fire me. Those were my options.

I reasoned I would be better off without a contract. Richard Burton had encouraged me to do just that when we met. I thought I could get out and start making the types of films I wanted. No longer would there be a studio boss in my way, insisting that his choices were best, whether they be bad films or more television. He was interested in commerce and what was best for his studio. I could do a better job of choosing material because I cared more about my personal development as an actor.

Diane was in control of my decision-making process, which was definitely out of whack. Although the studio had in some ways held me back, it had also given me the opportunity for a career in the first place. The studio had provided all the accoutrements of stardom, such as important event invitations, arranged dates, limousines, and a wardrobe department at my disposal. The studio arranged all the publicity, juggled my schedule, and booked my personal appearances, all the things needed to turn an ordinary girl into a star.

To accomplish and maintain the same level of stardom to which I had become accustomed, I would have to hire expensive publicity professionals and managers, who would take as much as 25 percent of my income. I needed to maintain a high profile in order to attract good scripts, and I would need to have money stashed away to carry me through the slow periods. I had to be able to refuse work with confidence and never take a role that wasn't superb.

Along with so many other young contract players who were cut loose, I was blithely ignorant of what it really took to be a star without the power of a major motion picture studio behind me.

Still, I passed on *Sex and the Single Girl*. I just couldn't bring myself to accept such a throw-away minor role because the studio couldn't see me in anything else. I told them I wouldn't take the part. I was politely shown the door. They told me I was relieved from my contractual obligations to them. In October 1963, I gathered my few belongings and left Warner Bros. Studio as a contract actress for the last time. I was twenty-two years old.

Chapter 12

Ralph sensed my feelings of insecurity while I felt that my career was crumbling before my eyes. We had seen each other steadily since meeting. We were not the most companionable couple, but I was terribly impressed with his ostentatious wealth and his bulletproof self-confidence. He was kind to me in his way and lavished me with expensive gifts. He gave me platinum rings, gemstone necklaces, and a white gold Piaget watch.

Unfairly, I took advantage of his affections and affectations at a time when my own future in show business seemed tenuous. We flew first class, stayed in the best hotels, and were squired around in limousines. After a trip to Houston, Ralph offered to rent me a house so our affair could continue more easily. He found a lovely two-bedroom house with maid's quarters, a landscaped backyard, and a swimming pool. The house was comfortably furnished. I was feeling very vulnerable after my departure from Warner. I knew I made the right move, but I was concerned about maintaining my lifestyle and earning a living independent of the studio.

Shortly after Christmas, I moved into the house that Ralph rented for me, with my friend Mary and her young daughter. I wanted her there with me, and her presence provided the perfect cover for my affair with Ralph.

His gifting escalated. My drinking escalated, as well. He was a social person and a social drinker. I prided myself on my ability to match him drink for drink, and I did. I was uncomfortable with the situation I had put myself in. Again, I was involved with a married man. Ralph didn't seem to have any interest in leaving his family. I accepted the house, the jewelry, the furs, and shopping sprees, and tried to numb my discomfort with alcohol. Moreover, I relied on diet pills to wake up each morning.

Ralph had a taste for fine food, which suited me, as well. We dined often at the best restaurants in Los Angeles including Cyrano, La Scala, Scandia, and La Rue. We basked in the "Feast of the Seven Seas" at the exotic Luau Restaurant. The nightlife beckoned us to the Beverly Hills Hotel, the Coconut Grove, and even Chuck Landis' Largo strip club on

Sunset Boulevard. Ralph liked the Italian food at Villa Nova next door to Largo. I had never lived so large.

Ralph loved expensive cars, too, and kept several at his home. He had a black 1961 Bentley Continental convertible coupe. He was a genuine "show-boater." I loved being driven around in that sleek car with the top down and my hair flowing in the breeze.

My first foray into a non-Warner television production came in the winter of 1963. I was cast in an episode of *Kraft Suspense Theatre*, which was filmed at Universal Studios. This one-hour dramatic anthology was a big hit for NBC for a couple of years and showcased some reasonably good dramatic fare for its time. I was hired by director Richard L. Bare to play the femme fatale in "My Enemy, This Town" opposite the darkly handsome and talented Scott Marlowe. Philip Carey, with whom I had worked in *Black Gold*, was cast as the friendly parole officer. He, too, was at loose ends since Warner Bros. had dumped all its contract players that year. Barbara Nichols starred as the bimbo who sets up the innocent Marlowe. The story had guts, and I enjoyed working with all the actors, especially Scott. We all commiserated about the demise of the contract system, and we shared our troubles about how to reinvent ourselves and take control of our own professional destinies. Barbara's once promising film career hit the skids and she scrambled for television work to survive. Scott's personal life dogged him. He was gay and the revelation of his affair with Tab Hunter a few years earlier was too much for him to overcome professionally. Philip and I were licking our wounds after being shown the door by Jack Warner.

"My Enemy, This Town" was well-watched and reviewed when it aired on February 6, 1964. A more prophetic title there never was!

Next, I guest-starred for producer Aaron Spelling in an episode of *Burke's Law*. Aaron was beginning to create a television empire for himself, and *Burke's Law* was a very entertaining one-hour detective show. Gene Barry starred as the rich and debonair chief of Los Angeles detectives, who lived in a mansion and drove to crime scenes in a Rolls Royce. Gene was wonderfully droll as each murder was investigated. The show was notable for casting well-known actors in numerous roles in each episode. I played the part of Susan Shaw in "Who Killed Marty Kelso?" The mystery unfolded when a movie producer was murdered at a party celebrating his most recent marriage. His three ex-wives, oddly in attendance, were all suspects. The show was smartly directed by Don Taylor and also guest-starred Glynis Johns, Luciana Paluzzi, and Marie Wilson. This was another very pleasant work experience.

As 1963 ground to a close, I filmed an episode of *Arrest and Trial* at Universal Studios. The ninety-minute crime-drama starred Ben Gazzara and Chuck Connors. The story of "Tigers are for Jungles" concerned a mobster set to testify before a Senate committee who was targeted for

"My Enemy, This Town" for Kraft Suspense Theatre. PHOTO COLLECTION OF MICHAUD

death by a hit man. The guest-cast included one of my favorite actors, Richard Conte, and a very young Marlo Thomas. I liked working with them both. They were exemplary professionals and generous actors.

I enjoyed the roles I was given after leaving Warner. The dramatic material gave me something to work with, but the press still reductively thought of me as just a "looker." The *Cleveland Press* reported, "The powers of a pretty woman should never be underestimated. Diane McBain, the charmer on *Arrest and Trial*, tames a tiger of a criminal."

It was a challenge at the time to find women's roles that were not one-dimensional. Most of the television writers were men, which may have clouded the way women were depicted in television scripts. The so-called "fairer sex" was most often portrayed as temptresses, coquettes, and big teases. They usually left the man high and dry, or more accurately, blue and wet. If they were effectual at all, it was because they were decorative and manipulative, or they just so adorably stumbled into the role of heroine. It was never by her intelligence or skill, but rather by her evil intent, or by innocent accident that her importance became known. In fact, most women's roles were written as if the women were inanimate objects rather than living, breathing people.

In the 1940s, women's roles were far more interesting. As written for the matinee market of homemakers, women were depicted as very strong and stoic. They had career opportunities, but were usually encouraged to chuck the career and settle down with the "right man." During World War II, women were needed in the work place because so many men served in the armed forces. Women were empowered by their importance, became self-supportive and self-sufficient, and felt as though they were contributing to the war effort. When the war ended, men returned home and to their jobs, and women returned to their womanly duties at home. Of course, once a person has a taste of independence and personal accomplishment, it's awfully hard to accept a lesser role in life.

As the release date approached for *A Distant Trumpet*, I went on a grueling five-day publicity tour that took me to Boston, Philadelphia, and New York. I appeared with Johnny Carson on *The Tonight Show* on April 13, 1964.

The one bright and unexpected light was a chance encounter I had with Richard Burton in New York City in April. Richard won a Tony Award for his performance in *Hamlet*. My friend Freddie Amsel took me to a Tony Awards after-party. Since I had last seen him, Richard had married Elizabeth Taylor. I thought he had long forgotten about me, but nothing could have been further from the truth. He saw me a across the room in a dark, uptown restaurant, and immediately approached me. He sat next to me, put his strong arm around me, and drew me to him. Of course, for me the world disappeared. We picked up where we had left off. We talked for a long time that wonderful evening, and poor dear Freddie was out in the Manhattan cold.

Despite the hype, *A Distant Trumpet* opened to a disinterested audience. The only jobs I had landed since my exit from Warner were television gigs. My agent at William Morris tried to find appropriate feature film projects. Plans were announced for me to star in a film based on the novel *Spring Is for Crying* by James Henderson. Production was set to begin in Bath, England in July. After numerous, disappointing delays, the film was shelved.

A few months later, I signed on to star in a film called *Halcyon Years*, written by Girard Rayburn and based on an English novel by Vincent Purvey. The romantic story was especially appealing to me. I would play a young, widowed US government worker in Paris, who fell tragically in love with a French military officer. Jean Paul Belmondo was supposed to play my leading man. The film was scheduled to begin in August in France. Again, nothing came of this project. I needed to re-establish a presence on the big screen, and the poor showing of *A Distant Trumpet* sabotaged my best efforts. I wouldn't appear in a film again for more than two years.

The trade papers were polite. *Variety* reviewed on May 25, 1964, "Miss Pleshette and Miss McBain would make any picture look good. Their roles hardly tap what histrionic resources may lurk beneath those beautiful facades." On the same day, the *Hollywood Reporter* wrote, "Diane McBain is lovely and sultry as Troy Donahue's fiancé." John L. Scott reviewed the film in the *Los Angeles Times*. He wrote, "Misses Pleshette and McBain are decorative and capable in their respective roles." On May 1, *Time* magazine nailed us, "Donahue is an animated Ken doll with golden hair, caught between the Barbie and Midge dolls impersonated by Susanne Pleshette and Diane McBain."

About *Time* magazine, Suzanne's words rang in my ears, "Well, fuck *them!*"

Chapter 13

Earlier in the year, Philip K. Scheuer reported in the *Los Angeles Times* the results of the *Motion Picture Herald's* 23rd Annual Exhibitor Poll. I placed fourth on their list called "The Stars of Tomorrow." George Chakiris, Peter Fonda, and Stella Stevens claimed the top three spots. Scheuer explained that some of the winners were already stars but were nevertheless judged as "heading toward top-star values."

I certainly didn't feel that way in the summer of 1964. I couldn't land a feature film, and I lost a two-part episode of Gary Merrill's detective series called *The Reporter*. Though my appearance was publicized, the series was cancelled before I could shoot my episodes.

I took little comfort in being cast as a guest-star in the season premiere episode of George Burn's new television situation comedy, *Wendy and Me*. George actually acted as the on-air narrator of the show, which starred Connie Stevens and Ron Harper. Since Connie was blonde, and the star of the show, I was required to wear a dark wig. I looked awful. Adding insult to injury, the "Molehills to Mountains" episode was filmed at Warner. It was my first job on the lot since leaving months before. The only redeeming feature was being directed by the talented and handsome Richard Crenna.

I then filmed two more episodes of *Burke's Law*. "Who Killed Mr. Cartwheel?" was broadcast on October 21. My fellow guest-stars included veteran actors Ed Begley, Patsy Kelly, and Sheldon Leonard. The story was set in a tourist-style Wild West Town. The "Who Killed the Tall One in the Middle?" episode aired a month later on November 25. I played Lana De Armand, a member of a sister trio act. One of the girls was poisoned, and the other surviving sister and I were the prime suspects. Steve Cochran was the leading man, and Barbara Horne and Juliet Prowse played my dangerously competitive siblings. I always enjoyed working on this show. The cast was always professional, yet playful, and both of these episodes were directed skillfully by Don Weis.

My television work, though less frequent, was pleasant and profitable. Being a free agent allowed my representatives to negotiate better salaries on my behalf. Nevertheless, I was very uncomfortable with my personal life. Ralph was kind to me and quite attentive considering he was married. My discomfort manifested itself in my being impatient and even unkind to him at times. Moreover, I drank way too much.

With Barbara Horne and Juliet Prowse in Burke's Law. PHOTO COLLECTION OF MICHAUD

The truth of my situation became glaringly apparent to me in the bathroom mirror of our hotel room late one night during one of our numerous trips to New York City. I was drunk and became fixated with my eyes, or more accurately, with my soul, which seemed to look at me while I contemplated washing the makeup from my face or simply stumbling into bed. I was suddenly struck with a blinding truth, one that should have been obvious. Ralph was a married man who was taking advantage of his wealth to keep a young mistress. In spite of what he wanted me to believe, my role in this pathetic scenario was that of a kept woman. Little wonder I couldn't utter his name in the press. I would never become his wife. In any case, why would I want that? A man who would sneak around behind his wife's back and keep a mistress was not the kind of man I wanted to marry. So, why did I carry on with him? He was a dangerous man with nefarious business connections.

At that point, I wasn't fully aware of his questionable business practices, but he was very friendly with his attorney, the famed "mob" lawyer, Sidney Korshak. Sidney first became involved with Ralph during the ill-fated RKO purchase. At the time, Sidney was retained as labor counsel for RKO. He was a Chicago attorney and not licensed to practice law in California. Ralph said Sidney had worked for Al Capone when he was young. Sidney's real power stemmed from his ability to act as a go-between between legitimate businessmen and underworld figures who controlled the unions. He was very important as a "backroom player" in Hollywood. Some people said he could start or stop a strike. Like Ralph, he was taken by the glamour of show business.

Sidney was an investor in The Bistro Restaurant in Beverly Hills, which opened on November 1, 1963. Ralph took me to The Bistro occasionally, and Sidney had his own table. Since he couldn't legally practice law in California, his unofficial "office" was the table he kept at the restaurant.

I could see I was involved quite deeply in Ralph's life. We had been together more than a year. Even my mother had met him. She tried desperately to understand what I saw in him. He was many years my senior, a more appropriate age for her actually, and he wore a toupee. Since he wore the rug to bed, I didn't realize he was bald for some time. I had a hard time explaining my attraction, too. I asked myself why I needed to associate with powerful men. I was attracted to power, and I was attracted to men who were slightly different. Perhaps Diane loved the power and Danny loved the untamed maverick. Ralph had humble beginnings and became successful in his own right — by hook or by crook. There was something intriguing about a man who traveled with armed bodyguards and had surveillance cameras around his property. He was not an ordinary man, and I wasn't sure an ordinary man, rich or poor, could hold my attention. Boredom was my worst enemy. I'd rather be poor than bored. Still, I was overcome with the feeling that the time had come to break it off with Ralph, but I didn't know how.

One night, a short time later, a bad dream wakened me. I was in bed with Ralph, enfolded in his hairy arms. Drowsy, and without thinking, I crawled away from him and moved to the other side of the king-size mattress. He groaned with disappointment and rolled out of bed. The next morning, I found him in the breakfast room, cold as ice. He was livid that I had moved away from his embrace.

"Sorry," I mumbled, "I must have been dreaming." I could tell he wasn't buying my explanation.

A little later, I was sitting on the brick wall in Sidney Korshak's beautiful backyard garden at his Beverly Hills estate. He was an interesting and charming man, and I could easily see how he had earned such a reputation as an effective negotiator. Behind the scenes, he was arguably the most powerful man in Hollywood at the time. In my view, he was one of the nicest men I had met in Ralph's circle of associates.

I had wanted to mate my poodle with another poodle and Sidney's was the only one available. It wasn't a perfect match. His dog had only one testicle and wasn't pedigreed. I didn't care about breeding show dogs; I just wanted my poodle to have puppies. Sydney was happy to oblige. So was his dog, so, there we sat watching our dogs humping.

"Diane," Sidney said, "I have a question for you."

"Fire away," I answered cavalierly.

"Do you really love Ralph?"

"If I were to answer your question, would it be reported back to Ralph, or is this for your sole consumption?"

"Well, I don't really care one way or another, so the information isn't going to affect me."

"Oh, my gosh, Coquette got her paw caught in her collar," I evasively chuckled as we watched my black mini-poodle hopping around on three legs trying to balance while her champagne-colored paramour was doing his best to remain connected.

My comment was meant to give me time while I thought about how to respond. I answered, "Ralph is married, isn't he?" My question was rhetorical. I wanted to rush in and help Coquette out with her improbable bondage problem.

"I want to be in love with him, Sidney, yet I have to be honest with myself. He doesn't say it, but I know his wife is still very involved in his life. He implies that the only other female occupying his time is his daughter, but I know better."

Finally, I rushed in to help my poodle out of her embarrassing, three-legged predicament.

I don't know what Sidney did with that information, but soon after that I started dating producer Aaron Spelling. He was well-dressed, perfectly groomed, and a real gentleman. He knew how to have a good time. We occasionally went to the Daisy, a private discotheque on Rodeo Drive in Beverly Hills. It had opened a couple of years earlier and quickly became the hippest spot in California. The club flourished, the founder once said, because celebrities needed someplace "evil" to go. The dance floor was packed with beautiful people drinking and doing the Watusi. I don't know how "evil" the place was, but it was a dangerous sea of jerking elbows and hips. I loved the dancing. Aaron was a member. With annual dues set at $500 per year, the only way I made the Daisy scene was as a member's guest. Because of the exclusivity of the club, you could easily find yourself dancing next to Cary Grant, Grace Kelly, or Paul Newman on a Saturday night.

Aaron had produced the television anthology series *The Dick Powell Theatre* and *Zane Grey Theater*. When we dated, he produced the then hit television series, *Burke's Law*. He seemed to know everybody, and those who didn't know him, wanted to. He was invited to every major event and Hollywood happening in town.

Aaron and I attended the world premiere of *The Greatest Story Ever Told* at the Cinerama Dome in Hollywood. The event was a benefit for the United Nations Association and the Eleanor Roosevelt Memorial Foundation. The circular lobby of the theater was aflutter with the flags of the United Nations. The ostentatious spectacle of a movie premiere always amazed me. Traffic was backed up for blocks. The red carpet was rolled to the curb. Hundreds of movie stars and politicians filled the theater that evening. The luxurious gowns, glittering jewels and exotic furs were stunning. The theater was so crowded that we had to be careful not to step on each other's flowing dresses.

The attending women had been asked not to wear "low-cut" gowns out of respect for the subject matter of the religious-themed film. It was quite cold on that February night, so the fashion directive was appreciated, but the chill brought out of cold storage every fur coat in Hollywood. Abbe Lane wore a full-length chinchilla coat that could have stopped traffic. I wondered how many little chinchillas were sacrificed to keep Abbe's legs warm. Polly Bergen, with whom I had labored in *The Caretakers*, wore an equally grandiose sable mink coat. I had my own fur coats then, but in 1965, we hadn't considered the cruelty involved in harvesting real fur.

After the endlessly long movie, we were all ferried in black limousines to the Coconut Grove at the Ambassador Hotel for a late-night, champagne supper. Many of the film's stars were there, and most of Hollywood's reigning movie "royalty." I chatted with actors and actresses with whom I had worked, but after sitting through a four-hour movie, most of us were more interested in the free flowing, bubbling champagne. The next day, newspapers reported that more than $75,000 had been raised for the charities, so the extravaganza was worth the trouble.

Aaron certainly knew how to take care of himself, but he was a nonstarter for me. He took it a bit hard that I didn't fall for him the way he had for me. He was very sweet and "comfortable," but he was far from being my type. He was just too nice. There was no chemistry, and I always thought chemistry was so important. I couldn't be comfortable having sex with someone when there was no chemistry. I had tried. There were a few men who seemed worth the effort, but ultimately a romantic relationship never worked out. Aaron was like that. He was a successful television producer, but his real successes lay ahead. Marriage to Aaron was not to be. It's too bad I didn't know with whom I was dealing. I liked Aaron's face, but he was so short and slight of build I felt like I might smother him. My father later told me that Aaron had asked him about marrying me. I thought he may have misunderstood as Aaron never proposed. Or maybe I missed something, a mumbled "Will you marry me?" could go unnoticed in a noisy room.

How different my life would be today, but I walked away from him. I was still trying to disengage myself from Ralph. What really ended my relationship with Aaron, though, was an accidental meeting with one of the most famous tennis champions in America. I was taking tennis lessons at the Beverly Hills Tennis Club when I met Richard "Pancho" Gonzalez.

One night, Ralph and I returned to my rented house after dinner. We had a nasty argument on the drive, which was the proverbial last straw. I told him I was through with him. I bought the house across the street. I moved Mary and her daughter into the two-bedroom, Cape Cod-style house with a huge back yard at 2155 Coldwater Canyon. I finally owned my first home. Ralph Stolkin became a part of my past.

Pancho was thirty-six-years-old. From 1954 until 1960, he was rated the #1 tennis player in the world. In a career that spanned twenty-five years, he won 113 titles, including the US Open, twice. We began to date, and I fell hard for him.

Tall and darkly handsome, Pancho was the image of a great tribal chief with shiny black hair and a sharp nose that would make any man proud. He was king on the courts. His smile endeared him to me. Mexican-American, he was born in South Central Los Angeles. He did not have a deprived childhood, but struggled nevertheless to make his mark in the world of professional tennis that was dominated by white men. Make his mark he did. There was a lot to admire about him.

He had a wonderful family, too. His brother, Ralph, and his sister-in-law, Carol, had two great kids, who became almost like our own. We went on double dates with Ralph and Carol. We loved to bowl, and enjoyed many dinners on the town. We even took short trips together. There was no pretentiousness, just lots of love. Danny was all at once thrilled and content to be in his presence and to feel so welcomed by Pancho's brother and sister-in-law.

My house in Beverly Hills had a warm and friendly atmosphere. The spacious back yard was perfect for Mary's daughter and Panchos's niece and nephew. I secretly yearned that the house with its homey sounds and smells would draw Pancho to me permanently. I knew he wanted to have a normal family life, too.

There was one problem. Pancho was married. Again, I was trying to take something that didn't belong to me. He had twin daughters with his second wife, a bit actress named Madelyn Darrow. His marriage, he said, was very shaky, and indeed it was. Madelyn didn't care for his family at all. In fact, her agenda in life seemed to be at odds with her husband. He loved his children and loved being with his large Mexican-American family for holidays and picnics. Madelyn wanted nothing to do with his family and wasn't enthusiastic about their daughters spending time with them. She seemed embarrassed to be around them, and didn't appreciate his Hispanic heritage. I was almost certain this would be the issue that would end their marriage. I could hope anyway, and that's exactly what I did — hope for the impossible. He actually left his wife when he started seeing me, but he soon "officially" returned to her when she threatened to separate him from his daughters, who were very precious to him.

I filmed another episode of *Kraft Suspense Theatre* in the summer. "One Tiger to a Hill" was directed by Jack Arnold, and my co-stars included

Peter Brown, James Gregory, with whom I'd worked in *A Distant Trumpet*, and Barry Nelson from *Mary, Mary!* I loved working with old friends, and James and Barry were fine actors. The episode, which had a surprising plot twist, was broadcast on December 3 on NBC.

With time on my hands, I took the opportunity to romance Pancho. I surprised him one night. He was going on tour, beginning in Cleveland,

With Barry Nelson in "One Tiger to a Hill." PHOTO COLLECTION OF MICHAUD

so Mary and I drove him to the airport in my car. My bags were packed, and I'd planned for Mary to leave me there at the airport with my tall, handsome lover, and to drive my car home.

"Where do you think you're going?" he asked, as I headed for the trunk of the car to get my things.

"I'm headed for Cleveland, too, on the same plane," I answered, smiling ear to ear. "That's where I was born, and I'd like to see it again." My plan was to accompany him on this tennis tour. Skeptical at first, he soon warmed to the idea when he saw my enthusiasm. His wife had never followed him anywhere. She wasn't interested in his sport. I hoped he would recognize how badly I wanted to be with him. Joining him was a bold move, but I really thought I could win him over.

The tour was so exciting. I loved hanging around the courts, playing tennis myself, and rooting for him as he advanced to the finals each week in a new venue. He swore off sex until he won the championship. I could hardly wait for him to win. At one point, he met Rod Laver for one of the greatest final matches of both their careers. They fought valiantly, until at last, my man prevailed. He was older than the hot, young contender, but with the will and pacing of a wise warrior and the tenacity of a shark, he won the match. Howard Cossell was there and reported that their duel was the greatest tennis match he'd ever seen and Pancho was the greatest athlete he'd ever known. Howard didn't know the half of it. That night, I had the greatest athlete of all time in bed, and the love-making was well worth the frustrating wait. There was no stopping him. We didn't sleep a wink. *Game, set, match*, I thought! I had finally won my mate.

I was set for a film called *Brown Eye, Evil Eye* to be directed by film veteran Ray Milland. The independent feature to be produced in Jamaica was to star British actor Hugh Griffith, and Maria Schell's younger brother, Carl. I was excited at the prospects, but the project got bogged down with financial and legal issues and was never made.

When the studios were forced to give up control of distribution and could no longer direct where and when their films were exhibited, the door opened for independent filmmakers. Young, creative mavericks finally had the chance to make small-budget films. The problem many of these young producers now faced, though, was a reliable source of production funding. Without a studio behind them to bankroll the production, many projects never got off the ground because of lack of capital.

In December, 1964, I landed a guest role on *The Chrysler Theatre*. The one-hour television anthology was an odd mix of drama, variety, and event-specials, *all* involving Bob Hope. The variety specials were pure Hope, often featuring his USO overseas holiday tours. I appeared with Lauren Bacall, Jack Kelly, Hugh O'Brien, and Zsa Zsa Gabor in a drama called "Double Jeopardy." While I was happy to be in such good company, there was only one scene in the entire show for me to do. I played a showgirl with no name. I remembered how Richard Burton had lauded the British actors' practice of doing anything no matter how small the part. What was most important was to keep working. I comforted myself with that memory because I had to keep going.

Chapter 14

My heated affair with Pancho continued. The passion was overwhelming. I had never experienced such window-rattling, satisfying sex before. We saw each other off and on for quite a while. He was torn between me and his wife and children. His devotion to his daughters had become a hindrance to our relationship. But for his children, I believe he would have permanently left Madelyn for me. I had not born any children to him and this was a definite disadvantage in keeping his attention. I continued to cling to the hope that he would recognize the hopelessness of his marriage.

Feature film work proved illusive. After years of contract service to a studio, auditioning for a role was a new phenomenon for me. One of my first experiences was an embarrassing eye-opener. In early April, I tested for the title role in *Harlow*, a biographical film about the 1930s movie actress and sex symbol. *Harlow* was to be shot in "Electronovision," a newly invented, shortcut process used to produce films utilizing high resolution videotape. The film was scheduled to be recorded in eight days, an unbelievable feat for a feature motion picture.

I bleached my hair the whitest blonde and wore nothing beneath the sheer negligee I lounged in for the test. This was a bold thing to do in 1965. I was so self-conscious of my naked body beneath the folds of nylon and lace that I struggled with my lines.

The test was shot on a television stage, and director Alex Segal was hidden away in the control booth. The inability to see the director — a rare experience on movie sets — made me unable to get a feeling for what he wanted. My dependence on his negligible direction was all too apparent, and I clumsily fumbled my lines. Momentarily, I heard the voices of Segal and producer Bill Sargent coming from the control booth.

"You don't think she's going to do it like that, do you?" the director asked Sargent. Stunned silence gripped the sound stage where everyone could hear what he said. Thunderstruck, and feeling very naked in my negligee, I flatly said in response, "I can hear every word you're saying, you know." I needed reassurance at that moment, rather than callous criticism.

My reaction disappointed me. Rather than jumping up and storming off the set like a diva, or even standing up for myself and asking for some direction so we might stop wasting each other's time, I cowered like a shrinking violet. I was always capitulating, giving up my power for the sake of being professional and a "good girl." Carol Lynley ultimately got the part.

Though our dating had ended, Aaron Spelling remained professionally loyal to me and offered me another television job. On March 31, I again appeared on *Burke's Law*. "Who Killed Nobody Somehow?" concerned the search for the person who attempted to poison an author at his publication party. My guest co-stars included Tom Ewell, Rory Calhoun, Kevin McCarthy, and Lola Albright.

My desire to work weakened my powers of reason, and in March, I accepted the co-starring role in an American production to be filmed in Spain called, *Huyendo del Halcon (Flying from the Hawk)*. Mary and I flew to Barcelona in April. The film was about an estranged couple, whose son disappeared when they were on holiday in Spain. John Ireland played my husband. He was professional, but a bit distant. The film was directed by Cecil Baker, whose directorial credits consisted of numerous episodes of *The Red Skelton Show*.

I needed the money. I needed a getaway. I needed a rest. We worked and stayed in Malaga, a coastal city in Andalusia, on the Costa del Sol of the Mediterranean Sea. It was warm, sunny, and beautiful. We then relocated to Torremolinos, a municipality just west of Malaga. A tourist mecca, it was quite liberal for the very Christian Spaniards. The first ever gay bar in Spain had opened in that town in 1962, and there was a large, joyful gay population. I was in such a mood that I normally would have been happily distracted by drinking and dancing with some fun-loving gay men, but instead, I had a short and fervent affair with the handsome young American producer of the film.

This is a film best forgotten, which I successfully did within weeks of completion. *Flying from the Hawk* was never released in the United States.

The next few months were professionally uneventful. I appeared as a celebrity contestant for a week on the NBC game show, *You Don't Say!* I then taped a television pilot with Dean Jones called *Alec Tate*. I played the role of an "alluring blonde" set up on a date with Dean's swinging bachelor character by his little sister. The show wasn't picked up, but was broadcast on *Vacation Playhouse* on CBS in July.

It was nearly impossible for Pancho and me to stay away from one another. I experienced a passion with him that was exciting and very satisfying. Still, he wouldn't leave his wife, and our reunions were frequent but brief. I wanted to tell the world about my love for him. Of course, his marriage made that impossible and forced us to hide from the public eye. I found the whole affair mentally exhausting, but I couldn't seem to quit. It was like driving a car with no breaks toward a road sign that boldly warned, "Dead End."

I was also terribly frustrated that my agent couldn't land me a proper feature film. Since leaving Warner, I had assembled a good professional team. Bill Shiffrin, my agent, represented many actors ranging from Jeanette MacDonald and Jayne Mansfield to Clint Eastwood. My money manager, Irving Leonard, famously represented Eastwood and James Garner. My press agent was a formidable veteran named Gene Schwamm. My personal life, real and fictionalized, still managed to end up in the hands of the eager Hollywood press. Gene did his best to field questions about my carryings-on, but perhaps the stories were too much for him to handle. The few scripts offered to me were awful, and I didn't know what to do to bring the slump to an end.

To make matters worse, Mary decided to move back to Hawaii with her daughter. My house, which had been filled with friendship and liveliness, was suddenly empty and very lonely. I felt despondent.

In late July, my family decided to take a road trip to the Painted Desert in Arizona, and Daddy asked if we could trade cars for a week or two. I was driving a big Lincoln Continental that Ralph had given me, while my parents drove around in a little Chevy Nova. I was happy to lend them my comfortable, air-conditioned car. I always liked being able to help my family, and they rarely asked me for anything.

While they were gone, I got antsy and decided to take a trip of my own. The loneliness at the house and my "non-relationship" with Pancho were depressing, and so was the state of my career. I loved driving to the illustrious Del Coronado Hotel on Coronado Island near San Diego. The drive was a few hours and the road followed the glorious coastline between Los Angeles and San Diego. I first visited the Victorian hotel in 1962, when I took part in a film festival on the tiny island. *Some Like It Hot*, starring Marilyn Monroe, was filmed there in 1958.

I wanted to get away from the turmoil that I perceived had engulfed me, and I wanted to know what it felt like to be an ordinary person again. Fame had turned my life into some sort of freak show, and Danny didn't like the act. I was treated as though I was something more than a human being. When Diane wasn't asserting her ego and desires, I was just a normal girl with average desires and dreams. My dreams had been simple when I was young. Celebrity had changed all that. I quickly lost sight of who I really was when those around me handled me with kid gloves. I was willing to go back to my old plan, to get married, have a family, and maybe even teach school.

By the time I got to the hotel after the long and unexpectedly lonely drive in my folks funny little Nova, I decided to check in as "Marilyn Miller," a nondescript young woman looking for a few quiet days by the sea. I brought my dog and cat along for the charade. Danny needed Coquette and my black cat, Pyewacket. I opened the patio windows in the room, collapsed in a chair, and stared at the rolling surf.

Bad weather drove my family back from Arizona a few days early. They called my house several times, without a response. Daddy got worried since I hadn't said anything to them about leaving. I hadn't thought it was necessary since I didn't expect them home so early. He drove the long distance from their house in Covina to mine in Beverly Hills. I hadn't been very careful about hanging up my clothes as I packed, and had left things in a bit of a mess. Daddy sensed trouble. He remembered I had reported an incident a few weeks earlier concerning a stranger who found me washing my car in my driveway. The self-confessed fan boldly walked up to ask for my autograph. Daddy recalled, too, that I had been vexed recently by some strange midnight telephone calls. My number was private, so the calls were particularly disconcerting. In fact, one midnight caller claimed to be Dodger baseball star Sandy Koufax.

Years earlier, when I was just beginning my career as a model, a man made several obscene phone calls to my house in Glendale. He had threatened to throw acid in my face. When the police were called, they determined the culprit was in close proximity to our home because he could describe exactly what was going on around our yard. The calls abated and nothing came of the threat, but the incident made us all a little wary of strangers.

So, my father was alarmed when he found my empty house on Coldwater Canyon. Even my pets were gone. He fretted on his drive back to Covina. He decided I had been kidnapped and worried my mother with his deduction. They reported my suspicious absence to the Los Angeles Police Department. My father was frantic and my poor mother was in tears. The police contacted my team, Shiffrin, Leonard, and Schwamm, and Pancho's brother and sister-in-law. They even called Mary in Hawaii. With the police facing a dead end, they released news of my disappearance to the press. The next day my photo was on the front page of the *Los Angeles Herald Examiner* with a banner headline, "Missing Star: Koufax Hoax Bared."

The article read, "Two mysterious phone calls from a man who falsely identified himself as Dodger pitching star Sandy Koufax today added to the mystery surrounding the disappearance of actress Diane McBain. Friends and relatives have expressed fear for the life of the 24-year old blonde, former star of TV's *Surfside Six*, missing since 1 a.m. Saturday.

"Today, her father, Walter McBain, 4356 N. Enid Ave., Covina, revealed to the *Herald Examiner* that his daughter had told him of getting two phone calls from a strange man shortly before her disappearance, 'He said he was Sandy Koufax and asked her for a date. She hung up on him'.

"Her father officially reported her missing last night at Hollenbeck police station, and detectives took up the trail from Miss McBain's $70,000 home at 2155 Coldwater Canyon Drive."

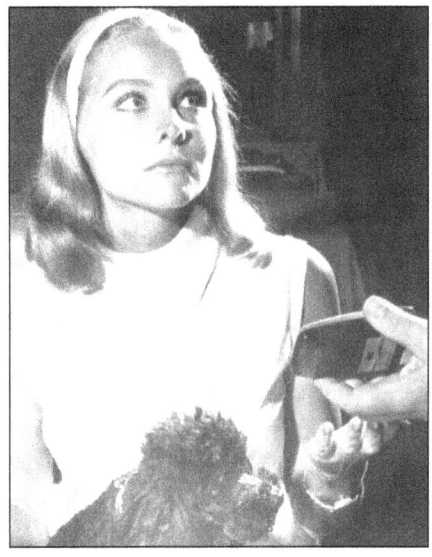

I was as uncomfortable as I looked while being interviewed by the press at the Del Coronado Hotel after being reported "missing." PHOTO COLLECTION OF MICHAUD

As I read this report today, I have to laugh. If a stalker didn't know how to find me *before* this incident, this reporter gave him all the information he needed to locate me and my family.

The truth was I'd secretly hoped my poor father *would* jump to such a conclusion. The disturbing thought momentarily occurred to me in the car on the drive south to Coronado Island. As I mused about using an alias, I'd fantasized how everyone would frantically look for me. Danny wasn't sure anyone would notice my absence, but Diane was sure she'd be missed. Now that the ill-conceived ruse had come true, Diane was red-faced and Danny tried to explain the situation to the reporters after a hotel employee found me underneath an umbrella near the tennis court. I was daydreaming and doodling while Coquette and Pyewacket slept near me. He showed me a newspaper headline heralding my mysterious disappearance.

Mortified, I immediately thought of my parents and ran to a telephone. I assured them that I was fine and everything was all right. I could tell they had been frightened to death, and I felt terribly guilty and self-indulgent.

The press swarmed to the hotel to find me feeling quite chagrinned. I mumbled something about needing "a change of scenery, faces, and attitudes." I told a reporter from the *Los Angeles Times* that "I just wanted to be Miss Nobody from Nowhere."

I had no idea the story of my disappearance had been picked up by the national news services. Even the FBI had been notified. No one believed my disappearance was an accident. Many people thought I'd set up the whole incident on purpose as a publicity stunt.

I returned home a couple of days later with my dog and cat, and my own tail between my legs.

A new series premiered in September, 1965, which quickly became an enormous hit on CBS. *The Wild, Wild West* was a one-hour adventure series starring Robert Conrad and Ross Martin. The stories revolved around a 007-style secret agent working for President Grant in the 1880s. Conrad starred as Agent James T. West, and Ross Martin starred as his sidekick, a master of disguise named Artemus Gordon.

I guest-starred in "The Night of a Thousand Eyes" as Jennifer Wingate, a beautiful assassin who tried to kill agent West. Ross Martin was a terrific gentleman to work with. Robert Conrad was his usual jackass self. Once again, the man with the Napoleon complex ordered any actor taller than him to stand in a hole.

In September, I filmed an episode of the hit television series, *The Man from U.N.C.L.E.* The one-hour spy spoof, broadcast on NBC, was a take-off of James Bond. Two super-spy agents, Napoleon Solo played by the suave Robert Vaughn and Illya Kuryakin played by the handsome David McCallum, were teamed up to fight an international crime syndicate. I played Joanna Lydecker in "The Deadly Toys Affair." The whimsical story concerned criminals who were anxious to get their evil hands on a boy genius, played by precocious Jay North, who had starred in television's *Dennis the Menace*. The villains hadn't counted on dealing with the boy's crazy aunt, played by the indomitable and hilarious Angela Lansbury. John Hoyt rounded out the guest-cast. Angela wiped me off the screen with her abundant personality.

This wonderfully written and directed episode was filmed at MGM Studios in Culver City. Professionally, it was a great experience. On a personal note, my sagging ego was boosted by a brief but intense dressing-room affair with McCallum. His native Scottish accent and Beatles-style blond haircut were impossible to resist. Of course, David was married to actress Jill Ireland at the time, but I had no romantic interests. I simply surrendered to the strong, physical attraction. David had recently become a major television sex symbol.

I was then cast in a comic book-inspired program that had taken television by storm. *Batman*, a unique half-hour comedy, flew into unsuspecting American households in 1965 with a "Wham," a "Whack," and a "Bam," making television history. Adam West starred as Batman, and Burt Ward as Robin, the Boy Wonder. The show was a sensation and placed in the top-ten ratings each week.

Like me, Adam had been under contract to Warner. We ran into each other once in awhile on the lot. Burt Ward was just twenty-years-old. When he wasn't fist-pumping on the set or chasing girls, he was locked in his dressing room with a female fan.

In 1964, writer Susan Sontag redefined the word "camp." In an essay published in the *Partisan Review*, she wrote that camp was a "sensibility — unmistakably modern. It is not a natural mode of sensibility. The essence of Camp is its love of the unnatural, of artifice and exaggeration. It is the love of the exaggerated, the 'off,' of things-being-what-they-are-not."

In 1965, there was nothing more "campy" than *Batman*. However, Adam didn't like the word "camp." He told me the show was a comic farce. For me, the experience was like being in a funhouse on acid.

I had never seen such elaborate sets on a television production before. The villain's hideout was opulent and elegantly furnished with extravagant furniture and fixtures. It was themed to suit the criminal's personality. One interesting thing I noticed was that the villain's hideouts were filmed at an angle. Villains are crooked, I was told, so their scenes were filmed at a crooked angle.

I was struck by the attention to detail on the set. I had never seen such excess before. This was remarkable to me considering the pittance Warner Bros. had spent on *Surfside Six*, where the sets were so flimsy one of the boys held up the wall while we were shooting. Our sets were rarely "dressed." Sometimes, they consisted of little more than an empty room and a table and chair. Of course, *Surfside Six* was shot in black and white, and *Batman* was shot in color. The comic-strip nature of the show necessitated glorious and brilliant colors in the sets, props, costumes, and makeup. The first time I stepped onto the *Batman* set it looked like a rainbow had exploded. I'd never seen a more indulgent but effective use of color.

The show was especially exuberant, and thus attracted one of the most impressive lists of guest-stars in TV history. Appearing as a guest villain became something of a status symbol in Hollywood.

Batman was shot as weekly, two-part episodes, which aired on consecutive weeknights. It took two weeks to shoot the two thirty-minute chapters on the lot at 20th Century Fox Studios, and on Stages 15 and 16 at Desilu-

Burt Ward as Robin, the Boy Wonder, me, and David Wayne as The Mad Hatter on Batman. PHOTO COLLECTION OF MICHAUD

Culver Studios. My episode arc was called "The Thirteenth Hat/Batman Stands Pat," and starred the charming and debonair David Wayne as the villainous Mad Hatter. I played his conniving assistant, Lisa. Our hideout was the defunct and abandoned Green Derby Restaurant. The job was as fluffy as marshmallow crème, but a very pleasant experience. David was bemused by the silliness of the job, but seemed to relish the over-the-top histrionics. I hated to admit it, but I did, too.

For actors like David and me, this was an entirely new way to act. David was a distinguished Broadway actor. We were both curious about all the goings-on. He was professional, delightful to work with, and very warm. Between shots, we chatted and he was genuinely interested in what I was doing with my life. He was a stimulating conversationalist. The highly stylized fashion of delivery and movement could only be likened to actually being *in* a comic strip. Gentle David Wayne transformed himself into a sneering, unctuous character. At first, it was hard not to be self-conscious, but within minutes, it was freewheeling and pleasurable.

At times, the dialogue was so silly that someone would break up during a take, and then we'd all follow suit. Once the giggles started, we struggled to regain control. Sometimes it took a half hour to shoot a ten-second scene. Adam used a teleprompter to help him with the contrived scientific mumbo-jumbo dialogue. I'd never seen a teleprompter used by an actor on a television show before.

Our far-fetched story arc concerned a fellow named Jervis Tetch (aka The Mad Hatter), who set about abducting all the twelve jurors who had convicted him of a crime wave. He mischievously collected each juror's hat. His ultimate target was the capture of Batman, whose key testimony had secured his previous conviction. He wanted revenge, and he wanted Batman's cowl.

"The Thirteenth Hat" and "Batman Stands Pat" were broadcast months later in February on ABC to an enormous and enthusiastic television audience.

Soon after I completed work on *Batman*, I got a call from Pancho. He wanted me to meet him at his brother's house. The news was heartbreaking. He was going back to his wife and his children.

"I do love you," he said for the first time. I froze. Diane was furious that he would tell me this right now, just as he was ready to walk out the door. Danny, on the other hand, was so crazy about him that she would have tolerated anything he did. I was conflicted, I could say nothing. I just sat there stammering how I wished he would stay, but my voice conveyed no emotion whatsoever. I later chastised myself for not seizing the moment and begging him to stay with passion and commitment. I could have dragged him into the bedroom and stopped him in his tracks right then and there.

But, I did nothing. He walked out the door. My tumultuous relationship with Pancho drew to a painful close. Our affair had become less and less about love and more about sexual liaisons. We were sexually compatible, and couldn't stay apart. He was the first lover who completely satisfied me. He would come to me and our intimacy was exciting and mutually climactic, but as soon as we were finished, I was consumed with sadness because I knew he was going to leave.

It took me a long time to realize that was the extent of our relationship and it would always be so. No matter the emotional pain, I was in my comfort zone. I had become accustomed to this dead end emotional pattern.

I was still unable to realize that the rape in Las Vegas and my failure to acknowledge the attack had taken a terrible toll on me. The assault had all but destroyed my sense of self-worth. Why did I settle for so little for so long? Perhaps I thought I deserved no better.

I ended up alone, on a therapist's couch, and very unhappy. I wouldn't learn until much later that all my romantic decisions were informed by the rape and subsequent blackmail, and by my reaction to it. I was damaged. I couldn't seem to make a logical decision in terms of my romantic pursuits. I could hardly maintain a logical thought.

Dan, the therapist, was a fatherly-looking, white-haired man. His sparsely furnished office was punctuated by a painting of a melancholy woman. I later bought that painting.

"I couldn't take Pancho from his wife," I told the therapist. "That would have been so wrong."

"Tell me," Dan said, "What do *you* think is your worst sin?"

I stared at the painting. The woman appeared intensely introspective. The somber message I perceived was that I had failed, and now I was being properly punished. "I committed adultery," I replied dully. *Forgive me Father, for I have sinned*, I thought.

Dan sat for a moment, seemingly stunned. "Gosh," he said, "is that the worst thing you have ever done?" He sounded dismayed.

"What else could I have done that is worse?" I asked, cringing. "Murder, maybe?"

"Well, a lot of people might have answered betrayal or duplicity or thievery as the worst things they had ever done. All you did was create pleasure."

"But it *was* betrayal," I protested. "It was duplicitous. I was trying to steal a husband!"

"And to whom did it do harm?"

"Obviously, the wife."

"Do you know her?"

"No," I answered, a little piqued. "Why? Do I have to know her?"

"Well, she may have lovers of her own, or maybe she's tired of her husband's incessant demands and has accepted his prowling in other beds."

"Are you saying I don't have to feel bad because she isn't my concern?"

"Wives have their own lives and you might be surprised how convenient you are to their purposes."

I began to see his point, but I was still inconsolable. Adultery was wrong. The Bible said so, and society said so, too. Otherwise, why would we make the indiscretion such a big deal? I couldn't just chalk this up as "something that served someone else's agenda."

"Maybe we shouldn't make it such a big deal," he proposed. "So, you believe in God and believe He would disapprove?"

I nodded my agreement.

"What if your actions are serving God's purposes?"

"Would God's purposes include people committing adultery and betraying one another?"

"I don't know," he answered wryly, "I'm not a priest. But, I've read a little of the Bible and I've noticed a lot in there about adultery, betrayal, and even murder. And it seems to me that people become stronger when they go through adversity. Either they become stronger, or they become embittered and depressed. Isn't it God's will that they become stronger?"

I tried to understand his point of view. He had good points when he argued that I could spend my time better by serving the poor, for instance, than by chasing after men and marriage. His philosophy seemed a strange mixture of excuses for the sins of selfish pleasure. Many people in the world needed help, he said, and so few actually helped them.

He was right about that. I had been spending precious little time thinking about other people. Being a celebrity, I had opportunities to serve others, and so I began accepting invitations to participate in fundraising events for charities. I volunteered for several telethons, too, but those activities also offered good publicity. I was getting back more than I was giving. This foray into volunteerism was clearly not enough to assuage my guilty conscience.

Perhaps to counter the negative affects of "living on the edge," I became obsessed with my parents and grandmother. I had happily done a lot of things for them in the past, but as Christmas approached, I wanted to shower them with gifts. So, I decided to go Christmas shopping. I bought my mother and grandmother fur coats, and my father, a new golf bag and clubs. Most fun of all, I planned an elaborate scheme to reveal their gifts. I placed gift boxes under the tree with little notes buried inside tissue paper. The notes led my family on a treasure hunt throughout the house that finally revealed the actual gifts. It was exciting for each person to follow the other on his gift-seeking journey. There were plenty of teary eyes that year. Daddy was taken with the golf clubs. Mom and Grandma loved their fur coats. I knew such a luxury was beyond their means and they would probably be uncomfortable wearing them among their friends.

I had felt the same way, but quickly got over my hesitance. I hoped they would, too. We all had such a great Christmas that year, and I hoped we could continue in such a lavish manner.

My house in Coldwater Canyon harbored too many memories of Pancho Gonzalez. Unsure of my personal and professional future, I decided to sell the house I had once loved. I moved to a small one-bedroom apartment in nearby Sherman Oaks. After all, I reasoned, no decent man would ever come near me if I already owned my own home. I thought men wanted their women a little dependent, vulnerable, and in need of rescuing. I talked myself into thinking I would soon meet and marry a nice man who would provide me with a home as lovely as the one I had owned. I was so certain, I would have bet on it. Where these notions came from, I have no idea. I can only attribute such ideas to growing up with fairy tales about "Sleeping Beauty" and "Prince Charming" — hardly the sort of life lessons that serve a person well in their adulthood!

At the end of February 1966, I began work on my first Hollywood film since leaving Warner. *Never Say Yes*, soon re-titled *Spinout*, was Elvis Presley's 22nd feature film. Elvis played the sexy lead singer in a band. A carefree, avowed bachelor, he was also a part-time racecar driver. The enigmatic "King of Rock 'n Roll" was chased by three women: the female drummer in his band (Deborah Walley), a spoiled rich girl (Shelley Fabares), and me, playing the role of an author named Diana St. Clair, who was investigating the sex lives of the typical American male for her new book, *The Perfect American Male*. Elvis, of course, was hardly typical. My character was based loosely on Helen Gurley Brown, author of *Sex and the Single Girl*. The cast was completed by Jimmy Hawkins, with whom I would later become good friends, the very funny Warren Berlinger, Carl Betz, Cecil Kellaway, Una Merkel, and Will Hutchins, the latter with whom I had worked so many times before.

Veteran producer Joe Pasternak was in charge of the film and engaged Norman Taurog to direct. Taurog had numerous film credits as director, including *Boys Town* and *Mrs. Wiggs of the Cabbage Patch*. More importantly, he was a favorite of Elvis and had directed the star in several feature films.

The director had looked for three typical leading ladies to star opposite Elvis, though each had to be as different from one another as possible.

Being involved with a big picture got my heart pumping. I later learned that my future friend, actress Tippi Hedren, was originally offered the role I played. She turned it down because the producer wouldn't meet her price. My agent had negotiated for five times less than what Tippi would have considered acceptable. In fact, the money was much less than I should have considered acceptable. Without the financial constraints of

With the "King," Elvis Presley, in Spinout. PHOTO COLLECTION OF MICHAUD

my previous contract with Warner Bros., I didn't know what to ask. My agent didn't seem to know either.

Nevertheless, I was excited to be working on a feature film again, and I thought my career might have a chance of recovering after all. My loneliness had taken a toll on me, along with my heavy drinking and pill popping. I had been feeling out of sorts, and I determined the time had come to clean up my act and get sober. Working on the film would do the trick. I was far too busy to think about booze and pills. I quit cold turkey.

My foray into therapy was an attempt to find some balance in my life. I began searching in odd, little esoteric books for answers to the problems that seemed to plague me. Dan, the therapist, had tried to be helpful, but he had his own agenda. I soon realized why he was so casual about sexual issues. He was recently divorced. He began to invite himself over to my place. In a sad, classic case of patient/doctor transference, he came on to me. I wasn't the least bit interested in him, but I didn't want to start over again with a new therapist. What a terrible decision I made. What little confidence I had in men was completely shattered. Again, I blamed myself, never thinking that Dan was responsible for his inappropriate advances.

With Elvis and Shelley Fabares in Spinout.

In any case, I had come to the depressing conclusion that no one was going to help me, except myself. If my past didn't kill me, it would make me stronger. I decided to become stronger.

The excitement of being on a movie set helped me. The cast and crew were terrific, supportive, and great fun. Elvis was a huge help, too. He was slim and gorgeous, at the top of his form. I hadn't really been a big fan, so I didn't know what to expect. The rumors that preceded him were true. He behaved like a complete gentleman. He was relaxed and accessible. He was often surrounded by a bunch of guys who were essentially "yes-men" or "gofers." They were patronizing to him, and terribly polite to the rest of us. I thought it was amusing that they all copied their boss's slick pompadour hairstyle.

Elvis had a spiritual side that surprised me. We incessantly talked on the set about our favorite books and what we were currently reading. Elvis gave me a little book called, *The Impersonal Life*, and several books from a series called, *The Life of the Masters of the Far East*. I became fascinated by these different ideas about God and the spiritual life. Because of my Christian background, these were things I never considered before. Elvis was reared as a Christian, too. We were like a couple of kids thrilled to share our ideas about what we were seeking.

Elvis serenades me with his hit song, "All That I Am," in Spinout.

Diane and Danny finally agreed on something. They *both* loved Elvis. When I kissed him in the film, I melted in his arms, and secretly wished he would melt into mine.

Spinout was shot at MGM Studios in Culver City and at five local locations, including the Ascot Park Speedway in Gardena, and at Lake Malibu, a small man-made lake in the Santa Monica Mountains. When we were at Lake Malibu, Elvis arranged for some of his motorcycles to be delivered to the set. He and his entourage of guys took rides during our breaks. Deborah Walley rode off a few times, sitting on the back of Elvis' Harley Davidson, for rides up through Topanga Canyon. I would love to have gone, too, but I wasn't invited.

The racing sequences were filmed locally at Dodger Stadium and in Hidden Valley and Thousand Oaks. Elvis was a very popular singing and movie star, and there was great "industry buzz" about the film. President Johnson, apparently an Elvis Presley fan, visited the set one day in Culver City.

The film opened nationwide months later in November 1966. There was a big publicity push because the film marked Elvis's tenth anniversary in the movie business. "It's Elvis with his foot on the gas and no brakes on the fun!" publicists squealed. "…singing!…chasing!…racing!…romancing!…swinging!"

Spinout included nine songs on the soundtrack. The album didn't sell especially well, and neither did the film. On October 14, 1966, the *Hollywood Reporter* wrote, "Shelly Fabares and Diane McBain are supposed to be lovely and little more, and they are that." The *New York Times* wrote on December 15, "Elvis Presley in Spinout, which landed heavily at local theaters, is neither a bargain nor a colorful Christmas bauble. Mr. Presley has made more than 20 films, but the minor variation this time is that he prefers racing cars and bachelorhood to the cuties his crooning captivates."

It was hard to imagine how anyone could make Elvis Presley banal, but Norman Taurog managed it nicely.

After a professional drought lasting several months, I filmed another guest-starring role on *The Wild, Wild West* in October. "The Night of the Vicious Valentine" also starred my old friend Sherry Jackson and the legendary Agnes Moorehead. The theme was murder. An evil matchmaker fixed up her "girls" with rich and powerful men, then killed them for their money. Agnes was wonderful to work with and won an Emmy Award for her performance as a murderous madam. Except for yet again standing in a hole for the insufferable Robert Conrad, I had a pleasant time on the set with Sherry and Agnes.

In November 1966, I began work on another feature film, *Thunder Alley*, for American International Pictures (AIP). I didn't know at the time, but this film would mark the beginning of the end of my career in motion pictures. AIP was founded by Samuel Arkoff, and earned a reputation for producing low-budget films for a teenage audience. The studio's "B" films usually went straight to the drive-in theaters. Most famous for a string of very popular and very silly "beach party" movies starring Frankie Avalon and Annette Funicello, and for a slew of campy horror films, the studio decided to turn its attention to a new genre of film, one that celebrated the teenage "hot-rod" culture.

The John Kennedy era and its pre-Vietnam War days represented a very optimistic time — and AIP produced countless films about innocent, sweet kids who loved fun. In 1965, the studio turned its attention to another type of exploitation film, one that capitalized on a burgeoning period of protest and social revolution. Mild alienation between kids and their parents was replaced by the depiction of dramatic change, violence, and youthful rebellion. Arkoff was no arbiter of taste. His savvy choice of movie themes had less to do with social conscience than box office appeal. In the mid-to-later-1960s, the considerable teenage audience demanded films that more reflected the way *they* felt about personal and social issues.

I found myself riding that wave in *Thunder Alley*.

A young director named Richard Rush tried to make something of the cliché-ridden script, concocted by veteran television writer Sy Salkowitz. The ludicrous story concerned a professional stock car racer, played by teen singing idol Fabian, who was forced to join a thrill circus after his blackouts caused a fatal accident. I played Fabian's girlfriend. Fabian was a pretty-faced twenty-three-year-old, whose music and once promising movie careers were in a free fall. The rest of the cast included Annette Funicello, Warren Berlinger, and Jan Murray.

Walt Disney must have been shocked to see Annette, his former television Mouseketeer, play the part of a young woman who threw orgies and became a drunk driver. Disney died weeks later. I wonder if he got wind of what Annette was doing!

The movie was shot in a couple of weeks at Producers Studios in Hollywood. *Thunder Alley* was *less* than a low budget movie, if that's possible. I could spend more money at the grocery store. Thankfully, I don't remember very much about filming this drive-in dud.

In the Heat of the Night was filmed at the same time, next door at Raleigh Studios. Most of my off screen time was spent watching Rod Steiger and Sidney Poitier at work. I had lunch with Steiger on the lot one day. I admired him very much. I was most excited to meet Sidney Poitier, however. He was so wonderful, charming, and incredibly appealing. I think I first "fell" for Sidney in the film *A Patch of Blue*. It was a

Sidney Poitier graciously agreed to a photograph with me and Coquette on the set of In the Heat of the Night.

wonderful, provocative film, and Sidney was dreamy and captivating. In my mind, the romantic possibilities seemed endless.

I recalled sitting at the dinner table at home when I was very young and overhearing a conversation my parents were having about one of my cousins, who had married an African-American woman. My parents were none too thrilled about my cousin's choice and speculated if the couple

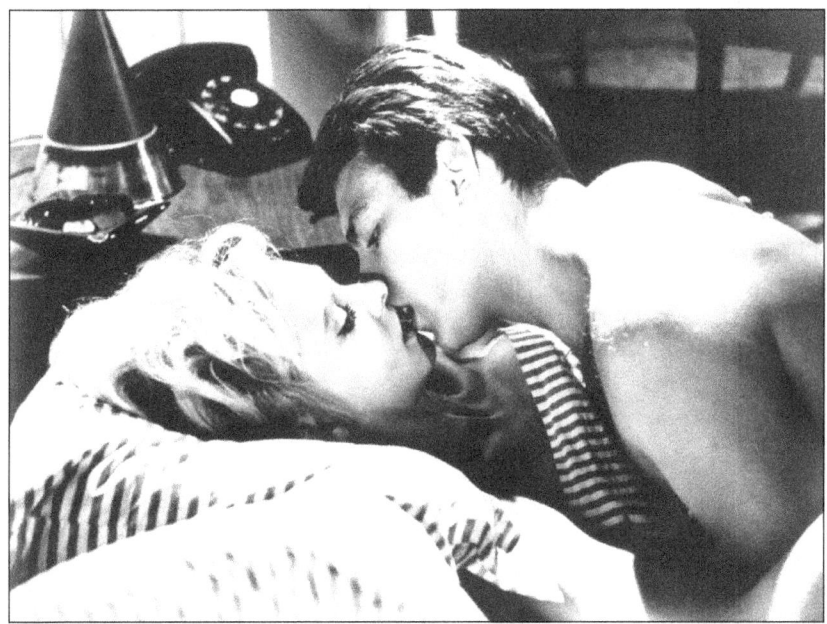

With Fabian in Thunder Alley. PHOTO COLLECTION OF MICHAUD

would have polka-dotted children! Even at my young age, I thought that was just about the stupidest thing I'd ever heard.

Movie stars do not impress me, but Sidney Poitier was a rare exception. I was thrilled to meet him, and daydream about him, and watch a master at work.

Thunder Alley was released months later in March 1967, with the advertising tag "Their God is Speed…their pleasure an 'anytime' girl!" I was required to do publicity for the picture. On February 25, I appeared on the television show, *The Dating Game*. I was the "movie star publicizing her upcoming film" bachelorette, who had to choose one of three eligible bachelors (hidden from my view) to accompany me on an arranged date. Normally, such an offer would not have interested me in the slightest. In this case, however, the date we were to win was an all-expense paid trip to the Canary Islands! I was no "anytime girl," though. As soon as we landed on Grand Canary, my "date" (a lovely man I'm sure), our chaperones, and I, hit the ground running — all in opposite directions.

The filmed racing sequences (shot at the Daytona Speedway in Florida) for *Thunder Alley* earned better reviews than did the actors. *Variety* reported on March 23, 1967, "Diane McBain seems much too level headed and fresh to be a track tramp." I should have sent them a thank-you card. On May 5, the *Los Angeles Times* wrote, "Diane McBain having done her part numerous times before is more than ready to go on to better things…" I should have sent them a fruit basket.

As *Thunder Alley* roared into drive-ins, *Doctor Zhivago*, *Alfie*, and *Taming of the Shrew* (starring Elizabeth Taylor and Richard Burton), not surprisingly dominated the box office. As far as my career as a movie star was concerned, I sensed the writing was on the wall. I wouldn't appear in a big-budget, major motion picture again.

Chapter 15

Johnny Grant, a talk-show host, and the self-proclaimed honorary mayor of Hollywood, contacted me in early December 1966. He wanted me to accompany him on a "visit-tour" to Southeast Asia. By that time, the United States had become entrenched in a terrible war in Vietnam. The press, some of whom were embedded on the ground with our troops, had never before covered the brutality of war so closely. Shocking images were broadcast on television news nightly to mortified Americans here at home. Bob Hope famously staged annual holiday shows in the area, often near combat zones. His touring company of performers was too large to reach all the smaller bases throughout South Vietnam, so the USO sponsored Johnny Grant and a couple of female stars to go each year to bring some holiday cheer to our fighting men. Tippi Hedren joined me on the trip. Tippi had starred in the Alfred Hitchcock films, *The Birds* and *Marnie*. She was a tiny woman, bold and beautiful, whose healthy sense of self made her appear much bigger in person than she actually was.

Jerry Buck, writing for the Associated Press, reported on December 12, "Disc jockey Johnny Grant, making his 29th overseas tour, is taking along actresses Tippi Hedren, and Diane McBain to cheer up servicemen from Saigon to Da Nang. 'The soldiers call me the GI Santa Claus who brings them pretty girls,' Grant said."

Images of Vietnam and the raging battlegrounds are burned into my mind. So many moments stand out vividly like watching a movie replay in my head. The incredible shades of green that blanketed the landscape, the startling blood red color of the iron-rich soil, and the dull browns and muddy greens of military fatigues paint my memories. The steaming heat was stifling, and the ever-present deep wetness of the air was palpable.

I had never experienced such an uber-masculine, testosterone-soaked environment in my life. There was no fragrant after-shave lotion in the jungle. Those beautiful soldiers smelled sweaty and a little like the metallic gun oil used on their weapons. They were musky, earthy, and mildly stimulating. They were so excited to see us. Some were uninhibited. They yelled our names out when they saw us. Tippi and I sat around, sipped beer with them, and listened to their stories. They wanted photographs and autographs. Many just wanted to talk with someone from home, whose mood and manners were not yet informed by the suspicion and self-defensiveness caused by battle exposure. Tippi and I simply provided smiling faces. Some of the boys were shy and just stood off a bit and stared

With a couple of handsome soldiers at the USO in Saigon.

at us. I tried to make eye contact with each soldier, and smiled when our eyes met. There was an element of ever-present fear in their eyes that was so disconcerting to me. Obviously, they craved female attention. I also felt they were always on the alert for someone to scream out "Incoming!" — when they would all hit the deck for cover. Within minutes, I also shook with panic. I couldn't imagine what the experience had done to those young men (so many barely out of their teens), who were stuck in such a foreign, dangerous, and inhospitable environment.

Although my parents never told me they were worried about my trip, I knew they were concerned for my safety. I promised to write to them everyday. The military facilitated the prompt delivery of my notes.

December 19, 1966. Dear Mom and Dad. We, of course, arrived safely and soundly. Took the northern route through Anchorage and Tokyo. It was a pleasant trip since we slept most of the way. I haven't been able to gather my wits about me as yet because of the change of time. I feel like I'm walking in a fog and I'm sure I look that way as well.

Everyone here has been great. They are very enthusiastic about the fact that we are here. Although it is hard for us to tell, they assure us we are doing a tremendous lot of good. We visited a couple of hospitals today and although the wards are fairly empty, the boys that are there have had it rough. We saw a lot of purple hearts and a lot of sad faces. It is difficult for me to talk to these boys. I just can't think of anything to say. Tippi and Johnny are very good at it. They seem to know what they are doing. Well, I guess once I get the hang of it, I'll be alright too.

Saigon is a lovely city. That is, it could be once they get their problems settled. This could be a great place to come and visit in peacetime. Most of the people are very poor and the city is over crowded so some people have to sleep on the sidewalks. This is indeed a pitiful state of affairs.

December 19, 1966. Today I ran into an old friend from Glendale Centre Theatre days. Gary Ramage is a Captain in the Army here. I guess I never thought I'd meet anyone I knew over here. Funny isn't it, how one separates one's friends from the possibilities of war and hardship. He apparently is making the Army his career.

It is very hot and humid. A lot like Hawaii in climate, although it is dirty, which makes it seem hotter and stickier.

Tomorrow we leave for our tour of duty. We are going to the Northern part of the country. I can't wait to get started.

Rather than write a diary, I thought I'd try to write a letter each day about our progress. So please save these letters as they arrive, so that I might have them for memories.

Tippi is a very nice girl. Always very cheerful. And Johnny's jokes are getting dirtier every day. Of course, he can be very funny. I guess he just takes a little getting used to.

Well, that's all for now. Please don't worry. We are well protected at all times.

Until later, take care.

We weren't as safe as I let on to my parents. Danger lurked all around us. I did not tell them what happened to us on our first day in Saigon, where I was able to test my powers of survival. As I quickly got to know Tippi, I discovered an indomitable woman. In fact, for me she became someone to emulate.

Don, a man I had previously dated in Los Angeles, worked for Bekins Van Lines, and was their point man in Vietnam for the armed services.

He had been there a while and asked if we might have lunch and do some shopping while I was in Saigon. I got permission to go with him on an excursion into the streets of the hot, steamy city.

We met for tea at the hotel where we stayed, and later Tippi joined us when we drove his jeep to a section of the city where he said we could find some great souvenirs. It was a clammy day, but we braved the relentless sun to shop for a couple of wonderful handmade ceramic elephants. They stood about two feet tall, were hand-painted, and very colorful. I wanted a pair for my new apartment. Since Don could easily ship them back to the States through Bekins, I was determined to get the best buy. So was Tippi.

Having made our purchases and completed the arrangements for shipping, we lazily wandered back to Don's jeep. As we approached, we could see that a gang of young Vietnamese men had commandeered the vehicle while we were gone. There were several sullen men draped all over it. They gave me the chills. They were defiant and apparently felt little reason to move, even though we were clearly the owners and needed the jeep back.

"V.C.," Don whispered to me.

"What?"

"Viet Cong," he hissed.

"Oh," I sighed. They were covert operatives — terrorists really — who worked for the enemy. The enemy was especially cunning and had infiltrated South Vietnam from the lush jungles to the asphalt city streets of that tropical land. They ultimately had complete control. It would take years for the United States to realize this sad fact, but, in truth, the Viet Cong had dominated the hostilities from the beginning.

Now, we had come face-to-face with the enemy. I was shaking, unsure of what to do. I tried to remain unruffled, and I knew Don had a revolver with him, but I didn't think our chances would be worth much if these fellows decided to take us on.

"Don," I tugged at his sleeve, "let's get out of here."

"How are we supposed to do that? They have my jeep!"

"We can walk."

"The hotel is on the other side of the city."

"How about a taxi?" Tippi volunteered cheerfully. She hadn't heard Don's warning and was clueless, perhaps mercifully so. She showed no fear.

I stepped behind Don, not wanting to go a step closer. "Come on, Don. Your jeep isn't worth our lives."

Suddenly, Tippi stepped forward, raised her hands and unreservedly shooed them off, "You guys, there! Get off that Jeep!" she yelled.

I prayed we would not end up in the middle of an international incident that would be reported on the front pages back home while our remains were returned in body bags. I could picture the headlines, "Tippi Hedren shoos Viet Cong!"

We stood in the middle of the street not knowing what to do next when, slowly, moodily, they unwrapped themselves from the jeep. As they moved, they deliberately displayed every ounce of menace towards us they could. It was like a beautifully choreographed number from *West Side Story*, only far more sinister.

Finally, we were able to take control of Don's vehicle. He started the engine and slowly drove away. Once we were out of eye and earshot of the menacing group, we let out a collective sigh of relief, and laughed all the way back to our hotel. Not that we thought anything was funny at all, but the tension had been so palpable it was the only way, other than crying and screaming, to let it out!

When Johnny Grant learned about our dangerous encounter, he railed at us. "You girls aren't in the States, you know! It's different here!"

"Oh, it's not so different," Tippi bristled. "Those guys were just blowhards, puffing themselves up to look good to the local girls." Tippi was intrepid. She wouldn't be bullied by anyone. There was something empowering about being strong and not crumbling in the face of evil. Tippi had been phenomenal, and her bravery was infectious. I felt like I might be able to get my own courage back.

> *December 20, 1966. 8:30 a.m. We were up at 4:30 this morning and on our way to Plieku. You won't believe our mode of transportation. It's an Air Force Transport plane (C-130). Well, we're in the Army now! We should arrive in about an hour and a half.*
>
> *We are going to visit I Corp. and II Corp. in the Northern part of South Vietnam. We will be in areas that don't often get people like us. So, we will be doing a lot of good.*
>
> *8:30 p.m. We just returned from dinner in the officer's mess. It has been a long, rewarding day. Pleiku is not a city, but a small village surrounded by a huge base. We went all around the base today visiting with the guys, serving mess in three places, and generally getting hot, sticky, dirty and conceited. These boys do wonderful things for your ego. You know how I've always complained that there are no decent men around anymore. Well, now I know where they disappeared to. They're right here in Vietnam. They're nice, good looking, clean cut, and they're men!!*

We have great quarters here. It is very clean and the water, they say, is potable. The soldiers have it pretty good. They can even get portable record players, etc. It is rough for them, but not as rough as it was during the Korean War. Frozen foods have made mess potable, too. And fattening. That's about all for now. Hope all is well at home.

Visiting with a wounded soldier in Vietnam.

Pleiku is a town in the highland region of central Vietnam. The town was strategically important as a military supply corridor and the main center of defense for the entire highland region of the country. Camp Holloway was an important U.S. Army helicopter base. The Viet Cong had launched a devastating attack against the camp less than a year before our visit, killing and wounding many. History states that attack prompted President Johnson to begin bombing North Vietnam.

I Corp. and II Corp. were corps of the U.S. Army headquartered in the region. A corps was usually composed of from 20,000 to 45,000 soldiers.

December 22, 1966. Yesterday was truly a day of days. We started out late, 8:30 a.m., or in Military terms, 0830. We boarded our choppers and were thrillingly whisked away. We flew high, 5,000 feet and low, 3 feet. Boy, what a ride. We arrived at the 3rd Battalion safely and soundly. They are great pilots so there really wasn't anything to worry about. It was just that the doors were wide open. It's a strange feeling to look straight down at 5,000 feet. Of course, I sat right by the door. Wouldn't have it any other way!

The boys or men (preferably referred to as men) were great. We just can't believe their war-worn eyes. I wish I could get a picture of some

Soldiers taking pictures of me taking pictures of them.

of the expressions. One thing they have plenty of is cameras. The press never was as well equipped. Click, click, click, they go. Each one has a picture taken with us. They are so adorable, you wouldn't believe it. We went to 3 or 4 different places. Some so remote all they ever see are the mountain people who live there. This is where the war is really fought.

In one place they were sending out a fresh strike force. We were able to say goodbye to them as they left. You know, a few of those boys won't come back.

Then we went to a special forces camp. They were living right in there with mountain people. The Lt. donned his Santa Claus suit for us. It was very funny. These guys have a great sense of humor. They have to. They'd die if they didn't.

12-22-66. In another place they were firing artillery. A Howitzer 85mm. The first time it went off we were ready for it, but the second *time we had our backs turned. Boy, I shot up about 10 feet! Have you ever been goosed by a Howitzer, Daddy?*

On our way back to the base we took a little detour. The pilots spotted an air raid on the Viet Cong. Well, we flew over it and saw some pretty fancy fighting. Those planes were doing acrobatics like you see in the movies. They buzz down in there and drop their bombs. It was terribly exciting and scary. Our doors were open so we could see everything and I'm sure they could see us. We are protected by shot-gunners on each side, but, even then, it is a dangerous proposition. Our escort officer was furious that they took us in there, but it was truly an exciting experience. I wouldn't have missed it. This is something few civilians can boast of having seen. After that, we tree-topped it all the way back to Pleiku. Well, how's that for a first trip out to the field! We came back very tired and dirty. Don't think I've ever been so filthy. We've been dry cleaning our hair every night because of the limited water facility. We have the best room at the base and it is the best we've seen, but even then it's a little inadequate. We felt lucky we didn't end up in a tent!

December 23, 1966. Yesterday we moved on to Da Nang. This is, again, a busy metropolis like Saigon. There are mostly Marines and Air Force people here. Our billets are very nice although we must go through the living area to go to the bathroom. It's an old French house with a lot of charm. We visited a hospital and an Air Force Base and served lunch to the Marines. Again with the unbelieving expressions. We are known as 'round eyes' here. I guess they think they are dreaming when they see us.

Last night we had a fascinating dinner with General Lew Walt. He's a great man and his troops adore him. He took pains to explain to us what and why we are here. We, back in the U.S., only hear about bombings, skirmishes, and casualties. Well, this is a very small, however important, part of the war. The real war is in winning the hearts and minds of the people. It is a political war, not a war for land. There are so many things he told us that I shall explain when I get home. It was truly a grand evening. After dinner we went to the officers' club to meet the men there. And guess what? We ended up in a crazy poker game. When I left I had them believing I could play a good game. I did all the things you told me, Dad. I expect we'll be invited back for another go at it.

Da Nang is a major port city in Vietnam, situated on the coast of the South China Sea. This city was home to a major air force base used by both the South Vietnamese and the U.S. Air Force. With an average of

2,600 air operations a day, the base was one of the world's busiest airports during the war.

At the time of my visit, General Lewis "Lew" Walt was the Commanding General, III Marine Amphibious Force, and Senior Advisor, I Corps and I Corps Coordinator in the Republic of Vietnam. A year earlier, General Walt introduced an innovative program called Combined Action Company

My holiday dinner with (left to right) *Martha Raye, General Lew Walt, Tippi Hedren, and Johnny Grant.*

(CAC). The program sent U.S. Marine volunteers into the countryside and tiny villages to train and advise the local civilian militia men known as "Popular Forces." The Marines were ordered to help protect the villages, befriend the people, find any Communist infiltration, and put it out of business. For a time, General Walt's CAC was quite successful.

> *12-23-66. This morning we were up and at it at 5:30. We were due to go to Hue, but, because of rain, we didn't get to go. While waiting at the airport we witnessed a couple of jet fighter take offs. That was pretty exciting! Before I go on about our day, I want you to know that this was our day of rest.*

After breakfast at the Press Club we boarded a chopper and were off to Hill 55. These poor guys have had a lot of trouble with the V.C. lately. This is a hot spot in this area. There was fighting on 3 sides of us while we were there. Don't worry, we weren't close enough to be in immediate danger. However, we could only stay for about a half hour since it takes the V.C. that long to launch a mortar attack when they spot a gathering

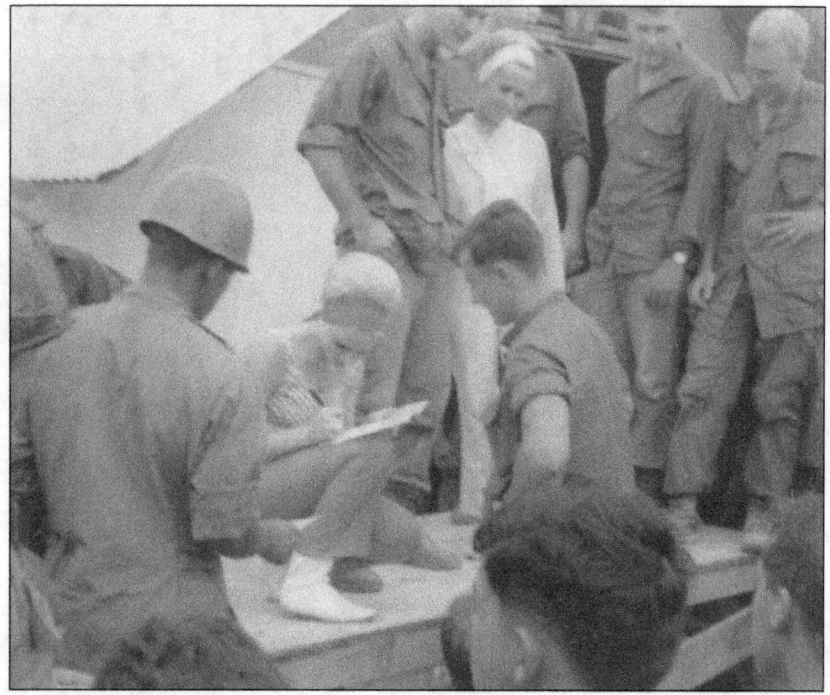

Signing autographs for the boys with Tippi Hedren.

of any size. Sounds awful, but there was no problem. We went there at the request of General Walt. Those boys haven't seen a round eyed girl for four months. Then at the request of the chopper pilots we went to where they are stationed. These guys weren't shy at all. I must say that the reception here was fantastic! Most of the guys we meet kind of hang back until they are coaxed a little. But, these pilots were something else! Good God, one of them even came up and kissed me! He asked permission first, of course.

Well, all in all it was a pretty exciting day. We, of course, got another hell of a ride back. Then Tippi and I with our escort officer went into the market place. It was not unlike the market places in Cusco, Peru. We also went for a short tour of the local museum.

"Hill 55," also called Nui Dat Son, was a strategic hill southwest of Da Nang. The Marines regained control of the spot from the Viet Cong, and established a base and sniper school there in early 1966. Nui Dat Son was the site of many historically devastating battles.

We visited the Museum of Cham Sculpture in Da Nang. Mostly carved in sandstone, the statues and objects were created by Champa artisans between 500 and 1,500 AD. Most of the art reflects religious themes that synthesize elements of Hinduism and Buddhism. All of these amazing pieces are indigenous to Vietnam. The post popular subject matter is the God, Shiva. Many of these precious sculptures were destroyed by bombs and invading Viet Cong. The U.S. Marines were instrumental in saving many of these pieces and moving them to safe shelter in Da Nang. It was surreal to see these amazing sculptures enshrined in a beautiful and serene oasis in the middle of a war.

> *December 25, 1966. Well, it's Christmas. Although around here it isn't much different than another day. In fact, it's almost embarrassing to go around wishing everyone a "Merry Christmas."*
>
> *Yesterday we started early again and went to Chu Lai. It was pouring down rain and the mud was knee deep. It was rough trying to get to all of the various units, but somehow we made it. We got wonderful receptions everywhere.*
>
> *Last evening we got all dressed up for our Christmas Eve. We ate dinner in the mess hall with the guys. Then we went to the church services with General Stiles. He, too, is a very fine man. Later, after fighting off the liquored men at the officers' club, we went to the General's quarters for our Christmas and opened our gifts.*
>
> *It was a very pleasant evening. We were lucky to have our gifts around a Christmas tree.*
>
> *Now I know how rough it is for these poor guys out here. Some of them are out knee deep in mud and water being forced to break the Christmas treaty. Some are just holed up in their quarters getting drunk so they don't have to think about Christmas. And some are being killed by Charlie Cong. Christmas treaty? Oh, sure!! It's a treaty for Lyndon Johnson with his voters. That's what it is. For these boys it's just one big ambush. For Charlie Cong it's a chance to reinforce. It's a chance for him to hit harder when it's over.*

The seaport of Chu Lai was a U.S. Marine Corps base when we visited at that time. Brigadier General William A. Stiles was the Commanding

General of the 5th Marine Division in Chu Lai. He formed a special tactical unit for combat operations within his Division, called Task Force XRAY.

12-25-66 Today, Christmas Day, we chanced to witness men being brought in from the field. These were wounded men. One had been shot

Christmas dinner with Johnny Grant (far left) and General Stiles (far right).

in the eye. Another was going to lose his arm. I don't know exactly what happened to him, but it was bad. Well, Merry Christmas.

Today we spent in Phu Bai. This used to be a Buddhist grave yard until the Marines moved in. Some of the graves still remain, but most have been moved. We had a very nice Christmas after a long day of visiting with the guys. Again, tonight, they will all get drunk if they don't have to work. If they do have to work, they'll just get high.

On our various tours through the hospitals we have seen a couple of V.C. prisoners. They looked so frightened. I guess they figure we'll treat them like they treat our guys. They hate us so because we are white like the French who oppressed them for so long. They have been brain washed by the Commies since they were kids that we are like the French were. It is no wonder they fight like they do.

Right now we are waiting for our plane to arrive to take us back to Da Nang. General Walt has made our traveling in his area much easier. These planes have orders to drop us off first before going anywhere else. They have had to go out of their way to accomplish this a couple of times.

We tried to call you last night from Chu Lai to wish you a Merry Christmas, but, as was expected, there was too much static. But, we did try.

In the field with our soldiers.

December 27, 1966. Well, we are now concluding our stay aboard the U.S.S. Enterprise. You may have heard of this little boat. It is a nuclear powered aircraft carrier. Most flight operations come from here. And to watch them take off and land is one hell of a sight. Have you ever seen a giant sling shot at work? Well, it's fantastic.

By the way, this little thing holds 5,300 people. It is virtually a small city. The only complaint I've heard here is that there are no women here on the Enterprise Hilton.

We walked this ship until our legs are ready to fall off. Of course, we haven't seen all of it. There are some guys here who have been aboard for months and still haven't seen all of it.

This is generally where we have been located. There is little fear of attack since the enemy is not well equipped with aircraft. And, the ship is well escorted with I don't know how many other ships.

> *On one of the reconnaissance planes there is a camera that cost us $1,000,000. I'm told that it is well worth it from the pictures it takes.*
>
> *The men here are wonderful, although not nearly as in need of attention as the ground forces. These guys go into port far more often than the others. The reception has been great just the same.*

Tippi, Johnny, and I flew to the *U.S.S. Enterprise* on a C1-A Trader plane usually used for mail and package delivery. Johnny got off the plane wearing his 20-gallon hat pinned with four little silver stars. He was a cigar smoker. In fact, he rarely took the cigar out his mouth. It just bobbed between his lips when he spoke. The weather was miserable while we were on the ship. It was raining and cold, and the sea was very rough. We spent forty-eight hours onboard and met many of the crewmen.

> *12-27-66. Cardinal Spellman was aboard yesterday and held mass for the men. It was very beautiful. They had a regular church set up on deck, complete with organ and choir. It certainly felt more like Christmas then it did in Chu Lai. Before the services we had a formal dinner with the Admiral. It was Admiral Curtis. I figured out the time and it was exactly the time you would be eating your Christmas dinner. So, I thought of you and how it might be if I were home.*
>
> *They start their flight operations at 0200 every morning. I am told that the catapult makes a tremendous noise and makes the whole ship tremble. I didn't hear a thing until 0700. Thank God!*
>
> *Tonight and all day today we visited and ate with the enlisted men. We also taped a half hour show for the ships television. Yes, they even have their own station. We also taped a couple of Good Nights to the guys. These will be shown every night just before sign off. Bet they'll like that!*

His Eminence, Francis Joseph Spellman, was the Archbishop of New York. He was an outspoken supporter of the Vietnam War, and occasionally spent time in South Vietnam. Rear Admiral Walter L. Curtis, Jr. was the Commander of the *USS Enterprise* when Tippi and I visited. The ship, the longest naval vessel in the world, had been tied up at Subic Bay to take on supplies in early December 1966. When we arrived, the ship had just taken its position at Yankee Station, a point in the Gulf of Tonkin off the coast of Vietnam. At the time, I could not reveal our actual location to my parents.

During the interview we taped in the ship's television studio, Tippi emphasized that she and the rest of us represented many Americans who believed in the justice of the cause, which kept so many young men away from home at Christmas. These sentiments seemed to make a difference to the boys who were hearing little bits of news from America that people were beginning to express dismay about the war effort. They were already in such a terrible circumstance that I felt they only needed to hear kind words from us, and not protestations.

Tippi Hedren, Johnny Grant, Bob Hope, and me in Da Nang.

> *December 28, 1966. We have just had one of the most thrilling experiences of our lives! We were just catapulted from the U.S.S. Enterprise. Boy, what a feeling. It is indescribable. I think I even let out a scream. And I'm not one to scream for nothing.*
>
> *12-28-66. We are on our way back to Da Nang. I guess we are meeting Bob Hope over there. We are also scheduled to visit a Special Forces Troop of Australians. That should be fun! I will add to this letter when I have more to report.*
>
> *I have just been told that we were one of the Truce violations! We were not aware of it, but we were fired upon by the V.C. while talking to the troops in Phu Bai. That was on Christmas Day. I can't imagine how it happened without our knowing about it unless it happened while the guys were cheering, which they did quite a lot. It must have been very quick or from pretty far off.*

December 29, 1966. Yesterday was a grand day. Our first stop was the Bob Hope Show. The G.I.s had built a nice amphitheater for them to perform in. There were 5,000 guys there to see the show. Bob arrived via General Walt's helicopter and the first thing I knew we were in the copter with them. We took a marvelous tree top tour of Da Nang and stopped for coffee at the General's. Then back to the amphitheater

With Phyllis Diller backstage at the Bob Hope Show in Da Nang.

to start the show. It was great. Those guys out there really enjoyed every minute of it. They screamed and cheered like nothing I've ever seen before. And, it was raining most of the time. They even brought some guys in from the hospital to see Bob. And some of them had been there all night waiting.

12-29-66. Then at the finale Bob introduced us and we received a cheering welcome too. We all sang "Silent Night" for the closing of the show. The tears came to our eyes on that one!

After lunch we all went out to Bob's C-141 to say goodbye. General Walt had earlier promised us another chopper tour so we could take pictures. After that exciting run we had afternoon tea (Coca-Cola) at his quarters and were invited back to dinner.

After taking great pains trying to look half way decent for the General, I took one of the muddiest spills of my life. On our way to dinner we stopped off to see some guys at the Enlisted Men's Club. It had been raining like hell for three months, so the mud was just a little too deep for our lady like shoes. Boots up to the waist might have been more appropriate attire. So, most gallantly, our escort officers picked us up and began to wade through the mud. Only my escort officer, bless his heart, didn't make it. He landed spread eagle with me right on top of him. I only wish someone could have gotten a picture of this. He had the most stunned expression I've ever seen in my life. The poor guy felt so bad about it he almost cried. So did I when I saw the mess. And, he didn't stop apologizing until he had taken me all the way back to our billets to change and got me safely in General Walt's care.

The General, bless his heart, really took a shine to us. After a lovely dinner and a long chat he presented us with three beautiful silver stars. That was the fastest promotion in the history of the U.S. Marines. From Private to Three-Star General in ten days. The girls from the Hope show had to steal theirs off the General's lapel, but we were formally presented. Gosh, we were so-o-o proud! The General even wanted to know who he could write to on our behalf. To think he would take time out of his busy schedule to do this for us. He truly is a wonderful man. He always wishes to do for others. I bet that's one big reason why he is where he is today.

You might say that yesterday was our *day with the General and a great day it truly was. I cannot say enough for him. And such a strong, kind face. It may sound like I've fallen for him, but I haven't at all. He's just the kind of man you can't help but have tremendous respect for.*

By the way, speaking of respect: I must add that Johnny Grant has truly won mine. I know I mentioned earlier that I was tiring of his jokes, but I discovered that this was just his way of blowing off steam. He certainly has been nothing but a gentleman all the way. He's been kind, considerate, fatherly and, yes, even motherly at times in his concern for our welfare. Underneath all of the sly fox façade there is a man who is as wholesome as blueberry pie. If anyone ever dares to speak against him again, I will be the first to stand up on his behalf.

12-29-66. We are now on our way back to Saigon. The General gave us his plane so we could get there in time to do some shopping, etc. See what I mean about the General? I'm sure you do.

A year later, on December 22, 1967, *The Chrysler Theatre* presented "Bob Hope's Christmas Variety Special" on NBC. The one-hour television special included on-location footage of our holiday show for the troops in Da Nang. Tippi and I appeared with Bob's company of stars, including Martha Raye, Phyllis Diller, Frances Langford, Anita Bryant, Joey Heatherton, and Vic Damone.

> *December 30, 1966. The last couple of days have been terribly hectic. As soon as we arrived back in Saigon we went on our shopping spree so that we could bring back some souvenirs home with us. Shopping in any foreign country is fun with the language barriers, etc. So, generally speaking, it was a good time. Our Escort Officer, who is a handsome black man, had studied Vietnamese at a special school before he came to Vietnam so that he could become one of their advisors. He has worked in a Special Forces Camp ever since up near Heu. Ernie was invaluable to us in this respect. English is spoken here, but mostly by those who work with Americans. The rest speak French, if they have gone to school.*
>
> *Last night, our last night in Vietnam, we taped a show for a Vietnamese girl who is well known there in motion pictures. She had been given this show and was desperate in finding people of interest to interview. She apparently has to do everything from office boy work to producing.*

Kieu Chinh was the Vietnamese actress we met in Saigon. A beautiful, young talent, she was caught in the crosshairs of the war as she tried to get her father and brother out of the north. Nine years later, as Saigon fell to the Communist invasion; Chinh escaped the city just in time. She left on the proverbial "last flight" on Pan Am from Ton son Nut Air Force Base. Tippi was instrumental in getting her into the United States. We became lifelong friends, and Chinh later excelled in American films such as *Hamburger Hill* and *The Joy Luck Club*. In the later, she played a beleaguered Chinese mother, who must abandon her two babies on the side of the road as the only hope for their safety. Chinh had a lot of real life experience to draw upon for that role!

> *12-30-66. We had met her before going on our tour and had promised to do the show upon our return. We had also asked her to get us a couple of Vietnamese dresses which she did. Johnny was giving them to us for Xmas, but she insisted that they would be from her. These must have cost her more than she makes in two weeks. They are just beautiful. We are thrilled with them.*
>
> *After the taping, we had a lovely dinner at a French restaurant in Saigon. Then back to our rooms to pack and get ready to leave for home.*

I will just have to skip over all that happened this morning since everything was such a rush that it's not worth mentioning. Except for one stop we made. That was for our appointment with General Westmoreland. About one out of every ten groups gets to see him before leaving because he's so busy. But, we made it! Before we left he presented us with a certificate of commendation for our contribution to the morale of the troops. And with it is an autographed photo of the General. He seemed so very nice. It was an honor to meet him. The guys really love him. He is well respected by all.

That was the grand finale of our tour. It couldn't have ended on a better note. Now that we are on the plane, I have to admit, I'm exhausted.

U.S. Army General William Westmoreland commanded the United States military operations during the peak (1964-1968) of the Vietnam War. His controversial position advocated a brutal war of attrition against the Viet Cong and the North Vietnamese Army. During his command, U.S. ground troops increased from 16,000 to more than half a million men.

We didn't spend very much time with Westmoreland. His demeanor was not completely humorless, but he was very stoic. I'm sure he felt the weight of the lives of his men on his back. He asked about our travels, what we had seen, and what our impressions were.

For two weeks, we had flown around in dusty C-130s and hedge-hopped in helicopters to get to our numerous remote destinations. Our grueling circuit took us through many U.S. positions in the country, from a Special Forces jungle camp among the Montagnard Mountain tribesmen to a Marine encampment in the Mekong River Valley. There were days we made as many as nineteen stops! Those were exhilarating times and I felt like we were right smack dab in the middle of the conflict! Being caught in a mortar attack, however, was going a bit far. I didn't write to my parents about the warfare we had witnessed, or the horrors we had seen. I didn't want to upset my mother, and, besides, I couldn't find the words to effectively express my deep feelings. But we survived the entire trip — as well as all of its uncivilized conditions — with many good memories. War does that to people. Everything that happens becomes so much more acute and meaningful. I didn't expect to be so profoundly affected by the trip. My experiences changed my feelings about politics, war, duty, and sacrifice. There was nothing "abstract" about the experience. Seeing the war firsthand deepened my sense of compassion for every one and every thing swept away by warfare. Every sight, sound, and scent is as fresh in my mind today as it was in 1966. The experiences haunted my dreams for a very long time.

Two weeks after I returned to California, I received a hand-written letter from General Lew Walt. He wrote, in part:

"I have told several people that you are the most beautiful woman I have ever seen and I know that the remarkable beauty you have is not only skin deep. I am deeply impressed by your immediate

Meeting General Westmoreland in Saigon.

grasp of what this war is about. It is about the minds and hearts of people. The military part is only a small portion and it really isn't the most important part. We could go on killing V.C. for the next twenty years but we still wouldn't win this war. We must 'build a nation' at the same time we are fighting the V.C. We must reconstitute the local governments and reconstruct the local communities which have been destroyed by the V.C. We must build up the local economy, raise the living standards, open the schools, repair the churches. Once the V.C. have been driven from the countryside; the communities have been rebuilt; the children are educated — 10 to 15 years from now — this little country is going to be strong, and will be the corner stone for the Free World in S.E. Asia. It has great natural resources and the people have remarkable potential.

"I've become emotionally involved with my job here, I guess, after 15 hours a day — seven days per week for nearly two years. I believe in what we are doing with all my heart. I have to or I wouldn't be able to live with our casualties — 1,600 dead and 12,000 wounded Marines — since I've been here.

"Diane, it was a thrill to meet you and I pray that we shall meet again. If you come back in June, I may still be here. I don't know, but I am sure they won't let me stay until Xmas, even though I'd like to."

I was very touched that the General had taken the time to write to me and share with me his philosophy and thoughts about his mission. Within months, General Lew Walt was ordered to leave Vietnam. He returned to the States where he served until his retirement.

Chapter 16

Immediately upon my return home from Vietnam, I shot another two-part episode of *Batman*. In the year since my last appearance, the show had become a pop culture phenomenon. I was back on the funhouse-style sets, and the candy-colored costumes and makeup were more eye-popping than ever. I was dressed all in pink. I looked like cotton candy. My pink hair and pink lipstick matched my pink dog, and my character — heroine Pinky Pinkston — owned the Pink Chips Stamp Factory where Batman and Robin were hoodwinked by the notorious Colonel Gumm.

The deliciously flamboyant Roger C. Carmel played Gumm. Roger was very funny on and off screen. He took direction well, but he exuded an enviable air of self-confidence and he managed to infuse so much of himself into his character. He accepted direction, but took it one step further in every take. Alex Rocco and Seymour Cassel were the conniving colonel's henchmen. We were all thrilled when Edward G. Robinson made a cameo appearance.

The producers of *Batman* had introduced *The Green Hornet* to television audiences in the fall of 1966. Unlike *Batman*, *The Green Hornet* was not played for laughs; the show took a serious tone. It starred my old friend and co-star Van Williams as the title character, and a young man named Bruce Lee as Kato, his sidekick. *The Green Hornet* hadn't caught on with the television audience and was struggling in the ratings.

The decision was made to create a "cross-over" two-part episode that brought Batman and the Hornet together for the first time. Colonel Gumm, the evil foreman of Pinky's stamp factory, ran a counterfeit stamp business on the side. Pinky became suspicious and enlisted the help of her friend Britt Reid (aka The Green Hornet). The police of Gotham City mistook the Hornet and Kato for criminals, and called upon Batman and Robin to intercede. The story was filled with mistaken identities, kidnappings, life-size stamps, and Colonel Gumm's "Enlarged Perforation and Coiling Machine," and, of course, my runaway-train-stopping pink bouffant.

I had a wonderful time with Adam and Burt again, and a terrific time with Van Williams. We had worked together so often in the past, it was like old times. We talked about our career woes and successes, and he proudly talked about his lovely family.

Bruce Lee was quite a marvel. He later became a big film star, but then, he was playing second string to Van. He was very polite and quiet on the

Roger C. Carmel (Col. Gumm), me (Pinky Pinkston), and Adam West (Batman) in Batman. PHOTO COLLECTION OF MICHAUD

set, often retiring to his dressing room to read a book, but he also wowed us with incredible demonstrations of his karate skills. He playfully kicked cigarettes and cigars out of the mouths of trembling crewmembers. He had been a martial arts instructor, and even at his young age of twenty-five, seemed very self-assured. He'd take his shirt off to limber up and stretch outside the soundstage. He was lean and muscular and walked

Pinky Pinkston (yours truly) with her two pink canine accomplices. PHOTO COLLECTION OF MICHAUD

with a dancer's grace. Still, I didn't pay much attention to him, he was so unassuming.

I loved watching the special effects experts working on the set, and I always tried to watch the "fight" scene rehearsals. These supposed brawls were choreographed as skillfully and gracefully as a ballet.

One scene called for Robin to fight with Kato. The scene was rehearsed for hours, first with stand-ins, and then with Burt Ward and Bruce Lee. Both young men knew each other off the set and had sparred and trained with each other before. Bruce decided to play a joke on Burt. Poor Burt was the only person not in on the prank. When they got ready to do a final run-through, Bruce became very serious. His eyes narrowed and he circled Burt like a stalking animal. He actually got in Burt's face, unblinking and threatening. Burt didn't know what was going on. He began to stammer, "This is not for real, you know; we're just shooting this." Bruce wouldn't back down. When the director got the actors in position, Burt was trying to prepare for the worst. Suddenly, Bruce jumped back, stuck out his tongue, and cracked, "Robin's a chicken!" Burt looked more relieved than amused, but the rest of us fell to the floor laughing.

Adam West (Bruce Wayne) and me as Pinky Pinkston in Batman. PHOTO COLLECTION OF MICHAUD

Part I, "A Piece of the Action," aired on March 1, 1967, and Part II, "Batman's Satisfaction," aired on March 2. A testament to the fanatical appeal of this show is that to this day I am often recognized as Pinky Pinkston. I thoroughly enjoyed working on *Batman*. It was one of my few forays into comedy.

I also returned to the television series *The Man from U.N.C.L.E.* to film a two-part arc called "The Five Daughters' Affair." Kim Darby, Jill Ireland, Herbert Lom, Curt Jurgens, Telly Savalas, and a somewhat physically diminished Joan Crawford completed the guest cast. Fortunately, I never ran into the faded movie queen on the set. The story about an eccentric scientist who discovered how to extract gold from seawater, before his mysterious murder, was written by Norman Hudis, and directed by television veteran Barry Shear. Since David McCallum's wife was on the set (actually playing the role of my sister), there were no dressing room dalliances between puckish David and me.

The two episodes, which aired to an appreciative audience on March 31 and April 7, were later edited into a feature film called *The Karate*

With Telly Savalas and Robert Vaughn in The Man From U.N.C.L.E.

Killers, which was released in Europe. This way, producers managed to use and reuse an actors' work without having to pay additional moneys. I was required to film an extra scene wearing pasties for the European film market to give the impression I was nude.

My artistic integrity seemed to fly out the window. There was a quiet voice in my head trying to tell me what was best, but the murmur

With Gardner McKay and Edy Williams in I Sailed to Tahiti with an All-Girl Crew.

just became a small part of the chaos of other voices giving me advice. Somehow, I didn't seem to have any more faith in my professional decisions than I did with my romantic choices. The cacophony of voices told me what I should do and how I should look. I needed to be more positive, I was told, more energetic, more this, more that. The noise drowned out any honest sense of who I really was and what was really best for me. I felt there was nothing to do but ride the prevailing tide.

Since I didn't have any money, I was forced to take any job that came my way. I didn't have the luxury of waiting for that all-important, career-changing screenplay that would catapult me into super-stardom. Instead, I accepted a role in a piece of celluloid trash called *I Sailed to Tahiti with an All Girl Crew*.

Richard L. Bare produced, wrote, and directed the film for a small, independent production company called United National Pictures. He was a television director with many programs to his credit including *Petticoat Junction*, *The Virginian*, and *Twilight Zone*. The cast included the extremely tall, extremely handsome, and extremely boring Gardner McKay, Fred Clark, Pat Buttram, Richard Denning, and Edy Williams. Gardner had starred in the television series *Adventures in Paradise*. He was an introspective man, and seemed most content when he was alone in his cabin. This film would be Gardner's last work as an actor. He later moved to Hawaii and became a novelist.

I Sailed to Tahiti with an All Girl Crew told the story of two rival sailors (McKay and Clark), who bet one another $20,000 that one could beat the other in a race to Tahiti by using an all-girl crew. Filming began in Honolulu on May 23, 1967. I needed the work and I loved Hawaii. To make the most of the opportunity, I treated my mother to the trip, and she had the time of her life. We stayed four weeks at the beautiful, newly opened Ilikai Hotel on the western end of Waikiki Beach. My Grandma Ray had passed away from cancer, and mom needed an exotic getaway to cheer her up. Mai-Tais and hula dancing! My dear friend Robbie had moved to Oahu a short time before. We had a lovely reunion at a time when it was sorely needed.

Mom loved the beautiful, balmy beaches, the great food, and the exciting nightlife of Honolulu. She also loved the attention bestowed on the mother of a movie star. Carla Beach made herself available to me again, and made sure my mother went everywhere she wanted to go, especially when I was busy filming. Robbie introduced us to the gay community there, and they loved us. Gay men love glamour, even when the glow is fading, as I felt mine was. Women and gay men are often alike in relying on their beautiful, youthful appearances to attract partners. I think gay men can easily relate to the problems created by dependence on the physical façade when that all begins to fade. Robbie and his friends took us to all the best spots on the island. I loved seeing Oahu anew through mom's eyes, and it was wonderful to have her close by. No matter how old I got, having mom around always felt good.

Filming the picture had its own rewards. We shot in coves that were the most beautiful in the world. Glassy lagoons that reflected the mast of our sailboat, and the occasional overhead clouds made the work dreamy.

On other days, we sailed the high waves off the coast of Oahu. I stayed below deck retching into a pail! I am a landlubber and no amount of sailing is going to change that. I somehow managed to do my scenes between retches, and was quite happy to finally get back to solid ground.

The actresses in this picture were delightful. The working atmosphere was playful and daffiness ruled the day. Loved by all, Edy Williams won the prize for portraying the over-sexed, ditzy female sailor who wore falsies to boost her already estimable bosom. In a scene, the sailboat becomes

Johnny Grant talked me into this appearance on behalf of Richard Nixon during his 1968 Presidential campaign.

stranded at sea during a calm moment in the race to Tahiti. The young women are not allowed to use any mechanical means to propel their boat. So, the resourceful girls jump into the water and peddle the boat forward with their frantic kicks. In the process, Edy's ten falsies, (five a breast), popped out and floated to the surface. The sight, and the laughter it engendered, made the whole trip worthwhile.

Since my trip to Vietnam with Tippi, Johnny Grant had called upon me on several occasions to support the USO by attending events that were political in nature. I wasn't politically savvy at the time, so I didn't really care that Johnny was conservative and supported Ronald Reagan for Governor of California and later, Richard Nixon for President. I unwittingly supported both.

On September 6, 1967, we visited Governor Reagan at the California State Fair in Sacramento on USO Armed Forces Day. Johnny, Sherry Jackson, Robert Stack, Hollywood USO Overseas Committee Chairman George Chandler, and I presented Reagan with a certificate naming him

Left to right: *Jimmy Sheldon (West Coast Director, USO Shows), General O'Donnell, Robert Stack, Johnny Grant, me, Sherry Jackson and Governor Ronald Reagan. USO-Armed Forces Day at the California State Fair on September 6, 1967.*

Honorary Chairman of the California State USO. Later, with Johnny's urging, I supported Nixon for President at several rallies in the state.

In October, I began work on another film for AIP called, *Maryjane*. I never signed a contract with AIP. Each film was contracted on an individual basis. I was just lucky, I guess, to make several films at the biggest "non" studio in Hollywood. *Maryjane* was written by Peter Marshall (host of *The Hollywood Squares* game show) and comic actor Dick Gautier (Hymie the Robot on *Get Smart*), and directed by "B" movie veteran Maury Dexter. This gem paired me once again with Fabian. The story about a marijuana ring in a middle-class, small-town high school, starred teenage actors Patty McCormack and Kevin Coughlin. Fabian played a high school teacher who was framed and then arrested while trying to convince the principal that pot was not harmful. I played a drug-selling history teacher! The movie attempted to give an *honest* portrayal of marijuana abuse, which was a hot topic at the time.

Maryjane was quickly filmed in and around Los Angeles, and at the

Back to American International Pictures with Fabian in Maryjane. PHOTO COLLECTION OF MICHAUD

impressive, castle-like Greystone Mansion in Beverly Hills. In keeping with the "quick production-quick release" philosophy of AIP, the movie was distributed to drive-in theatres within months — double-billed with a Vincent Price stinker called *House of 1,000 Dolls!*

The reviews were mediocre. Howard Thompson wrote in *The New York Times* on March 14, 1968, "The dialogue is generally wooden, the pace is static, the acting is generally second-level." On March 3, Kevin Thomas reported in the *Los Angeles Times*, "The script avoids the preachy approach... but at the climax it degenerates into melodrama, complete with a surprise twist cliché." About me, Thomas added, "As usual, Diane McBain seems superior to her material." I couldn't have agreed more, but Mr. Thomas and I were shouting into the wind.

"Mother, are you ready to go again?" Johnny Grant's robust voice on the phone roused my memories of Christmas in Vietnam the year before. I'd earned the moniker "Mother McBain" on my first trip. Oddly, I felt proud and yet chagrined that I was becoming known as a "mother figure." My experiences during the first trip emboldened me to accept Johnny's invitation in late 1967 to join actresses Melody Patterson, who played

Melody Patterson, me and Sabrina Scharf back in Vietnam.

Wrangler Jane on *F-Troop*, and Sabrina Scharf, a former Playboy Bunny, who had starred in a couple of pictures including *Hells Angels on Wheels*.

On the long flight to Vietnam, cocktails were flowing as Sabrina bent my ear. I listened to her stories about the ever-increasing number of draft dodgers, and of young men who were now frequently speaking out about dying in a conflict in which our country had no business being involved. They felt the war was just for the sake of a few politicians and their political careers. The war in Vietnam was not about defending freedom, she explained. The conflict was about business and keeping the war machine and military plants in operation. She called this vague group of war-mongering businesses "the military industrial complex." I remembered Ralph Stolkin talking about the need for business profits to be nurtured and encouraged at any price, but Sabrina talked about the political motivation behind such a notion, and the thought frightened me. I had been raised to believe that politicians and our government should not be challenged about such things. Sabrina had very different — and radical — ideas.

Sabrina's words about unjust wars and government cover-ups caught my attention. There were rich resources in Vietnam that our government coveted and wanted to keep from the Communists in the north. We were not in Southeast Asia to save the Vietnamese people from Communism,

Flying high above Vietnam in 1967.

Sabrina explained. We were solely protecting our economic interests in the region. Since President Kennedy had been brutally assassinated, I became disenchanted with our government. To make matters worse, it wasn't completely clear who was responsible for the killing, and there were many disturbing theories. Great suspicions developed about our role in the Vietnam War, too. Sabrina seemed very informed and convincing. She gave me a book to read about politics in Southeast Asia.

My second trip was different. There was a foreboding in the air in South Vietnam, and a subtle, bitter odor of smoke that passed in waves. In the months since my last visit, violence had intensified, and unedited word of atrocities was reported to the outside world. Whatever humanity (at General Walt's directive) that may have influenced the mission had vanished with Walt's departure months earlier. General Westmoreland had become a controversial figure. He seemed to be disdainful of the growing anti-war sentiment at home. He advocated a "take-no-prisoners," aggressive approach to battle. Aggression and impatience were palpable.

Again, we shot up and down the coastal areas of steamy Vietnam in our C-130's and helicopters, and worked our way into the interior of the country, visiting every base we could reach. Unlike my trip a year before, I did not meet commanding generals, or pose for publicity photographs.

With the bravest and most appreciative men I've ever met. Vietnam, 1967.

I did not dine in officers' quarters. In December 1967, we were in remote outposts in the bush, and in the mud.

The men we visited were adorable. Each time we arrived at a new bivouac, the boys had prepared a tent for us. Thinking we would prefer a little hominess in the face of war, they painted the chairs and tables, hung ruffled curtains, and provided other little amenities for our comfort. Where they got those things could be a story in itself, but we were absolutely charmed by their efforts to make us feel at home!

They, of course, were thrilled by our presence, happy to see a few good old American girls. We ate with them, and then we would do a brief show with Johnny, singing a few songs and telling silly jokes. The men lovingly huddled around us and talked about being homesick.

Visiting field hospitals was the most difficult part of our trip. Most of the time we'd visit the main hospitals in the larger bases where men were recuperating or resting until they could be shipped back to America. Occasionally, though, we'd visit a hospital in a combat zone.

The military police picked us up at the airbase and drove us to a particular field facility, the 91st Evacuation Hospital in Chu Lai. The hospital had been recently completed and had the latest and best equipment. Our hosts were very proud and bragged about what we would see on our tour after lunch. We were told we would see several actual operating rooms.

Just then, we heard some anxious voices from around a corner. An aide whispered into the adjutant's ear, and soon we were being hustled down a long, screened-in corridor that led to the surgical rooms they had told us about.

The adjutant instructed us to look through a porthole-like window into an operating room. He seemed assured we would be duly impressed by what we would see. We were impressed all right, but not in the manner he had hoped. Bodies of freshly wounded soldiers, bloodied and half-dressed, were laid out on operating tables as far as the eye could see, while nurses and doctors scrambled to save their lives. The men were dripping in blood, limbs gorged by gaping wounds or blown off altogether. I had never seen such a grizzly, shocking sight in my life.

I was light-headed when we were led toward a triage center, where soldiers were taken after arriving by helicopter. Most were carted in on stretchers, and some were stacked on makeshift racks in the waiting area until medical personnel could attend to them. They were frightened and loudly moaned in pain. These men did not have life-threatening injuries, but their trauma was just as intense as those with grave wounds. I could hear the panic in their voices as they cried out to us for help.

I was ashamed of my reaction. The stench of blood and death was overwhelming and I felt sick to my stomach. I wanted to run screaming from the room. Outside, the roar of the medivac choppers was deafening. I couldn't overcome the feeling that I needed more help than those brave men did. I felt like I was about to faint and sadly realized I couldn't do anything for them. I couldn't hold and comfort them as I dreamed I

In a chopper in the sky above South Vietnam.

would do when I was a child. My reaction made me ill and I faded from the room back into the long, dark corridor.

Suddenly, voices from behind me ordered me to move aside. I backed up against the wall as soldiers hurried past carrying a body on a stretcher. The body was covered from head to toe with an olive-green Army blanket. I knew, of course, that the man they carried was dead. As his corpse was carried by me, huge sobs erupted from my chest. Tears stung my eyes as waves of grief swept over me. I didn't know who this fallen young man was, but I imagined he had had his entire life ahead of him. Perhaps he left behind a young family. He had fought in a war, which many questioned, and now he was gone.

Tears continued to flow long after we left the horrific scene. I couldn't stop crying. My heart was heavy with the memory of my own childhood. I recalled how my father left me to fight in World War II. I hadn't realized how deeply his absence had continued to affect me long after he had returned. I wondered what had happened to my high school boyfriend, Joe Hudson, who loved the armed forces and left to attend military school. What had happened to Dr. Richard Monte who had done his residency in the military? He could have been ordered away to serve in this Godforsaken place. How many men might I have known throughout the years had been caught up in this conflict, never to return home? American casualties numbered 50,000 by the end of the war. I believe I wept for every single one.

An emotional dam burst inside me that day in the muggy heat of Vietnam. Ever since being victimized by B.S. all those years before, I hadn't shed a tear for anyone, least of all, myself. All of my sorrows had been locked inside my heart, eating away at me for so long and making it impossible to give myself over to real feelings of any kind. I was also still heartbroken over my failed romance with Pancho Gonzalez. The emotional pain and resultant depression had even showed up in my work on the screen — I looked tired and despondent. I didn't have the energy that was vital for acting.

The tears wouldn't stop, as we drove away from the field hospital and back to the base. I loved that dead soldier on the stretcher, a man I never knew. I mourned for his precious life. He had died for his country, and in some sense he had died for me. I could do no less than weep for him.

We stood by and watched many soldiers deploy from bases to battle sites. The look in their eyes was like that of condemned men. No matter how well-trained they were they knew the possibility and, depending on their mission, the inevitability of injury or death.

I flew home a changed woman. The trip made an indelible impression upon me. Sabrina introduced a new way of thinking to me. She later acted in the counterculture classic film, *Easy Rider*, and then retired from show business to enter politics. A few years later, she was elected to the State Senate of California.

I am not a war strategist and I'm not a politician, but I read newspa-

A last farewell to a few soldiers before departing Vietnam.

pers and magazines. I watched the news, and I read many books about what went wrong in Vietnam. More importantly, I know what I saw and heard and felt on the ground. War means one thing — failure to communicate — and nobody wins.

After returning to the States, I visited many Veterans' Administration hospitals. The men seemed to appreciate my visits and I appreciated the soldiers beyond measure. Most of the time, we would chat for a minute and pose together for a picture. Often I would give a kiss on the cheek to express my acknowledgement and gratitude for their service.

Tippi Hedren and I traveled to Tacoma, Washington for the grand opening of the city's first "million dollar theater." Arthur O'Connell, Troy Donahue, and John Russell (friends and co-workers from my Warner Bros. days), Jody McCrea, and Madlyn Rhue also made the trip. Theater owners paid celebrities to appear at special events and theater openings, and I went on several such sojourns — often with Tippi. In Tacoma, we were treated to a special preview screening of *Guess Who's Coming to Dinner*.

While we were in the city, we spent an afternoon visiting wounded G.I.s at nearby Madigan Army Hospital. Many of its patients were recent returnees from Vietnam, and most had suffered devastating injuries.

Signing an autograph for a young soldier in the field in Vietnam.

I met a young man there who was a quadriplegic. I can still see his beautiful eyes. His lush eyelashes looked dreamy. He resembled Montgomery Clift. This fellow in the wheelchair fascinated me. As I sat talking with him, I actually fantasized about him.

When I was about to leave, I planted a kiss on his cheek that left him startled. I surprised *myself*, and blushed. I'll never forget the look on his face. He nearly lifted himself off the chair when I turned back to wave at him. I could tell he wanted to come with me, but I was not brave enough to take on a man with such serious issues. I thought of him for days afterward. I asked God to bless him abundantly, but felt unable to do anything else. I didn't have the courage in me, and I didn't understand why. I wondered if I could live with such a constant and dramatic reminder of what I had seen in the war.

Chapter 17

Tippi Hedren's husband, Noel Marshall, was an agent. He later produced a few "B" films starring his wife, and in 1972, more notably produced *The Exorcist*. When we became acquainted, though, he was a minor agent with basically one client: his wife. Tippi had told him about my professional struggles, and Noel expressed an interest in managing what was left of my career. The fact that Tippi and I generally competed for the same roles wasn't lost on me. She had been offered, and turned down the role I played in *Spinout*. Noel was the first person who'd shown an interest in my career except for some people I recognized as "parasites." He assured me he could get me the sort of publicity I deserved. Having toured Vietnam with Tippi and befriending her, I trusted her and thus trusted Noel.

I still managed to get into movie gossip magazines now and then, but after many attempts to get me into some respectable publications, Noel came up with an idea. He suggested I pose as a nude centerfold for *Playboy* magazine.

"This is the sort of publicity I deserve?" I asked wryly. "I don't know, Noel. That's a big step for me to take. I intend to have a family someday and I would hate for my child to become aware that mommy posed nude in a magazine."

"The money is good and this will all be history by then and they'll never know. Even if they do, what's the big deal?"

"Noel, it may not be a big deal to you, but it is to me. And you know the photographer?" I asked.

"Don't worry; I'll be there to supervise."

"I'm not sure that's such a good idea!"

"What are you ashamed of? You have a wonderful body!"

"I've never thought it was so wonderful. Maybe they won't want my photographs once they see me."

"That's not going to happen."

I went ahead with the shoot. After all, Carol Lynley, whom my mother thought looked just like me in *Under the Yum Yum Tree*, was a *Playboy* centerfold a couple of years before and the exposure hadn't hurt her career. Even as a teenager, I had admired Carol. I wanted to look like her, in fact. We were modeling at the same time. She graced the cover of *Seventeen Magazine* while I was doing cover shoots for *True Love* and *Modern Romance*. I thought she was the most beautiful girl I had ever seen. Carol was still working in spite of her nude photos, maybe even more than before. So, I surmised the photo session was worth a try.

Me in The Mini-Skirt Mob.

I met the photographer and we slowly managed to complete the photo shoot. When I later saw the pictures, I thought they were quite beautiful but I *was* bare-ass naked.

Diane's voice kept me up all night after the shoot, arguing with Danny, who was much more adventurous than her up-tight counterpart. *You will regret this*, Diane said with some authority. *One day, your innocent little children are going to come to you and ask why you embarrassed them by appearing nude in a magazine.*

By the next morning, I was terrified and regretful of what I had done. I called Noel to let him know that I would not agree to release the photos. Forget what Carol Lynley did, I didn't want anyone under *my* yum yum tree. He was disappointed, but got the photographer to agree not to sell the photos to *Playboy* or any other publication. My palpitating heart could rest. Despite the photographer's assurance, though, I had a funny feeling about the incident, and feared the photos would someday come back to haunt me.

In late January 1968, I began work on another film for AIP called *The Mini-Skirt Mob*. The film was written by James Gordon White, and I was again directed by Maury Dexter. The cast included Jeremy Slate, Ross Hagen, Patty McCormack, Harry Dean Stanton, and my old friend, Sherry Jackson. The picture was shot on location in the Coronado National Forest in Arizona, and in Old Tucson, a western-style movie location ranch in Tucson, Arizona.

I played the role of Shayne, "a hog straddling female animal on the prowl," as the movie posters boldly declared. I don't think I was an obvious choice for this film. I was the actor with the most recognizable name. Shayne was the tough-talking leader of a female biker gang called the "Mini-skirt Mob." After she was jilted by her man, who then married a straight-laced young woman, she rounded up her gang to terrorize the happy couple. Shayne's sadistic revenge backfired, though, when her little sister was killed by a Molotov cocktail, and she was left hanging from a cliff at the mercy of her ex-lover's sweet bride.

The Mini-Skirt Mob was an unusual script for women. The role actually attracted me to the film. I thought it would be interesting to play a sadistic killer. I did my own stunts, and actually hung off the mountain attached to cables. Sherry and I also did our own fight scenes. We all got along very well. Harry Dean Stanton was the most interesting fellow, for sure. He was an accomplished and prideful drinker, and he always had a little spark in his eye that gave you the impression he was keeping delightful secrets.

Brawling babes in mini-skirts, and a climax that led to the "good girl" taking revenge against her rival into her own hands was intriguing. Ultimately, however, the film was sentenced to the lower half of drive-in double-bills.

Danny was thrilled at the idea of riding a motorcycle on screen. She loved the idea of managing a big engine between her legs. Actress Sabrina

With Jeremy Slate in The Mini-Skirt Mob.

Scharf, my fellow traveler in Vietnam, rode a Triumph 650 like an actual "hog straddling female" in real life, and she taught me everything I needed to know. Flying around town on a motorcycle was just what Danny needed. The feeling of the wind, and the power of the bike as it sped through traffic, were a natural high. When I arrived on the film set, I was given a little Honda 160 to ride. The producer was afraid the women wouldn't be able to handle anything larger. I felt ridiculous trying to play tough zipping around in the dust on little more than a scooter.

Variety reviewed the film on May 23. "A curious moral point is made here. After showing Miss Jackson as the one uncontaminated soul, the film allows her to let Shayne/McBain fall to her death, and thus stain herself. While this is unmistakably vengeance, and the mouse finally does in the snake who has tortured her, it is nevertheless weak, both morally and story-wise." I thought the ending of the film satisfied the audience's desire for retribution against a vile human being. Such an ending was shocking in a 1968 movie.

The critics were not impressed. "Miss McBain invests her nasty role with a touch of credible, if one-dimensional, evil," wrote the *Hollywood*

Me as a "hog-straddling female" in The Mini-Skirt Mob.

Reporter on May 23. Perhaps *Boxoffice Magazine* summed the film up best when they wrote, "Creamy thighs straddling motorcycles should offer the big draw for the summer drive-in trade." Though not a great film, this was a good excuse to learn how to ride a motorcycle. Furthermore, I enjoyed playing the part because I could act out some of my subconscious anger.

I wanted to do something different with my career. I was just a teenager when I was absorbed into the old-fashioned movie studio system. Then, my looks dictated the way I would be presented to the public. I had no choice in the matter. They groomed me, dressed me, coached me on what to say in public, and assigned roles that easily fit the model they were trying to create for me. Then, as the conservative, Republican 1950s came to a close and the swinging, radical 1960s began to bloom, the blonde glamour puss that Warner Bros. had created was suddenly out of style.

Filmmakers were in a quandary. They didn't seem to know their audiences anymore. The public was less and less interested in carefully groomed beauty on the screen. They clamored to see more natural-looking actors, who tackled more challenging subjects in their movies. The changing tastes reflected what was happening in our society.

Like it or not, I didn't seem to fit in. I tried playing tough-talking motorcycle mamas and track-tramps, but I wasn't physically suited to be believable in such roles. I couldn't really sing or dance. Westerns had become passé. Independent filmmakers began to dominate the Hollywood landscape, and they usually were not interested in hiring anyone who represented a Hollywood that no longer existed.

I decided to chuck the Hollywood scene and try something completely different. In June 1968, I accepted an engagement in a summer stock theater tour in the Neil Simon comedy, *The Star Spangled Girl*. I played the role of Sophie Rauschmeyer, a daffy, all-American loyalist, who falls for the editor of a counter-culture news rag. The play was a fluffy comedy about the classic conflict between the political right and left in America. Starring Connie Stevens, Richard Benjamin, and Anthony Perkins, the play originated on Broadway in 1966 and was a failure. Summer Stock Theater seemed a more appropriate setting. The folks in the countryside were less picky than their Broadway counterparts.

Carleton Carpenter, a veteran movie and theater actor, joined me on the road. He was very talented, funny, and a delight to work with. My other co-star, though, was a different story. There are a few people in the industry with whom I had to work that could really get my goat. They were usually men who had a problem with hubris. Their giant egos made it impossible for me to take them seriously. Edd Byrnes was one of the worst. The smug expression frozen on his face was mocking and self-righteous, and I wanted to smack him every time I saw him. He was unctuous and weasely. Funny, but years later, Edd revealed that he had been kept by an older man when he was a young actor. Not really surprising. Keir Dullea and George Hamilton starred in two other touring companies of *The Star Spangled Girl* that summer. I would rather have worked with either gentleman, but I drew the short straw and got stuck with pain-in-the-ass Edd Byrnes.

While Carleton was prepared and always pleasant, Edd just barely managed to learn his lines. He walked through the part. No matter how much he rolled up his sleeves, I could never believe he was a counter-culture anything. I, of course, had no trouble looking all-American and appropriately daffy in my red, white, and blue wardrobe.

In early June, we spent ten days in New York rehearsing. We were scheduled to tour the Eastern Seaboard, making one-week stops at ten different theaters. I looked forward to the tour. I had always dreamed about spending time in New England. I was enchanted by the postcard-perfect little towns where the treetops touched across the middle of the streets.

On our first night in New York, Edd decided he'd better bed me, since the only other cast member was a man. Carleton is gay, and Edd might have had better luck getting *him* in the sack. The fact that Edd was married to actress Asa Maynor didn't seem to slow him down. It gets lonely on the road, but I'd rather be lonesome than spend one minute with that droopy-eyed lothario, whose hair looked spray-painted onto his head. Edd did not deal well with my rejection. He became very cold and nasty tempered. Those weeks on the road were lonely for me. Carleton was a sweet man and I wish we could have spent more time together, but he had his own agenda and his own private pursuits. Fortunately, I had my poodle, Coquette, to keep me company.

The little towns and villages we visited were truly beautiful and possessed an old-world charm I had never experienced before. Summer Stock was still in its heyday. Most of the theaters were decades old and some were converted barns. Those cavernous, shingled firetraps with trellised verandahs and rolling croquet lawns were a honeymooner's dream and an accommodating vacation spot for the elderly. The air was fresh and clean, and the sold-out audiences were overwhelmingly appreciative.

On June 24, 1968, I made my professional stage debut at Elitch's Theatre in Denver, Colorado. We then traveled to Charlotte, North Carolina, New Haven, Connecticut, the Town and Country Playhouse in East Rochester, New York, and then east to New England.

Just before our opening in East Rochester, I was interviewed for the local *Times-Union* newspaper. "It's hard to play the part," I said. "Occasionally, the girl loses a quality of reality since it is a comedy. That makes it hard. It's very exciting and very grueling. I haven't decided if I like it yet. In Denver, the people were open about laughing. In New Haven they were almost as open. It makes you nervous when there's no reaction. Actually, this is not one of Simon's best plays. I like it though. I understand Simon wrote it about his own experience." What a great way to ingratiate yourself to the playwright!

"My director says I'm a natural for more comedy on stage," I rambled, "I'm more used to drama and I do prefer making movies. It might be different though if I were able to stay in one place, like Broadway."

The Candlewood Theatre in New Fairfield, Connecticut and the Lakes Region Playhouse in Laconia, New Hampshire were especially charming. I met some fascinating people along the way. Those old theaters traditionally had sponsors and season ticket patrons who were very supportive of the arts. They were impressed by the visiting stars and invited me to luncheons and other functions. Some well-to-do families invited me into their homes. I found nothing but the nicest people, who were happy to show me around their lovely towns and kept me busy during the otherwise lonely days.

By the time we reached our seventh stop, the Ivoryton Playhouse in Ivoryton, Connecticut, we were all pretty worn out — and we had three weeks to go! I met an interesting character named Fred Knapp, a local real estate magnate, who believed flying saucers were really space ships from an undiscovered planet on the other side of the sun. Fred was also a self-proclaimed warlock. He took my picture, a lock of my hair, and some small item from my purse that he burned to ash in order to create an amulet that I could wear in a ring on my finger. Fred "charmed" the amulet, he claimed, to attract a suitable husband for me. The idea was intriguing, but seemed a bit ridiculous, though he was convincingly zealous. Nevertheless, I wore that silly amulet long after the ashes had disappeared from its core. I hadn't really believed what Fred told me, but he was interesting and eccentric enough to draw me into his spell. I was always very interested in the off-kilter, whimsical people who crossed my path, and spaced-out warlocks interested me! Danny certainly liked him.

While we played the Cape Playhouse in Dennis, Massachusetts, I met a lovely gray-haired lady in her sixties, who was an heiress to the Otis elevator fortune, and lived in a house more than 200 years old. Coming

With the insufferable Edd Byrnes on stage in The Star Spangled Girl.

from Los Angeles, where nothing is 200 years old, I was intrigued by the sense of permanence and longevity in the East. Grave rubbings were a popular hobby at the time. A piece of paper was placed over the stone and rubbed with a pencil thereby transferring the words on the old stone to the paper. My new friend, Miss Otis, took me out to some small cemeteries hundreds of years old. I was fascinated by the names and dates

Curtain call for Byrnes, me, and the delightful (and very tall) Carleton Carpenter in The Star Spangled Girl.

delicately etched on the tombstones and the amazingly short life spans.

Our last stop was the Lakewood Theatre in Skowhegan, Maine. Not surprisingly, the playhouse was located on a beautiful lake in the woods. There were two restaurants and bars on the grounds, tennis courts, a motor lodge, cabins, and a golf course and club house. The spot was truly idyllic. I met an attractive young man there to play with. We had a wonderful time romping in the lake and enjoying the romantic surroundings. He was very nice, but "geographically" out of the question. Moreover, I still struggled with my feelings and unwillingness to be vulnerable again. The trip helped to show me how much I needed to deal with my fears and straighten myself out. The time away also produced in me a loneliness that was acute enough to pursue a change of conscience.

To supplement my unpredictable income, I tried to go into an interior design business, which was not successful. I also became involved with a cosmetics line that included a product called "Smylon," a dental eraser that whitened teeth. I got a little press for that venture, and some advertisements and a few interviews in some periodicals and in the *Los Angeles Times*. My foray into cosmetics, though, was not lucrative.

I made two motion pictures in the autumn. I was again paired with Ross Hagen in yet another low-budget motorcycle exploitation film. *The Sidehackers* (sometimes called *Five the Hard Way*), was an experiment in filmmaking utilizing new cameras that projected in a type of wide screen format called "Fantascope." Ross produced the film for Crown International Pictures, and a young man named Gus Trikonis was the director. The film also starred Michael Pataki, with whom I had worked years before at the Glendale Centre Theatre. The slim story, written by schlock writer Tony Huston, was about a motorcycle racer, who sought revenge against a maniac who murdered his fiancé. For a change, I played a good girl in this picture, and, as a reward, my character was killed early in the film.

Trikonis was a professional dancer, who had appeared on screen in *West Side Story*. *The Sidehackers* was his first directorial effort. He was dating Goldie Hawn at the time. She had wanted the film role that was played by Ross's wife, actress Claire Polan. Ross was the producer, so Goldie didn't stand a chance, but she hung around with us on location in Perris, California, and appeared in the film as an extra.

"HARD RIDERS! Mounted on Burning Steel!…With only their leathers between THEM and HELL!" (Who wouldn't want to see that?) The movie was finally released in 1970, and double-billed with another winner called *She-Devils on Wheels*. Kevin Thomas wrote in the *Los Angeles Times* on January 8, "*The Sidehackers* is one of those movies that are as much fun to watch as they are blatantly trashy. It's enjoyable because it has the courage of its badness…" Fortunately, Mr. Thomas didn't mention my name in his review.

In November, I flew to Mexico to make a film for a writer/director named Myron J. Gold. He had made a couple of low-budget movies in Mexico. *Savage Season* was a sexy action/adventure spoof with little originality. I played a scientist. The cast included Ron Harper and veteran actors Slim Pickens and Victor Buono.

Victor was an absolute delight. He was sly and terribly funny. I enjoyed our long chats about literature and culture. Victor was a rotund Renaissance man, who had a taste for good food and good booze — my kind of fellow. We had a delightful time experiencing the fine restaurants in the area. Las Mananitas Hotel in Cuernavaca was a hidden paradise. We had a sumptuous meal and delicious margaritas in the dining room

With Ron Harper and Victor Buono on location in Mexico filming Savage Season.

of the rambling pink hotel. The expansive, manicured lawns provided free range for wandering flamingos and peacocks. Wild parrots squawked at us from the palm trees. We also enjoyed the centuries old Hotel Hacienda Cocoyoc in nearby Cuautla. The gourmet Mexican cuisine, delicious wines, strolling guitar players, dreamy gardens, and historic fountains made for a magical distraction from movie making. Such exotic delights always softened the sting of a less-than-interesting acting assignment.

Victor and I had other things in common, as well. We both began our careers at Warner Bros., and we both got dumped by the studio. He had appeared on *Batman*, too, playing the villainous King Tut. Victor was a truly accomplished actor with wonderful film and television credits and an Academy Award nomination. Because he was bald and so over-weight, he looked much older than his twenty-nine years. I never decided if he was gay or straight. He didn't seem particularly interested in women *or* men. In fact, in one of our many conversations, he called himself "very self-sufficient." I was so saddened when I learned of his death at the age of forty-three.

This was Ron Harper's first feature film. He had starred in a television series called *Garrison's Gorillas*. Our location work took us to Veracruz,

Me in the rarely seen film, Savage Season.

Cuernavaca, and Mexico City, as well as Santa Fe, New Mexico. The film languished in the can for a long time and was eventually released in Mexico as *Temporada Salvejo* in May 1971.

While we were on location, we all felt a little isolated and I had an affair with Ron. It was little more than a show-biz romance. As soon as we got back to California, Ron was nowhere to be found.

Chapter 18

Noel Marshall managed to land me an audition for a Broadway play set to star Dustin Hoffman. Emboldened by my summer theater experience, I thought acting in New York City would be a good pursuit. The *Hollywood Reporter* wrote on January 13, 1969, "Diane McBain has been pitched to make her B'way stage bow in Henry & Phoebe Ephron's new play, *I Giveth and Giveth*."

I flew to New York and auditioned, but I failed miserably.

While I was on the East Coast, I finally made it to the White House. It was not handsome John Kennedy who greeted me at the door, but Richard Nixon, whom I now regretted having endorsed in his Presidential bid. He had invited celebrity supporters to a reception in Washington, D.C. following his inauguration. I joined Dorothy Malone, Anita Louise, Buddy Ebsen, and Dale Robertson at the breakfast get-to-together. We were greeted by Nixon and his wife, and were served champagne with Danish pastry. I don't know if it was the stomach-turning repast or Nixon's "used-car-salesman" smirk, but soon thereafter, I joined the Green Party, and sometime later became a Democrat.

The White House was truly something to behold. Upon our approach, two things struck me: the stately and tidy mansion looked a little like a dollhouse plunked in the middle of manicured but icy grounds, and the structure was much smaller than I had imagined. It was regal, opulent, and steeped in history. I felt the building had a strong and stoic sense of self. People were scurrying about, which made the place seem "alive." As I gazed around the beautiful rooms we were allowed to see, I couldn't help thinking about the average little girl I used to be and how far that child had come. To top off my Washington experience, that evening I attended the Inaugural Ball.

Noel sent Tippi and me to South America for a few days in February on a press junket to publicize the opening of a television station in Cartegena, Colombia. I loved travel and couldn't turn down the free trip.

Such engagements were not unusual. A few years earlier in October 1965, I had gone to Peru to promote a new television station in Lima. Actress Ina Balin accompanied me. I spent a day in the clouds touring the Incan ruins of Machu Picchu. Ina and I were special guests at a bullfight where we met El Cordobes. The handsome matador had quickly become a legend for his theatrical style in the bull ring. He was a feast for the eyes,

In Peru, Ina Balin and I model beautiful matador suits to the amusement of one of the greatest bullfighters of all time, El Cordobes.

but I found the sport of bullfighting to be repulsive.

We also went to the city of Cusco, the site of the historic capital of the Incan Empire. We toured the beautiful ruins and the bustling market place. One evening, we dined at a local entrepreneur's private residence. Actually, the house looked more like a palace. The host showed us his collection of priceless gold artifacts he stored in his specially constructed basement. When he turned on the lights, the glittering objects nearly blinded us. The walls of another massive room in the mansion were covered with stuffed heads of exotic, big game animals he had hunted and killed on safari in Africa. He even had a stuffed tiger and a stuffed elephant in the room!

I remembered attending a circus when I was much younger. A lumbering elephant was paraded past my seat. I was close enough to look into his eye. I could see deep depression and sadness. I don't know if I imagined those feelings, but the sight made me cry. Danny always shed tears for mistreated animals. The display of hundreds of dead creatures in the man's home was obscene. Even then, before there was any concerted effort to protect the planet and its creatures, I felt as if I had walked into a chamber of horrors. The mink coat I was wearing, a gift from Ralph Stolkin, suddenly felt like dead weight on my body. I didn't wear it again on the trip.

Noel Marshall's idea for a publicity photograph of me in 1969.

My time in Colombia was not nearly as interesting. Except for the hair-raising drive to and from the airport in Bogota, Tippi and I never left Cartegena.

I was then professionally inactive until the summer.

In June, I worked on a film in Nashville, Tennessee. Tay Garnett was an accomplished director with many film classics to his credit, including *Mrs. Parkington*, *A Connecticut Yankee in King Arthur's Court*, and *The Postman Always Rings Twice*. Based on a novel by contemporary mystery writer Mickey Spillane, *The Delta Factor* was adapted, produced, and directed by Tay. The spy spoof chronicled the adventures of two CIA agents (played by Christopher George and Yvette Mimieux), who were on a secret mission to rescue a scientist imprisoned by terrorists on a remote island. The film also starred Ralph Taeger and Yvonne De Carlo. Because any star-power I may have had seemed to have disappeared, I was third-billed behind Yvette and the adorable Chris George. For me, it was another lonely trip and another vapid role.

After I was finished, Tay took me aside and confided that he was sorry he hadn't hired me for the female lead. "You are the most professional actress I have ever had the pleasure of working with," he said. Gossip on the set was that Yvette had given him some trouble. Knowing his many directorial credits and the legendary film stars he had worked with, I felt honored. At the same time, I wished he had said nothing. His words, though kind, only made me feel worse about the state of my career. I really could have used the leading role, and it was bittersweet knowing the role might have been mine under different circumstances.

While I was in Nashville, I visited a few tourist attractions, including a full-scale replica of the Parthenon, the Doric temple of Athena in Athens, Greece. The Nashville version was built in 1897 for the Tennessee Centennial Exposition in Centennial Park. I was struck by the incongruity of this beautiful building in such peculiar surroundings. It was great to look at, but seemed out of place. That was exactly the way I felt about myself and my career.

Taking in the beautiful sight both inspired me and stirred feelings of wanderlust. I needed something new in my life. I decided to go back to school. The fall semester began in a couple of months. So, at the age of twenty-eight, I invested what little money I had to pursue a higher education. Suddenly, I felt young again.

Pierce College is a two-year community college located in Woodland Hills, California. Though Pierce began as an agricultural school, more than a hundred curriculums are currently taught there. The large campus is like a nature preserve with expansive rose gardens, a cultured forest of redwood trees, and a 225-acre working farm with an equestrian center and small herds of cattle, sheep, and goats. The campus is an oasis from

With Christopher George in The Delta Factor. PHOTO COLLECTION OF MICHAUD

the hustle and bustle of Los Angeles, just the respite I needed.

The college was warm and welcoming, and I liked the professors. I enrolled in a two-year Associate of Arts Program. Never quite comfortable with my formal education, I poured myself into my studies and landed on the Dean's List by the end of my first quarter. I was astonished that I could pull such a good grade average. I was terribly proud of myself.

The discipline of school was very appealing to me. Still, I was at loose ends. Self-promotion was not my forte. With neither a studio force-feeding me acting roles, nor a publicist working on my behalf, finding work was difficult, and so was staying in the public eye. I managed to make some public appearances by turning Diane loose. *She* was the showgirl, but Danny was always behind the scenes rolling her eyes in horror at the situations Diane got herself into!

A few of the less-than-satisfying jobs were game show appearances. On one of these, Joe Landis, a television producer, told me his esoteric interests one day and we got into a discussion about religion and spirituality. Since the time when I spent talking about such things with Elvis, I had begun looking into the subject of "spirituality" and had become quite interested in the writings of Edgar Cayce. I was fascinated by his teachings. I explored more arcane religions and even some occult practices. In the process, I stumbled upon Buddhism and found the teachings engaging. Landis said that he knew some Buddhists. They chanted a mantra, which would supposedly reward them with all their wishes. *Well,* I thought, *since I never seem to get anything I want, I should attend a meeting!*

"Nam Myoho Renge Kyo, Nam Myoho Renge Kyo," a man boomed, chanting authoritatively in the small crowded living room. The furniture had been pushed aside, and a dozen men and women knelt on the floor. A large, wooden box containing a hanging scroll sat on an altar-like table in the front of the room. The scroll, called the Gohonzon, was covered with what looked to me like Japanese writing and was delicately framed in green brocade. Candles flickered on both sides of the box. Incense was burning, and bowls of fruit and water were carefully arranged on the table. The formality of this Buddhist ritual instantly appealed to me.

The Gohonzon, I was told, was like a mirror. When chanting, your life condition was reflected back to you so you could address your personal issues and affect a change from within. I was assured that all things were possible. I wondered if I could turn my life around as these people claimed I could. The process sounded a lot like magic, but I was willing to try anything.

Immediately, I wanted to know if I was going in the right direction with my career. No longer an ingénue, I had become a woman fast approaching thirty. Hollywood didn't see me as an intelligent, thoughtful woman, but as a mindless, self-serving, publicity-seeking sex symbol. I didn't like the image, but I had to agree. Changing their perception of me required that I hire a proper public relations manager. Unfortunately, I didn't have the money to do so. I wondered if I could change my own perception of myself and if that would make a difference.

I wanted to meet the "senior leaders" of this group to get the guidance that my fellow chanters told me I needed. Wobbling around in obscenely high heels, wrapped in a mink coat, and wearing my Ralph Stolkin diamonds, I arrived at the small wood-frame house in West Hollywood where the meetings were conducted.

The house was nearly devoid of furniture. The Gohonzon and altar were in the tiny front room. Gary, the chapter leader, was unpacking a suitcase in the bedroom. "I just returned from Japan where I prayed before the Dai Gohonzon. It was impressive," he said in a sonorous voice.

The simple surroundings and casual nature of this meeting made me feel enormously self-conscious and out of place. I stammered as I made my request. I wondered if he would be able to understand my lifestyle. Would he find my concerns superficial?

"What should I do? I've tried everything in my power to change my situation, but I'm not getting the kind of work I want. Things aren't going very well for me, and haven't for some time."

"Chant," he said.

"Chant? Just chant?"

"You'll get all the answers you want from chanting. Saying the words 'Nam myoho renge kyo' is making the highest cause in the universe. When you make the highest cause, you get the highest result."

"Just *chanting* words is the highest cause?"

"Those words contain the highest vibrations and will produce results. If you don't have proof in your life, then you are practicing the wrong philosophy."

I was weary and felt I needed immediate results. Chanting seemed like a colossal waste of time, when instead, I should be *doing* something about changing my life. Sitting in front of a piece of paper and saying words that I didn't understand felt odd. Then, I remembered that Christians talk about speaking in tongues, so it occurred to me that these odd words might be the "tongues" they were speaking in!

I was desperate, and I believed in anything that might bring some order to my life.

"Just chant," he said. "Don't sweat the rest."

I removed my stifling mink coat and chanted my heart out that night. I continued this practice for some time. In a few weeks, I got my own Gohonzon and had the scroll installed in my living room.

On the day of the installation, several members from the local Shibu (chapter house) arrived at my home to assist in the ceremony. A woman named Janet led her friends into my little living room. She was a former Catholic and carried the Gohonzon in her hands as if the object was a Dead Sea scroll. I memorized long, complicated prayers in Sanskrit, which I chanted five times each morning and three times each night. The process was arduous, and I threw myself into the practice with gusto. I liked the sound of the chant. I also liked sharing a feeling of oneness with my fellow chanters.

Not only did I consider the sad state of my professional affairs, but also thought of the men I had met. Some felt they had some sort of "sexual proprietary claim" on me. My business manager, Irving, had proven to be ineffectual. He had invested some of my money in a bank deal that failed. To make matters worse, he developed an inappropriate interest in me. Noel Marshall also harbored an infatuation for me. His wife, my friend Tippi, somehow got the idea I was chasing after Noel, and she broke off our friendship. I fired Noel.

For a time, Kurt Frings, Elizabeth Taylor's powerful agent, considered me as a client. He literally chased me around his office and then threw me out when I refused to have sex with him. I was reasonably certain I could outrun Elizabeth, and wondered what terrible fate may have befallen her in Frings' office. Then again, she was a working, million-dollar movie star. Perhaps that was my answer.

Dr. Goldfarb, a "Hollywood" doctor, took me out for dinner one night. Without my knowledge, he was snorting cocaine in between bites of food. When he took me home, he went upstairs to use the bathroom. He returned stark naked and insisted he would not leave until we had sex! I spent the night with my neighbor.

My career was in no better shape. I had decided to turn down television offers in order to concentrate on feature films, but the several films I made did nothing to improve my waning star-power. Each lousy film led me to still another.

I had come to expect the worst. Now when I first met a man, I waited for his inevitable and unwanted sexual advances. I cringed at the thought, and then I cringed because my refusal guaranteed he would not call me again. They all wanted to bang Diane McBain the Movie Star — and I didn't like that role.

Perhaps the chanting cleared my head. My interest in the writings of Edgar Cayce made me think about visiting the institute dedicated to studying his work. The Edgar Cayce Association for Research and Enlightenment is located in Virginia Beach, Virginia, and the foundation's extensive occult library there is well known. I wanted to learn more about his predictions and his life. If he was a fraud, I wanted to know that, too.

I also became interested in television news programming. I thought a change of scene might do me good. I wrote to several local stations in Virginia and inquired if anyone would hire me as a television commentator. My chanting became obsessive and passionate, and soon I received an answer. A station in Virginia Beach contacted me about doing an early morning talk show. The proposition sounded promising, and I flew to Virginia. The meetings went well but the salary offer was paltry. I couldn't manage to live there on such little money, and such a commitment would prevent me from doing any film work in California. I returned home to think.

In Buddhism, there is no notion of God as there is in Christianity. Still, I had not abandoned the idea of God. The Buddhists I met believed the universe was the ultimate expression of life. This made sense but left me feeling "alone." I never quite articulated this, but I felt there had to be another identifiable figure to who I could direct my prayers. For me, the God who occupied the faith of my childhood was the other figure, and I continued to pray to Him though I used the Gohonzon as a way to focus myself. I thought that perhaps the chanting was a human expression of God. The Jesus of my childhood got lost in the process. He was a long-ago personage who had been the highest expression of God, and like Buddha, a good example of what to aim for. I had never really thought that Jesus was God himself, the way some Christians do. So, as I prayed, I thought of God as I always had, the wisest and most loving Father.

Now, if only I would listen to His urgings.

I had stopped listening to God a long time before, and although I was willing to follow His advice and guidance, I was reluctant to believe He had my best interests at heart. In faith, I supposed that He did have, but my experiences of late had made me skeptical. Of course, it was difficult to realize the extent of my own complicity when I considered the state of my life and affairs. I had been making my decisions without spiritual counsel for years, and I didn't feel like giving up that responsibility. Blind faith was at odds with Diane's sense of practicality. Danny was most often silent in these matters. She didn't know what to think. Her idea was to *feel* God's presence.

Moving across the country, away from my friends and family and a career I had earnestly pursued for all of my adult life, would not be easy. If that was God's intention for me, it was certainly hard to hear His message.

In the midst of all these possible upheavals, my agent called and arranged a meeting for me with a film producer. It was the first such meeting I'd had in a long time, and I was overcome with excitement. I felt this was a sign. God wanted me to stay in Hollywood!

The television producer in Virginia required my immediate response to his offer. I thought the recent film offer was in the bag, so I decided to stay in California.

If God had wanted me to go to Virginia Beach, He hadn't presented much monetary incentive! To jump into such a new aspect of the entertainment business with no experience whatsoever was very daunting. Mostly, the thought of being so far away from my loved ones was unbearable. I simply wasn't ready for such a big change.

However, I didn't get the part in that movie, either. That's when I began to curse God. I recalled the uninvolved deity that Elvis had introduced to me in the book *The Impersonal Life*. To me, Buddhism's "impersonal" universe was less disappointing.

In September, I taped at Paramount Studios an episode of *Love, American Style*, a comedy anthology series on ABC. I played a character named Jill in a segment called "Love and the Roommate." The light-hearted episode was wonderfully written by Emmy Award-winner Allan Burns. My fellow cast mates included Ted Bessell, John Beck, and Anjanette Comer. The episode aired on November 17.

Love, American Style was my first appearance in episodic television in two and a half years. I needed the money, but I was actually more excited by the role after I read the script. I was offered so few comedic roles, I jumped at the chance. Each episode was a collection of short plays starring many big name actors who worked with a repertory company. Each story dealt with the all-important theme of "love." The work was a real pleasure and I hoped doing comedy might lead me in a new direction.

My zealous chanting may not have increased my job offers or earning potential, but the peaceful practice lowered my blood pressure and gave me a sense of camaraderie with a group of gentle people. During the Cold War, there had been an unspoken threat of nuclear tyranny that seemed ominous and quite real. My fellow Buddhist followers believed the world needed a religion that could deliver true peace by changing the *hearts* of the people. Buddhism seemed the most likely possibility, and the people of the Nichiren Shoshu organization were determined to change hearts. Surrendering to something greater than me, and being committed to that effort, gave me the strength to get through the next four tumultuous years. The one thing I didn't expect was that my obsession with Buddhism would drive away some of my best friends.

Ralph Riskin, the man I had met and dated in Hawaii a few years earlier, reappeared in my life. He had decided to follow in his father's professional footsteps and become a television producer. My earlier insecurities had motivated me to go back to school. I became a voracious reader and a pseudo-intellectual who knew a lot about nothing, but I could *talk* my way through anything. I was determined that no man would ever dump me again just because I had let him do all the thinking and talking.

I fell in love with Ralph all over again. We spent a special evening together. We shared feelings and experiences like never before. After Ralph left, I credited this second chance to be with him to my devout chanting. At last, I thought, I was getting what I wanted and, most importantly, I felt loved. When Ralph left that night, I danced through the living room like a child. I felt light and unencumbered as if all my cares and woes had melted away.

I felt so full of love that everything in my world changed. Everything suddenly took on a newfound clarity. I felt like I was in an animated film with beautifully painted layers of light, color, and rhythmic movement. The next morning as I got my car from the garage, I saw the usual garbage bins and detritus in the alley, only now the refuse looked as colorful and dramatic as a Van Gogh painting! Not only had my world become brighter but the colors sparkled with a luminosity I am still unable to describe. I can only say that the revelation was extraordinary.

The wind was tossing fluffy white clouds around the stunningly blue sky. I drove to the Nichiren Shoshu headquarters in Santa Monica to drop off the monthly column I wrote for their newsletter. When I got there, I walked along the shoreline, reluctant to let the incredibly grace-filled day pass me by.

A flock of seagulls rose up as if on cue and flew across my vision. The teal blue sea sparkled like diamonds and sapphires behind the gulls. The scenario seemed meant for me. Surely, God was saying "I love you." My soul felt uncluttered, and my view of the world became intensely sharp. The moment made me feel whole again. All seemed pure. At once, it was clear to me that witnessing this unique moment made me a part of creation itself. My new ability to see my surroundings so plainly told me that I was intrinsic to God's creation, because without my attuned senses and expanded consciousness, His creation would go unnoticed and unremembered. The world would have no meaning. This had to be what God intended. He wanted to share His creation. I believe He created humankind just for that purpose. What meaning could all of this amazing life in the universe have without anyone to see, experience, appreciate, and remember it?

I tried to remain open, but the experience lasted only for a couple of days, and I soon reverted to my "old" self again. I wondered why Christianity had never given me this sort of profound feeling. It was natural for me to seek answers by returning to my religious traditions and the symbols that would help explain the meaning of this unfamiliar experience. Preferring the Judeo-Christian symbols to the Buddhist ones, which seemed "foreign" to me, I was particularly disturbed that this special intuition which I had felt was associated with the new, strange religion — one that didn't believe in a Creator!

While I was taken by Ralph, he was unmoved by me. I wanted a relationship so badly that perhaps *I* wasn't seeing clearly. Perhaps I saw a romanticized, fairy-tale picture in my mind. There was to be no romance with Ralph Riskin.

Chapter 19

Among the men who always seemed to be on hand were those I characterized as "hangers-on." One fellow named Joe was tall and gorgeous with a strong jaw line and sexy, prematurely white hair. He was an actor of little note, but he was fun to be around. I told him about my recent experience of seeing everything so clearly, and he claimed that I could, at will, have experiences like that all the time if I wanted.

"How?" I asked.

"LSD."

"It's illegal, right?"

"Well, yes. But everybody does it anyway. It isn't likely to get you put in jail, if that's what you're worried about."

That isn't something to worry about, I wondered.

"It's important to stop worrying when experimenting with LSD. A person could take their paranoia into the experience. The best thing to do is to fast and pray in preparation."

"Is it safe?"

"Sure," he said, "you'll be with me and I'll take care of you."

That was hardly the case. My first experience was horrendous. I wasn't prepared and I couldn't shake my fears. I was so paranoid that I literally felt frozen for most of the night. I wore my mink coat, piled on all the blankets in the house, and shivered for hours. When I was finally able to crawl out from under the covers, I wandered into the backyard and found the trees filled with slithering snakes, and the bushes were alive with gargoyles!

I was determined to have a better experience the second time, so I properly prepared myself. I ate fruit and vegetables and drank purified water for several days, and then I fasted for twenty-four hours. I prayed and meditated with more enthusiasm than I had the first time, and gathered a lot of art books that I wanted to study while in the drug-induced state.

The experience took me beyond the music I listened to and the books I had set out in my apartment. I moved past my ego and my sense of self and realized that without my ego, my unfettered self was Universal. My identity was so mixed up with His that I ceased to have a separate "sense of self." I found that the 'I' of me was *all* that is — not I, not me, not Diane, nor Danny. My ego was gone and now pure consciousness, pure thought, pure instinct, or God, had taken its place. "I am that I am," God said. My limited self, the self I called Diane or Danny, was just an extension or an expression of "I am." Only the true self can be the one that says "I am" in the purest sense of the word, which is a statement of being. This seemed to be what He meant. In striving to find the essence of truth, I discovered that there is no other true identity but God, and no other time but now.

When I returned from this amazing inner journey, I became convinced that life was meant to have a broader range of experience. People would say that I simply had an hallucination, but I felt that our ordinary experience was the illusion, a dream from which we would some day awaken, just as I had, albeit temporarily. It bothered me that I had to use a drug to accomplish that awakening, and I wanted to believe that this state of mind was possible with meditation and prayer alone. Enlivened by the incident and convinced that I had undergone something that monks and shamans had previously felt; I began a relentless campaign to discover the secrets of our origins. With little film work available, I had nothing else to do.

In the fall of 1969, I accepted several acting assignments. Reading every esoteric, spiritual book I could find took a back seat to my financial survival. Within a couple of weeks, I filmed "Blind Mirror," an episode of *Mannix*. The detective series, one of the most violent on television, was filmed at Paramount Studios. The program starred Mike Connors as a "private eye" and Gail Fisher as his secretary, which at the time, was an important and groundbreaking role for an African-American actress. I played a woman who feared for her life after she witnessed an attempted murder. Mike Farrell (a wonderfully, dear man) played the heavy.

I did my own stunts on the show. The director asked me to back off a cliff into treacherous ocean swells. Robert Lansing, with whom I was doing the scene, was amazed I would take such a risk. He was concerned that I would miss the water and land in the sand on my posterior. I thought that this small leap was tame compared to the other challenges in my life!

Land of the Giants was the brainchild of producer Irwin Allen, who had created several science-fiction television series. At 20th Century-Fox Studios, I filmed an episode called "Panic" with fellow guest-stars Peter

Mark Richman and Jack Albertson. This fantasy, starring Gary Conway, was about seven earthlings stranded on a planet inhabited by giants. I played a housekeeper (who was not what she pretended to be) to Jack Albertson's kindly inventor. As a giant, I liked the idea of walking around squishing the little people. I pretended they were all the "suits" who had turned me down for proper roles during the past few years.

I then filmed an episode of *To Rome with Love* called "To Go Home Again." The situation comedy starred John Forsythe as a widower who had moved to Rome with his three daughters. John was handsome, charming, and a true gentleman. The faux Italian sets of *To Rome with Love* were created at the CBS Studio Center in Studio City.

Unexpectedly, I was the queen of television in January 1970. *Mannix* aired on January 24, and both *Land of the Giants* and *To Rome with Love* aired on January 25. Casting agents weren't watching, though, and I didn't work again for months. With so much time on my hands, my ego took leave. I wrote letters to directors and producers whenever I heard they were considering projects I thought might be right for me. I received no replies. I tried not to let their indifference get me down. Instead, I immersed myself in the world of religions and mythology, and I even dabbled in the occult.

It was disturbing to see the dependence on magic that occult practices seemed to promote. Magic is illusion, and illusions are transitory and disappear. Nevertheless, my curiosity and fascination with the topic took me away from the reality that I needed to confront: how to make a viable living as an actress, yet remain relevant in a changing world that was quickly becoming obsessed with youth. My search for enlightenment was often a diversion from dealing with my issues. If I had spent half as much time *looking* for work as I did *chanting* about it, I might have gotten somewhere!

I was concerned that the lack of attention my career was getting might have a negative long-term effect, so I sought the guidance of senior leaders. Mr. Kikamura, the leader at the Santa Monica headquarters of the Nichiren Shoshu, offered his advice. To believers, seeking guidance from a senior leader was tantamount to speaking with God directly. Mr. Kikamura said I should concentrate on getting married and beginning a family. A career in the movies was nothing compared to being a mother according to this wise sage. The Danny in me concurred.

In the midst of my conundrum, my mother was dying. She had had a mastectomy, but the cancer had spread to her liver. I knew she wanted to see me married and perhaps with a family of my own before she died. I wanted to make her happy, and since Danny had always wanted to have a family, I felt the need to get the ball rolling.

I was thirty years old, and no one except a paranoid schizophrenic had ever popped the important question. Joe, my actor friend and LSD pusher, returned one day after a long disappearance. In a weirdly romantic moment, this very handsome young man just casually dropped by to ask me to be his wife. It quickly became apparent to me that his drug use had taken a toll. Before he asked the all-important question, he said the police, FBI, CIA, and "other-worldly aliens" had been trailing him for weeks. He was very frightened but said he knew if we married, he'd be okay. He was delusional, which is probably why he asked me to marry him.

I lead him to the door. I told him I was in a hurry and would have to get back to him. Then, he disappeared again. I tried to call him some time later, but was unable to find him. The odd experience was a good lesson to me and another admonishment about the negative results of drug abuse.

I began to date an attractive, charming, and humorous man named Noel. He was a Buddhist. He was a struggling photographer, still supported by his father. My Buddhist senior leaders told me that if I didn't love him, it didn't matter. I would learn to love him over time!

I told Noel I would marry him. I knew the news would make my ailing mother happy.

The terrible call came early on a hot, smoggy August morning. My mother had passed away, the attendant told me, with only a nurse by her side. I was overcome with guilt. I should have been there with her. I was my mother's only child. Being with her in her final moments was my responsibility. My mother was the only person in the world I could completely trust. Now she was gone. Mom was the sweetest, kindest person I had ever known. She was only fifty-five-years-old when cancer killed her. Dying so young wasn't right, and when she needed me to help her through her most difficult time, I wasn't there. In her final days, she was more concerned about my well-being than she was about her own. While I could count on her completely, she couldn't rely on me at all. At that moment, I realized I didn't like the person I was. There was a lot that had to change.

During her final days, I had been running between my apartment in the San Fernando Valley and her hospital in Covina, and to the Shibu in Santa Monica. The night before she died, I stayed at the Shibu chanting Diamoku for her life. The leader told me if I had enough faith and chanted diligently all night, my mother's life would be saved. When I should have been at my mother's bedside holding her hand, I had spent the night mumbling mumbo-jumbo!

In spite of her own faith, my mother had tried to embrace my new belief system. Only a few weeks before, ill as she was, she drove all the way to the Buddhist temple in Etiwanda to help me plan my wedding to Noel. She loved me enough to kneel down with me before the Gohonzon — to her mind a false idol. Mom was accepting and tolerant, and I loved her more for that than for anything she had ever done before. I knew how *compromised* she must have felt.

I selfishly asked the funeral director to place my Buddhist chanting beads in the casket with her. She was cremated, but I wanted to have my beads with her. No cross, no Christian artifact, nothing *she* would have preferred. I was thirty years old, and I was still thinking about my own needs and wishes — not those of the person I most loved!

As soon as my mother died, I told Noel I couldn't marry him. I didn't love him. My mother's death affected me profoundly. I thought of her marital situation and the futility of marrying someone for whom I had no love. Her death left me with many questions.

I had chanted for her good health. Instead of being with her on the night of her death, I chose to do a Toso, a chanting marathon...and I *quit* before the night was over. Diane got *tired*. Danny thought Diane was spoiled. If my mother had really known the conflicts going on inside my head all those years, she might have been reluctant to nurture Diane. She might not have encouraged my career as an actress. Danny, after all, had the bigger heart.

A publicity photo from 1969.

Starburst

Chapter 20

I needed a roommate. Aunt Dorothy, looking for something new in her life, had joined me in chanting Daimoku to the Gohonzon. She agreed to move in with me. We found a small two-bedroom house in Glendale. By returning to live in Glendale, I had come full circle. My mother's death left a terrible void in the family. She was the glue that held us all together. There was a gaping hole in my life, and living with my aging aunt gave me comfort. We spent the next year crocheting together. She was a master craftswoman, and I enjoyed listening to her stories about our family.

My father could not bear the loneliness. He soon found someone to take Mom's place. Isabel was an old family friend. I liked her, but I thought their romance was a bit rushed. My father had actually dated her when they were teenagers, and years later, my parents called on her to baby sit me. Six months after Mom's death, Isabel sent my father a note saying she was about to divorce her husband. She wondered if Dad would be interested in renewing their friendship. He met her in Texas and quickly married her.

I had a terrible time finding work. Eventually, steadfast Aaron Spelling tossed me a bone. In November 1970, I guest-starred on a successful television series he produced. *The Mod Squad* was filmed at Paramount, and concerned three young people who had gotten into legal trouble. They avoided jail by going undercover and working with the police to infiltrate the counter culture. The episode called "Kicks Incorporated" was directed by veteran Gene Nelson. The storyline was comedic. Barbara Rush and I played damsels in distress. Working with fellow guest-stars Jack Cassidy (perhaps the most shamelessly flirtatious man I've ever met), Danny Thomas, and Kim Milford was not unpleasant by any means, but I had a strange feeling of finality when the job wrapped.

The very public Diane slipped into a period of forced professional retirement. I continued to support charitable causes when called upon. Most notably, I made an appearance at the Inglewood Forum to promote a basketball game between the Harlem Globetrotters and some

Hollywood celebrities. The sporting event was a fundraiser to benefit the March of Dimes, but I wouldn't work again as an actress for more than a year.

For the first time since I was a youngster, I sought employment outside show business. I didn't know what else to do. I had only worked as a model or an actress since I had been a teenager. My skills were very limited. I went to a "temporary employment" agency, and accepted secretarial jobs in Los Angeles. Each assignment was short-term, but at last I was bringing home a paycheck — albeit a *small* paycheck.

After many months of inactivity, I traveled to Seattle, Washington to attend the annual West Coast Buddhist Convention. I turned around and was suddenly peering directly into the crystal blue eyes of a very handsome young sailor with a yachting cap slung over one brow. The encounter seemed like kismet! We boarded a ship for a tour of the Seattle harbor. Rodney Burke was a member of the organization's Young Men's Division. He helped with crowd control and directed passengers to the upper decks. He, too, was visiting Seattle from Los Angeles. He was too cute to resist, and soon we made plans to get together back in Los Angeles.

Rod promised to call but never did! I was nonplussed. No one had done *that* to me before. I found him so intriguing that I called his senior Buddhist leader to ask if he would ask Rod to call me. I didn't think it proper to simply call Rod myself.

Rod called eventually. We met and quickly discovered we had absolutely nothing in common except Buddhism. He worked for a collection agency and made telephone calls to debtors. Diane was still, though a bit tarnished, a movie star. Rod was interested in drag-racing. I loved tennis. He was a member of the paramilitary outgrowth of the Nichiren Shoshu, innocently called the Young Men's Division. I loved ballet and the arts. As a senior leader in the Young Men's Division, he wanted nothing more than to be at the center of the Kosen-rufu movement. Kosen-rufu is an important core concept in Buddhist Practice, which is commonly defined as "world peace through individual happiness." I aggressively solicited my friends and acquaintances to join Nichiren Shoshu. "World peace was the worthy cause," I pleaded. Soon, no one came near me.

The chanting had lost its luster. In spite of my best efforts to save my mother's life, she had succumbed to cancer. The Gohonzon hadn't produced the human revolution that was promised. I had no work offers, no betrothed, and all my furs and diamonds had been stolen from my apartment when I lived in the San Fernando Valley. I wasn't getting anything I wanted. In fact, I was losing the few things I had left and was now back in Glendale living with my aunt!

I was also uneasy with my careless abandonment of our family religion. My journey of faith had taken me far afield. The world around me was changing so rapidly that I missed the tradition of my earlier religious beliefs. Though dating a Buddhist was at odds with my Christianity, I was so focused on getting married that I simply overlooked a lot of the basics.

Rod and I ignored our obvious differences and managed to forge a partnership that would eventually be called a "marriage." Putting aside any reservations, we spent the next months getting to know each other, trying to understand each other, and generally following the guidance of the senior leaders of the Nichiren Shoshu. They expected us to remain focused and to demonstrate our readiness for a marital commitment. They obviously remembered what I had done to poor Noel the year before and wanted to protect Rod from "the insensitive movie star." The senior leaders were right, but I didn't share their concerns. I was trying with all my heart to find a way to love someone who was actually open to and available for marriage. Determined to change, I surmised that a good test of the Gohonzon's validity would be my ability to embrace change. Clearly, stealing other women's husbands was not the way.

I worked hard at being the "right kind" of woman who would make a "good wife." I set aside the pursuit of a career, also my feminist leanings. I reserved my judgments of Rod, which I now know were inappropriate. I worked hard to see him in the best possible light. It wasn't easy. He had little education and didn't even speak proper English. My mother had taught me diligently to speak correctly, because my grandmother who lived with us had been raised on a farm in the Mid-West and her command of the English language was limited and comical. I found it embarrassing to hear my husband-to-be abuse the English language in much the same way my grandmother had done.

No one in my family or among my Buddhist friends ever said anything about Rod's failings. His deplorable grammar was the elephant in the room. Perhaps I was being too picky and judgmental. It seemed that others were more tolerant. Perhaps I needed to be more forgiving. (I learned much later that everyone was whispering behind our backs about Rod's lack of education and manners, and questioning the intelligence of my choice for a partner in marriage.) I decided to put any concerns aside and concentrate on loving someone who was imperfect.

In Buddhism, if something gets in the way of a stated goal, it is thought to be an obstacle that needs to be overcome through zealous chanting. In Christianity, such an obstacle may be God's way of keeping you from making a terrible mistake. As such, the warning is meant to be heeded. I ignored it.

With my hair and makeup in place and my wedding dress carefully laid out in the backseat of the car, Aunt Dorothy accompanied me to the Myohoji Temple in Etiwanda for the ceremony. The car's water hose blew out on a freeway incline, and we sputtered to the side of the road. I now believe the breakdown was a last ditch attempt by God to make me reconsider what I was about to do. I thought about that while stranded on the roadside, but I was a Buddhist, after all. We were supposed to chant our way through obstacles. So, Aunt Dorothy and I chanted. Suddenly a Volkswagen van filled with hippies pulled up and stopped. They were headed to a mountain resort called Big Bear. The temple was considerably out of their way, but they generously accommodated us. I arrived an hour late. My hair was a mess, and my make-up smeared by tears. Nevertheless, I was determined to seal this marriage deal.

Japanese custom dictated that my father was not to walk me down the aisle. I walked by myself, while a little voice in my head said, *There aren't any vows to God in this ceremony, so if it doesn't work out, you can always leave him.* What a way to start a marriage! The conniving Diane was hedging her bets.

Aside from Aunt Dorothy stepping on my wedding gown and ripping the hem, the ceremony was uneventful. I felt ironically fortunate because someone had pointed out to me that a torn wedding gown meant bad luck. If only I had been conscious enough to recognize the warning signs! With a smile frozen on my face, I married Rod Burke on February 6, 1972.

My gown (designed by my friend, John Brandt) was lovely, a friend provided me with a spectacular bouquet of white lotus and orchids, and my father and his new wife staged a lavish banquet at our reception. Nevertheless, here I was marrying a man who was completely perplexed by celebrity! Furthermore, I represented a way of life to which he was completely unaccustomed. He was a parolee from Federal prison, convicted of harboring a criminal. He was a divorced father of two children he rarely saw. His mother was a diagnosed paranoid-schizophrenic residing in a halfway house in Oxnard, California. Instead of getting married, I should have been having my head examined.

We spent our honeymoon at Lake Arrowhead in the nearby San Bernardino Mountains. A friend lent us his condominium. The village was freezing cold, with a dusting of snow on the ground. I was exhausted and couldn't muster much enthusiasm for our first night as man and wife.

While we cuddled on the sofa and watched the glowing logs in the fireplace, Rod said he needed to tell me something. He was nervous and a bit hesitant. He wanted me to understand how outrageous what he was about to tell me sounded even to him, but, it was important for me to know that I

My wedding to Rod Burke.

had just married a future President of the United States! That's right — the man who hadn't finished high school, didn't know how to parse a sentence, could barely speak intelligible English, who couldn't vote because of his parole, was going to be President! Chanting to the Gohonzon had revealed to him his fate, he explained, and *I* needed to be prepared, as well! What I needed to prepare myself for, I feared, was a padded cell.

To make ends meet after our honeymoon, I continued to take temporary secretarial jobs. As I drove to work along Wilshire Boulevard, I looked at "For Rent" signs along the road. I fantasized about telling Rod I had made a terrible mistake and couldn't continue our days-old marriage.

I hadn't been able to sleep. My belongings were still in boxes. I assumed my acting career was long over. I couldn't imagine remaining another minute in the marriage. What had I done?

Yet I stayed. I didn't want to be a quitter. I didn't want to accept the failure. My first priority was to have a family. So what if Rod had delusions of grandeur? I would be tolerant because the time had come to grow up. If things weren't as I imagined they should be, then one day they would be. I had to be patient. I needed to create my own family or I might be looking at a very lonely old age.

We moved into a house in Santa Monica near the ocean. In the late spring of 1972, my agent (a voice from the distant past) called with an offer to star in a "really scary monster movie." *The Deathhead Virgin*, written by two struggling actors named Jack Gaynor and Larry Ward, concerned a treasure hunter who found a sunken Spanish galleon off the coast of a Philippine island. However, the murderous spirit of an ancient Moro princess guarded the ship and its treasure. It turned out to be a "monstrous" film in more ways than one. The film, clumsily directed by Norman Foster, was shot in the Philippines, where it was cheaper to make a movie than anywhere else on earth. They didn't spend any money on my wardrobe as my costumes consisted of an assortment of string bikinis.

I wanted to work. I wanted the money and I wanted to get away from Rod.

I didn't know how bad the experience was going to be until I arrived in the tropical Philippines. Besides Gaynor and Ward, there were several Filipino film stars. Vic Diaz, known as the Filipino equivalent of Peter Lorre, was the king of Filipino exploitation cinema. During his career he had made more than 100 mostly horror low-budget films. The people who watched us shoot on location certainly knew who he was. They followed him everywhere and paid no attention to any of the rest of us.

I played the role of Larry Ward's wife. Our director, Norman Foster, was seventy years old. This film would sadly be his swansong. He began his career in Hollywood by directing the *Mr. Moto* films of the 1930s. His 1928 marriage to Claudette Colbert lasted seven years. Although it might have been fun to compare notes with him about his ex-wife and my co-star in *Parrish*, I don't think he remembered their union. He certainly had forgotten how to direct a film.

The script was appalling, the special effects laughable, and the working conditions unspeakable. *The Deathhead Virgin* was supposed to be a horror movie, but the only horror was making this mish-mash. The lousy salary and overwhelming stress of working with people who had no idea what they were doing made me ill. I hadn't worked in a film for a couple of years, and this atrocity was to be my comeback vehicle. I was feeling devastated.

When I got home, my agent called with another job offer. William T. Orr, my old television boss at Warner, was set to executive produce a new horror film for an independent company called United National Productions. He had a distribution deal with MGM. Richard L. Bare was the writer and director. I was asked to replace an actress who had dropped out of the project. I'd worked with Dick Bare before, and felt good about working with him again.

Dick wanted to create a suspense film like Hitchcock's *Psycho*. *Wicked, Wicked* was about a series of grisly murders in a sprawling California hotel. Single, blonde women checked in and never checked out. A weird electrician, traumatized by his foster mother, murdered shapely blondes and embalmed them in the hotel attic. The curious cast included a handsome, deep-voiced model named David Bailey. His single acting credit was a television commercial for Mitchum deodorant. A young Vietnam veteran named Randolph Roberts, who had no acting experience, played the leading man — a psychotic killer. Tiffany Bolling, a singer and *Playboy* magazine playmate, played a potential murder victim. Film veterans Scott Brady, Madeleine Sherwood, and the genteel Arthur O'Connell rounded out the cast.

The gimmick of *Wicked, Wicked* was its introduction of a new film process, which Dick Bare called "Duo-Vision," more commonly known as "split-screen." This type of film involved an "active" screen and a "passive" screen, with action playing on *both* sides of the screen simultaneously. Dialogue came from only one screen at a time, though, while silent film played on the other. The music in the film was the original organ score from the 1925 silent film classic, *Phantom of the Opera*. Essentially, the viewer could watch the stalker pursuing his victim, and see the victim fleeing, all at the same time. The finished film, which took months to edit, was a mess. Dick Bare said, "It's high camp. Nobody can take it seriously. We call it half *Grand Hotel* and half 'Grand Guignol.'"

The movie was filmed at the Hotel del Coronado and on the lot of MGM Studios in Culver City. The small-budget film was shot in six weeks, beginning in October 1972. The job was uneventful, except for the fact that I had recently become pregnant. One morning in September, after having sex with Rod the night before, I was in the shower and suddenly felt woozy. I felt as if a force had entered me. My doctor soon confirmed the pregnancy.

During the filming of *Wicked, Wicked*, I had lunch with Lydia Lane, a reporter for the *Los Angeles Times*. She interviewed me for an article that appeared in the newspaper on January 11, 1973. No periodical had been interested in talking with me about anything for a couple of years. Diane, the movie star, answered Lane's question about why I appeared "thinner, gayer, and much more outgoing."

Danny was embarrassed as Diane rambled, "I am a new person, thank heavens! And I owe it all to my visit to Nichiren Shoshu of America in Santa Monica. You do not have to believe to get results. Well, it certainly worked, and I have been able to reach goals that were unattainable before. It helped me to achieve a self-identity, a human reevaluation that I did not find with a psychoanalyst. Chanting puts you in touch with a universal rhythm that helps you draw upon your potential power. Now I have a mature attitude toward myself and toward life."

These pronouncements were all hype; something Diane had become skilled at when the subject was a show business career. Diane was thrilled she was getting the attention she felt she so richly deserved.

When I was six months pregnant, the publicist for *Wicked, Wicked* asked me to attend the special premiere of the film at the Hotel Del Coronado. I recalled my embarrassing "disappearance" in 1965 at this hotel. I didn't want to be photographed at the time and begged off, but the invitation was more like an order. Rod was invited to accompany me in my delicate condition, so we decided to make the most of an expense-paid getaway to the glorious old hotel.

We were shuttled to Coronado Island on a tour bus. When we climbed off the bus, I came face to face with the waiting press and snap-happy photographers for the first time in years. Diane was horrified by the way Danny was dressed. Embarrassed beyond words, Diane wanted nothing more than to run into the restroom and rip off the little red and white gingham top. I was so relieved, however, when Rod and I were whisked away to our room to prepare for the evening festivities.

We actually had a nice time eating extravagantly and dancing together into the early hours. I had one glass of wine, my first since my pregnancy. Once we got into bed, my baby began a dance routine of his own, flip-flopping, twirling, and kicking. Thank goodness, my days of heavy drinking were behind me. I'm sure the wine set the infant to dancing, so I never had another drink while pregnant.

"TWICE THE TENSION: TWICE THE TERROR!" *Wicked, Wicked*, with that tagline, was released in April 1973 to generally terrible reviews, including my own — TWICE AS BAD! On April 26, Kevin Thomas wrote in the *Los Angeles Times*, ". . . all 'Duo-Vision' really accomplishes is to give the viewer two terrible pictures for the price of one. Edd Byrnes as a shady lifeguard and Diane McBain as one of the victims are similarly unimpressive." The *Los Angeles Herald-Examiner* was equally unimpressed. On April 27, the reviewer wrote, "Diane McBain steps from a shower to meet her hideously-masked and knife-wielding killer whose thrusts are edited just slowly enough to cover the screen in tasteless vermilion." Roger Greenspun enjoyed the unintentional humor and wrote in the *New York Times* on June, 14, "*Wicked, Wicked* emerges as an oddly pleasant movie about which there is not too much good to say. Everybody is at least professionally competent. There should always be a place for the low-budget hotel movie, where the same six extras as guests continually crisscross the lobby…"

My baby did not enter the world with ease. However, the pregnancy was a wonderful time. Rod and I attended Lamaze classes, and my spirits were high. My acting goals were on the back burner, but I was finally getting the family I had yearned so long to have.

Danny was in her element. I found myself in shapeless gingham dresses with ribbons in my long unbleached hair. With no makeup, no manicures, and my natural mousy-blonde hair, I looked quite bland. Danny was in heaven!

Sunday, June 24, 1973 was hazy and hot. As I stumbled out of bed, my water broke. Rod was not at home. In the year since our marriage, he had become scarcer around the house. I was feeling more and more alienated and alone.

Pregnant in gingham and no makeup.

In between contractions, I called the doctor and was told to get to the hospital at once. I called Rod at the Nichiren Shoshu headquarters and left a message for him to get home immediately.

Rod finally arrived and we hurried to the hospital. My primary physician was off duty that day, so his brother was called in, which interrupted his early morning golf game. He seemed annoyed at the disruption. His face was expressionless and unnatural looking. It looked very much like plastic. If someone had told me he was an alien from another planet, I would have believed him.

Suddenly I was nauseated. The baby was presenting headfirst, but I had dilated only two centimeters. The room went into a panic. The doctor announced that the umbilical cord was caught between the baby's head and shoulder. With every contraction, he was losing oxygen, and a quick delivery was critical.

Amidst the pain and confusion, I couldn't help thinking that the doctor might simply have been impatient because his golf game was disrupted. I wasn't even *his* patient. I didn't want an anesthetic; I wanted a natural childbirth, which is what Rod and I had prepared for. However, the doctor insisted I needed a caesarean section immediately, which of course required anesthesia. I could barely look at the strange doctor's odd face, but Rod seemed to agree with him.

"It's for the baby, Diane," Rod said earnestly, as though he was announcing something I hadn't considered or didn't already know. I would have punched him in the nose if I'd had the strength.

I relented. *Go with the flow, Diane,* I told myself. I hoped a C-section was truly for the baby's safety and not to facilitate the doctor's return to his golf.

I was whisked into the delivery room and an anesthesiologist introduced himself. As he placed the mask over my face, he said, "Don't worry, you'll be fine. You're in good hands." I was out, or so I thought.

The next thing I remember was extreme pain. The doctor was pushing and pulling something from my incised lower abdomen. It felt like he was ripping me open. I tried to scream, but couldn't. I tried to flail my arms to let them know the anesthesia had worn off, but couldn't move. Awake, I was paralyzed, in excruciating pain, and couldn't communicate my feelings. I wanted to move but my body couldn't respond. Suddenly, the baby's cry of freedom pierced the room.

"It's a boy," the doctor announced. I lost consciousness. When I awoke again, I was being wheeled to the recovery room. I turned my head in the direction of Rod's voice and saw my baby's skinny little body, arms, and legs squirming in the incubator next to me. He wasn't crying, just quizzically looking around at the lights and the people scurrying around us.

We didn't name him right away. Rod was a senior leader in the Nichirin Shoshu organization, and his superior named senior leaders' children. He would also receive a name from Daisaku Ikeda, president of the Japanese World Headquarters. Japanese culture, which I had earlier tried to adopt, was interfering with my own sense of tradition. Not being able to name my own child was a bit off-putting, but, I had to acquiesce. The first name chosen was Andrew. The second name was Eichi, which means glorious first son.

Danny fell into motherhood, happily. Movie stardom seemed a thing of the past. Life with Andrew had its difficulties. I insisted on breast-feeding him, but he wouldn't gain weight. I was a cigarette smoker at the time and was unaware how harmful nicotine was to a baby. Andrew was healthy and very active, but the pediatrician encouraged me to fatten up the little guy.

My secretarial skills were minimal. The job I took as a secretary after making *Wicked, Wicked* (to supplement Rod's meager earnings) came to an abrupt end. I was content, for the moment, to stay at home and work toward a more placid life. I expected Rod would become our little family's provider.

Months after Andrew was born, Rod and I contemplated having another child. Oddly, my husband became ill. He was admitted to the hospital in January 1974, and tested endlessly with no result or explanation for his illness. The days dragged on and on. Rod was actually in the hospital for a month. Eventually, he was sent home. Still mysteriously ailing, he was a changed man, whining and demanding.

Unable to work, Rod stayed in bed and had me running back and forth down the unimaginably long hallway from the back to the front of the house. I tried to care for him, but eight-month-old Andrew needed attention, as well.

Sometimes it takes an otherwise simple issue to blow up into an atomic explosion. I tried to be patient and considerate, but Rod's demands began to eat at me. One day he told me he didn't like cubes of ice in his juice. He wanted crushed ice. He demanded I crush the cubes in our blender. I knew it wouldn't work, and indeed, the blender broke. This prompted an ugly screaming match.

A few days later, while Andrew slept beside Rod, we erupted into another fight. At least the argument got Rod out of bed. He followed me down the hall, yelling all the way. When we got to the living room, I lunged at the Gohonzon, determined to rip the scroll apart. We were taught to be respectful of the object of worship and warned that if we ever damaged it purposefully, the resultant bad karma would damage our very life. All I could think of was, *Damn the Gohonzon and damn this marriage!*

Rod grabbed me from behind and slung me against a huge plate-glass window, which rattled in its frame. I couldn't defend myself and his sudden burst of strength surprised me. I nearly broke through the glass.

"Drop the Gohonzon!" he demanded. "Drop it or I'll…"

I had hold of the scroll by its brocade frame. "Here's your damned Gohonzon!" I screamed as I hurled it into his face.

Then I heard a cry.

We turned to find Andrew on the floor near us. He had been watching us, and his tears stopped us cold. He could hardly crawl on his knees yet, but he had somehow dragged himself by his little arms down the long hallway, through the dining room, and into the living room where we fought. The violence must have been terrifying to him — and certainly beyond his understanding.

Our fight ended, but not the war. Rod's illness, real or imagined, cost us plenty. I should say, cost *me* plenty. With him ailing, and neither of us working, I blew through the little savings I had left. My business manager actually released me because there was no business left to manage. Though Rod claimed he could not work, he still devoted time to the Young Men's Division of the Nichiren Shoshu organization. He managed to get himself back and forth to meetings.

One night I came home after attending a meeting of my own and found Rod holding court in our living room. He was sitting cross-legged on the couch, with a houseful of sycophants at his feet. Because he was a district chief, his ideas and training were supposed to make him knowledgeable enough to give these members guidance. I knew better. My husband could barely manage his own life. He was far from being in a position to tell others how to live. It was such a farce. My stomach turned, and I knew then that I could no longer maintain the front of a happy marriage. I tried to ignore my feelings of dissatisfaction, which caused them to build up to a boiling point. I didn't want Rod and I didn't want to be married.

Shortly after we married, I had joined a therapy group. I sought help in dealing with my marital problems. Finally, I had to admit to my therapist, the group and, more importantly, to myself, that I didn't love Rod. Though we shared a son and a religion, there was no real connection between us. There was no love, certainly not on my part. Our marriage was hopeless.

Rod was physically and emotionally unavailable most of the time, more dedicated to the Nichiren Shoshu than his family. In a desperate, ill-thought move, I took his small traveling Gohonzon, which he could wear on a chain around his neck, and tossed it into the corner mailbox. I addressed the package to my father. I thought this would get Rod's attention and that perhaps he could reassess his sense of propriety. However, my plan backfired horribly.

Rod kidnapped Andrew.

He turned our son over to his senior leaders until such time as I returned his Gohonzon. I was stunned speechless! This was questionable behavior by a balanced, enlightened Buddhist! Andrew was still breast-feeding, and should not be away from me. My breasts grew full and sore as the day wore on and I longed to get my baby home. I was terrified that Rod's vindictiveness might cause him to take Andrew away for good.

I managed to get the local postmaster on the telephone and tearfully coaxed him to send a postal worker to the mailbox. I got the package back and gave it to Rod. Andrew was returned to me.

Filled with an anxiety I had never felt before, I developed a terrible case of hives. No amount of medication could relieve the pain and itching. I was a nervous wreck. When Andrew cried, I couldn't let him be. I was compelled to be with him at all times to relieve his distress. However, my own distress needed relief. My anxiety was disturbing to my little son. Children are attuned to their emotional environment. He was growing physically, but I feared his emotional well-being was in danger. I feared for my own, as well.

The next time Rod left town for another Buddhist convention, I stayed home. I hurriedly packed everything I could and moved out. I stored the larger things, and then moved in with an old school friend in Glendale until I could find a place for Andrew and me to live. I was afraid Rod would try to stop me, even try to take the baby again. I couldn't risk the confrontation. I had had enough. I feared that Andrew had seen and heard enough for such a tiny tot.

My one regret was the loss of an old photograph of my mother I had left behind. It was damaged and terribly fragile and I was afraid the picture might be destroyed in my mad scramble to get out. I had planned to retrieve it later. When Rod got home, he threw out whatever was left of my belongings. The cherished photograph I had hoped to restore was gone.

Chapter 21

I needed to work. Seemingly out of the blue, I was hired to play a small role in *ABC's Wide World of Mystery*. It was, I hoped, a gentle reintroduction to the only profession I really knew. The anthology series was a revolving component of the late-night program, *ABC's Wide World of Entertainment*. "Tight as a Drum," produced by Aaron Spelling, was set in the midst of a formal military school graduation. The movie starred Howard Duff, Brock Peters, Anne Seymour, and Mariette Hartley. We shot on location at Pepperdine University in Malibu, overlooking the beautiful Pacific Ocean.

The women's movement had made some interesting inroads into the world of working mothers. I was a great believer in making the workplace more amenable to a woman's needs. There was much talk about breast-feeding at the workplace. I asked for and received permission to have Andrew with me on set so I could continue to breast-feed him. It was groundbreaking. This was one of the first times such an issue was broached by television producers. My gentle, discrete step back in front of the cameras was not to be. News of my on-set breastfeeding made it into the Hollywood gossip columns and prompted a national debate. Somehow, my seemingly harmless request had made me a heroine to some and a troublesome bitch to others. I couldn't win for losing.

"Tight as a Drum" was broadcast on February 11, 1974 with no fanfare. More than three years had passed since my last appearance on television.

Divorce is never easy. I had a vague plan to live apart for a while to see if I would have a change of heart. Rod was as ready to move on as I was. Four months after we separated, he served me with divorce papers and the formal proceedings moved forward. The truth be known, I had conceived the divorce while walking down the aisle.

Rod's attorney represented his client as penniless and unable to pay any alimony. I was declared by the court as the most likely parent to afford the care and feeding of our child. I had barely worked in two years. Rod was ordered to pay $40 a month in child support. Our divorce was finalized in May, 1974.

I moved into a guesthouse in Glendale. The little cottage was not unlike the one I lived in with my mother when we first arrived in California. There was so little room. I had to sell a lot of furniture that once belonged to my mom and grandmother, which broke my heart, but I needed the money.

One night, I was awakened by a noise to find a stranger sitting on the end of my bed. I tried not to panic. He was very strange, and said little. I remembered something I had read, and gently talked to him like a human being. I didn't scream, I didn't demand he leave, I simply tried to "reason" him out of the room and out of the cottage by saying, "You must have the wrong place. I'm sure you have the wrong place." All the while, I was terrified he would grab Andrew, who was sleeping in a crib next to my bed, and hurt him or use him in some way against me. Eventually, I was able to talk him into leaving, and I grabbed for the phone to call the police. He was caught, and suspected of entering other people's homes in the neighborhood in the middle of the night. I had to go to court to testify against him.

In Hollywood, the fall from grace (more like a plummet) is like the little snowball that begins to roll down from a snowy mountaintop. Before long, the snowball picks up speed and size until its descent cannot be stopped. People scurry out of the way. Nothing can stop the now formidable snowball until it crashes at the bottom of the mountain.

There are rules that accommodate the different levels of stardom. The biggest difference between being a star and an actor is the way you are treated by the people around you. There were no private dressing rooms, no catered lunches, no magical makeup artists, no hair stylists, no wardrobe designers, and no costumers. Rather than being treated with deference, I was treated with indifference. I did my own makeup and hair, I was asked to bring my own clothes from home to use on camera, and I stood in line at craft services. I wasn't insulted, but it was eye-opening. Diane was shocked, though Danny was indifferent.

This new circumstance became glaringly apparent in the summer of 1974. I was cast in a special two-hour episode of *Police Story*, titled "World Full of Hurt." I played the small role of the drug-addled mother of a boy in trouble with the cops. I had only a couple of lines. When I arrived at the set on Stage 6 at Warner Bros., I was treated like a bit player. The last time I worked at the studio, I was a star. This time no one knew who I was. It was a humbling experience.

Months passed, and Hollywood was not calling. Rod's small pittance of child support was sporadic, at best. Aunt Dorothy had been a bookkeeper, so I thought I might be able to follow in her steps. Of course, the fact that I didn't know the first thing about accounting didn't enter my mind at the time. For the purposes of such employment, I used my married name and presented myself as Diane Burke. I turned myself into the plainest Jane possible, wearing no makeup and my mousy blonde hair in a ponytail. I perused the classified ads in the newspaper and applied for the position of assistant bookkeeper for a company in East Los Angeles called Golden State Printers. The name sounded innocuous, and the business was located so far from Hollywood that I hoped nobody would know me.

I was interviewed by a jolly woman named Judy, with strawberry blonde hair and long carefully manicured fingernails. She took a liking to me and I was hired on the spot. At first, I didn't know that Golden State Printers published pornographic books and x-rated pictorial magazines. I had to shrug it off. I needed a paycheck.

On my second day at the job, Judy announced in the lunchroom, "I know who you are, you know. Did you really think you could hide your identity?" She smiled warmly. Judy turned out to be a fan, and that's how I got the job. She said she would never have hired anyone else with such a lack of experience!

Nevertheless, Judy was an excellent teacher. I didn't have a natural aptitude for the job, but I learned and soon enjoyed balancing the books at the end of the month, and posting to the general ledgers. Zeroing out the accounts to the penny each month was a challenge I enjoyed. I had to polish up my handwriting skills, too, because the entries had to be legible. My own sense of proportionality likewise demanded I make the books *look* good. Learning this new skill had Danny engaged, but Diane felt betrayed. It rankled her sense of self to have to keep anyone's books, or run after anyone's coffee.

The daily routine made it possible for me to reorganize my life in a more workable fashion. I hadn't known how to balance my own checkbook, and I had never really learned how to budget my time, either. The job and its inherent demands became invaluable to me in my personal life. I never realized until then how immature and out of control I had been.

I never thought that God would send me into the pornography business to teach me such lessons, but that is where I found myself. Most of the time, my particular work did not put me "face to face" with the product. I wasn't really interested in what was going on in other parts of the large building. I was told adjacent warehouses were crammed with porno awaiting distribution to the masses. On occasion, one of the bosses would bring a photograph into the office that was especially shocking or offensive, or revealed a particularly well-endowed male or female. As a single woman, I found it difficult and oddly frustrating to see such sexually graphic images. There was more to be learned from the place than originally met the eye. Photographs that would ordinarily have been repugnant to me oddly had the opposite effect. I hadn't realized how powerful my sexual needs were. I felt uncomfortable by the feelings pornography stirred in me, and I tried to avoid the bosses' photograph shows. I worked hard and managed to become a full-charge bookkeeper, and eventually, the office manager for one of the company's subsidiaries.

As time wore on, I found myself aching to get back to acting. In addition, I needed to earn more money. As Andrew grew, so did the costs of being a single parent.

I tried to juggle my full-time job with making appointments to meet with casting directors, or to audition. Though acting was the only profession I really knew, and was most suited for, times had changed since I was a working actress, and I felt a bit out of place. I was unused to auditioning for a role. Since my studio-contract days, I had rarely auditioned, and never had to "cold read" for a part. Cold reading consisted of showing up for an audition and being given some lines to read for casting agents, with no rehearsal time. This was a whole new world. Commercial ad men had set a standard that the rest of the casting agencies were now following. To save time, an actor cold-read on video tape for the role, the audition tape was then sent out to be reviewed.

I had always done well when I could meet and talk with the director and producer before any reading of the script took place. Now, though, the process was impersonal and cold as ice. My competition consisted of actresses who were fully prepared and relaxed, while I made a mad dash during my lunch hour to squeeze an audition into my day. It was nearly impossible to do a credible read in the audition room with that much stress. My bosses at the office were not pleased with me, either. I owed them a full day's work, but I was often late coming back from a lunchtime audition. More and more, my head just wasn't in the office.

All my life, well-meaning family members and friends had told me I needed something to fall back on if the acting didn't work out. I accepted the challenge to become whatever I needed to become in order to give my son a decent life. My old friend Mary called me one day from Honolulu. I was happy to hear from her, and we commiserated. Her problems seemed to pale compared to my own. "You didn't do your homework, Diane," she chuckled. "And now you're paying for it."

Shortly afterward, delayed by traffic, I returned quite late from a lunch audition. I was given an ultimatum. I quit. Although I played the role of bookkeeper well enough to be believed, I was playing to a pissy audience.

Nevertheless, I soon accepted the fact that I needed to find another bookkeeping job. As far as casting directors were concerned, I couldn't get arrested. I was hired by another publishing company, and I assured my new boss that I could deliver on the job and still make an occasional audition. Reluctantly, he agreed.

I was fired within in a week, when I returned late after auditioning for a television commercial that I didn't get.

In the summer of 1975, I finally landed a role in a new series called *The Barbary Coast*. Filmed at Paramount, the one-hour adventure series starred William Shatner and Doug McClure as hell-raising special agents. I played Myra in "Sauce for the Goose," a story about a fake séance planned by the heroes to entrap a corrupt civic leader. Bill and Doug, though personable and cute, were not as memorable to me as was Richard Kiel. Towering over all of us at seven feet two inches, Richard played the recurring villain called Moose. In terms of casting, if I had been a victim of my looks, so was dear Richard. He cornered the market on playing giants, villains, and monsters. In truth, he was a sweet man and the gentlest giant I ever met.

At the end of the year, I landed a small role on a two-part special episode of *Marcus Welby, M.D.* called, "The Highest Mountain." The shows aired in February 1976. I also reluctantly accepted a gig on a syndicated game show called *Cross-Wits* that aired in April.

A public relations man named Mike Druxman saw me on *Police Story*. He later described my bit role as a "scudsy character," but once we met, he became infatuated. Earlier, when I was still married, Mike had contacted me when he was working on a piece for *Coronet Magazine* called "Yesterday at the Movies." It was a sort of a "Whatever Became Of?" column. Nothing could have better described my career at the time.

We struck up a business deal whereby he represented me as a publicist for a mere 5 percent of my acting income. His percentage wouldn't amount to much in the short term. If his efforts could restart my career, however, it would benefit us both. We proceeded on that assumption.

He was faced with the difficult task of placing my name in the entertainment trade papers when I was doing nothing professionally. I suggested he tell the gossip columnists that I had recently returned from an extended stay in Europe. We thought the ruse would somehow trick the columnists into thinking I was occupied skipping around Europe rather than struggling for survival in Los Angeles. News of my employment by a pornographic magazine publisher would not be helpful. *Variety* ran the blurb in their "Who's Where" column on September 28, 1976. However, no one seemed to care who I was or where I had been. In fact, no one seemed to miss me in the first place. Perhaps they would have taken more notice if I *had* admitted to my job, though innocent enough, in the porno business. Nevertheless, I hired Mike to represent me, and news of our business relationship appeared in the *Hollywood Reporter* on October 28, 1976.

My career was as cold and dreary as were the oncoming winter months. My struggle to support my son and myself was depressing and desperate. My meager unemployment benefits expired at about the time Rod stopped sending his court ordered child support payments. We were both out of work. Out of despair, I took my son with me to the welfare office to seek relief. Asking for a handout was humiliating and demoralizing, especially when the stone-cold caseworkers recognized me. They probably thought I was trying to defraud the government. My request for assistance was turned down on a technicality.

Finally, in April 1977, I landed a part in a dinner-theater production in Wharton, Texas. Wharton, a charming little town on the Colorado River, is a suburb of Houston. I starred in a play appropriately called *The Pit*. In a peculiar move, the pre-publicity for the show addressed rumors of my death. In a letter to the editor of *The Houston Post* dated April 23, someone wrote, "Is the actress Diane McBain the same actress who stars in the television show, *Eight is Enough*? And is she the same actress found dead in her apartment a few weeks ago? And the one who will be playing at a local dinner theater soon? I'm confused." The editor politely responded, "Diane McBain does not appear in *Eight is Enough*. That show's star, Diana Hyland, died March 27. McBain will play a local show in Wharton in April."

These were my options — dead and buried or the star of *The Pit*. I worked diligently to make something out of practically nothing. Charles Meek reviewed the play in *The Wharton Journal* on April 27, not surprising considering we were the only show in town. He wrote, "Dominating the show is film TV star Diane McBain as an apparently cold, young sophisticate who overworks her cynicism until it wears thin and reveals the bare soul within. Ms. McBain's sensitivity and professionalism make for a performance which one is immediately thankful not to have missed."

In September, 1977, I was cast in a feature film called *The Silent Scream*. The movie was written and directed by a Denny Harris, an aspiring motion picture director. He cast me as a female detective, an uncommon assignment at the time. We shot on location, in and around Los Angeles, Eagle Rock, and Occidental College. The story concerned a group of college-bound students who rented rooms in a creepy, hilltop mansion, where they were murdered one by one.

During rehearsals in a rickety old Victorian house in Highland Park, I slipped on an area rug. I fell very hard, twisting my back and landing heavily on my tailbone. The small, independent production had just begun and the producer had yet to obtain State-ordered Workers Compensation Insurance. The producer paid for a chiropractor and begged me not to report the accident. I acquiesced, and carefully completed the movie.

The finished film was considered un-releasable, so the director brought in two brothers, Jim and Ken Wheat, who rewrote the script. In early 1978, new actors, including Yvonne De Carlo, Barbara Steele, and Cameron Mitchell, were brought in for reshoots. When all was said and done, only 15 percent of the original footage remained in the film. During the process, a decision was made that a female police detective was "unbelievable." The part was reshot with a man in the role. I was completely cut out of the film.

I was insulted and dejected. I felt I had delivered a good, balanced performance. Of course, my opinion didn't matter. Michael Druxman continued to champion me in the press, nonetheless. On September 12, he planted a story in the *Hollywood Reporter* that I was set to star for Guido Films in a "spaghetti suspenser" called *The Deadliest Foe* that would be produced in Rome, Italy. The story sounded amusing on paper, and it was a complete fabrication.

There is a thorny theory that life is regressive. Once a thread begins to unravel, the whole garment tends to go. I found this to be true. I dated an aspiring actor named Tony, and though he seemed like a nice enough fellow, I never intended to become intimately involved with him. One night when I was feeling especially lonely and vulnerable, we had sexual relations. I got pregnant. I discovered the pregnancy late. I was close to the end of my first trimester. After the fiasco of my marriage to Rod, I certainly didn't want to get tied up with someone who would become another burden. I didn't need another mouth to feed, and since I could hardly get my *own* acting career going again, I couldn't help Tony with his career aspirations. My resources were so scant; I did not think it fair to my young son to take on the responsibility of another child. Without someone to help me raise two children, I could not see a way for me to do it alone. There was no way out. After much thought, I reluctantly decided to have an abortion. Tony enthusiastically agreed with my decision and offered to pay for the medical procedure.

When I arrived at the clinic, I began to have second thoughts. I wondered how developed the baby was at that point in the pregnancy and I thought about the life I was choosing to extinguish. *Might this child discover the cure for cancer? Or might this child be a monster?* I didn't know what to think except I was depriving myself of another sweet child to love. I hoped it wasn't a girl, because I'd always dreamed of having a boy *and* a girl. However, my circumstances made having a baby impossible. It would be truly narcissistic to bring another child into the world that I was unable to support. Thankfully, the law was on my side. As I thought about my conundrum, I realized that a woman's decision to have a baby or not is between her and her god. No legislation should interfere in that relationship, nor should a law get between the woman and her doctor, or she and her partner.

There are no right answers to this question that countless women face every day. I wasn't practicing any particular religion at the time, so the moral issues that arise when the topic of abortion is broached weren't of concern to me. It was simply a very personal choice, and I was glad, frankly, to have the option available. I knew I couldn't handle another child like my beloved Andrew, who was a bundle of energy with a penchant for trouble.

As kind and attentive as the medical personnel were, I don't think I had ever felt quite so alone before. I wished my mother was alive to lend me the support I knew she would have had for my decision. On the other hand, had she still been alive, she could have helped me raise another child.

I wish she could have been there to hold my hand. The termination of my pregnancy was a horrible choice to have to make.

When the procedure was over, Tony drove me home and I promptly became deeply depressed. There was no way for me to find peace. I couldn't blame anyone but myself for my carelessness, and I couldn't reconcile my needs with my means. The recovery was physically, mentally and emotionally tough. I was not prepared for the long-term effects of my decision.

A few weeks later, I hemorrhaged badly. My sweet little boy helped me to the bathroom several times as my body tried to void the remaining aborted material. I felt as though the fetus was clinging to me, not wanting to leave. My heart was broken. I had been so cavalier with a precious life. Weak and lightheaded, I feared that I was in danger of bleeding to death. When I called the doctor, he reminded me to use the medication dispensed to me at the clinic. I did. The physical bleeding stopped, but the emotional bleeding had just begun.

Chapter 22

In early 1978, I began work on a television movie for NBC. *Donner Pass: Road to Survival* was directed by James L. Conway and written by S.S. Schweitzer. Based on the 1846 Donner Expedition in the Sierra Nevada Mountains, the story concerned a group of eighty-seven settlers trying to reach California. After being attacked by marauding Indians and running out of food and water, they found themselves stranded in a devastating snowstorm. The survivors of the historical trek were reduced to cannibalizing their deceased comrades in order to survive. Through the years, many filmmakers, including Roman Polanski, tried and failed to produce the movie.

I was thankful for the job, even though we shot on location in frigid Kanab, Utah. It was difficult for me to consider playing a character that could eat the remains of another human being. My research told me that the women were more likely to survive the terrible experience and they needed to eat in order to stay alive and care for the children.

The working conditions were harsh, but I managed to have some fun with my fellow players Mickey Callan, John Anderson, and Andrew Prine. We relieved the tension by making jokes about who would be eating whom.

When I returned home in March, I discovered someone had broken into my apartment. The culprit had trashed the place and stolen my jewelry and a few things of value I owned. The thief had also cooked a meal for himself and left the dirty dishes in the sink! What was stolen was worth more than what I had earned freezing my ass off in Utah.

Mike Druxman tried to book me on *The Tonight Show* to promote the television film. We thought jokes about cannibalism could be funny. We were sure the potential double-entendres would be too delectable for the host, Johnny Carson, to resist. We were wrong. Of course, Danny loved the idea of shocking everyone. It would have been funny to change the title, *Donner Party* to *Dinner Party*. On Carson's couch, I would have done so.

Joan Crosby interviewed me for *TV Parade* in October 1978. She wrote, "TAKING NOTICE — Diane McBain, a blonde beauty who was a regular on *Surfside Six* several years ago, eventually married. Now she is back, 'really back', she says, and she is having to overcome an obstacle or two. 'The attitude I find,' she said, '…Oh, is she still alive, they ask.' They also have an idea I have one foot in the grave instead of being a young, vital woman.' Viewers can check the youth, vitality and beauty in a short time when she shows up on NBC in the TV movie, *Donner Pass*."

I felt certain that my serious role in this film would make casting agents sit up and take notice. I scraped the money together to take a full-page ad in *Variety* on the day *Donner Pass* aired on October 24, 1978. The ad showed only a beautiful picture of me with my name. Later I realized that I should have used a photo of me from the film where I looked like I was starving to death, but I was afraid to let go of the one thing that had gotten me work in the past — my looks. No one of consequence mentioned seeing the ad or the film.

Druxman did the best he could with the press, but the reviews were lukewarm. On October 24, *Variety* stated only one scene in the entire film was believable. "There is a grisly moment when Diane McBain enlists bearded John Anderson in the snow-covered shelter to fix a cadaver for the stewpot, but it's the only convincing spot in the two-hour experience." Kevin Thomas was a wee bit kinder to me in the *Los Angeles Times:* "In an effective change of pace, Diane McBain, usually the hardened glamour girl, is Robert Fuller's staunch, and weathered wife."

Shortly before *Donner Pass* aired, I was cast in another snow-covered television production. *The Life and Times of Grizzly Adams* concerned a self-proclaimed mountain man, who lived in the woods with a full-grown grizzly bear. Dan Haggerty, a big bear of a man, was the star. The Christmas special, which also happened to be the television series' final episode, was called "Once upon a Starry Night." I played a woman reunited with her pioneer family by the assistance of Grizzly Adams and his bear, Ben, despite an array of obstacles.

Andrew was old enough to travel, so he accompanied me to Park City, Utah for location filming. We stayed in a fantastic, two-story condominium overlooking the majestic beauty of Utah. This was my son's first experience waking up to see snow outside our windows. I always loved seeing life anew through his innocent eyes.

My co-stars, Ken Curtis, Denver Pyle, and Don Galloway, were professional and pleasant. The sentimental story was something we all thought would please the television audience. All was not perfect on the job, though. Andrew loved playing in the snow. Unused to a movie set and all the trappings involved in movie making, he bounded into the craft services tent one day looking for a place to sit and take off his wet boots. There was a round metal heater in the middle of the tent that looked like a bench to my son. Before I could stop him, Andrew tried

With John Anderson in Donner Pass. PHOTO COLLECTION OF MICHAUD

to climb onto the heater by placing his hand on the hot surface. I felt his pain, probably more than he did. The blisters didn't slow him down one bit. He was too preoccupied with his new surroundings, and building snowmen.

When we returned to Los Angeles, I met up again with Janet, the woman who had installed my Gohonzon several years earlier. Janet was at loose ends. A single mother like me, she seemed determined to overcome her problems and make a life for herself and her young daughter, Mary. We found an enormous three-bedroom second-floor apartment on Sixth Street, just off Wilshire Boulevard. Comprised of a kitchen, laundry room, breakfast nook, dining room, two bathrooms, and a cavernous living room with a working fireplace, the apartment seemed more like a house. There was a goldfish pond in the back yard and plenty of room for our children to play. A good public school was nearby, too. With Janet and I both working, we could easily handle the rent.

Mary was a pretty, three-year-old when we moved in together. She was the daughter I never had. Andrew loved her like a little sister.

Our rambling apartment on Sixth Street became a salon for us and our friends. We had an enjoyable time. All sorts of creative types including artists, writers, actors, musicians, and quasi-intellectuals made their way through our welcoming doorway. Its central location in Los Angeles had loved ones stopping by almost every day to eat, drink, philosophize, and get high. I had some experience smoking pot before I moved in with Janet, when a friend would sometimes share a joint with me. Janet was an inveterate pot-smoker. In no time, we were all lighting up, pouring drinks, and sharing our liberal politics. What started out as a healing and relaxing respite soon became a little out of control and a bit reckless. Janet would travel to some of the most unsavory places in town to buy marijuana so we were never at a loss for a little toke.

In November, I was cast in an episode of *Charlie's Angels*. Produced at 20th Century-Fox Studios by Aaron Spelling, the show's primary ingredients were titillation and sex. The plot involved three libidinous female detectives played by Kate Jackson, Jacklyn Smith, and Cheryl Ladd. I played Marian in "Disco Angels," broadcast on January 31, 1979. I thought my appearance on this hit show would lead to more television work, but I was again mistaken.

Living with Janet added a bit of stability to my life. Our children shared a room and enjoyed each other's company. On a dare from Janet, I decided to quit smoking cigarettes. The decision to quit, something I had contemplated for years, was much tougher than quitting itself. During a particularly lucid moment, I had an epiphany about food, as well. One day we hosted a picnic in the backyard. Perhaps it was my nicotine-free vision, but that day I noticed the enticing colors of the fresh fruit and vegetables friends had brought. When Janet placed a platter of meat, a bit grey-colored after sitting in the refrigerator one too many days, I realized I no longer wanted dead meat in my body. I had begun to exercise for the first time in my life, and being cigarette-free, I was feeling quite healthy.

The new lifestyle seemed to clear my head, and it represented a "balanced" period in my life. I dated a few men, all unattached, although nothing serious ever developed. Work was almost non-existent, but I squeezed by on residuals and unemployment benefits for a while.

One day in early summer, I became reacquainted with Richard Donner, who had directed me in a commercial when I was sixteen years old. We had both gone on to bigger and better things. Donner achieved great success as the director of the hit films *The Omen* and *Superman*. He would later direct box office monsters, such as *Lethal Weapon* and *The Goonies*. He was a big bear of a man, who liked to have a good time. He had a loud voice and wasn't afraid to use it. He invited me to his house to meet Christopher Reeve, the star of *Superman*, who was flying into Los Angeles to begin a short stay at Donner's house.

"Come up and swim with us," Dick boomed into the phone, "we'll have a lot of fun!"

I thought Mary and Andrew would like to meet Superman, but honestly, it was my own interest in the very handsome Reeve that motivated me. The kids would be a perfect cover.

Dick's house was nestled in a hillside overlooking Beverly Hills. It was a hot and muggy day, so his swimming pool looked especially appealing. The children got into their bathing suits and joined us in the pool. Dick's other guests began to laugh before I realized what was the joke. I looked over to see my son clinging to a giant inflated — and erect — plastic penis. The testicles offered ballast to Andrew's weight. More shocking still was Mary's tiny hands clinging to a huge, floating red-nippled breast. Dick seemed to think it was riotously funny to see these innocent babes so blithely hanging on to the lewd inflatables.

Without making too much of a fuss, I gathered the children out of the pool.

"By the way, Di," Dick said, "Chris' plane is late. He won't be here until later this evening. We're having a party, and the kids may want to go home to bed."

He didn't have to tell me twice. "You know, Dick, that's a good idea. I'll come back later," I said. I was grateful for a gracious way out. This was no place for children.

Although the usual battle between Danny and Diane highlighted the reasons why I should or should not stay away from places like that, I couldn't resist going back. I left the children with Janet, who had planned to stay home that evening anyway.

By the time I returned to Donner's house, the company had changed dramatically. The house and yard were filled with groupies. They were drinking and smoking pot. Couples were intertwined in various stages of making-out. They were hanging over the banister, laying about the furniture, and rolling around the lawn. One young man followed me and tried to start up a conversation as I looked for Dick. *Sorry, buddy*, I thought, *my name is Lois Lane, and I'm waiting for Superman. You see, I have this assignment. I have to find out who he really is.*

Reeve's plane was further delayed and when he finally arrived, he came into the house with an entourage that included his girlfriend, Dana (later his adoring wife). They were exhausted, so she and several others went upstairs to sleep. Christopher stayed with us. Though it was well past my bedtime, I was too intrigued by this handsome young actor. Diane and Danny agreed. They were both equally curious about the real Christopher Reeve.

Within moments, recreational drugs were added into the mix. We'd all smoked a couple of joints earlier, but cocaine was suddenly being passed around. Pot was nothing new to me, and I had tried LSD before, but I stayed away from anything more serious than that. Janet liked to puff on her little pot pipe at home, so I'd been imbibing more often myself. Cocaine frightened me, though. However, Superman was sitting next to me. I felt safe, and I wasn't about to leave.

"I'm an actor, too," I stammered hoping to find some common ground. "A little before your time, but I had a bit of a career going there for a while."

"Wow, really?" he smiled.

"I liked you in *Superman*. You did a credible job."

"Thanks. I wish my father felt the same way."

"You mean he isn't enormously proud of you?"

"My father is an intellectual. He was okay with the idea that I might become an actor when I was in New York doing plays."

"You started out on Broadway with Katherine Hepburn, didn't you? Lucky."

"Yes, it was a good start and my dad seemed to be okay about it. But when I came out here it was different."

"He doesn't understand?"

"When I called him and told him I was going to play the part of Superman in a movie, he thought I was referring to *Man and Superman* by George Bernard Shaw."

"Richard Burton's favorite author," I mused.

"My father's too. No, he wasn't proud. He was pretty disappointed in me."

I felt sad for him. His father's opinion obviously weighed heavily on Christopher. We moved closer as we talked, sitting on the living room floor. The intimate revelation had pulled us together like magnets. We were both injured in our own way, on top of the world, me in my time and he in his, yet so unfulfilled. He was warm, affectionate, and very likable.

A mirror with thousands of dollars of cocaine carefully arranged in lines was handed to Christopher. Politely, he passed it on to me and said, "My father needs a little kryptonite for his brain. Maybe this would help."

The joke was silly, but my nerves got the best of me. I burst into laughter and blew all the cocaine into the tall, gorgeous movie star's lap. I was embarrassed and never so mortified in my life.

Christopher didn't seem to care about the cocaine and he instantly put me at ease. Dick, too, seemed amused by the wasteful accident. But I felt very out of my element, and very self-conscious. I didn't like myself very much because I had played games and compromised myself to suck up to Richard Donner. I didn't like "brown-noses" and didn't want to be one. I had never been a groupie, either. Whenever I was in danger of such behavior, Diane would emerge and stand guard with her icy façade. The specter of my babies hanging onto those pornographic pool toys was more than Danny's conscience could bear. I felt I had sunk to a new low. With no intention of drowning in a silly, meaningless state of affairs, I soon left the party.

In August, I was happy to go to Hawaii to appear in an episode of *Hawaii Five-O*, one of television's highest-rated police dramas. I was thrilled to see my good friends Robbie and Mary Muirhead, who were still catching rays on the white beaches of Waikiki. I brought Andrew with me, and we made a two-week holiday out of the trip.

One of Robbie's most intriguing friends was an older gay woman named Merle Kasten. I first met her on my previous trip to Hawaii. Merle owned a popular gay bar called the Cocktail Center on Waikiki. Robbie managed the establishment and tended bar. Merle had the bearing of a Chicago Crime Boss. I expected to see a cigar stuffed in her mouth, which was a description she heartily embraced.

With Paul Burke in Hawaii Five-O. PHOTO COLLECTION OF MICHAUD

Merle had a spectacular apartment in a high-rise overlooking the glimmering, glorious ocean. She kindly invited Andrew and me to stay there. My young son loved both Robbie and Merle, and lovingly called them "Aunt Robbie" and "Uncle Merle." They loved him, too. Merle harbored a romantic interest in me, which she had no trouble expressing. My dedicated attraction to men seemed to befuddle her, but she was an honest, funny, hard-working woman with a heart of gold. We forged a strong friendship, and along with Robbie, tore a pleasurable path through Honolulu while dancing, drinking, and laughing.

I was interviewed by Nancy Anderson for the *Tribune TV Week* on August 19, 1979. Anderson wrote, "Long-legged, tan and pretty in her light blue shorts and shirt, Diane McBain stepped off the *Hawaii Five-O* set, still looking very much like the girl who starred in *Surfside 6* nearly a generation ago. 'I'm playing a rather interesting character, which means

I'm now a character actress. But that suits me, because character work is usually the most interesting.'

"Yet she still looks like an ingénue. Slim and blonde, she's changed very little since she was Troy Donahue's leading lady and the star of youth oriented *Surfside 6*."

In the episode called "The Moroville Covenant," I guest-starred with Paul Burke. I portrayed a psychotic woman, who nearly destroyed her former high school boyfriend's political career. The star of the show, Jack Lord, proved to be another one of those egotistical males whose manners on the set needed some polish. Everyone handled him with kid gloves. The episode was directed by a journeyman director named Richard Morrison, who was actually the Director of Photography on the series. I guess they threw him a bone. The climactic scene was left to shoot on the last minute of the last day. Jack Lord's contract stipulated that he would not work past six o'clock in the afternoon, without exception. The last scene involved me and Lord. The difficult scene called for my character's mental illness to be exposed. At six o'clock sharp, Jack Lord turned his back to me and walked off the set without even saying goodbye! I was forced to shoot the scene with his stand-in, who had the acting skills of a head of lettuce. He just stood there, and gazed at me without blinking. I managed to get through the scene somehow, and Paul graciously thanked me. "You saved our show," he said, "you were wonderful." Words of praise from a fellow actor always meant more to me than what any critic had to say.

Chapter 23

To exist on the meager residuals that trickled into my mailbox was impossible. I had only one filmed acting role in nearly a year. My appearance on *Charlie's Angels* did absolutely nothing for me professionally. I enrolled in acting classes. I dieted, exercised, changed my attitude, and changed my attitude again. I tried to improve myself in any way I could think of. I tried to reinvent myself as an actress while pursuing the more ordinary roles of housewife or mother. At other times, I tried to take advantage of my looks. I had a face that defied "ordinary." It was almost a curse. I lacked the type of celebrity that opened doors to producers and casting agents, too. I was not famous enough. Danny was unconcerned, but Diane realized the package was flawed.

When unemployment benefits expired, I sought out temporary work through an agency. I worked in reception, as a secretary, and again as a bookkeeper. Janet and I had managed to keep our household together for a while. She began to sell art, but had a tough time collecting her commissions. In a short time, she began to unravel, too. Janet had never been very good with money, and her shortfall took a toll on me. When she couldn't pay her portion of the rent and expenses, I had to carry her. Our partying days were clearly over. We had basked in our wine-fueled salons and numbing pot smoke for long enough. I was pushing forty years old, and the time had come to straighten out and clear my head. To further complicate things, the building we lived in was sold to someone who wanted to move their family into our spacious unit.

At the time, we couldn't find anything that we could afford together. I was so preoccupied with my lack of work that a move didn't concern me (when such an upheaval clearly should have), and Janet was overwhelmed by change. She and her little daughter, Mary, moved to Sacramento to live with her mother.

Ralph Riskin had drifted in and out of my life several times. For a while, he worked as my agent. We were again dating when Janet and I had to move from our Sixth Street duplex. I had nowhere to go. I had no resources. Ralph suggested that I move in with him. He had a small but lovely house on Benedict Canyon with a kidney-shaped swimming pool in the backyard. Ralph didn't seem to be very interested in children, and he had always been awkward around Andrew. Still, we desperately needed to move, and he was kind to offer.

Ralph fascinated me. He was aloof, and I felt challenged by that. He was a busy television producer with several popular series to his credit, including *The Courtship of Eddie's Father*, *Bridget Loves Bernie*, and *Phyllis*. He was working diligently on a new series to be called *The Dukes of Hazzard*. His professional responsibilities made him slightly inaccessible. He was successful but nonplussed about his work load. I liked his lifestyle. We were sexually compatible. I thought he was a good match for me, and he was single.

I was able to enroll Andrew in the prestigious Warner Elementary School in nearby Holmby Hills. The school had a small enrollment and provided excellent hands-on attention from the teachers. I thought the learning environment would be perfect for my son.

Unfortunately, it didn't take very long to realize the living arrangement was awkward. My physical relationship with Ralph was satisfying, but he was emotionally absent. In a short time, he actually began to date another woman while I was still living with him! The biggest problem, however, was his inability to get along with my son. He teased him unmercifully. The teasing was mean-spirited and upset Andrew. In fact, Ralph would flat out make fun of him.

What started out for me as a serious romantic possibility soon turned sour. The entire episode was a crushing blow and utterly miserable. I was extremely unhappy by the way Ralph treated me and, more importantly, Andrew. Our move had been nothing but disruptive to my son, and now we had to find yet another place to live. This disappointing episode ushered in a dark period of despair for me.

John Brandt, who had designed my private wardrobe in the early days, lived in the upper unit of a duplex he managed on North Clark Drive near Beverly Hills. He offered me the downstairs unit. John lived alone and was flamboyantly gay. He wore long, flowing caftans around the house. He loved cats and practiced witchcraft. I liked John, though wondered what he was doing above us with his cats, candles, and magic potions. It was all a little creepy, but I smiled politely when he introduced me to his peculiar interests.

Very little sunshine blessed our downstairs windows, which gave an odd feeling of heaviness to the old building. The constant shadows were foreboding, and the place seemed a bit haunted. Nevertheless, John was a good person and he had stepped up to the plate when I was in need.

Our second move in six months was very tough on us, and cost money I simply didn't have. I was at my wit's end and became very disheartened. I questioned my own judgment and my attraction to a man who really didn't want me. I felt terribly guilty for dragging my son through that morass. I was incapable of holding down a normal job and I couldn't land a job in the only profession I really knew. I couldn't raise my son properly because I never had enough money. I was a terrible mother anyway, always distracted by auditions and trying to write screenplays that I never got around to selling. I should have given Andrew the full-time attention he needed and deserved. I tried to play the roles of mother and father since Rod was completely remiss in the latter. The situation was as confusing for me as it was for my son because my discipline was either "fatherly stern" or "motherly forgiving."

I convinced myself that Andrew would be better off if I were dead. Despondent, I decided I was not worthy of being alive.

I lost all reason. I convinced myself that I was doing this for the welfare of my son, but I now see my feelings of fear and despair propelled me in that far-fetched direction. I was the only parent Andrew had ever known, and despite my mistakes, I was a good parent. How selfish and reckless for me to consider suicide!

"I'm running away from home," I replied to Andrew's question. He'd sensed something was afoot. We were inching our way in my beat-up old Volvo toward the YMCA where Andrew was spending his summer days while I looked for work. The morning was oppressively hot, so we rolled the windows down. I was depressed beyond words — numb actually — except for feeling a heavy, anchor-like weight in the middle of my chest.

Andrew was more dear to me than I had ever imaged anyone could be. Because of my divorce, we were closer to each other. We were also pals. This was more for my comfort than his. I knew that at times I expected too much from such a young child. He went everywhere with me. We went to restaurants and movies, and he joined me on set, and usually on location, when I worked. Perhaps we were too close, and as a result, he may have sensed my dark moods. He seemed to know when something sinister was in the works.

The motor of a huge truck next to us had drowned out my voice. The perplexed expression on Andrew's face told me he couldn't hear. "Home," I said loudly, "I'm running away from home."

He slumped down in his seat. He'd heard me that time. I wondered what he was thinking.

"It'll be fun for you," I encouraged him. "You'll get to spend time with your daddy. He's going to pick you up today after you're through at the Y, and you'll get to stay at his house. Just think of all the 'guy' things you can do together," I said encouragingly.

Since the divorce, Rod had been less than attentive to Andrew. I would have let him take our son every weekend if he'd wanted to, but Rod only showed up sporadically. It irked me that he took such little interest in Andrew, and I wanted to encourage a more "father and son" relationship between them. I was playing the same role between them that my mother had played between my father and me. For years, Mom tried her best to bridge the gap between us. She worried that Dad and I would never be close. Until she passed away, we weren't. Our terrible loss forged a bond between us. Maybe that would work for my son and his father, I thought.

Andrew sank deeper into the bucket seat of the old Volvo. I was always amazed that the car still ran. I counted it one of the few miracles in my life. Andrew was a miracle, too. My only regret was that I wouldn't be able to watch him grow up and become a man. I would miss that, but I reasoned it was better to take myself out of the picture than destroy him, which seemed to me the most likely outcome if he remained with me. I didn't feel like a good parent.

The early morning traffic was especially heavy as we made our way to the Beverly Hills YMCA. The facility was close to the two-bedroom apartment we had moved to when Janet left. The new apartment was gloomy and thus matched the way I had come to feel about everything. Whenever my living circumstances were challenged, I would think about how foolish I had been to sell my house on Coldwater. That was the single stupidest thing I'd ever done.

Since the house sale, my choices in life hadn't gotten much better. Memories of all my failures crowded my mind, pushing out any hope or remembrance of the positive things that had happened along the way.

When we finally got to the Y, I took Andrew inside to meet his counselor. He had his bathing suit and his lunch. I handed his little suitcase to the counselor for safekeeping. Andrew hadn't spoken a word to me since I'd told him I was leaving home.

He trod slowly up the stairs, his little shoulders slumped and his head bowed as he stared blankly as his feet. At the time, I didn't grasp how dejected and abandoned he felt. "Your dad will pick you up after daycare," I called after him. "Don't worry. You'll be all right." Andrew didn't look back.

I had left a message and a note for Rod to pick up Andrew and to take care of him. Except for Nichiren Shoshu and his beloved Young Men's Division, he hadn't taken care of much. This would be good for *Rod*, too.

I drove north on Highway 101 through Santa Barbara, San Luis Obispo and past the imposing Hearst Castle in San Simeon. The winding road followed the rugged coastline and the ocean crashed against the shore to my left. I began to see around me some of the most beautiful terrain God had ever created. My thoughts, however, were far away from God. All I could think of were my countless failures. People had always told me to hang onto my dreams. If I did, I could soar like an eagle. At this point, all I had were failed dreams. Hope was gone. I felt mocked. *Look at you, you've had every opportunity, every talent, every power given to you and you squandered it all. You have come to nothing!*

If life was a string of failures, then I wanted no further part of it. I'd heard there were people who were born losers. If I was one, I would rather do away with myself than endure endless failures. All I wanted was for the sharp pain of constant rejection to go away.

I watched the terrain became greener and more lush as I drove northward by Redwood groves. There was something peaceful and soothing about this spectacular countryside. I was taken by the towering giants that reached heavenward. I knew that these trees, the oldest living things on earth, had endured draught, flood, and fire. Their determination to live was almost palpable. I felt my thoughts changing. They began to drift to happier, more uplifting memories. My successes were harder to recall, but almost imperceptibly at first, a comforting small voice made its case known. Slowly, one after another of my "good times" crept back into my mind. A moment or two of positive speculation about the future even managed to peak its head above my sorrowing heart. As my decrepit old car coughed its way closer to the majestic cliffs I was so eagerly anticipating, I felt a sense of hope rising in me. Maybe I *could* write screenplays. Maybe I could write a novel and get it published. I had artistic talents that could be developed. If I applied myself more diligently and relied solely upon myself, maybe I could achieve my goals.

I got to the edge of the cliff. Giant blue waves peaked and crashed into white foam over the immense, ragged-edged boulders below. This was the cliff and below it, the cold stones, that could quiet my roiling, regretful memories.

I don't know how long I listened to the sea and stared at the crashing waves. However, at some point, I felt a great weight lift itself from my shoulders and I decided I would rather live than die. I realized that suicide was not a remedy, but a selfish and cowardly act. I backed the car away from the cliff, and drove home.

Perhaps I needed to redefine what success means, I thought, as I drove. *Instead of looking for fame and material things, maybe I should be looking for an "inner" significance. I need to be like the towering Redwood trees that surrounded me. Instead of indulging in self-pity, I need their strength and endurance to find creative solutions that I could apply to my life. I need to be a better mother to my child, and I needed to be more attentive to his needs. This may be the only way to regain any self-confidence.* At last, I was listening.

I believe that God was with me.

With my son.

Chapter 24

With an old standard typewriter and a bottle of Liquid Paper to correct my many typos, I began to write. It wasn't the most practical endeavor for me because I couldn't type very well, but I kept hammering out stories and writing treatments for television shows and feature films. I also began to write a novel using my personal life as fodder for the story. With memories of my Sixth Grade teacher, Mr. Edgar, I began to trust my writing abilities. I never forgot how powerfully he responded to a little story I had written. My confidence began to build with that recollection.

In June 1980, I played the role of Sylvia Crewes in *The Tender Trap* at the Fiesta Dinner Theatre in Spring Valley, California. The tried and true comedy, written by Max Shulman and Robert Paul Smith, chronicled the romantic misadventures of a confirmed Manhattan bachelor. There was no star treatment for me. All of the actors were billed in alphabetical order. On June 19, Christopher Schneider reviewed the show for the local paper. About me, he wrote, "Diane McBain is humorous and deeply sympathetic in this role." I don't know how anybody found us, so far outside San Diego. We were stuck there in the verdant hills for a month, but I managed to have some fun with my cast mates.

I had a pleasant infatuation with my leading man, actor Dale Reynolds. He was cute and funny. Naturally, he was gay. Dale, who became a good friend, was the only working actor I knew at that time who was actually "out." He founded a support group called the Alliance for Gay and Lesbian Artists. They promoted a balanced portrayal of homosexuals in movies and television. I'm sure he lost roles due to his outspoken advocacy of gay and lesbian actors' rights. I admired his bravery and commitment and whole-heartedly supported his honorable and much-needed efforts.

Later that year, Hollywood smiled upon me and I landed a return guest shot on *Charlie's Angels*. "Angel on the Line" aired a few months later on Valentine's Day in 1981. I also worked on *Eight is Enough*. The story about a widower raising his eight children was a popular program on ABC. I played the part of an older woman dating the eldest son, played by the incredibly handsome Grant Goodeve. "Yet Another Seven Days in February" aired on April 4. I enjoyed my time on the sets very much. Both working environments were professional, personable, and pleasant. The money came at the right time, and the work gave my sagging confidence a bit of a boost.

I reconnected with my friend, actress Deborah Walley, with whom I'd worked on the Elvis film, *Spinout*. Deborah was a single mother of two boys. Tony was a teenager, and Justin was about the same age as Andrew. Like my own, her successful film career had petered out and acting roles were sporadic at best. She lived in a little country house by Malibu Lake in the westernmost section of the San Fernando Valley. She had fallen in love with the bucolic spot when we worked there on location for *Spinout*. Her lovely house and rustic surroundings were a wonderful respite from the "city static" of Los Angeles. We spent many weekends philosophizing, drinking wine, and smoking pot.

She was writing, too. She wrote mostly for children, and her books and plays were wonderful and very inspirational to me. She adored her two sons and loved animals. She was happy and grounded. We took long walks together in the woods near her home. One day, we were talking and I was grumbling about one thing or another. Deborah turned to me and said, "But Diane, you are an adult now." Her simple yet profound statement took me by surprise. I had to stop and think. Actually, I felt like a little girl in her company, like a child who had yet to mature, and at that moment, I felt like a little girl who "hadn't a clue." She brought me to my senses with that simple, uncontestable statement.

Technically, she was savvy. She was one of the first people I knew who worked on a word processor rather than a common typewriter. She gave me the courage to try it myself.

Our weekends together and many hours of conversation led to a business arrangement. Deborah had written a full-length feature film about a family of endangered blue whales and their struggle to survive titled, *Last of the Blues*. We decided to raise money to produce what Deborah envisioned as an animated musical movie. Along with her friend, a skilled performance artist named James Green, we founded Pied Piper Productions, a non-profit corporation. Famed architect R. Buckminster Fuller joined our Board of Directors in 1980. With a lovely endorsement from Tom Bradley, then the Mayor of Los Angeles, we created live theatre for youth groups around Southern California.

Our first production, *Tales of the Pied Piper*, was underwritten in part by Paramount Studios in order to promote their upcoming film, *Popeye*. We visited all of the Robinson's department stores in the area and performed our forty-minute show to crowds of enthusiastic kids. Paramount provided free tickets to a private screening of *Popeye*, a give-away of Popeye-themed toys, and a free breakfast for all the children who saw our performance.

We then toured elementary schools in the Los Angeles, Conejo, and Las Virgenes unified school districts. Because public schools did not provide the funds to pay our token honorariums, our performances were usually underwritten by local merchants. Performing for so many children was meaningful and gratifying. One letter from a fourth-grade student named Kim, at Warner Avenue Elementary School in Los Angeles, provided us with one of our most cherished reviews: "Dear Pied Piper Players, I think you did a great job. This was the best play I ever saw in my life. I hope it comes again. I think my brother would even like this play. HE IS NOT A PLAY FAN."

To raise additional funds, Deborah taught acting lessons for kids. However, with all our efforts, we didn't earn enough to pay ourselves anything, let alone raise money to produce a motion picture.

Deborah had a wonderful circle of creative friends. Vera was an artist who created our backdrops. She became a devoted friend of mine, and smoothed the way for me toward a broader understanding of life. As I got to know her better, she told me she was an atheist. This surprised me because she seemed so spiritual. Later she told me she was a lesbian. Vera added new dimensions to my thinking with this particular disclosure, and in other ways, too.

I didn't know very much about homosexual women. There were times, though, when I felt envious of their relationships. Two women together somehow seemed a much easier blend than that of a man and a woman. I surmised since they were more alike they would be better able to understand each other. I learned that this was not true. The dynamics of a gay relationship are not dissimilar to those of a heterosexual relationship. The same problems, challenges, and issues exist. Vera is a fascinating woman and a good friend.

Andrew and Deborah's young son, Justin, became chums. One day, I was taking an appointment and Andrew stayed behind to play with Justin. Justin had just gotten a pet baby mouse. The boys were playing together, and at some point the excitement level increased. Justin's screams brought Deborah and Vera to his bedroom door. Andrew had gotten too eager in their horseplay and had thrown the mouse across the room and against a wall. The mouse died. Justin was devastated and Deborah was livid. Vera tried to explain away the accident, but the horrible deed had been done. For a long time, Andrew was "persona non grata" at Deborah's house. I wasn't sure what to make of the incident, but it scared me that my young son could be so careless with a live creature.

Chapter 25

Andrew was usually quite hyperactive, running here and there trying to make sense out of his world. Our unconventional family situation was difficult for him, and my unreliable occupation didn't help matters. In addition, I was often overwhelmed by the demands of parenting. I took Andrew with me when I starred as Amanda in a production of Tennessee Williams' *The Glass Menagerie* for the California Repertory Theater in Pacific Grove, California in the fall of 1980. The three-month-long engagement was too much for Andrew, who was lonely and out of his element. I could not pay enough attention to him, memorize the intense script, and rehearse, so I put him on a twelve-hour Greyhound bus ride to go to my father and his wife in San Diego for a while. Sending him off without a chaperone was torturous for me, but I didn't know what else to do.

With Paul Laramore in The Glass Menagerie.

I reflected that everything we did seemed a bit out of the ordinary. Life was tough for me, and I can only imagine how perplexing it was for him, though I tried very hard to make the best of our situation. He didn't seem to have the normal controls on his behavior that other boys had, but since he was lively and very smart, I excused the hyperactivity as part of his intelligence.

To add to the strangeness of our new surroundings on North Clark Drive, the building next door was abandoned and looked a little like a black hole outside Andrew's bedroom window. At night, he would become frightened, run into my room, and climb into bed with me.

"There are monsters living there, Mommy," he whispered as he cuddled in my arms. I tried to calm his fears. He seemed to buy into my explanation that there were no monsters and the big empty rooms were just cold and creaky. Then, the next night, he'd be right back in my bed with the same fears.

"Mommy! Mommy!" I pounded away at the typewriter when Andrew's panicked voice alarmed me. He flew into the room and yelled, "Mommy, it's a fire! The house next door!"

I ran out of our apartment to find the garage at the rear of the abandoned building ablaze. The eucalyptus trees between the two buildings began to ignite.

Soon, fire engines crowded into the street and firefighters quickly extinguished the flames. The garage was gutted and acrid smoke filled the air. People in the neighborhood had gathered, and Andrew's mood seemed filled with elation.

We tried to settle down after the commotion, but Andrew was exhilarated. "Wow," he gushed, "that was close, wasn't it Mommy?" The fire was much *too* close, and any further delay could have ended with our own building burning. "I'd like very much for that *never* to happen again," I announced.

As usual, I brought candles to our dinner table. Andrew was still very excited. The fire seemed to have an effect on him, though it wasn't exactly fear. He told me he wanted to light the candles. I had always resisted his requests in the past. He had seemed too young to me to be handling matches, but now seemed the time to teach him how to use a match. I showed him how to cover the matchbook before striking the match, just as my parents had taught me. He finally got the hang of it, and then I lectured him about fire safety, using the fire next door as an example of what can go wrong. He seemed to listen, and I thought the experience had a positive effect on him.

A couple of days later, Andrew tore into the apartment again screaming, "Mommy! Mommy! There's another fire! This time it's *inside* the house!" I called the fire department, and again Andrew was elated by all the anxious activity.

The fire chief approached me and said he thought a vagabond was living in the abandoned building. He had likely started the fire. They found sticks of denuded marijuana and some clothing left behind. The explanation seemed logical, and Andrew had been complaining for weeks that the building was haunted or full of monsters. He must have heard the intruder and been frightened.

However, after two more fires in the space of less than two weeks, the arson squad asked if they could talk with Andrew who may have seen something or someone. I watched as Andrew was escorted back to the burned out garage. The tall investigator talked with him for a few minutes and then they walked back down the driveway to me. A police officer took Andrew's hand and the investigator took me aside.

"Miss McBain, I've talked to your son and he tells me that he saw a black man with blue eyes start the fire in the garage. It was some distance away and he couldn't tell me how he could see the man had blue eyes. And, of course, black men generally don't have blue eyes."

I braced myself for what must be coming next.

"The fire that was set today was started by someone sitting inside the closet. It was someone who didn't realize that you need to have a way to escape after you set a fire. Miss McBain, he's lucky he got out alive." I couldn't believe what I heard. "Oh, no… he could barely light a match at the dinner table. Are you sure?"

"We're sure. He used a Bic lighter."

"Oh, my God."

"Miss McBain, your son is far too young to arrest and charge with arson, but may we suggest that you take him to get some therapy. We really can't waste taxpayers' money keeping your son entertained with our daily arrivals."

I was embarrassed beyond words. "Of course not. I don't really have the resources to get help. What can I do?"

"We'll set you up with a community center affiliated with the Thalians nearby. They are associated with Cedars-Sinai Medical Center, and they'll give you the therapy you and your son need."

"My son *and* me?" I asked.

I had no choice but to agree. In the past, I had participated in fundraising events for the Thalians. Supported by show-business folks, the facility provides health care to those in the community who cannot afford services. The therapists focus on the family dynamic that affects attitude and behavior.

The counselor studied Andrew's drawings, which were filled with fire, red and yellow rockets, guns and bombs exploding, and havoc all over the page. With guidance, I soon realized that my earlier effort to end my life was at the bottom of Andrew's "fiery" mood. One night, we sat on his bed and talked about that day when I foolishly told him I was running away from home.

"I thought you were running away from me," he said sadly.

"Oh, no," I said, overcome with guilt. "That was the last thing on my mind. I was trying to make things better for you. I thought if I stepped out of your life you'd be better off." As I said the words, I realized how confusing they must have sounded to a little boy.

"You said you were running away from home," he said. "Aren't *I* home?"

Mortified, I could have just crawled into a hole. "Of course you are. And I love you more than anything and everything else in the world."

"Promise you won't run away again?"

"I promise. You don't ever have to worry about that again."

I was always reluctant to make promises because they are sometimes impossible to keep. Anything can happen to cause the sincerest assurances to go awry. I resolved to keep this promise, though. It was far too important to break, and I had come to realize that I didn't want to die no matter how bad things got. I certainly didn't want to leave my son behind as Rod was ill-prepared to nurture a child. *I* had to be there for him.

The fires had spooked my upstairs friend, as well. John was no longer comfortable with our living arrangement. It was curious to me that a man who practiced witchcraft could be so unnerved by the goings-on. Nevertheless, I understood, and shared his concerns. Our fears became a moot point, however, when the owner of the building notified us both that the property had been sold and we all had to move.

In my wildest dreams, I never thought that I would not have remarried by this time. Andrew was a hyperactive eight-year-old. His boundless energy may have kept suitors away. Most of the men I dated did not have children, and they didn't want to become too involved with a woman who had a rambunctious little boy. Andrew came first, and the men didn't last.

Though I was earnest about my writing pursuit, it seemed to be going nowhere fast. I finished several film treatments and screenplays and sent them on (with expensive baskets of goodies) to literary agents. The response was courteous, but no sales. Trying to find my place in show business and locate a new place to live and raise a child was daunting. I felt like I was pushing an enormous rock up a steep mountainside.

I finally found a two-bedroom apartment in West Hollywood near a busy intersection. The upstairs unit was cozy and had a porch that faced several fast food joints on Santa Monica Boulevard.

The landlady could be kindly described as a battleaxe. "How will you pay for the apartment?" she asked with a scowl on her face and her hands firmly planted on her hips. I lied. I told her I worked for Deborah Walley's production company, Pied Piper. I told her I was on the staff, but I didn't tell her I wasn't paid a salary.

Then she asked a strange question. "Do you think you will feel safe here?" As she spoke, she looked out the window at the nearby food stands. "Is there a reason I would not be safe?" I asked. I was already nervous since I was under the gun to find a place to live.

The woman's face was something to behold. I don't like myself when I am critical of people's looks, but there is an old saying, "When we are five, we have the face God gave us. When we are fifty, we have the face we deserve." Her face indicated a difficult, strained existence. She was shrill and appeared to be miserly. Though she was smaller than I was, she looked down her nose. All of my old prejudices came roaring to the surface. I had never believed in prejudging people based on race, religion, looks, sexual preference, or any of the various prejudices humans are prone to. I have always thought that intolerance is a condition of the culture or maybe even a product of human nature. I chose to discriminate against any discriminating thoughts I might be having. This was a lesson I wanted to teach my son.

I thought my cause was lost, but she offered me the apartment for $450 per month. I scraped together the security deposit and Andrew and I moved in on June 22, 1981. My friends helped us move, and managed to break, bruise, or scrape almost everything I owned. As soon as we began to settle in, I noticed many needed repairs to windows, cabinet doors, and drawers. The landlady ignored my requests until I finally gave up and hired someone to do the necessary work.

Because the apartment was small, I had to sell the things that simply didn't fit. I had a garage sale and regretfully sold family heirlooms for nickels and dimes. A woman talked me out of a box of costume jewelry for so little money I cried. I was heartbroken later when I realized the box had contained items belonging to my deceased grandmother. It wasn't the money so much; my surroundings and those things which fill my home profoundly affect my mood. The sale forced me to adjust my "sense of beauty" to accommodate my diminishing resources.

What was important was hanging on to the few things that were left. I acquired a taste for simplicity. Our little apartment came together in a way that was both pleasing to the senses and practical for a single mother with an overactive child. My creative skills came in handy. As Scarlett O'Hara had made a dress from her drapes, I did the opposite and made curtains from some of my old skirts in the closet.

For a finishing touch in our new home, Andrew, whose scavenging techniques were superlative, found a wooden sign with a picture of an adorable, disheveled little boy on it that read "Be gentle. God isn't finished with me yet." He proudly hung the sign above his bedroom door, and I endeavored to heed its warning.

Adjusting to our new surroundings took some time. Unlike other parts of the city where I had lived, a large number of homeless people sought shelter in the alleys beneath my apartment windows. In addition, the fast food stand nearby was open twenty-four hours a day. Many people congregated there after the local bars closed at two every morning. They would sit on picnic tables eating, chatting, and listening to the noise blasting from a radio inside the establishment. The proximity of the stand and the acoustics gave the impression that a party was going on outside our bedroom windows into the wee hours. I tried to complain to the employees of the food stand to no avail. I wrote letters of complaint to the owners. These, too, were ignored. One day, though, I had a brainstorm.

Years earlier, when I was under contract, I received some unsettling fan letters from obviously disturbed people. Fortunately, the studio filtered my mail. I did see a few letters that included stream of consciousness writings and peculiar drawings. Some contained veiled threats directed at me. I wondered what kind of mind could produce such works of madness.

Apparently, my kind of mind.

I wrote a similarly nonsensical but threatening letter to the food stand owner. I stated I was a neighbor and I had a shotgun. I wrote that, in the middle of the night, I often aimed it at their business because I could hear "rantings of the devil" coming from their blaring radio. I warned, if the noise didn't stop, I would have to use the gun. Not surprisingly, the late night, blaring radio music stopped.

Chapter 26

Andrew and I endured the therapy sessions for the next year. After the sessions ended, I anxiously watched Andrew's artwork for any signs of potential trouble. His fierce, fire-filled drawings continued, though, for many years after the therapy. I often lay awake at night wondering if the remedial treatment had really helped him, or if we would awaken one night engulfed in flames.

Therapy can produce moments of revelation and moments of oppressive despair. I was astonished to learn that children commonly play with fire. More than half of the children who set fires are between the ages of four and nine.

Of course, my primary question was why do children play with something as potentially deadly as fire? Deliberate fire setting is often linked to risk-taking, or individual or family pathology. The therapist initially assured me that although fire-play is a serious issue and warrants a psychological evaluation, typically, the dangerous action is not a sign of a deeper emotional problem. I was shocked to learn that I should not have been so willing to teach Andrew how to handle a match. I learned that children who were taught how to light candles, and tend a fireplace and autumn bonfires were actually *more* likely to play with fire.

Andrew's case was more deeply rooted. Beyond the issue of cognitive understanding, children's involvement with fire is related to family and socioeconomic factors. National studies at that time concluded that between 58 percent and 80 percent of children who started fires lived in broken homes with a single parent, and half of these children lived in families with less than $10,000 annual income. We seemed to fit the classic case.

Andrew lived with a single mother who usually struggled to pay the bills. He was hyperactive and did struggle to control his impulses at times. When I did work, I was away from him, and facing our problem was heartbreaking. Even more painful for me was to consider my shortcomings as a parent and my "complicity." My son had special challenges that I wasn't sure I could meet. As a single mother, I was ill-equipped to be all that Andrew needed.

Another result of our time with the therapist was Andrew's diagnosis of Attention-Deficit/Hyperactivity Disorder (ADHD). This chronic condition affects millions of children and has a combination of problems including a difficulty sustaining attention, impulsive behavior, and hyperactivity. Such children may also suffer from low self-esteem, have trouble with relationships, and perform poorly in school. In worse cases, a child can suffer anxiety disorder or depression. The therapist told us that various forms of treatment, including therapy and sometimes drugs, can help with symptoms, but won't cure the condition. We were assured, though, that most children with ADHD grow up to be "normal" adults. Andrew's ADHD manifested itself in the forms of an incessant tic and reading problems.

His condition explained many things. He was bright, curious, and had good comprehension, but he struggled with the disciplines of school and lessons. He had been hyperactive since he was a little boy. It was difficult for him to sustain a level of attention to certain tasks, and even at play.

I was not surprised by the diagnosis, though at first I didn't fully understand the nature of the affliction. I felt responsible, but was told this was most likely the result of a genetic disposition rather than external causation. I immediately referenced Rod's mother and wondered if any of her mental illness had been passed down to her grandson. I appreciated the clarification of something that I myself had recognized but couldn't properly identify. I was disheartened to learn that the condition, though treatable, was incurable. I was saddened by the many problems my little boy might have to deal with in his life.

As much as I was learning about my son during our therapy sessions, I was learning more about myself. The near tragedy of a fatal fire had forced me to confront our ghosts and demons. We weren't always anxious for our next appointment, but we never missed a scheduled session, and I felt appreciable relief when I began to see the forest through the trees.

Since I was squeaking by on residuals, I was especially annoyed to learn that I was in a movie titled *Legend of the Wild*, released in November 1981 by Sunn Classic Pictures. The film was edited from clips of previous episodes from the television series *Grizzly Adams*, including "Once Upon a Starry Night" that I had filmed in December 1978. I was not paid for my appearance in this patchwork movie narrated by Denver Pyle.

That fall, I landed a small role on the hit prime-time soap, *Dallas*. I was hired to play Dee Dee Webster, a friend of the female lead played by Linda Gray. Though the part was small, my agent told me it could evolve into a recurring role. I was encouraged and happy to work with Linda, Larry Hagman, Victoria Principal, and Patrick Duffy, whom I had known from my Nichiren Shoshu days. Sadly, I filmed only two episodes, which aired in January 1982.

In March, I was asked to do a play at the Cast Theatre in Hollywood. The rickety, little equity-waver theater was a popular try-out spot for local playwrights. A very handsome young man named Drake Hogestyn was cast to play opposite me. Drake was a former ball player, and just beginning to test the acting waters in Los Angeles. I became infatuated with him; though he was twelve years my junior and had a steady girlfriend he would eventually marry. Drake would later become a heartthrob on the soap opera, *Days of Our Lives*. Apparently, my unrequited infatuation was not humiliating enough. During rehearsals, the writer and director took a dislike to me and I was fired before the play ever opened. Later, I was told by the casting director that the writer was jealous of my intentions toward Drake. Apparently, he was infatuated with the handsome young man, too.

I hadn't appeared in a feature film in nearly eight years, nor were any television roles being offered, so I accepted a local theater engagement. *Who's Happy Now?*, written by Oliver Hailey, was originally produced in 1967. Hailey's television writing credits included *Mary Hartman, Mary Hartman* and *Love, Sidney*, the first series whose lead character was gay. Best described as a "black comedy," *Who's Happy Now?* depicted the foibles of a family in a small Southwest town. I was cast as the mother. We had a successful, month-long run at the Gene Dynarski Theater on Sunset Boulevard in Hollywood. The *Los Angeles Times* wrote, "Diane McBain, whose career was launched in local theater, returns to the stage in a sensitive performance as the mother who maintains an uneasy truce between her embittered husband and young son. She has matured gracefully and her performance is marked by intelligence."

I was then cast in an episode of *Matt Houston*, another series produced by Aaron Spelling for ABC. The one-hour crime drama was filmed on the Warner lot. I had a painfully small role in "The Rock and the Hard

Place," which concerned the investigation of a rigged professional fight. Interestingly, George Takei also appeared in the episode. I had worked with him twenty-three years earlier on *Ice Palace* on the same lot. It was a bittersweet moment for me. The years since our contract days at Warner Bros. had been such a challenge for me, but George enjoyed enviable success with his years on *Star Trek*.

One day in early 1982, my father felt a sharp pain and his wife took him to the hospital. He had suffered from heart disease for a short time. The doctor misdiagnosed the pain as being the result of his ulcer and sent him home. A day later, Dad had a heart attack in his yard while he was trimming the hedge. He fell into a coma and was placed on life-support. The move to a medical facility more suited to treating him was too risky. His wife Isabel called me and together we consulted with the doctors. They felt my father would not recover from the incident. After careful and painful consideration, Isabel and I decided to take my father off life-support. I went into his room and spoke to him. I told him I was sorry for not being a better daughter and sorry for not being the son he really wanted. He died within hours. My father was sixty-nine years old.

This was one of the hardest decisions I had ever made, yet another life and death choice with someone else's life. I was comforted in being able to make this fateful choice with Isabel. We both knew my father did not want to remain alive with only the aid of machines, but deciding the time has come for a person to die affected me profoundly. Now and then, I think about that decision and wonder if we made the correct choice. I think we did. I believe honoring his wish was the humane and compassionate thing to do.

Chapter 27

In the fall of 1982, I landed a part on an NBC daytime drama called *Days of Our Lives*. The steady employment afforded by appearing in a soap opera was very desirable. Accordingly, the goal of a soap opera actor was to negotiate a three-year contract. Unfortunately, I was hired as a day-player, which provided me with no job security. Nevertheless, I was thankful for the job. I had actually watched *Days of Our Lives*, so it was fun to step into the fictional city of Salem and play Foxy Humdinger, a manipulating madam with the proverbial heart of gold. I liked the schedule, which necessitated fast-paced work and pressure to get the work done correctly in one take.

Acting on a soap opera was a completely different type of effort for me. Besides the pressure to tape in a timely manner, there was little time to rehearse and less time to try to create an interesting character. I kept telling myself I was earning a paycheck as an actress, but I couldn't help feeling like I was working in a factory where quantity mattered more than quality. My first day on the job was an eye-opener. My wardrobe was culled from racks in the wardrobe department. I got the leftovers. This was very different from my days working with costume designers at Warner Bros. I felt as recycled and dull as the clothes being tossed at me on the set.

I cried myself to sleep many nights as I assessed my situation. In my early forties, I was a show business has-been, and a divorcee after only a year and half of marriage. I was unable to hold down a regular job that might allow me to create a future for my son. At times like that, the accomplishments of my life were difficult to see. When I found myself indulging in useless self-pity, I always tried to counteract the feeling by considering the job opportunity that had come my way. I was determined to make the character of Foxy work for me.

Playing Foxy was fun, though confusing at times. There are a number of writers working to produce the daily scripts for a soap opera. In the case of my character, the writers had a general idea of the story outlines, but sometimes had a different take on these minor characters played by day-players. Therefore, there were no consistent character traits for me to draw upon when portraying the role. Some writers wanted my kind-hearted character to be a bit of a threat to a married couple on the show, and some wanted Foxy to be a cold, manipulating bitch, who would be exposed in good time. I preferred the first characterization. Naturally, the producers preferred the second. I never knew which Foxy I was expected to play each day I worked. I was reeling from the schizophrenic machinations of her undecided upon personality.

One day, we were rehearsing a scene in a hospital room. One of the long-time leading men on the show was dressed in a hospital gown and lying in a bed. He was supposed to be sick, though his makeup was applied perfectly and his hair and gown in pristine arrangement. The actor, whose dimples looked like buttons in an overstuffed pillow, smiled at me. The script called for my character to walk into his room in tears. A teary-eyed Foxy seemed a bit disingenuous to me. She was a tough broad who wouldn't weep, but would instead provide a big shoulder for someone else to cry upon. Nevertheless, this was not the place for someone in my tenuous position to approach the director regarding disagreements about the script or characterization! I was expected to play the part as written on the page. There was no time to discuss or improvise.

When the stage manager called "Action," I was cued to make my rehearsal entrance. Wanting to break the tension and bring a little levity to the situation, I exaggerated a "boo hoo," a dry cry that was supposed to elicit a laugh.

"You aren't going to do it like that, are you?" the director's voice boomed over the intercom.

"It was supposed to be funny," I offered. I was trying to convey the need to have the emotional freedom to cry, to laugh, and to do whatever would viscerally emerge. Without that freedom, I was doomed to a phony portrayal of tears, but I didn't say that. Thinking fast on my feet while slow-witted Diane was in control was always problematic. Had Danny been in charge she might have said something like, "Can I help it if no one here has a sense of humor?" Instead, I froze. I wanted to sink through the floor.

"You aren't going to do it like that, are you?" the voice repeated loudly.

Instead of speaking up, I stood there in stunned silence. While Diane was embarrassed, Danny was rolling her eyes.

I was dealing with unseen directors and producers, whose voices boomed out of the darkness. However, I stuck to my guns. Foxy did not cry in the scene. When I saw the episode weeks later on television, I decided my choice was correct.

In a short time, Foxy Humdinger became an audience favorite. I began to receive fan mail again. There was no studio publicity department to handle things, so the mail and fan requests were directed to me. Fans purchased photographs of me from memorabilia shops and sent them to me to sign.

My earlier decision to bare all for *Playboy* magazine caught up with me in just the way I feared. Though the photographs were never supposed to be released, prints somehow began to float around in public. One day, Andrew retrieved the mail. He opened a large envelope from a fan, which he had never done before, and pulled out a color photo of his nude mother before I could stop him. I nearly fainted. I grabbed the photograph, ran into my bedroom, and tore it into tiny pieces.

"Mom!" he clamored, "why did you do that? It was beautiful!"

"Beautiful?" I was stunned by his comment. "That's not supposed to be beautiful to you!"

"You were beautiful then, Mom."

I melted. His innocent assessment of the nude picture made me smile. "Maybe you didn't see it the way I did," I replied.

Things seemed to be looking up. With a regular paycheck coming in, I was able to catch up with our bills and begin to feel more relaxed about the future. In November 1982, I traveled to England for a couple of weeks to visit a dear friend of mine from my Buddhist days. Barbara Wagner Joce had married an Englishman, moved to Britain and started a family. They lived in the countryside of Berkshire, near Windsor Castle. My trip was beautiful and memorable. We went into London a few times for sightseeing and shopping.

The most interesting part of my visit was a weekend side trip I made to Scotland. I felt the need to see the land of my ancestors. I was making the journey as much for my deceased parents as I was for myself. Since my father's death, and with no immediate family remaining, I felt a bit like an orphan. Exploring my family history had been in the back of my mind. My mother's family, named Ferguson, had roots in Scotland, and my father was a McBain.

What little I knew about the McBain clan was intriguing. They were from fabled Loch Ness and they were sheep thieves! I perused quaint little shops in search of my family tartans. A tartan is a particular plaid pattern associated with a certain Scottish clan. Kilts, scarves, ties, and blankets usually bore the pattern. I found a scarf with the Ferguson tartan, which I purchased. I could not find anything with the McBain tartan, however.

On my way back from Scotland, I sat next to a lovely, tidy gentleman on the train. We had a conversation about my sojourn, and he said he knew a woman in Dundee by the name of McBain! I gave him my contact information, and after I returned to California, Helen McBain contacted me and kindly sent me a gentleman's tie with the distinctive McBain tartan. We determined she was a distant relative! I spoke to her on the phone once, but with her heavy Scottish brogue, I couldn't understand a thing the dear woman said. We corresponded for several years until her death.

My appearances on *Days of Our Lives* attracted the attention of the media, and I was sought out for fan-magazine interviews. Soap operas had large, devoted audiences. My guest-starring episode of *Matt Houston* was scheduled to air on January 2, 1983. Having some money made a big difference in the way I felt about my life. I was working as an actress and earning enough money to make our life livable. Andrew and I looked forward to Christmas and the future.

Chapter 28

The headlines were withering. "Actress attacked on Christmas Day," trumpeted the *Los Angeles Herald Examiner* on December 29, 1982. Reporter Patricia Klein wrote, "McBain, an actress known for guest appearances on such television shows as *Dallas* and for earlier television and movie roles as a femme fatale, was raped and beaten in the garage of her West Hollywood apartment early Christmas morning...."

Funny things run through your mind during times of great distress or trauma. My father had died earlier in the year, and all I could think about was how glad I was that he wasn't here to deal with my attack. My physical injuries made me almost unrecognizable. For a time, I thought I would never look the same again. However, the ugly wounds healed and I was able to return to work on *Days of Our Lives* with the help of their wonderful makeup woman.

My two attackers were strangers. In a way, this made the ordeal easier to digest. I felt no guilt, as some women do after being raped. I was not at fault. I went public with my plight because I felt strongly that women were sometimes complicit in their victimization. This happens when they believe they cannot talk about the rape with friends, family, or the community. Hiding in shame only prolongs the delicate healing process.

I spoke up, publicly. Some people were uncomfortable around me, some were concerned and helpful, and some — remarkably — didn't believe the attack had happened at all. One day not long after the rape, a neighbor cornered me in the driveway. He put his arm around my waist and leaned into my ear. "You can tell me," he whispered. "It was fun, wasn't it?" Then he giggled.

Astonished, I pulled away from him and shouted loudly, "No, it was *not* fun!" His wife was standing nearby, and I hoped my other neighbors were listening too.

I went on a crusade to dispel the myths surrounding the act of rape. I wanted to help other women, but I also wanted to help myself — to deal with the rage I felt toward my two attackers. My agent tried to dissuade me and asked me to think carefully about my determination to go public in such a big way. These sensitive issues, he warned, could backfire and adversely affect my career. I didn't care. Because of the therapy I received at the Rape Trauma Center at Cedars-Sinai Medical Center, my survival instincts were fortified. I rejected the idea that I was complicit in any way. I was not a "victim" nor was it my fate to simply be in the wrong place at

Talking about my attack with Gary Collins on the syndicated talk show, Hour Magazine, *in January, 1983.* PHOTO COLLECTION OF MICHAUD

the wrong time. I was viciously and brutally attacked by two dangerous criminals. I wanted to show women that they could *survive* rape. If we can survive rape, we can survive anything! I spoke freely on television talk shows, radio call-in programs, and contributed written pieces and interviews to newspapers and national magazines.

Whether I thought of myself as a victim or not, others did. Suddenly, my job on *Days of Our Lives* came to an abrupt and unexplained end. Foxy Humdinger disappeared for nearly a year. The character was brought briefly back to the show the following Christmas to bring some closure, and then was written off the program entirely almost a year to the day after my rape. Oddly, I've never been invited back for the annual anniversary party thrown by the producers to celebrate their many successful years of broadcasting. Perhaps they were embarrassed by my outspokenness and willingness to talk about a subject that elicits discomfort in many people. Maybe they didn't believe the circumstances of my attack since other people had doubted the veracity of the incident. Maybe they thought it was some sort of misguided publicity stunt as a few people had suspected some years before when I had fled to the Del Coronado Hotel.

In the final analysis, I didn't care what anyone else thought. The public stance I took was helpful to many women. I received thoughtful and supportive letters from hundreds of women of all ages throughout the country. Women who had been raped and lived in painful silence and denial were encouraged by my shamelessness to step forward and speak up. Many women told me that after doing so, they finally got the help and counseling they so desperately needed.

The *Matt Houston* episode that I had filmed, "The Rock and the Hard Place," was broadcast shortly after the rape, and that was exactly where I found myself — between a rock and a hard place. My agent now experienced an icy chill from casting directors and producers when my name was suggested for employment.

In February 1983, I made the difficult decision to pursue legal action against the landlord of my building. I wrote to her, "We have a problem. As you know by now, I was attacked in the garage of the building and raped by strangers who spotted me as I came home from a Christmas Eve party early December 25th of last year. It was very dark in the garage since there was no lighting available to illuminate the area. We believe the lack of sufficient lighting contributed in an important way to the fact that no one located nearby could see what was happening to me, even though I screamed for help well before the men closed the garage door to hide what they were doing. I really hate to do this to you, but I am sure you have insurance covering any problems that arise, so you will be hearing from my attorney soon. This isn't personal. It's just necessary to recover what I have lost which is considerable. I hope my actions will not cause any trouble between us."

I was naïve. The trouble caused by the lawsuit was considerable and long-lasting. Even though the landlady eventually settled out of court, she was vindictive and harassed me for years afterward.

"What is rape, Mommy?" My son was understandably perplexed. He was far too young to be learning about such things. I was faced with destroying some of the innocence to which he was entitled at his age.

Should I try to tell him about sex, and then tell him that rape is a hateful aberration of what should be a loving act? I had to tell him something, and it seemed right to speak the truth rather than sugarcoat my response and confuse him even more.

I believe in introducing children to small amounts of information about sex early on, so that learning the "facts of life" isn't such a shock later. I remember being absolutely flummoxed when I first heard about sex as a child. I heard it from a friend my own age. She had walked in on her parents, and her description of her father's big penis and her mother's nakedness was shocking. I was aghast. In my perception, he was rough with her mother, perhaps even hurting her. Though my mother's chaste intentions had been good ones, I later thought it would have been better if she had prepared me a little earlier about the birds and the bees, instead of letting me learn about such things from my inaccurately informed little friends. Early on, I tried to tell Andrew in little bits and pieces about sex.

"Rape is a bad thing that a man does to..." *God*, I thought, *this is complicated*. "It's a hurtful thing, but usually..." This was more difficult than I thought. I wanted him to learn that sex was something that happened between two people who love each other and that rape, though sexual in nature, is not about sex and love at all.

I began again. "There is a thing that women and men do together when they love each other. It is private and it should only be done when two people are really in love with each other. It's supposed to be about affection between two people. People do this when they want to make babies and have their own families. But some men..."

"I thought those men hurt you."

"Yes. They did. But it doesn't hurt when it is done with love." I stopped for a moment, hoping he could absorb what I was struggling to explain. "It only hurts when it is done with hate. The men who attacked mommy really hated mommy."

"Why?"

How do you answer a question you've been asking of yourself? "I don't know why, honey. Maybe they don't like *any* women, not just mommy."

His little face twisted as he tried to understand what I was trying to tell him.

"I will protect you," he finally concluded. "You don't have to worry anymore, mommy. I will get those guys." He jumped into a defensive kung fu pose.

At night, I cried myself to sleep. The rape itself paled in comparison to the seemingly endless fallout. From that day on, and for a long time,

Andrew would approach building corners or any other blind spots with his kung fu pose, ready to protect his mother from evil men. What my son was going through was, I believed, far worse than anything that had happened to me. I thought maybe I should have said nothing, but he had asked "What is rape?"

Later, when Andrew was eleven and had developed some carpentry skills, he built shelves for planters on all our upstairs windows so that the "bad men" couldn't crawl up the wall and in through the window to get to me.

My friend, Janet, and her daughter, Mary, moved back to Los Angeles in 1983. They took up residence just a block away, and I was happy to have them nearby again. Andrew and Mary, the little girl he considered his sibling, picked up where they had left off — squabbling like a brother and sister. Andrew had so little family that he adopted almost every significant person in his life. My long-time friend, Freddie Amsel, who always arrived with an armful of toys, became "Uncle Freddie." Robbie and his friend, Merle, in Hawaii were lovingly known as "Aunt Robbie" and "Uncle Merle." It was wonderful to have people close by who could be counted on in good times and bad. I didn't have a husband, a large family, or a satisfying career, all of which I craved. My friendships were therefore indispensable. Now, without the sparkle of "celebrity," I could tell who was a real friend and who was not.

Janet was a loyal friend, and Mary was like a daughter to me. Life, like flowing water, finds its own way, and the spirit its own level. If the spirit can't enter in one direction, it finds another. I felt that God had sent Mary to me as a sort of substitute for the daughter I was supposed to have. After my abortion, and the night of dangerous hemorrhaging, I sensed that the little life that had been inside me "didn't want to let go." Mary was born in San Francisco shortly after my abortion, and I wondered if this little soul might have found another way to enter my heart.

Chapter 29

I gradually came to terms with my rape, but the physical damage lingered. The vicious and prolonged sodomy I was subjected to aggravated my existing problem with hemorrhoids. Surgery was required, and the procedure was successful, but necessitated the removal of much delicate tissue in the area.

While convalescing at home, I experienced hunger pains. Foolishly, I ate some boiled white rice and chocolate-covered almonds. The terrible food combination instantly made me constipated. Amidst my physical discomfort, my cat gave birth to a litter of kittens! She refused to care for one tiny runt in the bunch. I was overcome with grief, and in a panic tried to save the little reject. The kitten was weak and became very distressed. In the meantime, because the doctor had ordered me to sit in a hot bath as a means of coaxing a bowel movement, I did so.

I sat in that hot bath for hours ruminating about what had brought me to this place and to my struggling, perhaps in vain, to save a little feline life. Finally, at about 3:00 a.m., I was struck by an epiphany and filled with an enlightenment that would become an immeasurable help to me as time went on. If I have love (God) and the off-spring of love, compassion (Jesus) for my fellow man, then I find the spirit (Holy Spirit) of forgiveness within myself.

As this realization dawned on me sitting in that bathtub, I was suddenly able to void my aching bowels. I was naked and humbled like a baby who comes to meet the Holy Spirit. I experienced a profound "knowing" that night. I believe that the Creator had come to meet me. He filled me with hope and the willingness to forgive.

The kitten died in spite of my best efforts and I mourned the loss as if it were my own baby. Janet reminded me that my deep grief and tears were inappropriate over the loss of a cat. Still, I was filled with sorrow. "You haven't mourned the loss of your unborn child," Janet said, referring to my earlier abortion. "This could be a substitute. Perhaps this is another way to mourn the loss." Truth is hard to swallow, but swallow this one I did. I knew she was right.

A similar thing happened when my mother died. All during the memorial service and her internment, my emotions remained solidly in check. Diane was in control and there would be no sniveling. Guilt had taken over, though. I had done little to help my mother when she was alive. My shame would not allow me to cry now that she was gone.

Years later, when my friend Robbie's mother, a woman I had known most of my life, died, I sobbed openly. I realized then that my self-indulgent tears were for my own mother, whom I had failed to mourn.

After my "bathtub baptism," it was time for me to find a Christian church, which I did the following Sunday. I wanted more than anything to find my authentic self, the self that God created.

I liked All Saints' Episcopal Parish very much, and the church was conveniently located in Beverly Hills. I joined the choir and became a Lector and Intercessor. I loved reading scripture on Sunday and felt I had found a home.

Janet and her daughter joined me, and we discovered Marianne Williamson lecturing at another church, which we attended each Saturday. Williamson's lectures, based on the popular book *A Course in Miracles*, were mentally stimulating. I felt a sense of spirituality long absent from my life. The church was my tradition. Whether I could agree entirely with the dogma or not, I could nevertheless appreciate the efforts of the clergy to make the subtext palatable. The parish had "right-wing" evangelicals, and I knew I could not engage them in a discussion about the tenets of faith without an argument. To me, the devil is in the dogma. Fortunately, my Episcopal parish tolerated many different views and approaches. While *A Course in Miracles* was considered to be heretical by the church, I found much reason to have faith because of trying to heed the lessons. My personal problems didn't simply go away — I was finding a new center, a new peace inside my core. I was opening up to the presence of God. I felt an inner glow, which warmed my heart. This was something I hadn't felt in a very long time.

My time of spiritual contemplation seemed to usher in a period of work. In the summer of 1984, I landed a guest-star shot on a CBS drama called *Airwolf*, which starred veteran actor Ernest Borgnine. Ernie was one of the sweetest actors I ever met. Jan Michael Vincent was his costar. Vincent, a genuine "Hollywood Hellion," was working with a broken arm, the result of a drunken fight with his wife. My fellow guest stars included Brett Halsey and Lola Albright. The "Sins of the Past" episode was broadcast in October.

A couple of months later, I guest-starred on *Crazy Like a Fox* and the phenomenally successful *Knight Rider*. Set in San Francisco, *Crazy Like a Fox* starred Jack Warden as a con-artist/private eye. *Knight Rider* was the story of a man and his talking car, and starred a very tall, blue-eyed David Hasselhoff and the disarmingly charming English actor, Edward Mulhare. Both episodes aired in the early months of 1985. I cherished

My son on the set of Knight Rider *with "Kitt" the talking car.*

the work, but I didn't act again on television for several years.

In July, I flew to Utah to shoot *The Red Fury*, a feature film advertised by the producer as a "Heartwarming Family Classic." Directed by Lyman D. Dayton, this was the first and only film written by Douglas J. Stewart and Royce Lerwick. The cast included Alan Hale Jr. and William Jordan. *The Red Fury* storyline concerned racism directed against a young American Indian boy in a small western town. The subject was provocative, and I thought the message was important. I appreciated working on the film and being away from home for a few weeks. With little else to do with my spare time, I played tourist and took advantage of the otherworldly beauty of the Utah landscape.

While I was working on location, I learned that Richard Burton had died on August 5. He was only fifty-eight years old. I mourned his death as if we had never been apart. I grieved the loss of what once was, moreover, what never became of our romance.

I recalled the time in 1977 when Richard was in Los Angeles and looked me up. I was stunned to hear his voice on the phone.

"Is this Diane?" he asked, "Are you the Diane McBain who acted in *Ice Palace?*"

On the set of The Red Fury *with Alan Hale, Jr.*

"Yes," I said, "and this sounds an awful lot like Richard Burton."

After some amusing reminiscences, he asked, "May I come and see you? I was always fascinated by you and often wondered what happened to you. I think it is because I could never quite…penetrate you." I could hear the smile in his voice. He hadn't changed a bit. Richard was still unabashedly sexual.

A limousine dropped him off in front of my apartment on North Clark Drive. I watched a considerably older man make his way to my front door, his little dog happily trotting along on a leash. Andrew answered the door and Richard appeared immediately charmed by him. Perhaps, I thought, he saw Andrew as the son he always wanted but never had.

I didn't have a babysitter, so Andrew joined us for dinner. We walked a couple of blocks to my neighborhood hangout on Robertson Boulevard for a steak. We were seated on the patio so Richard's dog could sit at his feet. Richard slipped the manager some cash to guarantee our privacy. We talked and laughed and he confided to me about Elizabeth Taylor and her amusing, self-absorbed habits. He was married to a new woman now, and there was little chance he and I could be together. He called me the next day before he returned to his home in Switzerland. "I love you," he whispered heavily into the phone. "I ache to be with you." My head reeled as I heard his words, and they echoed for days afterwards.

It wasn't long before he called again. I was taking a bath one afternoon and the telephone rang. I later mused that there isn't a woman alive who can get into the shower or tub without receiving that all-important, life-changing phone call! Andrew answered. Slamming the phone down, he ran to me and said, "Mommy, Richard is on the phone." Then he disappeared into the yard. By the time I got out of the tub and to the telephone, the receiver had rocked into its cradle and disconnected the call. I was horrified that he thought I purposefully hung up the telephone. There was no way for me to reach him. I wept, and I never heard from him again.

The television in my Utah hotel room reported the shocking news of Richard's death that sad day in August, 1984. I was surprised how his death seemed to bring him even closer to me. A couple of days later, I was in the bathroom when I had the strongest sensation of his presence in the room. He did have a way about him, a distinct energy, and a powerful presence that was as immediately recognizable as his voice. His spirit seemed to dance around me, happily informing me that there *was* a life after death. I knew he had never expected that because we had talked about such things in the past. Now, he wanted me to know that I was right!

Richard's considerable personality contributed to my realization that the essence of who we are never dies. I knew myself to be immortal, and I knew that life exists with or without a body. Richard's powerful soul validated my feeling. Being "present in the moment" seemed to be the one thing most people sought, no matter what religion or philosophy they espoused. I know a few people whose presence is intensely constant. They have powerful personalities because they are so available to the present moment. They aren't thinking about a thousand other things, they're not fretting over the past, not wishing for some illusory future, or worse, conjuring up a dreaded outcome. They are not worrying about what other people are thinking about them, nor trying to figure out their next sentence, but listening and responding to their present environment.

Whether they have a religion or not doesn't seem to matter. They have "presence" and that is where God dwells. Richard Burton had "presence" like no other person I knew, and his post-mortem visit seemed entirely real to me.

Loving a man like Richard, being a responsible single parent, and maintaining an acting career were goals worth keeping close to my heart. As I recalled the wonderful times I had spent with Richard, I was deeply saddened that I wouldn't see him again. And, more than a decade would pass before I appeared in a feature film.

A publicity photo from 1993. PHOTO COURTESY OF BILL DOW.

Starshine

Chapter 30

Ralph Riskin called my agent with an offer. He had never offered me a job before. He was co-producing a made-for-television movie titled *Gidget's Summer Reunion*, and he had me in mind for a role. I would have to read for the other producer, but with Ralph in my corner, I felt I had the job in the bag. Foolishly, I got my hopes up and felt the tide was turning in my favor. When I learned that I didn't get the part, I was devastated.

So, what happened? Producers and casting directors called and seemed enthusiastic, but they cooled before long and the offered role went to someone else. What was I doing wrong? I had worked with consistent professionalism all my life. I was always in the makeup chair on time. I was always attentive on the set to what was going on and what the director wanted. I knew my lines and I hit my marks. I rarely pulled a "diva act," though a couple of times I argued over certain issues with a director. I differed once with director Jim Conway on the set of *Donner Pass* regarding my hair. He wanted my blonde hair to be black and budget constraints prevented a professional hairdresser from simply dying my hair black and then back to blonde when we had finished filming. Instead, Conway wanted to use spray color on my hair. Spray color always looked fake, and I resisted. Though the women's hair looked dark in the actual tintype photographs, I thought their hair was probably lighter in natural daylight. Conway disagreed. From that point on, I was placed outside the frame of the film so my hair color couldn't be seen. He won, but surely that was not enough of a problem to steal future work away from me.

I did my own stunts, and I endeavored to bring creativity to my art. I'd even worked, against my better judgment, when I was hurt or ill. When my ability, experience, and professional reputation did not help, and the aid of friends and acquaintances failed as well, what could I do?

"It's your clothes," Ralph said. "You have to bring your wardrobe up to date."

"My *clothes*? Now it's my *clothes!*" I barked into the phone. It had been my hair, my makeup, my height, my weight, always some excuse that just didn't make sense. I was too young. I was too old. I was too famous, or not famous enough. What was wrong with my *clothes*? That's what wardrobe people are for on a movie or television set!

"Your hair could use some updating, too," he added. That comment made me want to throw the telephone across the room. Even Ralph, someone I considered my friend, saw me as an object, a lifeless thing to be dressed and coifed.

With everyone telling me how to act, what to wear, and what to say, it was hard to develop any healthy sense of myself. Once again, I felt lost in a business I depended on for my living and over which I had absolutely no control.

With no acting jobs on the horizon, I had to find an alternate means of support. I was hired as the front-office receptionist at All Saints' Episcopal Church. Mary, who was about eleven years old, surprised me one day when she asked me if she could be baptized in the church. She asked me to be her Godmother, and I was deeply honored. Andrew didn't want to be left behind, so he, too, asked to be baptized. I was very glad and made all the arrangements.

The children chose my birthday as their Baptism Day. It was Pentecost Sunday, which represents the day the Holy Spirit was released into the world. Andrew would turn thirteen in about a month, so we celebrated this as a time of rebirth.

Soon after he decided to be baptized, Andrew told me he wanted to change his name. He'd thought about this for a while, and I supported his decision. He had been touched on the head with the Gohonzon — the Buddhist baptism rite — and named Andrew Eichi. Now, a Christian name would be more to his liking.

We settled on Evan Andrew. The name Evan means John in Welsh, which appealed to me because Richard Burton was Welsh. My memories of Richard were now strong again, and my instincts told me he would like the choice.

My heart burst with pride on the big day. Mary became my Goddaughter and my son was baptized with his Christian name, Evan Andrew. The priest handed me a lit candle embossed with his new name and I felt I had finally broken the "cultural bonds" of Buddhism. I returned to my home church, now with my son at my side. Mary's baptism assured me a special place in her heart. On May 18, 1986, we were all born again. The day was joyful.

As we awaited the pending lawsuit against my landlord, my meager receptionist's salary paid our bills. I decided to make use of my extra time and returned to college. I was inspired to explore the priesthood, so I needed a Bachelor's Degree to pursue theological training. Dr. Nathanial Safian, a dear friend and a gift from God, covered all the costs. I chose to go to Antioch University in Los Angeles. My grades were very good, and I hoped that Evan would see this as a good example to follow. I enjoyed learning and wanted to inspire the same interest in my son. I majored in psychology. I discovered I was still intelligent and a good writer. I also learned I would make a lousy priest.

Instead, I became involved in a lay pastoral ministry at the church as a trained Stephen Minister. This meant I counseled parishioners who couldn't come to church for services. In my mind, my very diligent work was not enough. I soon decided I couldn't give these people what they needed. My own strong belief in God was not enough to make me truly effective. I did enjoy the field of psychology, however, and seriously considered it as a career pursuit.

I reconnected with the director of the Rape Trauma Center at Cedars-Sinai Medical Center, and she graciously invited me to join their board of directors. What little celebrity I had left was helpful in bringing much needed attention to the excellent services provided by the center. I became a trained counselor for victims of violent crime. I spent many a long night in hospital emergency rooms advising rape victims about survival and helping them through the horrible experience. Most of those I assisted returned to the center numerous times to sort out the intense feelings they were experiencing. Helping these women was a gratifying undertaking. Counseling others also helped me come to terms with my attacks.

I was invited to speak about rape victims and the criminal justice system to a convention of the Trial Attorneys Association. During my counseling, rape victims had complained to me about the insensitive treatment they sometimes experienced at the hands of attorneys. Many said they felt they were being raped all over again. I thought the lawyers wanted to know how victims felt so that litigation could be handled in a more compassionate manner. However, they didn't want to hear that the system of plea-bargaining — so widely used at the time by law enforcement and even prosecutors — was injurious to the victim. Not only did my message fall on deaf ears, I was "uninvited" to the next convention. I felt strongly that plea-bargaining should be considered only under strict and controlled circumstances, especially with rape cases. It seemed unconscionable to me for a rapist to be able to plea-bargain his way out of the strongest punishment, for any reason at all.

I continued to work with the Rape Trauma Center for the next five years until the program ended due to lack of government funding. All the people I worked with there practiced compassion, understanding, and integrity.

While still working at the church front office, I was instructed to hand out a bag-lunch and a bus token to each homeless person who ambled in. However, I was firmly instructed to limit the handouts to only three per person. How do you say "no" to someone who has humbled himself to ask for help?

I couldn't, and I felt the church shouldn't either. I campaigned for a civil treatment of the homeless men and women who approached the church for help. I felt very strongly that a religious entity should be the one to aid these people.

All Saints' Episcopal Church also had a wonderful program for senior citizens called "Senior Saints." Senior citizens needing a place to gather for lunch and fellowship met at the parish hall. Many needed a ride for the daily get-togethers. I volunteered my services, and I met a delightful woman named Marie, who became my "regular" pick-up. Our friendship endured until she died several years later.

I became acquainted with philanthropist Iris Cantor through my friend Freddie Amsel. He was a good friend of her financier husband, Bernard "Bernie" Gerald Cantor, who co-founded the securities firm Cantor-Fitzgerald. Freddie and I double-dated with Iris and Bernie occasionally. Iris had been a fashion model in her youth, and her philanthropic interests included medicine and the arts. Like my mother, Iris' sister died of breast cancer.

Iris had an interest in show business, and understood the value of celebrity to bring attention to a charity cause. I got involved with the Executive Committee of the Iris Cantor Center for Breast Imaging at UCLA hospital. The new technology available since mom's death helped women with early diagnosis and life-saving treatment. The Cantor Center performs state-of-the-art breast imaging, including screening mammography, diagnostic mammography, imaging-guided needle biopsy, and ductography. The Center was the first such facility in the United States to be certified by the American College of Radiology Mammography Accreditation Program.

I worked on several fundraisers for the organization. My celebrity, though waning, helped Iris raise funds for a special mobile unit that contained mammography equipment. This mobile facility, virtually a clinic on wheels, was able to reach countless women and provide free, low-cost mammograms.

Until my mother became ill with breast cancer, I didn't know very much about the disease. I learned that about one in eight women in the U.S. would develop invasive breast cancer. Though death rates have steadily decreased due to early testing and detection, nearly 40,000 women die each year in the United States alone. If detected early, though, the five-year survival rate for breast cancer exceeds 96 percent.

Of course, vigilance, self-examination, and proper testing are vitally important. These mobile clinics save countless lives, and mobile mammography vans now travel the streets in many American cities. Iris Cantor's dedication to a cause so dear to her heart was an inspiration to me. I so wished my mother had had the life-saving tools available to women today, yet I was gratified to know that I was making a noticeable difference.

At last, the lawsuit against my landlord was settled out of court. With a substantial amount of cash in hand, I decided to buy a condominium and a few other things I needed. I also wanted to take Evan on a rafting trip down the Colorado River. I invested most of the money in the stock market, and with the little left, I bought Evan and myself a ticket on a raft.

In August 1987, we headed for the Colorado River for my first genuine vacation in twenty years. I had promised myself when he was a baby that we would take a whitewater river-rafting trip as soon as he was old enough to go. Finally, we had the money and the time. Five days and nights on the rugged Colorado River was just what we needed.

The whitewater, while dangerous enough, didn't seem to be the most overwhelming element to contend with. For me, the ground on which we had to sleep was far more problematic that the rapids. One might think that a sandy beach would serve nicely as a mattress. Hardly. Evan and I shared a little tent that was cramped and stuffy. After a lot of tossing and turning, I left the tent and tried the outdoors. I smoothed out my sleeping bag and climbed in. Turning my face to the stars, I lay there dumbfounded. The night sky was so bright with heavenly bodies I couldn't close my eyes. The Milky Way was every bit as milky as I had remembered so long ago when I was sent to summer camp. I felt as if I could reach up and touch the twinkling stars. I'm not sure how one sleeps under those conditions. It was nearly bright enough to be daylight.

I got out of my sleeping bag and wandered closer to the dark river as it quietly washed by me. Sitting, I tucked my toes into the water and let the coolness wash over my feet, and through my soul. The weight of the water dragging against my toes reminded me of the current's undeniable power. One could fall into the inky depths during the night and be swept away before anyone would notice. I wondered how such dangerous power and such incredible beauty could be so entwined with one another.

Before long, Evan joined me. He couldn't sleep either. He sat next to me, awed by the rushing water and the moonless sky.

"Where's the moon, Mom?" he asked.

"You know the earth travels around the sun and the moon travels around the earth."

"It never meant anything before tonight," he said.

"For us city dwellers, the moon and stars are just rumors."

"I notice it when the moon sometimes moves along the horizon getting bigger," he said. "And it turns that weird orange."

"Did you notice it sitting directly over Oki Dog the other night?" I asked. "It was an image of orange that was unforgettable."

Evan sat quietly.

"Have you been going over there?" I asked. I had made a rule that he was not to visit that place after my rape. During the investigation of my assault, the police informed me that the ugly joint was a haven for all kinds of nefarious activities, including drug trafficking and prostitution. I was in the process of suing the hot dog stand. We thought the place was a breeding ground for rapists and murderers. The two rapists who attacked me had been sitting at a table outside the establishment when I arrived home that fateful night.

Soon the memories of that mirthless place paled in contrast to the exquisite evening. The starry sky was like a huge blanket that covered us in benevolent folds. Turning to Evan, I said, "Please stay away from there. There are reasons, and I mean it." I hated to be so stern in the wonder of that beautiful, spirit-filled night. Here on the river, so far away from any civilization, nothing seemed so important that I had to spoil the moment, except my son's safety.

Across the river's black chasm, huge walls of geological history rose like a cathedral in which to pray. Each layer of rock had different configurations that indicated the passage of time, as our tour guide had pointed out to us earlier in the day. They had the marks of flowing sandbanks with layers of flora and fauna. Then, just as suddenly, another change! The ground became dry topsoil upon which there was no water — just the glare of hot unremitting sun creating layers of hard dry shale. One after the other, these shifts proclaimed a vast and cataclysmic alteration to the Earth's ever changing face.

"It's the abruptness of the changes between these geological events that jar me," I admitted. "It scares me that life can go along in the same way for so long, then all of a sudden, boom! It changes completely. Nothing is ever the same again."

"It's like how can we ever count on things, huh, Mom?" Evan asked.

"Yes, but it can also be the result of a wonderful time. The alteration can be sudden and surprising, yet bring us to a very positive life-changing experience," I said.

"Like tonight?"

"Yeah, like tonight." My heart gladdened whenever we could communicate so well, which didn't happen often enough. The one thing I never imagined in my childhood was being the mother of a little boy. In my mind, my baby was always a girl. I felt oddly unprepared to know what a boy needed, and I felt inadequate to his needs. That night, however, I felt fulfilled as a mother. I felt like I'd done my job. There were other things to teach Evan, but I had managed to convey something positive about what had happened to me. I was grateful for the unexpected opportunity.

In October, not long after our idyllic vacation, the stock market crashed and my investments were wiped out. There was no money left for a down payment on a condominium. There was no money left for anything. The loss was ruinous.

Perhaps to make me feel better, Evan brought me two white Silky Doves that his neighborhood friend bred. We didn't have an appropriate cage for them, so we often took them out to waddle and peck around the living room floor.

By that time, we had quite a menagerie. Evan had a couple of hamsters, two parakeets, a cat he called Tuffy, and I had my beloved feline,

Moonshine. One night, they were all on the carpet together. The hamsters were running around in plastic exercise balls and the parakeets were climbing on Tuffy and Moonshine, who were lolling about on the floor. The cats certainly knew what birds were. They often sat on the windowsill and hungrily watched the birds outside in the tree branches. Now, the doves waddled right under their noses and the cats were content to doze in peace. They actually purred happily as if they were attending a friendly get-together. One could extrapolate from this experience that the spiritual expectations of the leader of the household, or any leader for that matter, are what set the tone for everyone in his or her care, even those that are the most wild among them. Since my experience with the Holy Spirit, there had been many unusual events like that. I began to believe what religions often preach: peace within begets peace without. However, peace for us was tenuous and short-lived.

Evan's formative years continued to be plagued with challenges. His ADHD symptoms and physical tic occupied our attention. The doctor put him on Haldol, a major narcotic. The drug relieved his tic, but his "general appearance" was "off." Evan is attractive, yet he was mercilessly teased at school for his big ears and nose. He eventually grew into his features, but at the time, his classmates were unforgiving and nasty. The teasing affected his self-esteem and his education.

Although numerous tests confirmed that he was very bright and possessed great comprehension skills, he didn't recognize his abilities and he under-performed in the classroom. I enrolled him in a private school for a year, but found the teachers were ill equipped to handle his problems. Finding a school geared towards the particular needs of special children was very challenging. He was always playing catch-up in class. Though he didn't appreciate school at the time, I knew how important it was for him to get a good education. For a while, he was forced into supplemental special education classes in public school. This took more time away from his regular classes, and did not help his self-confidence. I felt the more he worked, the more he fell behind.

Still, he was a creative self-starter. He became obsessed with skateboarding. I watched him build a large wooden skateboard ramp on a small vacant plot next door. He and his buddies did a great job, and for a little while enjoyed the ramp. The owner soon stepped forward and told the boys to get off his land. Evan devised a plan. He and his friends partially dissembled the ramp. They rested the large pieces on their skateboards, and with the help of a police car escort, wheeled the pieces several blocks up the street to a new location at the foot of the Hollywood Hills. Evan had canvassed the area until he found a property owner agreeable to letting the boys use his land. Evan had proved himself a natural-born leader and a good problem solver. Now, all I had to do was somehow harness his enormous energy and help to focus his attention on learning.

Chapter 31

In 1988, I returned to daytime television with a recurring role for six months on another soap opera, *General Hospital*. The longer an actor stays away from the business, the tougher it is to get back in. I got a call from a casting agent named Marvin Paige, who was a friend. He offered the role on *General Hospital*. I appeared as a character named Claire Howard, the pathetic victim of a love triangle. I appreciated the paychecks but again found the grind of such routine work to be barely tolerable.

I wrote screenplays into the wee hours of the night and managed to have a few optioned, though none were ever produced. A few nights a week, I worked as a counselor at The Response Center, a safe haven for victims of violent crime. I listened to so many of their awful stories, and tried my best to counsel, give support, and inspire a little confidence in them.

When called upon, I happily worked on charitable projects with Iris Cantor. During the course of her marriage to Bernie, he had amassed the largest private collection of works by Auguste Rodin. In July of 1988, Freddie and I accompanied Iris to the dedication of the B. Gerald Cantor Sculpture Garden at the Los Angeles County Museum of Art. The Cantors had donated for permanent display eight Rodin sculptures and five other impressive works by Emile-Antoine Bourdelle and George Kolbe.

To earn some extra money, I reluctantly appeared at a few "autograph fairs" where celebrities sold autographed photographs to fans that paid admission to the event. I felt like an animal at the zoo, as people slowly strolled past me to see what I looked like after so many years.

As challenging as my life was, Evan struggled more with his disabilities. He had a high IQ score, but he suffered from a learning disability that made reading especially difficult. He fell behind in classes and was embarrassed as his fellow classmates and friends advanced without him.

When he was seventeen years old, he quit high school. He told me he wanted to move out and live on his own. I didn't want him to leave, but I knew he would go whether I approved or not. I couldn't bear for him to leave in anger, and I wanted him to feel comfortable enough to come back home if he needed to, so I reluctantly agreed to his request.

I couldn't explain to him how difficult life might be for a teenage boy who failed to complete high school and had no real goals. Nothing seemed to hold his interest for long. He had worked at a few places including a shoe retailer, the Hallmark Company, and a Cinema Prop company that created miniatures for motion pictures. I tried not to worry about him, but he was constantly in my thoughts.

In 1989, Marianne Williamson put her words of compassion to work when she founded "Project Angel Food," an outreach program of the Los Angeles Center for Living, which helps people with life threatening illnesses. Specifically, "Project Angel Food" is a program that delivers free hot meals to people suffering from AIDS. In those early days of the disease, people who quickly and mysteriously became gravely ill desperately needed help. Many were treated disrespectfully and with disdain, as if a deadly illness was not enough to contend with. It was shocking to witness how badly human beings could act out of fear and misunderstanding. There were only a few volunteers when "Project Angel Food" began. In about a year, the operation moved into the kitchen of the Crescent Heights United Methodist Church in Los Angeles.

Mary, my Goddaughter, cleaned the kitchen, and her mother, Janet, was a cook. Originally, we prepared lunch for "drop-in" clients and people in need of a warm meal. As fewer and fewer were able to leave their homes due to illness, our lunches were delivered to them. I delivered meals, driving from one end of the city to the other with the back seat of my car full of food. At the beginning, we were delivering approximately ninety meals each day. Within the first year, that number tripled. This was a labor of love. I delivered meals for many months and returned whenever my schedule allowed. The work was gratifying and heartbreaking.

One of the more unusual non-profits I enthusiastically supported was the Roar Foundation, the brainchild of my friend Tippi Hedren. After making a film about the plight of the big cats in the wilds of Africa, she created a preserve in Acton, California called Shambala. The sprawling animal sanctuary on the Santa Clara River became home to more than seventy lions, tigers, leopards, and other endangered, exotic big cats. These impressive felines were either born in captivity or taken from illegal private owners and placed into protective custody. Tippi even rescued a couple of African elephants. She worked tirelessly on behalf of these wonderful animals. The preserve was also an exotic and peaceful oasis,

Not only were lions and tigers living outside Tippi's windows, some also lived in her house. I'm bravely cuddling a lion on Tippi's kitchen floor. Don't try this at home.

and I happily spent time there away from the grind of a Hollywood that Tippi and I knew all too well.

I participated in many fundraising events to benefit the Roar Foundation. One day, Tippi invited me to take part in a documentary filmed at the preserve by an Italian production company. We were interviewed on camera with several of the more docile big cats walking around us in a gated paddock. I sat at a picnic table. A lioness was positioned lazily on the tabletop. She casually gazed at my leg, and without warning, bit my thigh. I screamed, the movie cameras were ordered off, and the animal wranglers jumped to my aid and managed to wrestle my leg free of the animal's mouth. Thankfully, the 400-pound carnivorous feline did not break my skin, but the resultant bruises were hideous. The experience provided me with one of the most exciting and unbelievable stories of my life. I continued to support Tippi's worthy efforts, but stayed clear of rubbing elbows or knees with her lions and tigers!

Chapter 32

An old boyfriend seemingly called out-of-the-blue. Dr. Robert (Bob) Roos had become a Circuit Court Parole Judge for the State of California. He had also founded the Delta Institute, an inter-disciplinary group of legal scholars engaged in research in the area of criminal justice. The Institute organized an exchange program for American judges and Chinese judges to visit each other and study their respective criminal justice systems. The program was designed to create an understanding between the two cultures, which was especially important following the Democratic protests that rocked Tiananmen Square in Beijing, China the year before. People around the world had been shocked to witness the deadly confrontation when troops and tanks were pitted against unarmed Chinese citizens.

"Do you know anyone who can write a screenplay, Diane?" Bob asked me on the phone.

"I do," I said. "Me. I can. What do you want to write?"

An article titled "In search of...Diane McBain" had been printed in the Los Angeles Times on May 27, 1990. I was always dismayed by those types of headlines, which made it sound as though I was living under a rock. The short profile reported that I had stepped away from acting to pursue writing. At the time, I was taking screenwriting courses at UCLA Extension. I had completed a screenplay titled *The Spilling Moon*, about the first woman to ride the Colorado River through the Grand Canyon. My interest in the true story had been sparked by my time with Evan in that glorious region.

Bob was recently divorced and said he wanted to write about the pain of his breakup. The idea wasn't especially appealing to me. We had a warm conversation and he explained his involvement in the judicial exchange program with China. I had been riveted to the television during the uprising and massacre. Now, my creative side began to simmer. I felt that old, familiar stirring that meant the Holy Spirit was urging me on.

Shortly, I called Bob back and told him I had an idea. I wrote a treatment for a film that concerned an American judge, who haplessly found himself in the middle of the uprising and the subsequent violent clashes in Tiananmen Square. He loved the idea. He insisted that we should go to China to properly research the story and get a feel for the land and its people. With his judicial and political connections, he arranged a trip

Ren Jin Shin presents me with a gift. Bob Roos is seated between us, and our translator, Mr. Liu, is standing in the background.

that was paid for by the Chinese government. We began our month-long visit in late September 1990.

We flew to sprawling, bustling Beijing. The XI Asiad Games had begun in the city a couple of days before our arrival. Tourists from more than fifty participating nations crowded Beijing. China is overwhelmingly beautiful, imposing, and exotic. I played the part of Bob's assistant and took copious notes at his meetings. My unofficial function was to record my impressions of the country and the culture, and to learn about the rebellion for the screenplay I intended to write. I took hundreds of photographs.

Sept. 27. Mr. Ji Shu Li is the Communist party official who is in charge of our tour. He dresses in a dark, navy blue Mao jacket, buttoned to the neck. He is friendly, but officious. Mr. Liu is our translator. He is a judge in Shanghai who studied English in the States. He dresses in ordinary "western" wear. Both wear glasses and watches, which they often look at. They are both very nice, very accommodating, but Mr. Ji is very reserved. Mr. Liu is open and friendly. Yi Li is a very young woman who was referred to us, and will accompany us on several excursions in Beijing. She speaks English very well.*

We were treated like guests of State. On our first day, we visited the Hall of Prayer for Good Harvests at the Temple of Heaven. That evening, Ren Jin Shin, Chief Justice of the People's Supreme Court, hosted a lavish banquet in Bob's honor. Before dinner, we attended a formal reception, where Bob and Mr. Jin had a lengthy conversation. I was the only woman in the room, and although our hosts were gracious and accommodating to me, I was not invited to join the conversation. I sat quietly and sipped tea. As we prepared to move to the dining room, Mr. Jin presented me with a stunning jade bracelet.

Our meal consisted of many intriguing and delectable courses. Bob was seated to the right of Mr. Jin and I was seated to his left. With the aid of a translator, the two men talked about the concept of the death penalty. Wang Jen Liang sat to my left. He was a senior economist for the Foreign Affairs Bureau of the People's Court. He spoke excellent English, and was very charming. We had a spirited conversation about the concept of Capitalism and free markets. They were polite and tried to be personable.

The Chinese have no rules against slurping soup. It demonstrates you are enjoying your food. And, when they pick their teeth, which they do between each course, they do so hiding the picking behind a cupped hand.

After dinner, as we all left we shook hands with everyone and when I walked out the door, I glanced back to see Mr. Ren standing alone in the middle of the entry hall. Unsmiling, he fixed his gaze on us, and clasped his hands behind his back. He is a very formal man, very intimidating.

Based on my film treatment, Bob made specific requests regarding where we wanted to visit. Accompanied by our official guide, our interpreter, and various local officials dressed in conventional suits, we toured a section of the Great Hall of the People, located on the edge of Tiananmen Square. The Great Hall is used for ceremonial functions by the Communist Party of China and is the meeting place of the National People's Congress, the Chinese parliament.

> *Sept. 28. There are special meeting rooms for each of the Provinces including, surprisingly, a room for Taiwan. It was less opulent and less well-cared-for, but it was there. I took pictures of the exquisite art in the Great Hall, and of the Red Guard doing their military exercises in front of the building.*

We visited Tiananmen Square and were free to walk about, though we were watched closely. The large lampposts used to light the area at night were all fitted with cameras, which were used for around-the-clock, monitoring purposes. The huge open area (deceptively called a "square") can hold a million people. When we visited, the vast area appeared to be filled with schoolchildren. They laughed and chattered while the adults seemed more circumspect and subdued. I was overwhelmed by the desire to weep at the memory of what had happened there on June 4, 1989. I struggled to control my feelings because our hosts would not have liked such a display.

We then walked to the nearby Forbidden City, which is a collection of more than nine-hundred buildings built during the Ming and Qing Dynasties. For nearly 500 years, the Forbidden City was the home of the emperors of China. Puyi was the last emperor to live in the fortress. He abdicated his throne and was expelled from the Forbidden City in 1912. The former Imperial Palace is located in the center of Beijing. The building is gracefully magnificent. We were told that the deep red color of the walls historically represented "the emperor's hope for national stability."

> *Spotted a little boy dressed in a soldier costume on the way to the Forbidden City. He looked really cute, but one can imagine how such a sight might feel to a student or a worker after June 4, 1989. We walked for more than an hour, from one court yard to the next, until we reached the end. It is like walking into ancient history. We walked from square to square, from structure to structure beneath a seemingly endless stream of tile roofs. It was truly opulent. At last we reached the Emperor's garden where we saw trees that had been planted 1,500 years ago.*

An interesting thing occurred on our second day in Beijing. During the course of our three-hour luncheon, I believe I met my first Chinese homosexual. This young man was handsome and genteel. I wanted to ask our escort what was the general attitude toward gay people in China, but such a question didn't seem appropriate. Neither did I want to get the man in trouble by drawing attention to him.

I was surprised to see many city signs printed in both Chinese and English. Even the Communist Headquarters Building was identified with Chinese and English signage.

After lunch, we visited the High People's Court, which is the Chinese equivalent to the United States Supreme Court. I learned a little bit about Chinese justice in the smoke-filled room when Bob finally asked about

At the Forbidden City.

the fate of the "rebellious" students of Tiananmen Square. They adroitly ducked the question.

> *Sept. 29. Today, we were up-graded. Instead of an ordinary van to drive around in, we now have a chauffeur driven Mercedes Benz. We visited the Great Wall. Two thousand years old and three thousand miles long, I felt the strong presence of history while there. Many thousands of people have left their mark on the Wall. Its steep steps nearly wore me out.*
>
> *After lunch, we went to the Ming Tombs. They sure would be a neat place to explore. It seemed there were portals leading to chambers that weren't open to the public. The child in me wanted to investigate.*

Thirteen Ming Emperors were buried at the Ming Dynasty Tombs. A road called the "Spirit Way," which was lined with forbidding stone statues of guardian animals, led into the revered complex. The tombs, walkways and gardens were all designed according to Feng Shui principles to ward off bad spirits and evil winds. We were able to see the Dingling Tomb — one of only a few tombs that had been opened and explored. All excavations at the site had stopped in 1989.

> *Sept. 30. Beijing University is an especially beautiful campus, but I was surprised to learn that only 10,000 students attend school there. Out of a nation of so many people, it seems that university enrollment is low.*
>
> *A visit to the Summer Palace was a pleasant respite. A boat ride on this exquisite lake would be a very romantic thing to do.*
>
> *Bob and I talked about Yi Li today. To get his attention, she will slap his arm with the back of her hand, a charming touch. Chinese women are shy and it is hard for them to acknowledge a compliment comfortably. They are not very fashionable, but this is probably a reflection of their socialist upbringing and the general poverty of the land and its people.*

That evening, Bob and I were special guests at the State Dinner celebrating the eve of their National Day. On October 1, 1949, Mao Zedong had declared the founding of the People's Republic of China. The red-carpeted event took place in the Great Hall of the People, which is located on the western edge of Tiananmen Square. Li Peng, the Fourth Premier of the People's Republic was in attendance. Oddly, there was little security considering all their government leaders were in attendance. In America, there would have been secret service all over the place. I saw a soldier or two standing casually near the doorways.

We dined in the State Banquet Hall. I wore a beautiful off-the-shoulder white gown. The men were dressed in grey Mao suits or dark Western suits. All the women in attendance wore subdued dark ensembles. With my blonde hair and flashy white gown, I looked like an atomic explosion in the middle of the room! I'm tall in my stocking feet, and in my heels, I towered over every Chinese woman and most of the Chinese men. Our Communist escort quickly covered my bare shoulders with a delicate white lace shawl. Later that evening in my hotel room, I turned on the television to CNN. I watched as their cameras panned the State Dinner, and there I was — a glimmering, angelic flash of white in a sea of dark suits. I was the only white spot in the room! Diane was thrilled! Danny got a good laugh.

> *Oct. 1. Bob and I took a little side trip in a pedicab today to the Central Academy of Fine Arts where the Goddess of Democracy was built. When we got there, we took photos, but suddenly the guard at the*

gate approached Bob with his hand out as if to take Bob's video camera. He asked if we had a pass. It brought home the fact that just below the surface of this normal looking life, there is a threat to freedom of speech and movement.

The Goddess of Democracy was a statue made of metal armature covered with papier mâché. Created by students at the Central Academy of Fine Arts during the Tiananmen Square protests, the object slightly resembled the Statue of Liberty. The thirty-three-foot-tall sculpture was placed in the middle of the Square. Ultimately, it was destroyed by soldiers as they cleared the area of protestors.

Life here seems normal on the surface. But, if you wish to speak to someone about sensitive matters, you must take a walk down the street, or around the block.

This P.M. we went to Beihai Park, where we saw, about two and half miles around a huge lake, a string of stationary floats. They were lit and animated, often gaudy and cheap by Western standards. It was the Chinese version of an amusement park. The people here have very little in the way of amusement, so a place like this is entertaining. Every display has a story it tells. There are a few rides, but they are fairly primitive. The children's eyes light up over what may seem to a Western child a very uninteresting pastime.

Beihai Park is one of the largest imperial gardens in China. Located at the northwest corner of the Forbidden City, the park was built in the 10th Century. The small pavilions and displays imitate the most famous scenic spots and architecture from all over China.

Oct 2. A free day! It was hard for our hosts to let go of us for a day. It seems they fear for our safety. But, I have felt very safe in this place. There are no hostile faces anywhere.

We spent that day with Yi Li, traveling around Beijing in taxis and very crowded public buses. We returned to Beihai Park for a boat ride, then, we went to Tiananmen Square for lunch. The police closely watched us while we ate. Evidently, they were expecting to slap us with a heavy fine for littering.

Unbeknownst to our Communist escort, I spoke to many Chinese citizens about the massacre. I was amazed by how much I was able to learn. The government had been very effective in corralling the media and preventing much news from being broadcast at the time. I kept mental notes about sensitive conversations and never wrote them down for fear our bags might later be searched. I walked around many blocks, and people approached me and self-consciously spoke in hushed tones. The experience was unsettling.

We were able to visit the residence of a Chinese family in the old section of town, and dine in their tiny home. Their kitchen was part of an outdoor patio. Delicate lace curtains separated the rooms in the petite structure. They were kind and generous with what little they had to share. They guarded their words with us because a neighborhood watch committee would visit them for a debriefing as soon as we left.

> *I held their baby on my lap. They don't diaper children here; instead they cut open their pants and let them pee or poop through the hole. The baby peed on me. I noticed they don't circumcise their baby boys. There seems to be little evidence of obsessive/compulsive personalities here. Everyone seems quite calm. Perhaps this has something to do with the lack of early and forced potty training.*
>
> *Their house was very old and sparsely furnished. It belongs to their grandfather and if they wish to sell it, they must sell at the government regulated price or pay a stiff fine which equals the sale price. They only own the building, not the land. They were very sweet people. They took a big chance in having us there.*
>
> *We had dinner with Yi Li's family this evening. A huge pot of boiling water was placed in the middle of the table and we were served raw strips of lamb which we then dipped into the water and cooked. Then we dipped it in a mixture of sauces. It was very delicious. Garlic cloves were served along with cilantro as condiments, and noodles. Beijing beer proves to be quite delicious. It is a German recipe the Chinese have adopted. There are no dogs wandering the streets of Beijing. We were told they are not allowed in the city, but, in truth, they appear on the menus here.*

Traveling within China was nearly impossible. Their airports were models of inefficiency. The waiting was interminable and uncomfortable. It took nearly twelve hours to get from Beijing to Shanghai.

> *Shanghai has bugs and they bite! This city reminds me of New York, honking horns and too many people. But, it is fascinating. In a way, I like it better than Beijing. It has more character.*

Shanghai, the most populated city in China, was a mind-blowing spectacle of ancient temples, lush gardens, and glittering skyscrapers. The streets were teeming with business people, street venders, tourists, automobiles, and even rickshaws. I noticed how much capitalism had infiltrated the country. On one of our tours of Shanghai, we came upon an altar to MasterCard.® The Chinese had honored the credit card logo

Standing in front of the Shanghai Film Studio with Bob Roos and our Chinese guides.

by placing the image on an enormous billboard attached to a massive, white-columned building. The image shimmered in a long reflecting pool. MasterCard,® a major symbol of Capitalism, was literally enshrined in Communist China! In all these places, we visited with local Communist leaders. Bob and I took every opportunity to espouse the virtues of Capitalism.

On October 4, I had my moment in the spotlight. Bob and I visited the Shanghai Film Studio. The facility was founded in 1949 but had been shut down for a number of years at the beginning of the Cultural Revolution led by Mao Zedong. Much of their film negative library was destroyed at the time, and the studio was used to produce propaganda films to further Chairman Mao's political campaign. In 1990, the studio had begun to resume entertainment film production. The sound stages were smaller than those in Hollywood, and their equipment was outdated, but they seemed enthused to be able to exercise some level of creativity to make motion pictures.

I had taken a video tape of *Claudelle Inglish* to show an invited group of filmmakers and film students. They knew nothing about American films, or American "stars." They had never heard of Elvis Presley! I probably should have taken a copy of *Spinout* to show them. After we watched *Claudelle Inglish*, I participated in a question and answer session that was quite interesting. Although the young filmmakers were making movies for popular entertainment, each film had to be reviewed and approved by the Chinese government before being released.

Before leaving, we viewed film clips representing their current work. The technical quality was very good. The subject matter was a bit old-fashioned and very melodramatic. The storylines reminded me of traditional Chinese theater that arose in the late 18th Century. A few days before, we spent an evening at the Beijing Opera. We saw *The Legend of the White Snake*, based on a centuries old Chinese legend and the famous and much-performed opera, *The Monkey King Wreaks Havoc in Heaven*. We were in awe of the brilliant costumes and makeup, the acrobatics, and martial arts-style of movement displayed in the battle scenes. I'll never forget the loud, falsetto voices, the staccato music, and the graceful dancing. The production was nothing short of a spectacle. I noticed that there were not many Chinese people in the theater. Most of the patrons were visiting international athletes and their families. When I asked our interpreter, he explained that most Chinese people had to work six days a week. They did not have time or money to spend on such luxuries. I wondered how many of them had the time or money to go to the cinema.

The next day, we traveled for two and half hours to the garden city of Suzhou. The architecture was a bit of an anomaly. The city, which is located on the Yangtze River and criss-crossed with canals, looked like an old village in Europe. We visited the thousand-year-old Yunyan Pagoda, which is known as the "Leaning Tower of China." Suzhou is the center of the profitable silk trade.

> *Oct 5. We went to a silk factory where they make Liz Claiborne dresses, and saw a Chinese fashion show where they modeled clothes from ancient times to the present. I saw a couple of beautiful Claiborne dresses that I will look for in the U.S.*

At dinner tonight the subject of advertising came up. Because it is one of the areas of my expertise, it occurred to us China needs to advertise on U.S. television to regain American tourism, improve its image abroad, and to overcome the awful June 4 memory. The people here are saddened by the loss of the influx of American people and ideas over the last decade. Making a commercial is an excellent idea. Bob will write a letter to persuade the government along these lines and I will do a storyboard with a sample for them.

We requested a tour of the China Welfare Society Children's Palace in Shanghai. The imposing building is completely made of white marble. More than a million children attend this school, which aims to develop adolescent interest in the arts. They learn to sing and dance, and play instruments. Their studies cover traditional and folk performance to contemporary works.

Oct 6. The Children's Palace was delightfully different. Socialism works in three areas. One, their prices are very low. Two, their social control is effective — they have few criminals and they know how to rehabilitate them. This kind of treatment would probably grate on our Western sense of individual civil rights, but it does work on crime. Three, they know how to train and treat children. They are dealt with strictly, but kindly. The education system is a number one priority, so they get the best teachers. They are paid comparatively well so they live better than most workers. The Children's Palace is a free art school where children go after regular classes. They begin training there at three years old. I saw a nine year old girl play a classical piece on the piano. She was brilliant and I expect she'll be a concert pianist one day. The children learn many artistic skills. They only pay for the materials they use. When the Chinese convert to a free market economy, as they inevitably must, I hope they don't lose sight of such successful programs.

Oct 7. Our guide, Zhang, picked me up at the hotel and took me to a Buddhist Temple. He was impressed by my knowledge of Buddhism. Zhang is an attractive young man whose consideration of my every need was endearing.
Later Bob and our entourage went to a Mass at a Catholic Church. I think we must have freaked the worshippers out because Bob took a video of the service, and Mr. Ji wore his official Mao suit. The service was all in Chinese. Once in a while I recognized "alleluias."

Oct 8. Today, yet another meeting at a so-called "law school" — it was more like a school for police and corrections officers. Our hosts, Mr. Lee and Mr. Mao, graciously answered all my questions about re-education camps and recidivism rates, which are very low in China. Then, we ate in the "American" section of the dining room, separately from our hosts. It was delicious food, but I don't understand why they separate the Chinese from the Americans.

We left Shanghai for Xi'an. Fraught with delays. It was raining when we arrived and we were driven in royal style in a chauffeur driven limousine, escorted by a police car with sirens wailing.

The next morning, we toured the Qin Shi Huang Mausoleum, built in the third century B.C., and saw the bewitching Terracotta Army. Thousands of life-size terracotta soldiers stand in frozen, ancient formation in the mausoleum. Xi'an is also the eastern terminus of the Silk Road, a confluence of trade routes linking all of Asia.

Oct 9. We went to a Moslem mosque and photographed the Moslem people. Their free market bazaar was interesting. The sales pressure was intense. I bought a beautiful handmade abacus for Evan. Dinner was with the Mayor of Xi'an at our beautiful hotel. Since Bob is pushing for us to spend less time here in Xi'an and Chengdu, the schedule has changed often, but it looks like we won't be getting our way, after all. We want to get to Lhasa in time to take a land vehicle across the Himalayas to Katmandu.

Oct 10. I discovered last night that my writing material was missing from my hotel room! I dreamed an incredible dream and woke up with the completed screenplay in my head. I wrote up the treatment while I sat in a meeting where they discussed arbitration procedures at a plant that builds airplane engines and employs 16,000 people. They all live near the plant, are provided for in every way, except, of course, the freedom to choose to leave. They could leave, but the consequence of such a decision would be a drastically different life. The set up really forces these people to accept the intrusion of the company into their lives, which they do at every level. If there is a dispute, they think nothing of re-educating people in morals and behavior, an outrageous idea to most Americans.

When I returned to the hotel, I found that my missing writing materials had been returned to my room!

The trip from Xi'an to Chengdu took nearly twelve hours. We waited most of the day for the plane to arrive. What was supposed to have been our welcoming luncheon banquet was served to us after dark.

Chengdu is the capital of Sichuan Province. This beautiful city, dating back to the Bronze Age, was filled with contradictions. Chengdu was one of the most livable cities in the country, and had become an important

Up close and personal with a Panda cub at the Chengdu Zoo.

economic center. It was also legendary for its historic production of stunning Chinese brocade.

> *Oct 12. In the morning, we attended the Intermediate People's Court to witness a trial of three men who had stolen on several occasions. They were poor, uneducated farmers, who had no work. The case and their guilt were pretty much determined before they got to trial. There were three judges, the prosecutor, and the defense attorney. There was written testimony taken by police investigators, and one witness.*
>
> *In the afternoon, we went to the Chengdu Zoo to see the pandas. What a treat that was! One panda had twins. We were allowed to see the babies, which is a privilege reserved for very special people. Their eyes weren't quite open yet, and they were the size of little puppies. So cute! The mother panda was beautiful as she cuddled her babies. I got to*

> touch one of the babies on the nose. I felt extremely lucky — God surely is smiling on me, he gives me so much!

The Chengdu Zoo is the world's most successful breeder of pandas. Sichuan Province is home to 80 percent of the 1,500 giant pandas in the world. I was disappointed by the prison-like concrete cages at the zoo. The enclosures had dirty glass windows for visitors to gaze through. Even the pandas lived in concrete boxes. I thought their living conditions were deplorable.

> Later we visited another Buddhist Temple. Although it was impressive, it was not unlike the one we saw in Shanghai. The most intriguing feature was a spacious room filled with 500 smiling, life-size Buddhas, mostly made of jade! Each was different from the other. They also lined the corridors that spread out and away from the Buddha with one thousand hands. Great images!
>
> That evening, another lavish banquet. The officials of Chengdu seem more garrulous than the previous politicians and authorities we've met along the way. They love to party and did so with a very strong rice wine called Wuliangye. It tasted just like the Maotai in Shanghai. Very intoxicating! Maotai has a very high alcohol content, and is served at special occasions. They like to play Gam Bay (Chinese for "bottoms up"), challenging each other to drink more and more.
>
> Here I met the perfect prototype for my heroine in the screenplay. Her name is Yang Fan. She is our interpreter, a delightful young woman with an adorable personality.

Early the next morning, we flew to Lhasa, the capital of Tibet. It was cold, and the air was very thin. Bob and I caught colds. We visited the bazaar and watched the poor people pray and lay prostrate on the ground. One man ran through the street and repeatedly skidded on his hands to a facedown position in the dust. I wanted to tell him his sins were certainly forgiven. What a sight! Many people had prayer wheels and endlessly chanted.

> Oct 13. Trying to get our road trip to Katmandu is like pulling teeth. Mr. Liu is so angry that he must go with us to the border as interpreter on our drive through the Himalayas. Every time I see him, he asks me to change my mind. I sat with him and Mr. Ji at dinner and felt so uncomfortable that I've decided he should go home. Perhaps we can do without an interpreter.

We visited a Tibetan hospital. I must say it was interesting, but odd. Their religion is heavily involved in all aspects of their lives. No less in their medical care. They built shrines to the founders of medical treatment and revere them as Gods. The originator lived in the Eighth Century. The charts he composed about the human body are fascinating. But, it seems they revere the past so much they have become stuck in outmoded beliefs and antiquated treatments.

This afternoon we spent time in the countryside with the peasant farmers as they harvested wheat. It was incredible to watch the process done by hand as it has been done for centuries. My cold worsened, and I was glad to get back to the hotel, although I loved watching the children laugh and play behind the plows. Such beautiful simplicity. I pitied the poor skinny donkey that had to pull the plow, but the yak didn't look too unhappy!

A couple of days later, I toured the Potala Palace in Lhasa. The palace, consisting of more than a thousand rooms, had been the chief residence of the Dalai Lama until the fourteenth Dalai Lama fled to India after the Chinese invasion in 1959. Though officially stripped of any spiritual significance, the rooms and grounds still exuded a sense of peace and serenity. Being there reminded me of my earlier fears, fueled by Hollywood movies, of mysterious Asian temples filled with the thick smoke of incense and esoteric chants in monotone voices. Yak oil served as candle wax to the flickering candlewicks illuminating the smoky area surrounding the huge statues of Buddha. The mingling aromas, musky with a strange, temple-laden scent, created an overwhelmingly awe-inspiring spiritual space. Like magic, the atmosphere transported us from the world of the mundane to the world of the spirit.

Still more beautiful were the faces of the believers as they filed past us mumbling their chants and prayers, their hands folded together in respectful Namaste to the Buddha, their eyes aglow with innocence and hope. They were a noble but rugged people; their brown skin, eyes, and clothing reminiscent of South Americans and Polynesians.

Our days in Tibet were extremely special. High in the mountains and nearer the stars, I raised my eyes up to the brilliant celestial bodies. I was reminded of my time on the Colorado River with my son, his and Mary's baptism, our doves, cats, and parakeets. All that I had done since the rape to make life bearable again came flooding back. It seemed little wonder that the ancients had looked to the heavens for their answers. I realized then that I was truly living by the grace of God. My life was flashing before me in full, blazing, magnificent Technicolor.

> *Oct 15. Getting the Chinese to agree to arrange our trip through the Himalayas has been very difficult. They have done it, very reluctantly. They cannot understand why we would want to do such a thing. Hardship is something to be avoided, not sought after. Tonight, at our final official Chinese banquet with the President of the High People's Court in Tibet, there was a commotion outside the door that called our hosts away from the table. When they returned, they told us we were supposed to go to the countryside the next day to meet some herdsmen. Of course, we were leaving for Katmandu the next day. Bob had told me earlier that if they gave us anymore flak about the trip, he was going to apologize for being a poor guest and assume our own care, then cancel our road trip and leave by plane, which is exactly what he did. They were so embarrassed that they had forced him to take such a stand. They were all apologies. Bob was sincere, but it had been a ploy that he knew would work. They reassured us that all the necessary plans and supplies were ready. We were not to worry, we would leave in the morning by car as we had requested. Mr. Ji, a true Communist who is definitely a non-believer, told us he knew God would bless our trip through the Himalayas, and bring us to Katmandu safely. He brought tears to my eyes.*

We began our road trip to Katmandu on October 16. The road was treacherous, but the countryside was magnificent. The haunting topography reminded me of the otherworldliness of Mono Lake and Death Valley in California. One difference was the amount of waterways on the 160-mile drive from Lhasa to Shigatse. The area was rich for farming. We drove along a vibrant river, and I noticed a trail carved out of the mountainside. I thought it a perfect setting for a scene in my screenplay.

> *Oct. 17. The news came too late. Two feet of snow had fallen on the road during the night. We cannot proceed as planned. They don't have snow clearing equipment. We are so disappointed we will not be able to fulfill our dream plan. If we get to see Mt. Everest, it will be from the air. But, cancellation has caused problems. Our scheduled flight to Katmandu leaves from Lhasa International Airport tomorrow at 9:50 A.M. This means we must turn around and return tonight on these treacherous roads. It made us wonder if this was a passive-aggressive way for our hosts to punish us for insisting on the land trip.*

We arrived at the Lhasa Airport Hotel at one o'clock in the morning. The inclement weather had caused a blackout in the area. In addition, there was no running water. We had to awaken some disgruntled people at the hotel, but they didn't want to help us. They told us to go back to Lhasa, an hour away in total darkness! We finally got rooms. I had to feel my way around in the pitch black to find the bathroom. I didn't bother to

On the mythical, storied road to Katmandu.

undress, and fell asleep under a heavy quilt on a bed I couldn't see. At six in the morning, the lights suddenly snapped back on. I awoke, but there was still no water. We waited at the airport for three hours. The waiting rooms were crowded with smokers. I shivered outside in the freezing cold.

> *They do not make it easy, as expected. They thoroughly searched our suitcases, and scanned our papers. When it came time to board the flight, the most difficult part was saying goodbye to our hosts. Especially hard for me was saying goodbye to our interpreter, Mr. Liu. He is a very special man. I felt we had become very good friends. When I first met Mr. Liu, I thought he seemed nice enough, but his skin was bad, he has dandruff and his teeth are set too far apart. As time went by and we got to know each other, Mr. Liu became more and more interesting, more intelligent, and more spiritual. As I got to know him better he grew in stature, he turned out to be stronger and more independent in his thinking than I originally thought. He was more attractive at the end of our trip than at the beginning. It was cute what he said to Bob just before we left. "If she wanted to, I could do it for her." Coming from this rather shy and modest man, the statement was not only very endearing, but, I thought, given more time and different circumstances, I might consider it.*
>
> *Oct 18. Katmandu is far more pleasant than Lhasa. It is warm, I can breathe, and it is very cheap. The hotel is nice and the room is only nineteen dollars a day! The service here is overwhelmingly enthusiastic. In China, people were kind and helpful, but very laid back. You had to ask for everything. Here, they offer. It is less crowded. The people look exotic. Nepal is ruled by a royal family and King Birendra. It is capitalist on the verge of becoming more democratic. Change is in the air.*

At the hotel, I finally had access to a newspaper printed in English. Once we had left Beijing, I rarely saw the news. There were no news stands or newspapers and no English language news on television. Select news items were handwritten in Chinese on large "dazibao" posters that were posted on public walls. People could stop and read the approved news items. The Chinese people seemed basically uninformed about world events. They barely knew what was going on in their own country. I had difficulty talking to them about world affairs. They tended to parrot the official party line. Once in a while, someone might open up and discuss Chinese affairs, but they were not savvy and somewhat in the dark about their own politics.

Cows rule the day in Katmandu. We came upon a cow lying in the middle of the street and a bull standing over her as if to ward off any calamity. And, God forbid, don't run into one. If the cow is killed, it is 20 years in jail for the driver!

Transportation is difficult. They have pedicabs, buses, taxis, and little motorized carts. All conveyances are bursting. Buses have people stuffed into them and hanging from the roofs. The little carts are squeezed with little faces peering out the small windows. The pedicab drivers sweat and struggle up the hills carrying fat Americans. Bob had to sit forward because his fat backside wouldn't fit. I decided that would be the last of my pedicab rides.

When we arrived in Katmandu, the Tihar Festival was underway. The five-day-long Hindu and Buddhist festival, which honors and reveres humans and animals, is celebrated throughout Nepal. The second day of the festival celebrates the dog and his relationship to man. People string beautiful handmade marigold garlands around their dogs' necks. The dogs are fed especially well on that day and worshiped. This was quite a departure from China, where dogs were on the menu.

The third day celebrates the cow. In Hinduism, the cow is a sign of prosperity and wealth. They are draped with flowers and hand-painted with festive, colorful paint. It was quite a sight! The entire city was in a festive mood. Multi-colored flags were hung from windows and on ropes strung between windows overhead. Homes and businesses were decorated with candles and flowers. The people wore flowers in their hair, and were draped with spectacular floral garlands made of the most vibrant and beautiful blossoms. The people were blissfully unaware of the rest of the world. Steeped in tradition, the festival was gloriously beautiful, and I was so happy that we could be there.

The festival has made the city a cross between Christmas, with candles and twinkling lights everywhere, and Halloween, with children dressed in costumes going to all the hotels and businesses to perform for money. It was like the Fourth of July with loud fireworks. Lots of noise. Hard to sleep.

Oct 18. Hinduism dominates the culture. There is a lot of poverty and everywhere we go there are people begging, selling, or trying to con money out of Americans. As soon as they see us, their faces light up and they say, "Hello! You are from America!" That's all the English they know.

They think we're a soft touch. Their hounding is difficult to take when they're trying to sell or con something out of you. But, the ones who beg are the hardest of all. It is obvious how desperately they need money, and yet, you know the children with infants on their backs have been sent by the adults into the street to get money from the tourists.

After dinner, we walked back to the hotel past a small child curled up against the cold, sleeping alone on the sidewalk. It's a heartbreaker.

The next day, Bob and I traveled to the countryside to see a Hindu temple. I was not prepared for what I saw there. People were cremating their dead on funeral pyres next to the Bagmati River. The river flows into the Ganges, and thus is considered holy. The dead who had family members to tend to them were carefully wrapped in white and gold shrouds. There was one poor man who had evidently starved to death in the streets. He had no attending family. He was simply laid out in the clothes he had died wearing. There was no special ceremony for him.

Oct 19. After building the pyre, they carry the body around it three times before laying it on the tinder. The oldest son anoints the head with water and oils, and encircles it with flowers. The son lights the fire, then a professional takes over. It takes three to five hours to complete. The remains are then swept into the river. Children innocently play and swim nearby. Women wash their clothes in it. The contrast is startling to Americans who are used to hiding their dead. The smoke was hard to take. Not because it smelled unusual. The odor didn't bother me, just the thought.

Everywhere we went today we saw monkeys, cows, cow pies, poverty, filth, begging and selling. The temples are old and beautiful. At the temples, they make offerings of fruit, and then the flies come. Passing by, the flies rise up by the thousands. The streets have an old world charm, but the people here...it's too hard for me.

On our last day in Nepal, we drove up to the town of Dhulikhul, a typical Newari town with nearby Tamang villages, about forty-five minutes from Katmandu. The countryside along the narrow winding road was lush with tiered colorful plots of produce. We finally got a respite from the filth and the flies at the charming Himalayan Horizon Hotel. Located on a mountain crest at an altitude of 5,500 feet, the hotel commands a panoramic view of the Himalayans. Kings and Queens have stayed at this legendary spot. The hotel was old-world charming with tables outside to eat in the sunshine on a comfortable patio that was surrounded by stunning flower gardens. The food was decent and, for me, the mountaintop oasis was a huge relief from the throngs of begging children in Katmandu.

As we sat on the patio enjoying our view of Mt. Everest, something extraordinary happened as the sun slowly passed overhead. Everything around us — the buildings, the gardens, the trees, the hillsides, the mountains, and even the people — all turned a golden yellow color. Every man-made object, every living thing, even nature itself, glowed a warm, radiant gold. I had never seen such a breathtaking sight in my life. We all experienced the moment in awe. After our fascinating travels, it was the perfect ending to our adventure.

> *Oct 20. Travel day. The quality of travel improves as we have moved farther away from China. The Bangkok airport is a great improvement. However, Bangkok is a huge city with little charm or beauty. One big concrete block.*

On our last day in Thailand, we took an early morning tour of one of Bangkok's famed Floating Markets. We boarded a boat and trafficked our way through small canals crowded with boats piled high with rainbow-colored fruits and vegetables, fresh coconut juice in the shell, and local delicacies cooked on floating kitchens. The temples along the way were amazing, but a small zoo that displayed crocodiles stuffed into a small pond, a gorgeous tiger squeezed into a tiny cage, and reptile handlers playing with snakes, was very sad.

Early the next day, after an amazing month in Asia, we flew home on United Airlines. I had never seen such repression, social control, and rigid order, such abject poverty and filthy living conditions, such venerable ancient history, such a deep sense of tradition, and such faith and devotion of spirit in the face of adversity and hardship. I had never seen such beauty. I had jumped at the chance to go on the trip because I love travel, and I wanted to bring color and detail into my screenplay, but I took so much more than that away from my time in China, Tibet, and Nepal. I left with a newfound appreciation of the power of the human spirit and the importance of devotion to the soul, a truly life-changing experience.

In a very short time, I completed my screenplay, titled *West Wind*. The "big" story is filled with adventure, love, and politics. My epic has yet to be produced.

Chapter 33

My head was still awash with the seductive beauty of China when I guest-starred in an episode of *Jake and the Fat Man*, titled "I Know That You Know". Talk about going from the sublime to the ridiculous. There's nothing like the artifice of Hollywood to bring you back to your senses. The detective series was created by television's wonder-boy, Fred Silverman, for CBS. A rotund and genteel William Conrad played a Los Angeles District Attorney, and handsome Joe Penny played his assistant.

As the holidays approached, and after living by his own wits on the streets of West Hollywood, Evan called and tearfully asked to come home. Of course, I welcomed him back, but I noticed a new willfulness and impatient temper in my son. I knew Evan smoked pot. Since I did myself, I wasn't terribly concerned about his occasional use. Smoking marijuana seemed to relax him and help him focus, but I suspected any drug usage at all might compound the problems he was dealing with. I didn't know if he was using any *other* drugs, though I had my suspicions. Selfishly, I didn't ask, and he didn't tell. I was content to have him close by again.

This began a pattern of coming and going that, painful for both of us, would continue for the next several years.

With the exception of taping an unsold CBS television comedy pilot in early 1992 with Brian Keith called *The Streets of Beverly Hills* (I was cast as the mayor); there were no acting roles for me. To supplement my income, I continued to work in the office of All Saints' Church in Beverly Hills. My job there had me in a quandary about how to help the homeless without making them more dependent upon us. I thought the parish needed a more humane approach, if for no other reason than to give these people dignity by simply following the example of Jesus.

I had formed a committee of like-minded people at the church to research ways to aid the homeless. Janet was a committee member and she'd been on the lookout for someone who could help us.

"You've got to meet this man!" Janet said excitedly. "This man is amazing! He is so committed to the homeless problem that he refuses to leave homelessness himself until the problem is solved."

"He is homeless?" I asked.

"Oh, yes. He chose to become homeless, of course."

"Oh…" I replied a little sarcastically.

"You have to meet him, Diane."

"Okay. What can it hurt? Does he have a phone number?"

"Yes." She checked her phone book for the number. "Ted Hayes…"

I found it easy to pick up the phone, even though I had no idea what I would find on the other end of the line.

"Justiceville. May I help you?" The voice on the phone was pure honey.

"I'd like to speak to Ted Hayes, please."

"Speaking."

"Hi. My name is Diane McBain and I…"

"Hello, Diane," he said disarmingly.

"I'm calling you because your name came up."

"Get outta here… really?" He sounded genuinely surprised and pleased.

"No kidding. You seem to have made quite an impression."

"I hope it was good."

"It was all good."

"What can I do for you today?"

"I need a knowledgeable speaker to talk about homelessness to our group at church."

"You've found the right man," he replied. We quickly agreed on a date.

I felt very comfortable talking to him, feeling as if we'd been friends for years. His way of speaking was in tune with mine. Our friendly banter was almost like singing a duet.

"By the way," he added. "If you're interested, we're meeting next Tuesday about the riots. We're trying to form a West-side coalition to address the problems between the communities. We hope to stem the tide against any more discontent. Would you like to come?"

"I'll be there!"

I hadn't driven east of my apartment since the Los Angeles riots (dubiously called the "Rodney King Riots"). My neighborhood was spared the horrible violence that gripped the city for three days beginning April 29, 1992. The overwhelming civil unrest was the result of a "not-guilty" verdict for the policemen who were videotaped beating an African-American man named Rodney King following a traffic stop. Building after building displayed the scars of a rampage that had paralyzed the city of Los

Angeles and only ended when the Army was ordered into the streets. I passed countless buildings that had been looted, vandalized, and blackened from uncontrolled fires.

Ted's neighborhood just west of downtown was ethnic enough for a single white woman to feel a little nervous at sundown. I was apprehensive. Dressed for work, I looked horribly out of place. Luckily, there was a parking space directly in front of his office.

The simple storefront had nothing to indicate its purpose. There were heavy drapes covering the windows so I couldn't see inside. The front door was gated, and the windows were barred. When I entered, I noticed cheap overstuffed couches, a desk, and bulletins thumb-tacked to the walls. There was a full-color photo of an African-American man with a beard, whom I rightly assumed was Ted.

A woman swooped in from the rear of the office. She seemed a little surprised when she heard my name. I could tell she recognized me. She was warm, welcoming, and very attentive. She gave me some literature about Justiceville to read and something to drink.

Suddenly, Ted appeared in the middle of the room without seeming to have entered. He drew everyone's focus immediately. *Who was this man?* I wondered.

He was tall and reedy, with beautiful, ebony-colored skin. His long dread locks and beard were flecked with gray. He wore the kind of clothing you might find on someone who lived in the desert. He sported a yarmulke on his head. His hands were long and graceful, and the way he used them gave the impression of a man who knew what he was about. His eyes showed a deep understanding and compassion. He was strong, while still gentle, polite, and completely without defensiveness or guile. His eyes turned to me.

"Hi, Ted. I'm Diane McBain. We spoke on the phone."

"Right. All Saints' Church." His eyes were penetrating. I felt a strong presence, a shock of recognition even though I had never met the man.

I mumbled something about wanting to hear more about his organization.

For the next two hours, he had my undivided attention while he told me about Justiceville, U.S.A., a concept about transitional housing and the manufacturing of small biospheres by and for homeless people. An outgrowth of Buckminster Fuller's "Bucky-Ball Domes," these proposed dwellings were small synthetic igloos that could house two people each. There were larger communal domes for shared kitchens, as well as recreational rooms, toilets, and baths. Ted envisioned small domed villages in cities and towns throughout the country, where residents could work out their issues before moving into permanent housing.

"A chronically homeless person is suffering from shell-shock, much like a combat veteran does," Ted explained. "You can't take a combatant out of the killing fields and place him back into a domestic situation without giving him a little time to transition. The difference is too extreme. It's the same for the homeless. They need a transition period to readjust to civilian life again."

He continued without taking a breath. "Warehousing, which is the way most shelters operate, provides no space to really settle into. You get a bed, maybe a locker, and that's it. There is no availability of telephones or an address to use so you can seek employment. There is no time to become established, to find work, even if you want to. There aren't adequate places where you can brush your teeth and go to the bathroom, no privacy, and no responsibility to contribute to a community, which is required in my plan.

"The spirit of this country was founded on the backs of pilgrims, who were essentially homeless people. They were the persecuted ones. The people no one wanted. Then, there was a new land to turn to. Today, we don't have such a luxury. So, we have to find unused land here."

"That's a pretty big dream you have," I said.

"It'll work," he said, "because everybody wins. I've talked to people in the government and in business who say they like the idea because it solves a lot of their problems, too. Businesses are especially hampered when homeless people are sleeping in their doorways."

"But you have to form a coalition, right?" I asked.

"Right," he said. "They want to see grass roots support from the communities. And, domes or not, we still have to contend with N.I.M.B.Y. You know, 'Not In My Back Yard.'"

"Well, you couldn't have picked a better time to find willing helpers," I said. "Almost the entire Westside is filled with a sense of responsibility and a desire to see change since the riots."

"That won't last long," Ted sighed, "which brings me to the reason for this meeting."

I suddenly realized that as we talked, the room had filled with a few people of all sizes, colors and types. Their faces were friendly. Ted was passionate about his subject. I believed what he was saying because he believed what he was saying.

Ted eloquently spoke at our church committee meeting about how chronic homelessness occurs. In his view, the newly homeless come to learn over time that they are freer than they ever were when they towed the corporate, capitalist line and slaved in a nine-to-five workplace. I understood that very well. I could see how the lure of freedom could lead a person down that path. I couldn't imagine living that way myself, being a creature of comforts, but I could understand their feeling.

Soon after Ted addressed our group, I found myself involved with his Westside coalition that was comprised of several folks from my church, Rabbi Frehling from Brentwood, and members of the Justiceville team, who were essentially homeless people. We called ourselves "New Day L.A." and worked to raise funds by staging events that promoted the idea of community unity, which was the foundation of our mission statement.

After a while, I came to realize that chronic homelessness is a lot like drug or alcohol addiction, only in this case freedom was the intoxicant. The substance abuser tends to lose interest in personal hygiene and all the responsible behaviors that make for a productive citizen. In the same way, the chronic homeless person becomes unproductive and self-destructive.

One morning, an idea struck me: if chronic homelessness is so much like drug abuse, perhaps the problem could be helped with the twelve-step program of Alcoholics Anonymous. I set to work immediately editing the program into words that would be appropriate for the homeless person and turned the twelve steps into a recipe for healing chronically homeless people.

I took my plan to the community relations director at our church. "We can have a free lunch here once, twice, or five times a week and invite the people who come to a meeting afterwards. If they don't want to stay, they can leave, of course, but it would be a wonderful way for the homeless to help each other get out of the rut they are in and become more interested in society again."

The director's reception was cool, to say the least. "The church doesn't have enough money to offer free lunches every day. I'm sorry, Diane, you are just going to have to do what we have asked you to do. Three bag lunches, three bus tokens, and that's it."

"But it's important that we do what Jesus would do, and I just don't think it's befitting Him to offer so little."

"These are not the best of times and the church doesn't have the money." He was intractable.

This was the second time he dismissed my proposals. He had promised to expand the homeless lunch program during an earlier entreaty if I could cut the cost of the proposed extra lunches in half. With Janet's help, we did, but nothing happened. The homeless program never changed. I was very disappointed.

I called upon Marianne Williamson for help. As I knew Marianne at the time, I believed she was first a child of God, second a spiritual leader, and third a Jew. She was also strong-willed and polarizing. To some, she was a ministering angel, especially to people suffering the effects of AIDS. To others, she was the Devil incarnate. Neither extreme impressed me. When people come up with such divergent views, I look for the person within.

As far as I could tell, Marianne's integrity was unequivocal. She had always proven to be a principled and devout woman, though she was not always easy to deal with. She was intimidating and her intensity unnerved people, including me. Yet, I had long ago gotten to know her and found that whatever her momentary display of passion, her heart was always in the right place.

When I first saw Marianne during a lecture at a local church, we exchanged a knowing look. When we met a few minutes later, she indicated that she, too, felt a connection. We had been friendly ever since.

"So, what's on your mind," she asked.

"I'm finding it increasingly difficult to feel positive about my association with All Saints' Church. At every turn, I'm stymied and blocked when I offer new ideas to help the homeless and others in need." I told her what had happened with the program director. "These are normally very sweet, kind people," I explained, "but when it comes to the homeless, attitudes change.

"We are supposed to be Christians, for heaven's sake. I understand that budgets have to be met, and I know times are rough for everybody, but if we are to call ourselves a church, then we must lend a helping hand. We can't slap people in need on the wrist." Unexpectedly, I began to cry. "The whole thing makes me want to leave the church altogether."

"What do you want to see happen, Diane?" Marianne asked.

"I want to see a new program that could help the homeless help themselves." I told her about my free lunch plan at the church, and a new twelve-step program presentation that would be coordinated by homeless people for their own benefit. "I'd like to see it happen every day, but a free lunch and meeting once a week would be better than what we do now."

"How much would it cost?" she asked me.

"I have no idea. It depends on a lot of factors."

"Your time isn't up at the church just yet," she said authoritatively, "at least not in my opinion. I think God needs you there. You may not continue to work in the office, but as a member, you will need to remain for a while longer. Get me a budget and I'll fund the entire first six months of the program, whatever you decide it should be — $10,000 or $25,000 — whatever it takes. The donation will be anonymous. We won't tell anyone." Marianne smiled conspiratorially.

Marianne Williamson was unwelcome in most mainstream churches. She was perceived as a "New Age" monster. Her ideas about Jesus and who he really was were supposedly the antithesis of the church's position. To many, she was a heretic. In my opinion, her ideas were a step "above." The church was like the Pharisees in Jesus' day — protecting the status-quo. The church was the guardian of the past while the new covenant struggled to survive and prosper. I didn't know what Jesus would have said about Marianne, but I had a feeling he would have liked her. No, she wasn't perfect, but Jesus didn't require perfection. God always seemed to choose those who were damaged, wounded, and less than perfect to do His work.

I was called into a meeting with the program director at church. I excitedly thought that he had reconsidered my proposal and was receptive to my new approach. We were joined by a woman, who had recently come to church and promoted her own ideas about how to deal with homeless people.

"I hope you don't get upset about this, Diane," the director said, "but we've decided to hire Joanna here to head our homeless program."

Joanna sat with her hands folded in her lap like a penitent. She was wafer thin and gaunt, and her hair was pulled into a tight bun. She didn't appear to be malleable.

"She wants to put together a once-a-week lunch with services."

"Services?" I asked. "You mean church services?"

"No," she piped in. "I want to offer a roster of places where the homeless can get more help, and refer them there. We will do the calling around for them and send them where they need to go."

"Oh," I said. "Well, were you told about my idea for a self-help, twelve-step-program? Maybe we could do that, too."

"We don't think they'll be interested in that," she stated. "At the shelters, they are often forced into drug rehab and most of them have been in drug and alcohol related twelve-step-programs before. I doubt they'll go for it."

"Well, honestly, I doubt they'll be interested in your referral program either," I said.

"We think this is the best way to go, Diane," the director stated. "And we are very excited to have Joanna here to head it up."

I folded my papers and left the room. I never mentioned my program idea to Marianne again and All Saints' Church never got that anonymous donation. Ted Hayes later told me that people in the field of social services don't really want to solve the problem of homelessness because the outcome would put them out of work. He said, "They may not realize it, but they unconsciously do things to sabotage any real possibility of solving the problem."

I, however, involved myself at the service level, and when the once-a-week lunch program for the needy was launched, I worked in the church kitchen serving hot meals. It was satisfying to volunteer, and while people were eating, we would sit and talk with them. Most homeless people really appreciated the conversation because on the street, they were usually ignored.

"You really helped me out, Diane," a Vietnam War veteran said to me one day. "I don't know if I would have ever dealt with my situation without our talk."

"I also experienced the Vietnam War!"

We connected immediately. He had been a medic during the conflict and had euthanized some dying soldiers in the field. He believed he was doing the right thing at the time, but the thought of taking another's life, even for humane purposes, proved to be too much for him. He never told anyone about what he had done. When he returned home from Vietnam, he drowned his memories in drugs and alcohol.

I was gratified to know that I could be there and hear his confession. As a result, he changed his life and now helps others. Surely, this was what we, as Christians, are supposed to do.

In a short time, I was fired from my job in the reception office. All Saints' Church considered me too much of a maverick for their taste. I was relieved. I was glad to be away from some of the folks whose values I questioned. I felt it was hypocritical to love God and deny Him at the same time.

I had been working on a project for "New Day L.A." We scheduled a rally to talk about homeless issues in the city. Marianne Williamson was originally slated to appear with many other notables, including Rabbi Frehling from the synagogue in Brentwood, and some so-called "New Age" proponents. Before I had a chance to pass out flyers at church promoting our event, Marianne cancelled her appearance. With our meager funds, we could not reprint the announcements.

John, an associate minister at the church, invited me to lunch a couple of days before my last day of work in the office. "You are so gracious, Diane," he said. "I don't know many people who would take getting sacked as well as you." John was a nice man, and I trusted his counsel. However, he then told me that the "New Day L.A." flyers had to go. With Marianne's name printed on them, they were not acceptable on All Saints' property.

"Why?" I asked. "As it turns out, she won't even be at the rally, and it's too expensive for us to reprint the flyer."

"They feel that Marianne's view of Jesus is a misrepresentation and counter to that of the church."

"Rabbi Frehling doesn't even *believe* in Jesus and he's on the flyer."

John explained how the church felt about the "New Age" movement and how spiritually dangerous some of its practices were. Although I also felt some of their methods did not promote a relationship with God, the book, *A Course in Miracles*, did. In fact, that relationship was the thrust of the set of books from which Marianne had always taught. She never took any personal credit for writing or promoting the course. No one did. It appeared to me that Marianne had a powerful relationship with God. The church was taking a curious, hard-line position.

"The course is based on the Gnostic tradition which looks good in the beginning, but proves detrimental in the long run," John explained.

I had never heard of this Gnostic tradition so I knew nothing with which to counter his statement. I didn't even really know what it meant to be "New Age."

"Maybe the New Age movement is less than desirable," I said. "The Power of Positive Thinking is perhaps missing the point and misleading. But, having a positive self-image has value."

John said, "The church clergy agrees that nothing with Marianne's name should be allowed on the campus of All Saints' Church."

I was compelled to leave the church and never look back. What closed-minded people they seemed to be. When I approached the Rector some time later, I asked if she had read *A Course in Miracles*. She said she hadn't, but she depended on the assessment of church scholars who had dismissed the book. If she had read the work herself, without bringing to the experience all of her prejudices, I could not imagine she would have come away with the opinion she held now.

Nevertheless, I discovered that the bonds I had formed at church were too powerful to abandon. Forgiveness, I knew, was really the impetus to a happy life. The Twelve-Step Program recommends forgiveness. *A Course in Miracles* teaches that any resentment we retain toward others only eats away at us — rather than those who caused the ill will. Our old wounds project onto our lives, and create even more problems. We need to forgive. I didn't like the feelings of anger and resentment toward members of the church that consumed me. I needed to work on myself.

Chapter 34

While Ted and I worked together on his projects, we became closer. We were a good professional team. I lent a bit of stability and legitimacy to his mission. ARCO surprised us both and expressed an interest in underwriting Ted's planned dome village. The thrill of success inevitably spilled over into our personal relations. Though I tried to ignore our attraction, beneath the surface there was lots of sexual tension.

One night after working at Justiceville, Ted drove me home in his van. We parked behind my apartment. Instead of quickly going inside — as was my habit — I lingered to talk. Ted was warm, open, and hell-bent on telling me how unsuitable for me he was. I got "The Speech." Many men seem to feel the need to give a woman a "heads-up" about their many shortcomings. Perhaps they think that the woman who is forewarned is forearmed. He spoke about his marriage. He said he was separated from his wife, but not divorced. I'd heard the story countless times before. I'd sworn to God, Jesus, the Holy Spirit, the Gohonzon, the Buddha, and I'd sworn on my mother's grave that I would never get involved with another married man, but here I was — dismissing his confession as if his words meant nothing. He spoke of his many infidelities. He said he was incapable of monogamy. Because of the life he had chosen, he said he actually preferred to stay away from women entirely. He smiled and said he'd considered becoming a monk.

I'd heard all of this before. Ted was a natural leader and very much his own man. He exuded a strong sense of independence. These qualities made him dangerously attractive to women. I was certainly no exception. I didn't know what would happen between us, but I knew any relationship would be dramatic, emotionally painful, and I knew I would probably regret it.

Ted was an intense man. I loved his knowledge and intellect. Though unschooled, he was wise and thoughtful. Long a proponent of the homeless, he had distinctly original solutions to their problems. I also soon learned that other people's pettiness and shortsightedness were the major hurdles to overcome.

"I'm going on a cruise," I told Ted.

"Get outta here. Are you really?"

It was time to pick up the loose threads of my personal life. My friend Freddie, who had always harbored romantic feelings for me, had been in Bangkok during the Los Angeles riots, and hadn't witnessed the blatant anarchy. I came to realize that there is no effective government without the tacit approval of its citizens. We believe that our system of law and order is what keeps us safe. In my opinion, we are fooled.

While Freddie was in Thailand, he witnessed a revolution. The people of Bangkok pulled off a coup that brought democracy to their land.

"Have you ever seen 90,000 people in one place at the same time?" he asked. "It was an amazing sight."

"I'm sure it was," I said. *It was also quite amazing to see thousands of vandals and hoodlums loose in the streets of Los Angeles, wantonly torching businesses after they were looted,* I thought.

Ever since Freddie had returned from South East Asia, he was feeling a bit neglected by me. We had been good friends for such a long while. At the time, we were dating, hoping we could find something "more" in our relationship. He felt threatened by my newfound interest in being an "activist." Freddie was a "proper" and reliable date. He knew everyone in town, and they him. He had accompanied me to an AIDS benefit at my church and was my dinner date at Chasen's Restaurant to honor our friend Iris Cantor and her Center for Breast Imaging at UCLA. Freddie loved to travel and enjoyed my company, so he proposed we go on a weekend cruise together.

"Are you taking your son with you," Ted asked. "Or is this a romantic cruise?"

"Well, romantic isn't exactly it. Freddie and I have been close friends for more than thirty years. There's nothing terribly passionate. Just nice."

"Like a warm cup of coffee?" Ted had an uncanny way of taking my thoughts and turning them into words.

"Yes, that's it exactly."

"Good for you. You need that once in a while."

An odd feeling overcame me. I realized that I wanted him to be jealous and forbid me to go on the cruise.

"Have a good time," he encouraged. He genuinely wanted me to enjoy myself. I was hoping for another reaction altogether!

Freddie and I had a nice time, but he was like an old shoe — comfortable and "worn in." Though Freddie was my mother's age, he had a very youthful attitude. He was a lot of laughs, but I had trouble getting Ted off my mind. Ted had invaded my spirit and I couldn't shake him.

After the cruise, the Budget Director of the Federal Department of Health and Human Services visited us at Justiceville. He was attentive and seemed interested in our work. He encouraged us to continue to explore new, creative ways to deal with the problems that plague the inner cities. However, he offered no financial help or government grants to help us move forward.

When the meeting was over, Ted was severely depressed and lamented, "We've already devised many creative ideas to help the inner cities. What does he think we've been doing?"

I invited him over for drinks. Ted drank wine and brooded. I felt for him. As a performer, I understood the process of gearing up for the big moment and the emotional crash that always follows. He was a leader, whose life and ideas were at stake. I could imagine the pressure he must have felt to produce results and the disappointment when nothing came of his efforts. Boy, did I know what that was like.

I watched Ted closely, and found him watching me, as well. *It's in the close-ups!* I thought. In film, the drama happens when the camera zooms in for a close-up of a face. The camera searches for that instant when the eyes and heart connect. Ted sat across the room from me, but we were definitely connecting on a deep level.

At the end of the evening, I walked Ted to the porch and as he was leaving, I reached up to hug him. "Good night, Prince of Justice," I said.

His arm encircled my waist and his black cape wrapped us in a shadowy cocoon. His dark eyes penetrated mine and I went limp. At that moment, I knew we would become lovers.

He telephoned the next morning, still sounding like a defeated man. He was feeling the weight of failure. He said the pain in his heart was too much to bear. While we were talking, an aide dropped a bill needing payment on his desk. His voice cracked when he told me. I hadn't heard him cry before. I prayed he would be lifted up.

"I wish I could help you… financially, I mean. You need to get away. You need time away from making these impossible decisions." Before I could stop myself, I blurted, "Go make love."

"Yeah," he said, "I need that. I don't have that in my life right now. It's been a while."

"You need to get away."

"You're right. I know."

"Come over here and spend a couple of days." *What was I thinking?* I was appalled by my words, but they continued to slither from my mouth like slippery little snakes. "We won't tell anyone and they won't know where to find you." *Good God*, I thought. *What was I saying?*

Ted arrived at five that evening.

We sat and talked for hours. I served dinner, though neither of us was very hungry. For weeks, I had been losing my appetite. My stomach was filled with butterflies.

"I've never been good at monogamy, not for long, anyway," he said.

"Monogamy is *not* common to the *male* of the species," I stated.

Ted talked about his wife. His marriage, he said, was completely over. They were not divorced, but had lived separately for many years. His lack of money prevented them from formally divorcing. Though I had often seen his children, I rarely saw his wife so his explanation seemed plausible. I *wanted* to believe him, but I sensed there was something else keeping him from divorcing his wife, something he wasn't revealing.

We discussed my life, too. He listened attentively and sympathetically. It was easy to reveal myself to him because he genuinely seemed to care. Soon I was making my own speech about how many times I'd been hurt, my rapes, and my miserable marriage. He didn't criticize or judge me. I felt exposed, but loved. In the Garden of Eden, Adam and Eve were naked and not ashamed. I felt that way after we had revealed so much to each other.

We talked about our sexual histories. Ted had also been molested when he was only four years old by his blonde, blue-eyed babysitter. (I took note of the blonde hair and blue eyes. I thought he might be obsessed by blue-eyed blondes. His wife was blonde, and there had been a couple of photographs at his office of other women he'd dated. They had blonde hair and blue eyes.)

How strange it was that both Ted and I had been "sexualized" far too early in our lives. We were damaged. We believed that our chance for happiness was doubtful. Nevertheless, we were both compelled down a path, though we were also both reluctant to take that first step.

"If we do, it will mean that we must be careful in front of others," he said.

"I know," I sighed. "I know about discretion. At the very moment you want to yell joyfully from the rooftop, you are muzzled like a sorry dog."

"Worse," I added, "it's a sin. But sometimes God says, 'Disrobe my child.'"

"He says *what*?" Ted laughed.

We both laughed a lot on that passionate, steamy night.

The more I got to know him, the more I realized we were alike. Neither of us was chaste. We were God lovers, nevertheless. We didn't agree on everything. He was, at once, both more conservative *and* more radical than I was! However, where it counted, we were almost the same. We cared about the same social issues. I marveled at the contrast of our skin colors. He was as "black" as I was "white." Yet no such contrast existed in our souls. My hand resting on his was an image reminiscent of the "New Day L.A." logo: black and white hands shaking in peace.

"We are all pink on the inside," he said, almost reading my thoughts.

"Can we still be friends, do you think?"

"Best friends."

He broke into a sweet love song. His voice was fluid and distinctive. Entranced, I was feeling things I hadn't felt in years. Twenty years had passed since I swore, in the midst of despair, that I would never "let a man get to me that way again." Never was a long time and it felt good to be awakened from the twenty-year sleep — at the age of fifty!

The days became a time for remembering the passionate night before, and the nights became a time to make more wonderful and enduring memories. My heart swelled, and I was at peace when Ted was near.

"This is good for me," he said. "I've been much better since we've been together like this."

"Better for me, too," I said.

He sang to me again, and we laughed and swayed back and forth in time to the beat.

"This is nice," he said.

"It's the kind of nice you don't want to let go of," I answered.

Chapter 35

Though I was able and proud to put aside the racial differences that Ted and I shared, some of my friends were less accepting of our developing relationship.

Howard was a confirmed bachelor I'd met at a Marianne Williamson lecture. We had dated on and off for a while. He was born in the Deep South. Though he denied it vehemently, he was a bigot and a misogynist. His psychosexual history, especially his Freudian relationship with his stepmother, was fraught with emotional junk. He clung to his psychosis, perhaps hoping the hang-up would "protect" him from marriage. Because he was raised by an African-American nanny and came to love her like a mother, one might expect that he would have fond, or at least, cordial, thoughts toward African-American people. He did not.

After my dismal attempt at romance with Howard had failed, I occasionally saw him for dinner. He had a problem with monogamy, too, so I always felt like a mistress rather than a girlfriend. He spent his weekdays in Los Angeles, so that's when we spent time together. During the weekends, he stayed with another woman in Malibu Beach. He claimed she was only "a friend in Jesus." He said he wasn't in love with her and since she was ten years his senior, there was no sex. When I asked him to tell her about me and suggested that I meet her, he refused.

"I can't tell her about you, Diane," he said. "It would hurt her too deeply."

Since there apparently was no thought about how hurt *I* might be, I stopped sleeping with him.

One evening in my living room after dinner, he grabbed me around the waist and pulled me toward him. I was especially uncomfortable because Ted and I had been intimate there earlier in the day. I felt "cheap" being now in someone else's arms.

"Tell me again why we can't make love like we did before." His strong Southern accent made the question sound especially lewd. He tried to pull me closer.

"I am ten years older than Ted," I said, as I pushed him away. "Just because a woman is ten years older doesn't mean she isn't sexually desirable and active."

"What is that supposed to mean?"

"You are spending your weekends with a woman who you say is not sexually attractive to you because she is ten years older. Well, I am ten years older than Ted."

"Are you having sex with Ted?" he snapped.

"Yes." Anticipating his reaction, Danny couldn't help but smile.

"Diane! You are a white woman!"

"Yes. That would be true, Howard."

"He isn't with you because you look young and beautiful, which you are still by the way, it's because you're *white*! Do you want people to think you're some sort of Nigger arm-candy?"

I was shocked speechless.

The man I had met in a spiritual setting burned red with frustration. "You can't have sex with him! It's not smart! You will have worse problems than you do already! What about AIDS? He probably has it, you know!"

I wasn't completely surprised by his reaction, but I was stunned by his vehemence. When I criticized him for his ignorant, racist attitude, he justified his prejudice by telling me he wanted to protect me. (Many men had told me before that they wanted to "protect me." The only thing I needed protection from was them!)

"From what," I asked. "Do you think I don't know? Already we've been stopped twice by the police. That's the first time in my life that's ever happened to me on a date. We were stopped for no reason except the cop assumed I was in the car under duress. Why would he assume that?"

"You see?"

"I see a lot. It's about sex, isn't it? It has never been about a fear of African-American men becoming too powerful or controlling. It's not about crime, or business, or politics, or sports, or anything — other than sex. It's always about sex. You're afraid they'll abscond with all the white women if we allow this *integration* to go unchecked, right Howard?"

I edged him to the door, and said goodbye. It saddened me, knowing as I did, that so many shared his ignorant feelings.

One evening, Freddie and I were discussing politics and presidential candidates. Freddie joked that he'd rather elect a homeless person than any of the current crop of hopefuls.

"I may just have the person for you," I said. "He's homeless and he's political. He's smart and he has vision. He has a unique perception of the world and…"

"He's homeless!?"

I nodded.

"You're joking, of course."

"I'm not kidding. Ted Hayes. You met him yesterday. He was over to pick up the material I typed for him and I introduced you," I explained.

"You mean that black fellow with the…" He motioned with his hand to indicate dread locks and smiled ruefully. "We're not ready for him yet."

"What matters is what comes out of his mouth, not how he chooses to wear his hair. He has good ideas and I think he might make an interesting candidate. You're right, though. He'd have to change the way he dresses, at least in public."

"You're serious?!"

"Well, yes… and no."

"Is he the reason you've been so distant lately? Are you having an affair with him?"

I said nothing, but watched the color drain from Freddie's face.

"You aren't doing *that* are you?"

I couldn't help but smile. Danny was rolling on the floor in hysterics. She loved to shock people and thought their reactions were well worth the trouble. "Do you realize how racist you're sounding," I said. "I'm stunned. I'm really surprised. I thought you were so liberal. What happened?"

"Well, yes, I can understand having them in the neighborhood and the schools and working side by side with whites, but not *that*!"

I was shocked to find such prejudices in people I'd known for so long and thought I knew so well. Women friends had also expressed dismay and said they were just trying to protect me. They defended *their* feelings by saying they were simply concerned for my welfare. I believed that underneath all their protestations was a fear of sexual contact between the races. Prejudice, pure and simple.

In my old friend Nadine, I finally found a pair of sympathetic ears. She, too, was dating an African-American man. We spent a lot of time commiserating about the vicissitudes of multi-racial relationships. Such undertakings were fraught with problems.

I had met Nadine at a party in 1961. She was an aspiring dancer then, who had since traded in her leotards for marriage and children. There I sat — as she recalled — perfectly coifed and dressed, makeup thick and forbidding, as I quietly and coldly surveyed everyone and everything.

"Like a princess," she always said with a big laugh. Of course, a lot had changed since then. I no longer felt the need to hide behind Diane and her layers of makeup. I had never really been an "ice-queen," just a frightened imposter. I no longer felt the need to sit back and survey others out of fear that my "fraud" would be revealed. I now realize that celebrity is a huge burden to place on one who isn't ready. Nadine and I had a friendship based on a long history practicing Buddhism together, and later Christianity. We didn't see anything wrong with interracial sexual relationships or mixed marriage. It was nice to have her to talk to because we were both steeped in the "molasses-like morass" of love with imperfect strangers. *Not everyone was against me,* I happily thought.

Chapter 36

My relationship with Ted had developed quickly with intense passion. "I'm serving dinner 'bass-ackwards,' I told him.

"What?"

"Everything is coming out backwards. I mean, I didn't intend to have the salad last. However, I was born that way. My parents used to tell me that I have been doing things 'bass-ackwards' ever since."

"Breach?" Ted asked.

"Yes. And they told me that even though I had *not* been born with a silver spoon in my mouth, my life was charmed because I could fall into a pot of shit and come out smelling like a rose."

"I was born in a toilet," he chuckled, "and I was drunk, too, because my mother was drunk."

"Born in a toilet?" I laughed.

"It took me a long time to get over it."

"Talk about a lowly birth."

"No wonder I'm downtown doing what I'm doing, huh?"

"It follows. Mangers and toilets."

We roared. The irony was funny to us, but our conversation had a cutting edge. Life is never a picnic for a person who chooses to live by the dictates of his God-conscience. I knew — perhaps we both knew — it was only a matter of time before Ted's commitment to homeless causes would come between us.

Since the Los Angeles riots, my life had taken a turn that led me to believe that love and peace were possible on an intimate level as well as on a broad social level. At least, temporarily, I could believe so. My relationship with Ted had my head spinning. "New Day L.A." proved to be successful and influential. Neighborhood gangs had begun to reconcile. At last, a large corporate sponsor stepped up to help us when ARCO funded our first dome village.

I wanted to believe we could have a life together, but running away with Ted was unrealistic. He was still married, yet I wanted to be with him regardless.

We both had decisions to make. I thought love was all that mattered. Ted did not. That's what made him loveable to me. He had the courage and the conviction to make larger issues (such as the plight of the homeless or justice for the poor) his first priority. He lived that way and that made him a giant in my eyes. Ted was phenomenal with young people, too. He could inspire them and rally them into affirmative action. He was truer in his beliefs than the religious bigots who spoke a good line but didn't practice one. This is what I loved about Ted, until I realized his commitment to his cause was his way of avoiding intimacy. This was probably his reason for refusing to get a divorce.

The tenuous balance that was struck in the city was in danger of spinning out of control at any minute. Ted was in the midst of all the uncertainty. I wanted to support him in any way I could, but he was beginning to look at me in a different way. I was becoming a threat. He had a reputation with the ladies, and as distressing as it was for me to admit to myself, I was a part of the problem. I was not good for his career or his life.

"I am a mess," he said. "I have so much to say, but I don't have the character to do it. People don't believe me because I am so undisciplined with women."

"We've been all over this county to various schools, and city and county functions to promote "New Day L.A." and the dome village. The audiences are always very enthusiastic," I reminded him.

He gave people something constructive to think about but that was not enough for him. His self-image was at stake. He believed he should be a monk, but he was far from that! In truth, the community demands from its activists a kind of moral perfection. When the activists cross moral boundaries, their leadership abilities are compromised.

One hot July night, we left my apartment and walked down the street to get some ice cream. The two of us got quite a few glances. I suspect all the attention had something to do with the unusual elegance he bore. Ted looked like a regal personage. He was, in fact, at that time — a walking dichotomy.

Bathed in the light of a full moon, we sat on a cement wall to eat our ice cream.

"Do you see the man in the moon?"

"No," Ted said, "I could never see that."

"What do you mean? You can't see the man in the moon? I thought everybody could see the man in the moon!" I was astonished.

"Well, I can't," he replied. "I've heard, though, there's a rabbit in the moon."

"A rabbit?" I looked up. The shadows that created the image of a man's face wouldn't give way to the image of a rabbit. Ted pointed out the ears and the nose, but I couldn't see it.

He tried to see the man in the moon, but was completely unsuccessful. We can only see what our brains will allow us to see, or maybe what we want to see, or perhaps we've seen something one way for so long that we can't see it any other way. We laughed at our inability to see what the other saw.

When we made love, though, we had no problem communicating. We were one. When I woke up the next morning, Ted was laying on top of the covers fully dressed. His eyes were closed and he looked like he was lying in state.

"Are you all right?" I asked.

An eyebrow lifted. "Yeah," he said.

The man who lay beside me was the exiled king. This man saddened me. He was cold and distant.

"I have a problem with women," he stated flatly, "and it keeps me from concentrating on the things I need to do to accomplish my goals. That's why it's taking so long."

There wasn't much I could say to comfort him. The dome village would soon open. Either he couldn't see our success, or he was pushing me away.

Soon afterwards, I realized he was pushing me away. Suddenly, there were more women in the picture, his wife was spending more time at his side, and the domed community began to grow. Perceived as a threat to Ted, I was forced to step aside. A year would pass before I saw him again.

I was emotionally devastated by the ordeal. I had made a fool of myself in every way. Danny had found her perfect man and wasn't about to let go. Diane had her objections. She didn't like being trumped by other women. She was insanely jealous of the new females in his life. I was overwhelmed by my feelings, and shocked that I was reacting in such a manner.

I was excluded from the opening ceremonies of the dome village. The completion of the project had been my priority for so long. I had also involved my friends with in-kind donations and services for the cause. Yet, I was summarily banished. My emotions were boiling over. I'd never been so furious in my life.

I realized that I had to come to terms with my dependence on the kind of men who would never fulfill my irrational needs. I yearned for a man with strength of character; one who was capable of loving a woman sexually, and would offer consistent and monogamous companionship. I knew there were no perfect mates, but I found it difficult, if not impossible, to be attracted to a man without a libido strong enough to match my own. Such men were normally not the type to settle down. They were usually the ones who played around.

I joined a therapy group that explored dependencies on love and sex. I marveled at how different life had become in our modern world. Women who had been revered as saints in earlier days, because they "sacrificed" their lives for their men, were now told they were co-dependent and unrealistic. I had loved Ted too much. I had idealized him disproportionately. If not for his problems with other women, I would have cast him in the role of the Second Coming. He even looked the part; there was a statue of Jesus in downtown Los Angeles that looked just like Ted. I had fallen in love with an image. Yes, he had many good qualities. However, his inclination to love me one minute and resent me the next outweighed his kindnesses. The "push-pull" of our relationship had me reeling. My emotions were out of control. It was unlike me to taste the bile of jealousy in my throat, and hate anyone as much as I hated the women in Ted's life; including his wife. It was unlike me to pick up a bureau and hurl it, but I did! I was irrational and I knew I needed help.

I found a program for friends and family of compulsive sex addicts. Similar to the "Al-Anon" program for friends and family of alcoholics, the Twelve-Step program was invaluable to me. I gradually came to an understanding of why I fell in love with men who were unattainable to me because they were sexual addicts. It is rather easy for a person to fall into a pattern that involves bad choice. I had to recognize what had attracted me in the past to the wrong man, and unlearn my mistaken defense of my romantic carelessness. This was a difficult lesson for me. The program was very beneficial.

With my goddaughter Mary and Hillary Rodham Clinton at the Beverly Wilshire Hotel in July 1993. Mrs. Clinton received the first Iris Cantor Humanitarian Award at a luncheon to benefit the Iris Cantor Center for Breast Imaging at the U.C.L.A Medical Center.

Chapter 37

Reality slowly crept back into my life. I was unemployed and money was running out fast. I had dedicated so much time to Ted's pursuits, and to worthy charities that I had neglected my own financial wellbeing. I hadn't acted in four years.

In early 1994, I found a new agent and went to work on a film called *Puppet Master V, The Final Chapter* for Full Moon Entertainment. My scene was a one-day shoot in Culver City. The business had changed so dramatically over the years. Gone were the perks and all the great reasons that made it fun to work on a movie set. Again, I had to wear my own clothes and apply my own makeup. There was no one supervising continuity from one take to the next. I had never been on a set with so little attention to detail, but the producers didn't seem to care.

I never saw the finished product, nor did I see the four previous *Puppet Master* films. This series of ultra-violent horror movies was about maniacal puppets that come to life and wreak havoc. The films were filled with perversion and carnage. What a great way to step back into the movie business!

In the midst of trying to put Ted out of my mind and reestablish my acting career, I had an unexpected visit from an old love. Pancho Gonzalez's voice was soft and full of laughter over the telephone. When he later arrived at my door, we were both nervous, but I was certain sex would be as exciting and satisfying as it had been before. I didn't waste much time, and after dinner I lead him to my bed. However, time had taken a toll on him, and on his lovemaking skills. As we lay in bed, he talked about his young son with whom he lived in Las Vegas. He had divorced Madelyn years before, married and divorced again, and then married the younger sister of tennis pro Andre Agassi. There was still no room for me.

In July 1995, I heard the news that Pancho had died of cancer at the age of sixty-seven. I mourned his passing as if we'd been together all along, just as I had Richard Burton. Pancho died in poverty and nearly friendless. The sad circumstances of his death frightened me. Actually, they affected me profoundly. A few weeks later, I was God smacked out of my depression when a car hit me in an intersection. Neither I nor the other driver had insurance. The police officer instructed us to work out our dilemma. We did. I paid for my car and she paid for hers.

I had to find a job. I worked for a couple of local "throw-away" newspapers. I was a copy editor and sold advertising for one. For the other, I wrote an advice column. One of the papers was run by a couple of crooks who swindled their employees. Our paychecks, such as they were, constantly bounced. What little credit I had was destroyed, and my longtime bank closed my account.

I made a promotional film for Princess Cruise Lines, auditioned for acting roles now and then, but never seemed to appeal to casting directors. I wasn't very successful in the commercial market, either. I did make a national commercial for Merrill-Lynch, but had a terrible experience when I lost a national television spot for Sears because the client said I was "too famous and too recognizable"! Unbelievable, since so many people in casting didn't know who I was!

In a short time, Evan met a young woman and the two fell in love. They preferred to live on their own, and tried. Frequently, though, they moved back in with me to make ends meet, or until they could save enough for an apartment. She seemed to provide him with some balance and direction. On the fly, he formed a moving company with a couple of his buddies and began to forge a life for himself.

My old co-worker and long-time friend, actress Sharon Huegueny died of cancer at the age of fifty-two in July 1996. I hadn't seen her for a while, but was aware of her hard fought battle with the disease.

I wanted to attend Sharon's service, but I had an inexplicable sense of foreboding. "I'm anxious about this memorial," I told my friend, John Fulton, as we wended our way through the late afternoon Malibu traffic. John and I had been dating. On our way to where Sharon's life would be memorialized on a cliff overlooking the Pacific Ocean, I talked about her life and many struggles. She had died too soon.

The memorial spot on the cliff was spectacular. Sharon had come there as a young girl to sunbathe and soak up the peaceful atmosphere.

The ocean was smooth and there was a soft breeze, just enough to ruffle your hair.

As we slid down the loose dirt path toward a group of people, I saw a large photograph of a younger Sharon with those sad, brooding eyes peering from her sweetheart face, framed in dark curls. The picture surrounded by beautiful fresh flowers formed a shrine. As we got closer, her photograph became obscured by a crowd of people gathered around B.S., who appeared to be holding court. I was stunned. A deep chill swept over me. *My God*, I thought, *what is **he** doing here?* I couldn't believe my eyes.

His hair was dyed black and pulled into a small, tight ponytail. I thought ponytails only looked good on little girls and ponies, and chuckled at my own joke. I focused on his ill-fitting, out-of-style clothing. As I got closer, I could see dandruff flaked all over his shoulders. When he began to turn his head, his curly, limp ponytail bobbed at the back of his neck. It reminded me of the tiny dick between his legs when he arose from the hotel bed after raping me so many years before. The best revenge is a good laugh, I thought to myself. There are few things in this world as pathetic as a man who women are attracted to only for his wealth.

His reaction to seeing me was visceral. "Diane," he called as he turned to find me passing him by.

I suppose he was surprised that I didn't fawn over him as many others were doing. I simply walked past the inconsequential man I could now see him to be. He actually stammered as I walked away. I took my place on the other side of the bluff with John and some other people, and began chatting amiably. When I looked back, I could see his expression was one of perplexity. Did he really expect me to stop and chat?

I had told John the entire story about my horrible experiences with B.S. and my ultimate rape at his hands. I wasn't used to talking about that awful time in my life. The subject was difficult to resurrect. The violation still gnawed at me, even more so than the second rape. The assault in 1982 taught me to be on guard with total strangers, which was a painful, but useful lesson. However, my first attack at the slimy hands of B.S. had caused me to distrust the men I needed to trust — my dates. This rape had definitely hampered my relationships with the opposite sex. Betrayal by a person who calls himself a friend is much tougher to deal with than becoming trapped by a couple of thugs.

I was angry that B.S. had prospered in show business. Ironically, he was the most famous attendee at the memorial. Many people there seemed drawn to him. They were loudly laughing and talking about the "Biz." In true Hollywood fashion, fame eclipsed the purpose of the get-together. I hadn't kept tabs on his personal life, but I knew he had earned a fortune. I had not. Sometimes I wondered why God had favored him in spite of his sins and blessed almost everything he touched. My anger could take me to very bad places, and I tried to think about my own life and successes. I was thankful for my family, friends, lovers, and acquaintances. My charity work and church service were very gratifying. I felt those small acts of kindness outweighed any success I enjoyed as an actor. Sometimes, I thought that maybe my career had been a waste of time. There was nothing in the entire body of my acting work that made me genuinely proud. What matters is the love I carry and sustain, as I have come to realize.

B.S. clipped my wings just as I was about to take off, and I crashed hard. I *was* haunted by what had happened. I was angry, *still*. Though I knew anger was a foolish emotion, it ate at me! He had not suffered for what he did! I, on the other hand, had suffered enormously. I carried these feelings with me all through the years. Standing on that cliff overlooking the glorious, limitless ocean and feeling dear Sharon's loving spirit, I realized that the time had come to get rid of them. The time had come to forgive.

Later that summer, I was cast as "Granny" in a popular, situation comedy titled *Sabrina, the Teenage Witch*. Melissa Joan Hart starred as Sabrina, and I played her beloved, dead grandmother to whom she turned for sage advice. Most actresses avoid aging as best they can. I embraced the idea and was gratified that casting agents saw me as "grandmother material." I thought their change of perception might open up new doors.

"A Halloween Story" aired on October 25, 1996. As had often happened in the past, I was told by the casting director that my character would be a recurring role. Though my episode was popular with the audience, I never did return to the series.

My friend Vera met a terrific woman named Sandi and the two women "married." Of course, there were no marriage rights for gay men and women at that time, but I honored their union and respected their commitment to one another. Their partnership seemed more solid than many of the sanctioned heterosexual marriages I had known. They lived in a modest house in West Los Angeles. They cultivated a beautiful garden that was rustic and inviting.

Vera and Sandi had two house cats — Minou and Vincent van Cat. The threat of fleas and the expense of getting rid of them kept the long-haired felines indoors. Vera called me one day when Minou became ill. "We've tried everything," she cried. "It's a long story. Come over and you'll see."

I hung up the phone and hurried to their house. Minou was my own cat Moonshine's daughter. My cherished feline companion had recently died after many years of gracing my home.

Vera's little house was badly in need of paint. Her renovation plans were put on hold in order to pay the veterinary bills for Minou. She had decorated the entrance to her house with the beautiful background panels she had painted for Deborah Walley's Pied Piper traveling children's shows. Depicting German mountain villages and thick green forests filled with colorful flowers and animals, the panels were a unique way to welcome visitors to her world.

Her sad eyes met me at the door. "We decided to give Minou a party in the garden for her last hoorah," Vera explained. "She never gets to be in the garden, you know."

Overcome with sadness, I hurried through the house. Minou was a limp piece of white fluff languishing in the cool grass. Though weak, she obviously was at peace and finally able to experience the lovely garden. I gently stroked her and fought back tears.

"She is lucky to have so many people fussing over her," Sandi said. A healer by nature, she was a medicine woman who used homeopathic potions, herbs, and vitamins in her arsenal of curative secrets. She treated their cats, Vera, and anyone else who would submit to her ministrations.

It wasn't long before I was comfortably seated in a lawn chair and handed a glass of wine. My dear friends doted over me and made me feel completely at home. Since my mother had died, I sought out and occasionally found friends who were motherly, would allow me to snuggle up in their homes, and raid their refrigerators.

Languishing in Vera's garden had become a ritual that soothed my soul and separated me from the everyday world of frustration and worry that plagued my life. A respite in the greenery was a custom that helped me remain sane.

To me, rituals are a key ingredient in life, offering calm and strength. My church provided plenty of opportunities with which to center myself. Vera, a self-proclaimed atheist, performed various rites to keep peace and love flowing throughout her world. She found ritual in the upkeep of her beautiful garden, too.

A few years later, I again found myself in Vera's garden with an ailing friend. Deborah Walley had been diagnosed with cancer and fought a brave and valiant fight. Though she had moved to Sedona, Arizona several years earlier, where she founded the Sedona Children's Theater, she often visited Los Angeles. She languished in the colorful garden until her strength gave out. Deborah died of esophageal cancer at the age of fifty-seven. She had been so determined to survive, she had convinced us all she would beat the deadly disease. I was shocked when she lost her fight. Deborah's was another death that cut me to the core. She left behind her two beloved sons and her wonderful screenplay, *Last of the Blues*, which has yet to be produced.

Chapter 38

"Hello." There was no mistaking his voice. "Hello," he said again. I knew the voice was Ted. "Hello," he repeated. "Don't hang up, please."

I stared at the receiver, unsure of what to do. I had mourned the end of a relationship that was never to be. I had worked hard to overcome my grief at the prospect of a lonely future filled with unrealized dreams. *Why was he calling?* Ted's voice was the last thing I expected to hear. Part of me wanted to slam the phone down and part of me wanted to jump through the phone and kiss him madly.

Danny and Diane argued with wild abandon.

You're almost done with him. It's time to put him behind you for good, practical Diane said.

But he makes my heart rush, pleaded Danny. *He makes me feel alive and we mesh so well together in every way.*

That's what you think, but that is your fantasy!

You aren't above having fantasies, Danny argued. *You have to admit Ted makes you think of Prince Charming enough to turn you on.*

Well, that's true. He is magnificent. But you know from experience he is really a dog.

So, the debate went until I heard myself say, "Hi. Gosh, what a surprise."

In truth, I had expected to hear from him. There is an invisible tie that binds Ted and me. Our bond reveals itself whenever one of us is thinking of the other. I hadn't heard from Ted in ten months and hadn't thought about him for several weeks; yet, three or four days before he called, I started thinking about him constantly. I couldn't shake the feeling.

"I need to sit down." My voice shook and I felt faint.

"I know this is a surprise," he said. "Bet you never thought you'd hear from me again."

"I'm shaking and I never thought I would react this way." There was no use in trying to hide my feelings. My body quivered, and so did my voice. A lot had happened since we had last seen each other. The dome village, Ted's dream, had opened in downtown Los Angeles, but not without a hitch.

Before I left the project months before, we had spent hours trying to determine how dome village applicants should be reviewed and approved. Ted felt that anyone who wanted to live in the village should be acceptable. He had a point. How do you discriminate between a drug addict, a mentally troubled veteran, a mental patient, or a parolee? However, should criminals be allowed to live where children will be playing? Ted argued that if we relied on background checks, we would eliminate almost every applicant.

As chair of the Social Services Committee, I felt many strong reasons why we should run background checks on all village applicants. It was also wise to know with whom we were dealing. We could track the progress of our residents, but only if we knew where they came from. We certainly needed to know if they had drug problems, suffered from psychotic episodes, or experienced murderous or criminal urges. If an applicant was unable or unwilling to assume the rules and responsibilities of village life, then it was unwise to allow admission. I felt we needed to leave the space open for someone who was ready for the challenge of community living. Ted and I had been at loggerheads over this issue. He wanted nothing to do with applications or background checks.

My committee was disbanded when I left the project. Unfortunately, I was right.

The initial group of residents was an odd bunch. Some were honest folks trying to get back on track, some were drunks and drug addicts, and some were mentally unstable. Worst of all was a couple with a nefarious past. Unknown to the village, the man was a rapist and murderer on the lam, and the woman was his accomplice. Tragically, a young woman reporter, who was working on a story about the dome village, was raped there at knifepoint by this criminal. The resulting negative press proved devastating to the newly opened village, and Ted's reputation was publicly trashed.

I met the rape victim, who filled me in on the unadorned truth of what had happened. When the commotion eventually settled down, Ted became more circumspect about the people he would allow into the community he had created.

"I'm sorry. This is unfair to call you out of the blue this way," Ted said. "But I was thinking about you and wanted to know how you are."

Ted's mellifluous voice touched my soul and made me weak in the knees.

"You're right," I said. "I thought we were through. What are you doing calling me?" I just couldn't see the next bend in our story line, and so I allowed Ted to slip back into my life.

Our relationship took on a new tone. I was no longer a professional involved with him or his projects. Other women had moved into his professional life and I did not want to be around them.

I wanted a committed relationship with Ted and nothing less. He did everything he could to woo me, but he was not interested in commitment. If I agreed to his request, he would roller-blade ten miles uphill in the middle of the night to sleep with me. Yet, he wouldn't tell his wife he needed a divorce so that he could date me openly.

Dating was a concept he didn't seem to appreciate. Getting him to take me out to dinner and a movie was like pulling teeth. He didn't like to eat and he didn't like movies. He wanted to come over for sex whenever he felt the urge. Other than being very kind to me when we were together, he promised nothing.

Ted was kinder than most. He was the only person to come by and help me through a bad case of poison oak. He brought soothing creams, and said he still loved me even though the poison oak made me look hideous. He said he didn't care how I looked, which was infinitely freeing and wonderful. I couldn't help but love him. Ted's love, even with its manifest shortcomings, was better than anything else in my life. When we were together, our intimacy was just fabulous and seemed to get better as we went along. I rarely connected so deeply with another human being. When I did, it was harder to give up.

I knew my relationship with Ted was a dead-end pursuit. While Danny and Diane battled long and loud in my head, my prayers for strength were answered. The Holy Spirit finally prevailed. To think that Ted could be in love with me was pure illusion. I had to pull back in order to get a better perspective. With the help of dear friends from All Saints' Parish, I began to focus on what I was doing to myself. Fortunately, the Holy Spirit touched my heart, and I saw the light through my pain. My fear vanished.

Breaking up with Ted was one of the most difficult things I ever had to do, perhaps because the sexual relations we shared were the best and most satisfying in my life. It takes me a while to decide important matters, but once I do, I am determined. I still love Ted, but I am resolute about my decision. While we continue to be friends and speak on the telephone, the overwhelming physical attraction we share makes us reluctant to be in the same room together now that we are no longer intimate.

I realized that my decisions are possible only because of the loving support from the people who surround me. They are not here because I am famous, or pretty. My fame and youthful "freshness" are gone. They are simply friends — and I cherish them. My gratitude to God for them is boundless.

I wouldn't act again until I worked in an independent film called *Besotted*, produced, written, and directed by a friend, Holly Angell Hardman. I flew to Massachusetts in 1997, where we shot on location on idyllic Cape Cod. The story concerned a glum alcoholic lobsterman, who holds a torch for a fellow fisherwoman, but she has eyes for a handsome Harvard boy summering in their little New England coastal town. *Besotted*,

On May 13, 1997, Johnny Grant placed his hand and footprints in cement in the courtyard of the Chinese Theater in Hollywood. Connie Stevens and I attended the festive event to honor Johnny, who, amidst the high jinks, misspelled his name!

Holly's first feature film, premiered at the Provincetown Film Festival in the summer of 2001, and was later released to theaters. Even though I knew much more about moviemaking than Holly, I liked working with a female director. I was inspired to see a woman in charge of a feature film.

I thought the script was offbeat and full of literate and sardonic wit. *L.A. Weekly* called the movie "a starry-eyed fable," but audiences didn't appreciate it. Still, I enjoyed getting away to Cape Cod for a short time and eating lobster rolls to my stomach's content.

I filmed an episode of *Dr. Quinn, Medicine Woman* in November 1997. I was little more than an extra, playing a character identified as Old Woman in the episode called "Point Blank." Not long after, I was cast as a strange woman with a strange dog in a funny little movie called *Invisible Mom II*. This direct-to-video film concerned a mother who drank a magic elixir that rendered her invisible. Directed by Fred Olen Ray, the movie starred Dee Wallace Stone. I loved playing the zany Mrs. Chandler.

In June 1998, I was requested to read for a part in a television movie called, *Cab to Canada*. Based on a true story, the film starred Maureen O'Hara. I got the part, or so I thought. When I reported for work, I was in for a surprise. Rather than the part I had read for, I was assigned the bit role of a mourner at a funeral. I had two lines. They gave me a pair of large sunglasses to wear and an enormous floppy hat. I was unrecognizable. I was shocked, insulted, and humiliated.

I had been a celebrity presenter at the 1963 Golden Globe Awards alongside O'Hara. Thirty-five years later, I was little more than an extra in her starring film. I'm embarrassed to say that for the first time in my professional life, I threw a fit on the set. I don't know why they had called me in for such a trite part. I delivered my two lines, and then told the producer I didn't want to be in the film nor have my name in the credits. The entire experience left a very bitter taste in my mouth. Although I acted professionally a few more times, this demeaning episode was a turning point for me and all but destroyed any desire I had to pursue acting.

In early 1999, I attended a Screen Actors Guild (SAG) meeting in Hollywood with my friend, actor John Brandon. Many issues faced actors at the time — especially issues dealing with cable television and new media residuals. The meeting was spirited, to say the least. John talked me into running for the National Board of Directors of SAG. I had never considered running for any political office before. I knew that the issues we discussed that evening profoundly affected actors and our ability to earn a living. I have always been pro-union. Influenced by my father, who was a proud union member when he worked as a bus driver, I had always thought unions protected the common man.

To my surprise, I was elected to the Board! I received the most votes for a non-incumbent. Little did I know that a coalition of board members who supported my run had an agenda of their own!

Several issues dominated their plans. First, there was a move afoot to oust the then current president of SAG, Richard Masur. He was pro-union. I liked Richard, who was very smart and the right choice for the job. The contingent of board members who supported my election wanted to weaken Masur. They expected me to join them in their quest. I didn't, but within months, Masur was gone and William Daniels replaced him.

Members vigorously debated the pros and cons of merging SAG with the other major actors union, the American Federation of Television and Radio Artists (AFTRA). For many reasons, I supported the proposed merger, not the least of which was my belief that such a merger would strengthen the union and the ability of its members to control their compensation and working conditions.

The third issue was a controversial strike having to do with commercials, which was called in 2000. I reluctantly supported the strike. The action, though painful to most of us, preserved Pay-Per-Play residuals and increased cable residuals by 140 percent. Most actors celebrated this negotiation, but there were some who felt that the same terms had already been on the table, so a strike was unnecessary.

I spent the next three grueling and unpaid years fighting politically-motivated battles that riddled our precious brotherhood of actors during some of its darkest hours. I felt like I was running around putting out fires.

In late 1999, amidst the backstabbing and machinations that consumed me at the Guild, I made a charming Christmas-themed movie for Dreamvision Productions called *The Christmas Path*. Dee Wallace Stone starred as a single mother with two young children (in one of his first roles, Shia LaBeouf played her thirteen-year-old son), and Vincent Spano played the part of an angel. I was cast in the small role of a woman who saves the day at the end of the film. *The Christmas Path* went direct to video.

I also appeared in *The Broken Hearts Club*, written and directed by Greg Berlanti for Banner Entertainment. Young and talented, Greg would go on to produce the successful television series *Brothers and Sisters*. *The Broken Hearts Club* was a counter-culture movie about the infatuations, loves, losses, and heartbreaks among an endearing group of gay friends. The cast included John Mahoney, Zach Braff, Dean Cain, Andrew Keegan, Nia Long, and Mary McCormack.

Released in September 2000, the film was appealing and compassionate, and became a favorite with festival audiences. Although my contribution to this movie was minor, I was happy to be a part of such a fine film. My appearance re-introduced me to a whole new fan base that recognized me from my crazy days as an AIP motorcycle hottie.

In 2001, I filmed an episode of *Strong Medicine* called "Silent Epidemic." I played Lovey Carmichael in the one-hour drama for Lifetime Television.

Later that year, I was interviewed by a couple of independent production companies for glossy documentaries about Bruce Lee and Tippi Hedren.

The most dramatic moment, however, happened in May 2001. My duties as a Board member of SAG kept me very busy, but my position, in terms of preserving and strengthening the union, was displeasing to those who had helped elect me in the first place. They did their best to destroy me and drag my name through the mud in the entertainment industry press with false accusations about my conduct. Actors I had worked with and had held great respect for, (including Peter Mark Richman and Richard Crenna), came at me with malice, blatantly lying about my political activities and the activities of others in my coalition. I was brought before the Guild for "conduct unbecoming." I was accused of handing out pro-union merger brochures on Guild property. This was untrue. In fact, I was at home preparing invitations to my sixtieth birthday party at the time. I received the shock of my life when I walked into the boardroom and heard that actors I knew and liked had lied about my actions. After much ado between my attorney and SAG committee members, I was exonerated and the Board voted that my legal bills be charged to the Guild. I felt terrible at not having the resources to pay the expenses myself. These people were "union busters," and I had been utterly naïve in believing that all actors gave credence to their union membership and were in solidarity with one another.

I decided fear drove the opposition, fear engendered by a Machiavellian coalition — a small yet highly intelligent and crafty group of malcontents, who spread fear like wildfire. Their acting careers had all but ended years before, or maybe they never really had careers in show business to begin with. One man, for instance, had played the role of Policeman #67 in one movie, but the tiny part was enough for him to obtain membership in the Screen Actor's Guild. He actually ran for President of SAG while I was there. Another man had gotten his union membership based on his one and only television commercial! Membership in the union was a requirement of their employment and they had joined only under duress. To be forced to join was, in their opinion, an infringement on their freedom. Their intent was to weaken the union, thus making it easier — or so they thought — for new, young actors to get jobs. However, it is the purpose of the union to protect all its members from unfair trade practices, unsafe working conditions, and to guarantee that they are paid for years after their initial filming. The collection of residuals (royalties for performers) enables actors to survive between jobs. They have a right to these resources because their performances are repeated potentially forever.

As a result of my problems on the Board, my name became sullied in the press. All these folks had to do was to *accuse* me of inappropriate behavior and the trade papers ran with the story. Their false accusations were boldly printed in both *Variety* and *The Hollywood Reporter*. My exoneration, however, was barely covered!

In some perverse way, it seemed fitting that my own professional union would be the instrument to drum me out of the business once and for all. Of course, I cannot say for sure whether the overt mudslinging or the negative chatter behind the scenes did me in, but the fact remains that after my acrimonious stint on the SAG board, I never worked as an actress again.

On September 2, 2001, my old friend and most frequent co-star, Troy Donahue, died of heart failure at Saint Joseph's Hospital in Santa Monica. He was sixty-five years old. Troy was a sweet, gentle soul, and I think show business had proven to be too tough a career for him. He had struggled for twenty years with alcohol and illegal drugs before hitting rock bottom. He had finally found happiness with a lovely Chinese woman named Zheng Cao, and he had shared a home with her in Santa Monica for ten years before his death. We had stayed friends throughout the years. We saw each other occasionally and spoke on the telephone. He was a lovely man, and his passing deeply saddened me.

Around this time, Evan bought a small cabin in the mountains north of Los Angeles with earnings from his moving business. With great optimism, he moved there to begin a new life with his girlfriend. In addition to the moving jobs he managed in Los Angeles, he worked at clear cutting and sold firewood in the mountain village to earn a dependable living. Soon, he was able to leverage his finances and buy a larger house.

It became a little too quiet without my son's comings-and-goings in my apartment. With no acting work to distract me, I soon came to feel as though I didn't belong in Los Angeles any longer. I visited Evan and his girlfriend in the mountains whenever I could.

The clean mountain air, the fragrant evergreens, and the comforting winter snow proved seductive to me. I moved into Evan's small cabin, happily far away from the fading luster of Hollywood. My visitors became raccoons, deer, bobcats, rabbits, hares, and an occasional black bear that lumbered past my back porch. Danny, at last, was in her element!

With no small amount of joy, I gave up acting and sought to reclaim my "private life." I reveled in the quietude. I continued my writing projects and even took up quilt-making and watercolor painting. Snow falling in the woods and the crackling of burning logs in the fireplace were just too good to resist. I had come from a hard-working middleclass family. I had lived luxuriously and traveled the world. I had lived amongst the rich and famous and was often in the spotlight myself. I had fallen in love and had been loved. I had had more than my share of joys and sorrows. Through the grace of God, I had survived. All these thoughts comforted me.

The environment required that I be very physical in dealing with everyday life. I now routinely walk to the nearby village for supplies. I bring in the firewood that Evan provides for my use, and I cook everything from scratch. I remember becoming aware of all my senses. By returning to the values my mother had instilled in me, I got in touch with what is important to me.

One day, Evan and I took a little walk in the forest near my cabin. We went to his favorite spot just to sit and talk. I was in a reflective mood. The sky was a soft blue and the sweet-smelling air gentle to the spirit. I felt a million miles away from Hollywood and all that show business represented. I was intensely happy.

Evan had spent many hours in that spot creating rock sculptures. One looked like a Geisha girl doing a traditional dance. Another looked like an old man sitting in the forest contemplating his navel. The third was especially intriguing. Danny's sense of humor, as well as her love of shocking people, came to the fore. "That looks like a penis and vagina poised to make love," I laughed. Though embarrassed, my son had to agree.

"That is such a mom thing to say, Mom!" His ears turned red, but Danny was gleeful.

"On a more serious note," I said, "what you are doing here is meaningful."

"Why?" he asked.

"Life is a process of building, just like you're doing with these rocks. There's the bedrock — the rock bottom — of all that we are and do. The cornerstone determines the balance that the other rocks must find in relation to it. Then, you find another rock to place on top of that one; one that will fit perfectly and balance with the first.

"Sometimes, something will come along and destroy what you have built and you must start again because there is nothing else to do. When you have balanced the stones, one on top of the other, you find that you have constructed something that has substance and value."

"Smoking that funny stuff again, Mom?" he teased.

I smiled shamelessly and said, "When you've lived a while longer, you will want to step back, cast some light on the content of your life, and find some meaning."

Fade: To Light

I live by the forces of serendipity. God leads and speaks to me in this way. He inspires my thoughts and actions. In my view, Jesus was the embodiment of the Holy Sprit of God in the world, and I follow Him.

My experiences have taught me that the life God wants for each of us is different from a life based solely on ego-based gains. It is necessary to relinquish our self-made ego in exchange for the authentic Self created by God. His light burns up the egoistic system because it was a self-made illusion.

Giving love instead of ego is a daily struggle. My ego has been faithful to me for my entire life. However, when I allow it to control me, my life is without direction. God has transformed me into a person who is willing to surrender her self-made ego for the genuine Self that He intended.

There seems to be a moral law inherent in the universe that fosters the progressively intelligent evolution of life. Each of us must find that universal value and nurture it. We carry this quest in our genes. Losing perspective and going off course causes pain. Life is a gift, and bears enormous responsibility. Just as our democratic freedoms include responsibilities of community, life requires our dependability for all other life. I cannot believe there is a time when we do not have this obligation. When I learned to embrace my authentic Self with the help of prayer, my responsibilities became easy to fulfill.

Although I am not an expert, these things seem to be true in my life, and I believe they can be true for anyone. I also sense that all religions, theosophies, and philosophies contain aspects of the same truth-seeking ideas. I do not believe there is only "One Way."

The awful experience with B.S. never took away from me my intrinsic faith in a truth that I believe ultimately leads to a benevolent Creator. No matter what happened to me, even at my lowest point, I always knew there was something more to life than the despair that often clouded my view. Even when God's ways were so quiet that I could not feel His presence, His love always proved to be there when I was in need. God loves us unconditionally as parents love their young. Yet, we cannot deny our insignificance in the universe. Science reveals that we are literally in the universe and the universe is in us, just as the New Testament of the Bible tells us that we are in Christ and Christ is in us. Each of us contains the neurons that comprised suns millennia ago, and each of us contains the spirit of life. We come to know that we are an infinitesimal part of the vastness that is beyond our grasp. Our consciousness, and the love we have for one another, is the bonding agent that makes our uniqueness necessary to the whole. I may not have lived the most conventional success story; clearly, I was not famous enough to suit my acting career. Rather, my true success comes from knowing that God loves me and has been with me always.

Yet, I was on a path that was not complete. There were obstacles in my way. At times, they seemed insurmountable. Bathed in God's light or not, life is never without problems.

One morning after a difficult night, I awoke to a realization that was to take me to the ends of the universe and back. That day, I shot forth into the darkest of nights, the loneliest of solitudes, and the deepest of depressions. This was my "dark night of the soul," which is an expression commonly used to characterize the crisis of conscience that takes us on our spiritual journey. The vastness of the universe we live in is beyond incalculable. I understood myself to be one of the smallest of the small, and as infinitesimal as all atoms. I felt alienated and wholly insignificant.

In truth, I was *not* alone.

I made the journey, with the help of my Creator, to the sublimation of my ego. The journey had begun long before and culminated in a knowledge of the Self that is irreplaceable. Danny was reborn.

As I got to know Danny more — that is, once I became aware of the difference between my heart's desires and the desires of my ego, my life became more "honest" and inevitably more fulfilling. Danny wants integrity to rule her life.

As I pondered my personality, I came to a deeper understanding that Diane is my self-made self. Throughout my professional life, I have felt as if I was just "faking it." I now know that I was! Diane was created out of my insecurities, my fears of rejection, my vacillations, and my self-loathing, all of which increased as my career opportunities diminished.

"If you bring forth what is within you, what is within you will save you. If you do not bring forth what is within you, what is within you will destroy you." This quote is from the non-conical Gospel of St. Thomas unearthed in the Egyptian town of Nag Hammadi in 1945. To me, its truth is undeniable. Diane's hubris nearly destroyed me.

I was with a friend recently, who believes very deeply in God. He is Jewish, yet we share a community of spirit that is helpful to us both. I spoke of the "dark night of the soul," and his response was visceral. A hippie at heart — a person who believes that we must think *only* positive thoughts — my friend threw up his hands and said, "No, I won't go there!" I was astonished. "I don't think you have a choice," I said. "You should try it. You might be surprised by what you can learn."

Love is enough. If we want to know the reality of God, not a version we create in our minds, then we must make this spiritual journey. In truth, we cannot avoid the "dark night of the soul" if we are truly on the path to becoming Light.

Film and Television Credits

All features are noted with release dates, all television shows with the date of original broadcast. This listing includes only credited appearances of Diane McBain as an actress. Television talk show, game show, and radio show credits are too numerous, and not listed here.

Feature Films

Ice Palace, 1960. Warner Bros. PRODUCER: Henry Blanke. DIRECTOR: Vincent Sherman. SCREENPLAY: Harry Kleiner, from the novel by Edna Ferber. With Richard Burton, Robert Ryan, Martha Hyer, Jim Backus, Carolyn Jones, Ray Danton, Shirley Knight, and Diane McBain as Christine Storm.

Parrish, 1961. Warner Bros. PRODUCER: Delmer Daves. DIRECTOR: Delmer Daves. SCREENPLAY: Delmer Daves, from the novel by Mildred Savage. With Troy Donahue, Claudette Colbert, Karl Malden, Dean Jagger, Connie Stevens, Sharon Hugueny, and Diane McBain as Alison Post.

Claudelle Inglish, 1961. Warner Bros. PRODUCER: Leonard Freeman. DIRECTOR: Gordon Douglas. SCREENPLAY: Leonard Freeman, from the novel by Erskine Caldwell. With Arthur Kennedy, Will Hutchins, Constance Ford, Claude Akins, Chad Everett, and Diane McBain as Claudelle Inglish.

Black Gold, 1963. Warner Bros. PRODUCER: Jim Barnett. DIRECTOR: Leslie H. Martinson. SCREENPLAY: Bob and Wanda Duncan, from a story by Harry Wittington. With Philip Carey, James Best, Fay Spain, Claude Akins, Iron Eyes Cody, and Diane McBain as Ann Evans.

The Caretakers, 1963. United Artists. PRODUCER: Hall Bartlett. DIRECTOR: Hall Bartlett. SCREENPLAY: Henry F. Greenberg. Screen Story by Hall Bartlett and Jerry Paris, from the novel by Dariel Telfer. With Robert Stack, Polly Bergen, Joan Crawford, Janis Paige, Van Williams, Constance Ford, Sharon Hugueny, Herbert Marshall, Ellen Corby, Robert Vaughn, and Diane McBain as Alison Horne.

Mary, Mary, 1963. Warner Bros. PRODUCER: Mervyn LeRoy. DIRECTOR: Mervyn LeRoy. SCREENPLAY: Richard L. Breen, based on the play by Jean Kerr. With Debbie Reynolds, Barry Nelson, Michael Rennie, Hiram Sherman, and Diane McBain as Tiffany Richards.

A Distant Trumpet, 1964. Warner Bros. PRODUCER: William H. Wright. DIRECTOR: Raoul Walsh. SCREENPLAY: John Twist, adaptation by Richard Fielder and Albert Beich, from the novel by Paul Horgan. With Troy Donahue, Suzanne Pleshette, James Gregory, William Reynolds, Claude Akins, and Diane McBain as Laura Frelief.

Flying from the Hawk (Huyendo del Halcon), 1966. Zurbano Films. PRODUCER: Cecil Barker. DIRECTOR: Cecil Barker. SCREENPLAY: Jesse Goldstein. With John Ireland, Barta Barri, Antonio Mayans, and Diane McBain.

Spinout, 1966. MGM. PRODUCER: Joe Pasternak. DIRECTOR: Norman Taurog. SCREENPLAY: Theodore J. Flicker and George Kirgo. With Elvis Presley, Shelley Fabares, Dodie Marshall, Deborah Walley, Jack Mullaney, Will Hutchins, Warren Berlinger, Carl Betz, Cecil Kellaway, Una Merkel, and Diane McBain as Diana St. Clair.

Thunder Alley, 1967. American International Pictures. PRODUCER: Samuel Z. Arkoff and James H. Nicholson. DIRECTOR: Richard Rush. SCREENPLAY: Sy Salkowitz. With Annette Funicello, Fabian, Warren Berlinger, Jan Murray, and Diane McBain as Annie Blaine.

The Karate Killers, 1967. MGM. PRODUCER: Charles E. Sellier, Jr. DIRECTOR: Barry Shear. SCREENPLAY: Norman Hudis. With Robert Vaughn, David McCallum, Kim Darby, Telly Savalas, Joan Crawford, Curd Jurgens, and Diane McBain as Countess Margo De Fanzini.

I Sailed to Tahiti With an All-Girl Crew, 1968. National Telefilm Associates and United National. PRODUCER: Richard L. Bare. DIRECTOR: Richard L. Bare. SCREENPLAY: Richard L. Bare from a story by Richard L. Bare, George O'Hanlon and Henry Irving. With Gardner McKay, Fred Clark, Pat Buttram, Richard Denning, Edy Williams, and Diane McBain as Liz Clark.

Maryjane, 1968. American International Pictures. PRODUCER: Maury Dexter. DIRECTOR: Maury Dexter. SCREENPLAY: Maury Dexter, Dick Gautier and Peter Marshall. With Fabian, Kevin Coughlin, Patty McCormack, Teri Garr, Robert Lipton, and Diane McBain as Elli Holden.

The Mini-Skirt Mob, 1968. American International Pictures. PRODUCER: Maury Dexter. DIRECTOR: Maury Dexter. SCREENPLAY: James Gordon White. With Jeremy Slate, Sherry Jackson, Ross Hagen, Patty McCormick, Harry Dean Stanton, and Diane McBain as Shayne.

Five the Hard Way (aka The Side Hackers), 1970. Crown Productions/Crown International Pictures. PRODUCER: Ross Hagen. DIRECTOR: Gus Trikonis. SCREENPLAY: Tony Houston, based on a story by Larry Billman. With Ross Hagen, Michael Pataki, and Diane McBain as Rita.

The Delta Factor, 1970. Medallion Television/Spillane-Fellows Productions, Inc. PRODUCER: Tay Garnett. DIRECTOR: Tay Garnett. SCREENPLAY: Tay Garnett, based on the novel by Mickey Spillane. With Christopher George, Yvette Mimieux, Ralph Taeger, Yvonne DeCarlo, and Diane McBain as Lisa Gordot.

Temporada Salvaje/The Wild Season/Savage Season, 1971. Filmadora Universal/Panorama Films. PRODUCER: Felipe Mier. DIRECTOR: Myron J. Gold. SCREENPLAY: Myron J. Gold. With Isela Vega, Ron Harper, Slim Pickens, Victor Buono, and Diane McBain.

Wicked, Wicked, 1973. United National Productions/MGM. PRODUCER: William T. Orr. DIRECTOR: Richard L. Bare. SCREENPLAY: Richard L. Bare. With David Bailey, Tiffany Bolling, Randolph Roberts, Scott Brady, Edd Byrnes, Roger Bowen, Madeleine Sherwood, Arthur O'Connell, and Diane McBain as Dolores Hamilton.

The Deathhead Virgin, 1974. PRODUCER: Ben Balatbat and John Garwood. DIRECTOR: Norman Foster. SCREENPLAY: Jock Gaynor and Larry Ward. With Jock Gaynor, Larry Ward, Vic Diaz, and Diane McBain as Janice Cutter.

Legend of the Wild, 1981. Jensen Farley Pictures. PRODUCER: Charles E. Sellier Jr. DIRECTOR: Jack B Hively. SCREENPLAY: Brian Russell and James Simmons. With Dan Haggerty, Ken Curtis, Denver Pyle, Jack Kruschen, and Diane McBain as Jenny.

The Red Fury, 1984. Dayton-Steward Organization. PRODUCER: Richard Landerman and Fenton Terry. DIRECTOR: Lyman Dayton. SCREENPLAY: Joe Elliott, based on a story by Joe Elliott, Royce Lerwick, and Douglas J. Stewart. With Cal Bartlett, Alan Hale Jr., Juan Gonzales, and Diane McBain as Mrs. French.

Puppet Master 5: The Final Chapter, 1994. Full Moon Entertainment. PRODUCER: Charles Band. DIRECTOR: Jeff Burr. SCREENPLAY: Douglas Aarniokoski, Steven E. Carr, Jo Duffy, Todd Henschell and Keith S. Payson. With Gordon Currie, Chandra West, Ian Ogilvy, Nicholas Guest, Clu Gulager, Ron O'Neal, and Diane McBain.

Invisible Mom II, 1999. Concorde-New Horizons. PRODUCER: Ashok Amritraj, Joe D'Angelo, Fred Olen Ray, Alison Semenza, and Andrew Stevens. DIRECTOR: Fred Olen Ray. SCREENPLAY: Sean O'Bannon. With Dee Wallace, Mickey Dolenz, Mary Woronov, Barry Livingston, Kathy Garver, and Diane McBain as Mrs. Chandler.

The Christmas Path, 1999. Dreamvision Productions. PRODUCER: Bernard Salzmann. DIRECTOR: Bernard Salzmann. SCREENPLAY: Bernard Salzmann. With Dee Wallace Stone, Vincent Spano, Madylin Sweeten, Shia Labeouf, Allan Rich, Marcia Wallace, and Diane McBain as Laura.

The Broken Hearts Club, 2000. Banner Entertainment/Meanwhile Films. PRODUCER: Mickey Liddell and Joseph Middleton. DIRECTOR: Greg Berlanti. SCREENPLAY: Greg Berlanti. With Timothy Olyphant, Zach Braff, Dean Cain, Nia Long, John Mahoney, Justin Theroux, Andrew Keegan, John Brandon, Jennifer Coolidge, and Diane Mc Bain as Josephine.

Besotted, 2001. Surf 'n' Turf Films, Inc. PRODUCER: Holly Hardman, Amy Jelenko, Isen Robbins, and Aimee Schoof. DIRECTOR: Holly Hardman. SCREENPLAY: Holly Hardman. With Jim Chiros, Susan Gibney, Holly Hardman, Liam Waite, and Diane McBain as Mrs. Buell.

Television

Father Knows Best "Betty Makes A Choice." March 2, 1959, CBS-TV.

Maverick "Passage to Fort Doom." March 8, 1959, ABC-TV. Diane played Charlotte.

77 Sunset Strip "Six Superior Skirts." October 16, 1959, ABC-TV. Diane played Laura Stanley

Bob Hope Special "Deb Stars." November 9, 1959, NBC-TV.

Maverick "The Fellow's Brother." November 22, 1959, ABC-TV. Diane played Holly Vaughn.

77 Sunset Strip "The Starlet." February 26, 1960, ABC-TV. Diane played Paula Harding.

The Alaskans "Behind the Moon." March 6, 1960, ABC-TV. Diane played Harriet Pemberton.

Bourbon Street Beat "The Missing Queen." March 14, 1960, ABC-TV. Diane played Ginny Costello.

Sugarfoot "Return to Boot Hill." March 15, 1960, ABC-TV. Diane played Joan.

Bourbon Street Beat "Wall of Silence." March 28, 1960, ABC-TV. Diane played Lorraine Elliot.

77 Sunset Strip "Fraternity of Fear." May 6, 1960, ABC-TV. Diane played Doris Spinner.

Lawman "The Judge." May 15, 1960, ABC-TV. Diane played Lilac.

Bourbon Street Beat "Ferry to Algiers." June 6, 1960, ABC-TV. Diane played Christina.

Surfside Six "Country Gentleman." October 3, 1960, ABC-TV. Diane played Daphne Dutton.

Surfside Six "High Tide." October 10, 1960, ABC-TV. Diane played Daphne Dutton.

Surfside Six "The Clown." October 17, 1960, ABC-TV. Diane played Daphne Dutton.

Surfside Six "According to Our Files." October 24, 1960, ABC-TV. Diane played Daphne Dutton.

Surfside Six "Local Girl." October 31, 1960, ABC-TV. Diane played Daphne Dutton.

Surfside Six "Par-a-kee." November 7, 1960, ABC-TV. Diane played Daphne Dutton.

Surfside Six "Deadly Male." November 14, 1960, ABC-TV. Diane played Daphne Dutton.

Surfside Six "Power of Suggestion." November 21, 1960, ABC-TV. Diane played Daphne Dutton.

Surfside Six "Odd Job." November 28, 1960, ABC-TV. Diane played Daphne Dutton.

Surfside Six "The International Net." December 5, 1960, ABC-TV. Diane played Daphne Dutton.

Surfside Six "The Frightened Canary." December 12, 1960, ABC-TV. Diane played Daphne Dutton.

Surfside Six "Girl in the Galleon." December 19, 1960, ABC-TV. Diane played Daphne Dutton.

Surfside Six "Bride and Seek." December 26, 1960, ABC-TV. Diane played Daphne Dutton.

Surfside Six "Little Star Lost." January 2, 1961, ABC-TV. Diane played Daphne Dutton.

Surfside Six "Heels Over Head." January 9, 1961, ABC-TV. Diane played Daphne Dutton.

Surfside Six "Facts on the Fire." January 16, 1961, ABC-TV. Diane played Daphne Dutton.

Surfside Six "Yesterday's Hero." January 23, 1961, ABC-TV. Diane played Daphne Dutton.

Surfside Six "Thieves Among Honor." January 30, 1961, ABC-TV. Diane played Daphne Dutton.

Surfside Six "License to Steal." February 6, 1961, ABC-TV. Diane played Daphne Dutton.

Surfside Six "Race Against Time." February 13, 1961, ABC-TV. Diane played Daphne Dutton.

Surfside Six "Black Orange Blossoms." February 20, 1961, ABC-TV. Diane played Daphne Dutton.

Surfside Six "The Chase." February 27, 1961, ABC-TV. Diane played Daphne Dutton.

Surfside Six "Ghost of a Chance." March 6, 1961, ABC-TV. Diane played Daphne Dutton.

Surfside Six "The Impractical Joker." March 13, 1961, ABC-TV. Diane played Daphne Dutton.

Surfside Six "Inside Job." March 20, 1961, ABC-TV. Diane played Daphne Dutton.

Surfside Six "Invitation to a Party." March 27, 1961, ABC-TV. Diane played Daphne Dutton.

Surfside Six "Spring Training." April 3, 1961, ABC-TV. Diane played Daphne Dutton.

Surfside Six "Double Image." April 10, 1961, ABC-TV. Diane played Daphne Dutton.

Surfside Six "Circumstantial Evidence." April 17, 1961, ABC-TV. Diane played Daphne Dutton.

Surfside Six "Vengeance is Bitter." April 24, 1961, ABC-TV. Diane played Daphne Dutton.

Surfside Six "Little Mister Kelly." May 1, 1961, ABC-TV. Diane played Daphne Dutton.

Surfside Six "Spinout at Sebring." May 8, 1961, ABC-TV. Diane played Daphne Dutton.

Surfside Six "The Bhoyo and the Blonde." May 15, 1961, ABC-TV. Diane played Daphne Dutton.

Surfside Six "An Overdose of Justice." May 22, 1961, ABC-TV. Diane played Daphne Dutton.

Surfside Six "Count Seven!" September 18, 1961, ABC-TV. Diane played Daphne Dutton.

Surfside Six "The Wedding Guest." September 25, 1961, ABC-TV. Diane played Daphne Dutton.

Surfside Six "One for the Road." October 2, 1961, ABC-TV. Diane played Daphne Dutton.

Surfside Six "Daphne, Girl Detective." October 9, 1961, ABC-TV. Diane played Daphne Dutton

Surfside Six "The Empty House." October 16, 1961, ABC-TV. Diane played Daphne Dutton.

Surfside Six "Witness for the Defense." October 23, 1961, ABC-TV. Diane played Daphne Dutton.

Surfside Six "Laugh for the Lady." October 30, 1961, ABC-TV. Diane played Daphne Dutton.

Surfside Six "The Affairs at Hotel Delight." November 6, 1961, ABC-TV. Diane played Daphne Dutton.

Surfside Six "Jonathan Wembley is Missing." November 13, 1961, ABC-TV. Diane played Daphne Dutton.

Surfside Six "The Old School Tie." November 20, 1961, ABC-TV. Diane played Daphne Dutton.

Surfside Six "A Matter of Seconds." November 27, 1961, ABC-TV. Diane played Daphne Dutton.

Surfside Six "Prescription for Panic." December 4, 1961, ABC-TV. Diane played Daphne Dutton.

Surfside Six "A Slight Case of Chivalry." December 18, 1961, ABC-TV. Diane played Daphne Dutton.

Surfside Six "Pattern for a Frame." December 25, 1961, ABC-TV. Diane played Daphne Dutton.

Surfside Six "The Roust." January 1, 1962, ABC-TV. Diane played Daphne Dutton.

Surfside Six "The Quarterback." January 8, 1962, ABC-TV. Diane played Daphne Dutton.

Surfside Six "Separate Checks." January 15, 1962, ABC-TV. Diane played Daphne Dutton.

Surfside Six "Artful Deceit." January 22, 1962, ABC-TV. Diane played Daphne Dutton.

Surfside Six "Anniversary Special." January 29, 1962, ABC-TV. Diane played Daphne Dutton.

Surfside Six "The Surfside Swindle." February 5, 1962, ABC-TV. Diane played Daphne Dutton.

Surfside Six "Who is Sylvia?" February 12, 1962, ABC-TV. Diane played Daphne Dutton.

Surfside Six "Fine Leroy Burdette." February 19, 1962, ABC-TV. Diane played Daphne Dutton.

Surfside Six "Many a Slip." February 26, 1962, ABC-TV. Diane played Daphne Dutton.

Surfside Six "The Green Beret." March 5, 1962, ABC-TV. Diane played Daphne Dutton.

Surfside Six "Vendetta Arms." March 12, 1962, ABC-TV. Diane played Daphne Dutton.

Surfside Six "A Piece of Tommy Minor." March 19, 1962, ABC-TV. Diane played Daphne Dutton.

Surfside Six "Portrait of Nicole." March 26, 1962, ABC-TV. Diane played Daphne Dutton.

Surfside Six "Elegy for a Bookkeeper." April 2, 1962, ABC-TV. Diane played Daphne Dutton.

Surfside Six "The Money Game." April 9, 1962, ABC-TV. Diane played Daphne Dutton.

Surfside Six "Irish Pride." April 16, 1962, ABC-TV. Diane played Daphne Dutton.

Surfside Six "Green Bay Riddle." April 23, 1962, ABC-TV. Diane played Daphne Dutton.

Surfside Six "Love Song for a Deadly Redhead." April 30, 1962, ABC-TV. Diane played Daphne Dutton.

Surfside Six "Dead Heat." May 7, 1962, ABC-TV. Diane played Daphne Dutton.

Surfside Six "Squeeze Play." May 14, 1962, ABC-TV. Diane played Daphne Dutton.

Surfside Six "A Private Eye for Beauty." May 21, 1962, ABC-TV. Diane played Daphne Dutton.

Surfside Six "Masquerade." May 28, 1962, ABC-TV. Diane played Daphne Dutton.

Surfside Six "Pawn's Gambit." June 4, 1962, ABC-TV. Diane played Daphne Dutton.

Surfside Six "The Neutral Corner." June 11, 1962, ABC-TV. Diane played Daphne Dutton.

Surfside Six "House on Boca Key." June 18, 1962, ABC-TV. Diane played Daphne Dutton.

Surfside Six "Midnight for Prince Charming." June 25, 1962, ABC-TV. Diane played Daphne Dutton.

77 Sunset Strip "Leap, My Lovely." October 19, 1962, ABC-TV. Diane played Nina Maran.

Hawaiian Eye "Pursuit of a Lady." December 11, 1962, ABC-TV. Diane played Liz Downing.

Hawaiian Eye "Pretty Pigeon." January 22, 1963, ABC-TV. Diane played Charlene Boggs.

77 Sunset Strip "Nine to Five." March 8, 1963, ABC-TV. Diane played Lu-Ann Lynwood.

77 Sunset Strip "5: Part I." September 20, 1963, ABC-TV. Diane played Carla Stevens.

77 Sunset Strip "5: Part II." September 27, 1963, ABC-TV. Diane played Carla Stevens.

77 Sunset Strip "5: Part III." October 4, 1963, ABC-TV. Diane played Carla Stevens.

77 Sunset Strip "5: Part IV." October 11, 1963, ABC-TV. Diane played Carla Stevens.

77 Sunset Strip "5: Part V." October 18, 1963, ABC-TV. Diane played Carla Stevens.

Kraft Suspense Theatre "My Enemy, This Town." February 6, 1964, NBC-TV. Diane played Mary Jorgenson.

Burke's Law "Who Killed Marty Kelso?" February 28, 1964, ABC-TV. Diane played Susan Shaw

Arrest and Trail "Tigers Are For Jungles." March 22, 1964, ABC-TV. Diane played Elyse Binns.

Wendy and Me "Molehills to Mountains." September 14, 1964, ABC-TV. Diane played Linda.

Burke's Law "Who Killed Mr. Cartwheel?" October 21, 1964, ABC-TV. Diane played Xenobia.

Burke's Law "Who Killed the Tall One in the Middle?" November 25, 1964, ABC-TV. Diane played Lana De Armand.

Kraft Suspense Theatre "One Tiger to a Hill." December 3, 1964, NBC-TV. Diane played Diana Weston.

Bob Hope Presents the Chrysler Theatre "Double Jeopardy." January 8, 1965, NBC-TV. Diane played a show girl.

Burke's Law "Who Killed Nobody Somehow?" March 31, 1965, ABC-TV. Diane played Cissy Davenport DeWitt.

Vacation Playhouse "Alec Tate." July 2, 1965, CBS-TV. Diane played Sherry.

The Wild, Wild West "The Night of a Thousand Eyes." October 22, 1965, CBS-TV. Diane played Jennifer Wingate.

The Man from U.N.C.L.E. "The Deadly Toys Affair." November 12, 1965, NBC-TV. Diane played Joanna Lydecker.

Batman "The Thirteenth Hat." February 23, 1966, ABC-TV. Diane played Lisa.

Batman "Batman Stands Pat." February 24, 1966, ABC-TV. Diane played Lisa.

The Wild Wild West "The Night of the Vicious Valentine." February 10, 1967, CBS-TV. Diane played Elaine Dodd.

Batman "A Piece of the Action." March 1, 1967, ABC-TV. Diane played Pinky Pinkston.

Batman "Batman's Satisfaction." March 2, 1967, ABC-TV. Diane played Pinky Pinkston.

The Man from U.N.C.L.E. "The Five Daughters Affair: Part I." March 31, 1967, NBC-TV. Diane played Contessa Margo De Fanzini.

The Man from U.N.C.L.E. "The Five Daughters Affair: Part II." April 7, 1967, NBC-TV. Diane played Contessa Margo De Fanzini.

Bob Hope Presents the Chrysler Theatre "Bob Hope Christmas Special." December 22, 1967, NBC-TV. Diane as herself on tour in Vietnam.

Love, American Style "Love and the Roommate." November 17, 1969, ABC-TV. Diane played Jill.

Mannix "Blind Mirror." January 24, 1970, CBS-TV. Diane played Stella Diamond.

To Rome With Love "To Go Home Again." January 25, 1970, CBS-TV. Diane played Connie.

Land of the Giants "Panic." January 25, 1970, ABC-TV. Diane played Mrs. Evers.

The Mod Squad "Kicks Incorporated." January 12, 1971, ABC-TV.

The Wide World of Mystery "Tight as a Drum." February 11, 1974, ABC-TV

Police Story "World Full of Hurt." October 8, 1974, NBC-TV. Diane played Mrs. Thompson.

Barbary Coast "Sauce for the Goose." October 20, 1975, ABC-TV. Diane played Myra.

Marcus Welby, M.D. "The Highest Mountain." February 17, 1976, ABC-TV. Diane played Barra Dean.

Donner Pass: The Road to Survival (made-for-television-film). October 24, 1978, NBC-TV. Diane played Margaret Reed.

Once Upon a Starry Night (made-for-television-film). December 19, 1978, NBC-TV. Diane played Jenny.

Charlie's Angels "Disco Angels." January 31, 1979, ABC-TV. Diane played Marian.

Hawaii Five-O "The Moroville Covenant." March 29, 1980, CBS-TV. Diane played Eva Pritchard.

Charlie's Angels "Angel on the Line." February 14, 1981, ABC-TV. Diane played Penny.

Eight is Enough "Yet Another Seven Days in February." April 4, 1981, ABC-TV. Diane played Mrs. Hall.

Dallas "Denial." January 15, 1982, CBS-TV. Diane played Dee Dee Webster.

Dallas "Head of the Family." January 22, 1982, CBS-TV. Diane played Dee Dee Webster.

Days of Our Lives. Numerous episodes. 1982-1983, NBC-TV. Diane played Foxy Humdinger.

Matt Houston "The Rock and the Hard Place." January 2, 1983, ABC-TV. Diane played Marcia Bingham.

Airwolf "Sins of the Past." October 27, 1984, CBS-TV. Diane played Beatrice Meretti.

Crazy Like A Fox "Bum Tip." February 24, 1985, CBS-TV.

Knight Rider "Ten Wheel Trouble." March 24, 1985, NBC-TV. Diane played Mama Flynn.

General Hospital. Numerous episodes. 1988-89, ABC-TV. Diane played Claire Howard.

Jake and the Fatman "I Know That You Know." December 12, 1990, CBS-TV. Diane played Abigail Stevens.

The Streets of Beverly Hills. Unsold Pilot. 1992, CBS-TV.

Sabrina, the Teenage Witch "A Halloween Story." October 25, 1996, ABC-TV. Diane played Granny.

Dr. Quinn, Medicine Woman "Point Blank." February 28, 1998, CBS-TV. Diane played Old Woman.

Strong Medicine "Silent Epidemic." November 11, 2001, LIFETIME-TV. Diane played Lovey Carmichael.

With handsome David McCallum in "The Deadly Toys Affair" episode of The Man from U.N.C.L.E. PHOTO COLLECTION OF MICHAUD.

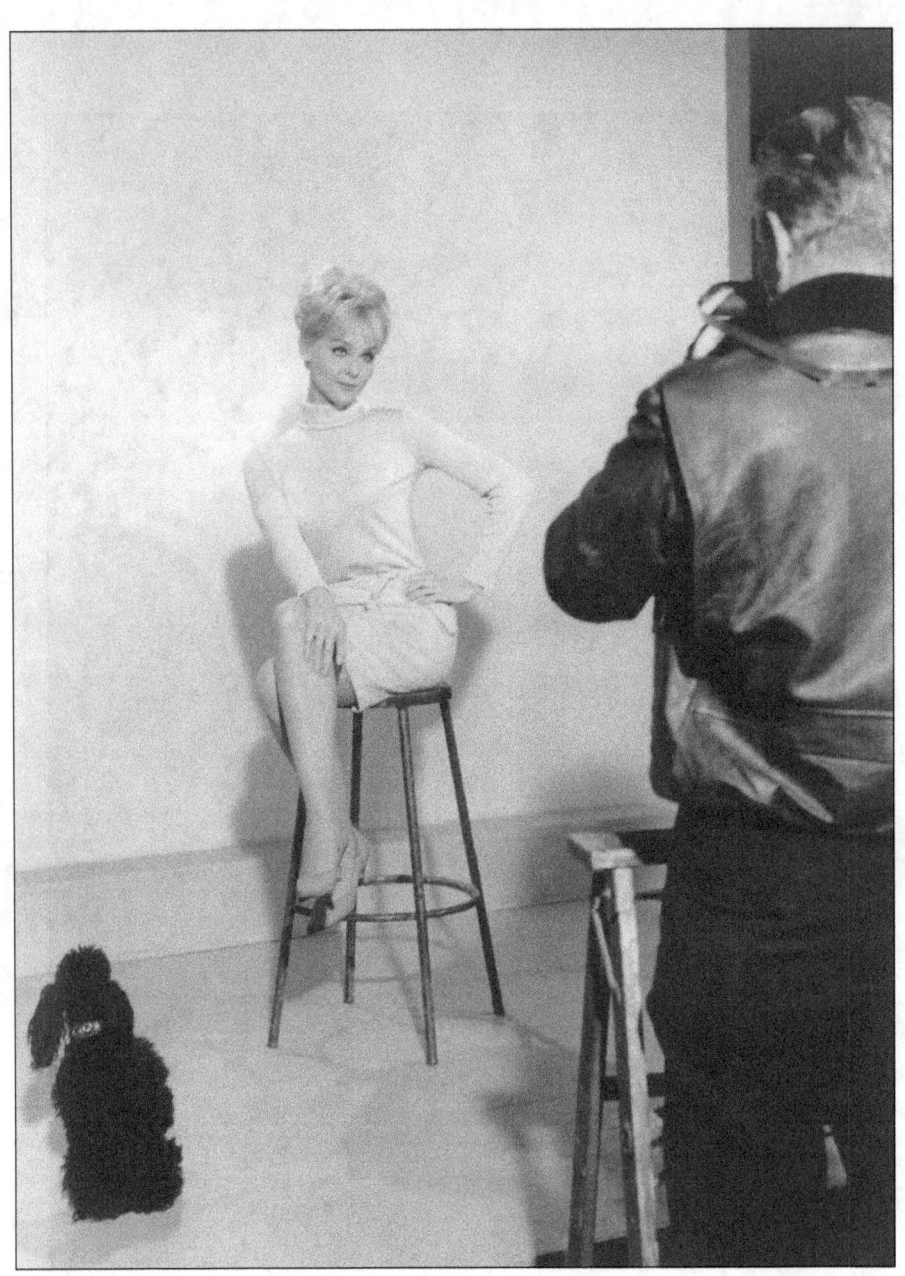
Posing for the camera while Coquette looks on.

Acknowledgements

When I started to write this book, "Serendipity" (another way of saying God's Grace) provided me with people who suddenly sprang from the proverbial woodwork with help and information to complete the work. My friend and co-writer, author Michael Gregg Michaud, stepped forward to help with the writing, research, editing, and marketing of the manuscript. His contribution is invaluable. He deftly juggled the (at times) vastly differing thoughts of Diane and Danny. I've never had such marathon long-distance telephone conversations with anyone in my life.

Thank you to the wonderful libraries and thoughtful librarians who assisted us. The importance of libraries can never be overstated.

Thanks to Ben Ohmart and Bear Manor Media for giving our story a home. And thanks to Michelle Morgan and Brian Pearce for all their work.

Sharon Huegueny's son, Shaun Aaron Ross, called me out-of-the-blue asking if we could meet and exchange information about his mother. We did, and he reminded me of many things that Sharon had shared with me through the years, which contributed to what I wrote about his mother in our book. Jerry Neighbors, a former Army MP I met in Vietnam, called to say, "Hello to one of the pretty actresses who came to visit us in Chu Lai." He provided the name of the place where we stopped at the 91st Evacuation Hospital. Phyllis Brockmeyer, with whom I had promised my undying devotion to Jesus long ago at Girl Scout camp, sent me some long-forgotten newspaper articles that appear in these pages. Eloid Ruis, a new friend, shared movie memorabilia books filled with information that was invaluable. Last, but far from least, Barbara Wagner Joce, a dear friend from my Buddhist days, helped with editing an early draft, and Richard McNalley for his early editorial assistance, as well. Thanks, too, to Jeri Coates for her editorial contributions.

These and many more coincidences within the space of a week told me I was heading in the right direction. I felt that God approved. That feeling has never left; it has only made me work harder to make the writing better.

Other people deserve mention for being a part of my professional life; former child actor (*It's a Wonderful Life*) and producer, Jimmy Hawkins, became a dear friend; actor Ty Henderson (*The Competition*) has been a good friend since my Buddhist days; actress and good friend Heather Woodruff and her husband, Jethro Tull drummer Doane Perry; Dale Reynolds, a fellow actor and dear friend; Henry Rackin, a Casting Director and good friend; and Tony Alexander, an actor and friend.

On a personal note, there are several people to acknowledge; my ex-husband, Rod Burke, has come through by effectively co-parenting with me at a critical time; Janet McMannis, a friend, mentor, and fellow spiritual path-finder; Mary Lynch Haber, a great human being and, proudly, my God-daughter; dear friends Vera Veronika Desmond and her partner Sandi; Deborah Rene Waynesmith and my "sisters" in Book Club; and my son Evan Andrew Burke.

Throughout my life, there have been many supporters and fellow "journeypersons" who helped me navigate the many challenges of life. They are too numerous to note here, but they know who they are.

The authors wish to acknowledge that some of the names have been changed to protect those who should be ashamed.

Diane and Michael attend a fundraiser for the Roar Foundation. PHOTO COURTESY OF BILL DOW

Diane McBain reached her peak of popularity as a Warner Bros. contract star during the early 1960s. She is perhaps best known for starring in the 1960-62 hit ABC-TV series, *Surfside Six*, and appearing opposite Elvis Presley in *Spinout*. Her more than twenty feature films include *Ice Palace, Parrish, Claudelle Inglish, The Caretakers, Mary, Mary, A Distant Trumpet, Maryjane, The Mini-Skirt Mob*, and *Thunder Alley*. She has guest-starred in dozens of television dramas, and numerous situation comedies. Diane supports many charitable causes, and is an outspoken advocate for victims of sexual assault. She received the "Special Service Award" from the USO for her visits to Vietnam in 1966 and 1967.

Michael Gregg Michaud is the author of *Sal Mineo, A Biography* (Harmony Books/Three Rivers Press), which was nominated for a Lambda Book Award in 2011. The acclaimed book was a pick of the month in *Los Angeles Magazine* and for Turner Classic Movies. *Sal Mineo, A Biography* was adapted for the screen by James Franco. Michael supports numerous charitable causes, and worked for more than a decade with Tippi Hedren and The Roar Foundation, which supports the Shambala Preserve. He is the Chief Financial Officer of the Museum of California Design, and is a founding Director of the Linda Blair Worldheart Foundation. Visit him at *michaelgreggmichaud.com*, and follow him on Facebook.

www.ingramcontent.com/pod-product-compliance
Lightning Source LLC
Chambersburg PA
CBHW051827230426
43671CB00008B/870